BATTLESHIP VICTORY

PRINCIPLES OF SEA POWER IN THE WAR IN THE PACIFIC

ROBERT LUNDGREN

NIMBLE BOOKS LLC

Nimble Books LLC
1521 Martha Avenue
Ann Arbor, MI, USA 48103
http://www.NimbleBooks.com
wfz@nimblebooks.com
+1.734-646-6277

Printed in the United States of America
ISBN-13: 978-1-60888-165-9

∞ The paper used in this publication meets the minimum requirements of the American National Standard for Information Sciences—Permanence of Paper for Printed Library Materials, ANSI Z39.48-1992. The paper is acid-free and lignin-free.

CONTENTS

CHAPTER 1: PRINCIPLES OF SEA POWER

Human perception is human reality and I offer a different perspective on battleships by applying the principles of several naval and military thinkers, including Alfred Thayer Mahan and Julian Corbett that may change the perception that battleships became obsolete? By the end of the World War Two the aircraft carrier had replaced the battleship as the reigning queen of the seas. No new battleships designs were created leaving the last four *Iowa* class battleships to be the last of their kind to serve the United States. What role did battleships, aircraft carriers, cruisers, and submarines play in the United States victory and Japan's defeat during the Second World War? I will argue here that, contrary to conventional wisdom, battleships continued to play a decisive role throughout the war.

Japan would abandon her battleships on the eve of hostilities believing air power had usurped their power and this decision would lead directly to her defeat. The United States would be forced to fight without them at the beginning of the war but would unleash their power in the greatest naval offensive in human history beginning in November 1943 that would see Japan's defensive perimeter crushed in eleven months.

Central to the thesis is the understanding of how naval power was employed to achieve a political objective. What application of force had greater strategic impact on the outcome of the war? Was it the direct attack on individual military units or was securing the right of passage and denying the right of passage to any adversary through the operational art of blockade an even more powerful tool? If one side established control of the seas through the use of its battleships and supporting cruisers and destroyers could any other weapon system break that control? The act of a naval air strike was an active use of power but to occupy a seaway and deny its use to any enemy was a passive use of power. The differences contributed to the perception that an air strike was more dominant. Over time the passive use of controlling a seaway will prove to be the dominant use of naval power and battleships would maintain this as their primary role in securing command of the sea. Why were modern battleships of the dreadnought era built to begin with? Battleships just like any other military weapon are a tool that allows a government to conduct politics and enforce its will through the use of force. Carl Von Clausewitz would define war as simply politics by another means once diplomacy had failed. What is important to understand is the political objective can't be separated from the weapon or tool that is used to achieve the objective. It is only through this lens that one can gain the proper perspective in judging if the tool was useful or irrelevant to the final outcome. Political policy is the objective and war is the means to the objective. Battleships, carriers, cruisers, and submarines are all tools used to obtain the objective. Every tool has a purpose.

War is probably the most important subject a society can discuss. Once a government chooses to conduct a military operation the currency that must be paid to achieve the objective is human life. War can be divided into two classifications of limited and unlimited wars, or may be seen as a spectrum between limited and total war. What are the people of a society willing to sacrifice for their political differences? In an unlimited war the political object is so vital an importance to both belligerents that they are willing to fight to the utmost limit of their endurance to secure it. In a limited war the object is of less importance, that is to say, where one or both belligerents did not find the objectives sufficient to justify unlimited sacrifices of blood and treasure.[1]

In an unlimited war if the political objective is so vital to the enemy that it would result in the enemy exercising his full war making potential it is reasonable to reach the conclusion that the struggle would not be decided until his ability to make war was entirely crushed. If there was not a reasonable hope of being able to do this then it was poor policy to seek this political objective through the use of force. In other words war should be avoided. If the objective is limited then the total destruction of the enemy's armed forces is unnecessary. The objective could be seized and a defensive posture could then be established so that the cost the enemy must pay to reclaim the objective would be too high.

The character of a war can be positive or negative. If the aim of the objective is to seize something from an enemy this is an offensive war and is considered positive. If the aim is to prevent an enemy from wresting some advantage this is a defensive war and is considered negative. This is a broad conception and more useful to establish trends and the character of operations required to obtain the political objective.[2]

---

[1] Corbett, Julian S., *Principles of Maritime Strategy* at 38-40.

[2] Ibid at 28-29.

Concerning maritime sea power two great naval theorists had a major impact in both the United States and Japan on how their respective navies were constructed and intended to be used to achieve such objectives. They were Alfred Thayer Mahan and Julian Corbett. Mahan's book, *The Influence of Sea Power upon History, 1660-1783*, published by Little, Brown & Co in 1890, introduced to the world the concept of geopolitics or a national policy based on the interrelation of politics and geography.

Mahan identified six principles in his first chapter that established the elements of sea power that a nation had to have in order to become a great naval power.

The first was geographical. An physically isolated nation that does not need to defend itself by land or seek extension of its territory by way of land must direct its aim upon the sea.[3] This basic principle showed why Great Britain as an island nation would be a greater sea power than the continental powers of France or Holland which had to maintain strong armies to defend their borders. This secure position gave such nations a strong advantage as a naval power. He argued that the Atlantic and Pacific oceans similarly offered a protective barrier that prevented continental invasion of the United States and therefore the United States shared this attribute of sea power with then superpower Great Britain. Japan as an island nation also had this attribute.

The second principle was physical conformation. A nation must have many natural harbors and easy access to the world's oceans. The more the better, and the United States having access to the Atlantic, Caribbean, and Pacific, gave it a significant advantage over other powers. Japan also had many harbors and easy access to the Pacific and Yellow Seas. The physical attributes of both countries were consistent with Mahan's second principle.[4]

The third principle was the extent of territory. If the country had a significant length of coast-line then this territory would need to be defended and without a Navy to protect this coast the first two principles turned into a weakness instead of a strength. Mahan then used the example of the U.S. Civil War and the South having the first two conditions equal to the North. However, the South without a

---

[3] Mahan, Alfred T., *The Influence of Sea Power upon History* at 29.

[4] Ibid at 35.

Navy to protect their coast allowed the North to blockade the South.[5] More than any other principle this was demonstrated in World War II in the Pacific. Islands are defenseless without a Navy to protect them. Islands surrounded by the seas were vulnerable to having all lines of communication cut off through blockade and this in turn opened the island to invasion.

Mahan's fourth principle was size and nature of population. In short the population must be a sea faring people with a strong ship building industry, with a strong merchant commerce trade over the oceans. The nation must have the resources and economic wealth to build such a merchant fleet and the goods that others need. The United States was 100% self-sufficient in natural resources and one of the wealthiest if not the wealthiest country in the world. Trade with Europe as well as Pacific nations was an important part of the U.S. economy. The United States also had a long established history as a seafaring people.[6]

Japan's naval history had included raids and pirates on Chinese and Korean shipping for centuries but in the 1800s Japan was in a period of self-imposed isolation from the rest of the world. On July 8, 1853 Commodore Matthew Perry entered Uraga harbor with *Mississippi, Plymouth*, *Saratoga*, and *Susquehanna* near Edo which was early Tokyo. This was not a peaceful overture but a demonstration of force to end Japan's 250 years of chosen isolation. When asked to leave and head to the port of Nagasaki, which was the only port open to foreigners, Perry refused, and demanded to present a letter from President Fillmore. After the Japanese agreed to receive the letter he left for China but returned to Japan in February 1854. Tokugawa Shogunate had accepted virtually all the demands in Fillmore's letter. Perry signed the Convention of Kanagawa on March 31, 1854.[7] These events are another demonstration of Mahan's third principle. An insular nation with long stretches of coast but without a navy to defend it was strategically weak, making such a nation extremely vulnerable to maritime aggression. From this point forward the feudal lords began to lobby for the construction of a modern navy. President Fillmore had achieved his political objective of dismantling Japanese isolation by using Perry's warships and this intervention had been a direct assault on Japanese sovereignty.

---

[5] Ibid at 42-43.

[6] Ibid at 44-45.

[7] Evans, David C., Peattie, Mark R., *Kaigun Strategy, Tactics, and Technology in the Imperial Japanese Navy 1887-1941* at 4.

Mahan's fifth principle of sea power was national character. A country to become a great sea power must be willing to use the seas for active trading and commercial pursuits, which, in turn, increases the prosperity of the people and the nation as a whole. Ninety percent of the world's commerce is still transported by ships even today in 2015. The government that controls the world's oceans can control the world's economy and achieve superpower status. Great Britain was the acknowledged superpower when Mahan wrote his book, largely due to the power of her Navy.[8]

Mahan's last principle was character of the government. Governments must have the will power and intelligence to create policies in favor of sea power in order to become a great nation. Mahan declared that the United States possessed all of the previously identified necessary qualities and all that was needed was the proper leadership, national will, and application of the required resources to achieve national greatness.[9] These six principles did not actually outline naval strategy but a national political policy that could raise such a nation to superpower status. Control the seas and you control the world's economies. Commercial expansion backed by a fighting navy would lead to mercantilist imperialism and the danger of future clashes with competing powers.

As a national policy to achieve superpower status Mahan's concepts were universally applicable to any nation that believed it had all of characteristics required to satisfy his principles and achieve greatness. Great Britain and the United States certainly had all the attributes but Germany and Japan aspired to these qualities as well. Germany with its inferior geographic position, long land boundaries, and authoritarian government had more challenges at sea, but its substantial population, industry, and strong military culture made it a major threat on land. The resulting arms race for superior sea power would be a significant factor in leading these countries to war in both World War One and World War Two.

Through the later chapters Mahan analyzed multiple naval battles during the age of sail between Great Britain, France, Spain, and Holland during the seventeenth and eighteenth century. Central to his theme was the idea that the primary purpose of the Navy was to defeat an opposing Navy to automatically gain control of the seas. He termed this "The Decisive Battle." This should not be confused with a decisive victory. The decisive 'battle was one that resulted in the total annihilation of the enemy fleet so the vanquished could no longer resist the will of

---

[8] Ibid. at 50.

[9] Ibid at 58-59.

the victor. This made the destruction of the opposing fleet a strategic objective to end the war.

During the age of sail the most powerful ship type was referred to as a ship of the line. They were the largest and carried the most guns of all the naval ship types and could destroy any lesser naval combatant. A ship of the line could only be defeated by another ship of the line. Once the age of sail passed away for the age of iron and steam this role was taken on by first the armored cruiser and then, with the advent of HMS *Dreadnough*t in 1905, the battleship. All were gun platforms, all normally entered combat in a battle line (although ensuing mêlées were not uncommon), and it was distinctly possible for any engagement to result in the total destruction of one side or another. Such major fleet engagements held out the possibility the war could be won or lost in a single afternoon.

Mahan did not argue, however, for a fleet of battleships only. He argued for a well-balanced fleet in which battleships only represented the top tier of the fleet. Being the most expensive ship type their numbers would be limited. However, numbers count and battleships were not meant to operate alone. A single battleship had only imperfect value. It was more a national symbol than a military force. Effective sea power required an integrated combination of battleships and supporting warships, a battle fleet that trained and operated as a unit.[10]

Developments in major world navies during the latter part of the 19th century were the background for Mahan's new doctrine. Prior and through the U.S. Civil War the American Navy was first rate with universal respect. The sailing frigates, ship for ship, were the finest in the world. The introduction of the U.S.S. *Monitor* with its heavy armor and rotating turret with huge guns had rocked the science of naval warfare to its roots. However, after 1865 the U.S. Navy would go through a period of decline as former Civil War generals dominated political life and focused on internal expansion. The war had destroyed much of the nation's maritime commerce and there was little sentiment for spending money on a large merchant marine or warships capable of protecting them. Technology in steam engines, armor, guns, and projectiles were rapidly expanding and these changes tended to create obsolescence among ships that were only a few years old or even before they could be completed.[11]

Secretary of the Navy William E. Chandler in 1883 called the U.S. fleet a subject of ridicule at home and abroad. President Chester A. Arthur on March 3,

---

[10] Friedman, Norman, *U.S. Battleships* at 1.

[11] Alden, John D., *the American Steel Navy* at 3.

1883 signed a bill for four steel ships that were later named *Atlanta, Boston, Chicago,* and *Dolphin.* They would become popularly known as the ABCD ships. They represented the birth of what would become the modern U.S. Navy.[12]

On September 14, 1862 British nationals were attacked (one killed, two wounded) by Satsuma samurai for not showing the proper respect for a daimyo's regent and this incident became known as the Namamugi Incident. Lieutenant-Colonel Neale demanded from the bakufu (Japanese central government), led by Ogasawara Nagamichi, an apology and a huge indemnity of £100,000. Britain also demanded of the Satsuma domain the arrest and trial of the perpetrators of the outrage, and £25,000 compensation for the surviving victims and the relatives of Charles Lennox Richardson.[13]

The Satsuma province refused to apologize, pay the indemnity, or arrest the samurai responsible for the murder. Negotiations with Satsuma lasted over a year. Finally the British Government decided to use force to achieve its political objective. A British squadron left Yokohama on August 6. It was composed of the flagship *Euryalus* (with Colonel Neale onboard), *Pearl, Perseus, Argus, Coquette, Racehorse* and the gunboat *Havock.* They sailed for Kagoshima and anchored in the deep waters of Kinko Bay on August 11, 1863. Japanese envoys exchanged letters and the British gave an ultimatum that its demands be met within 24 hours.[14]

After the deadline passed the British seized three Japanese ships that were at anchor. Japanese costal batteries opened fire on the British ships and in return Colonel Neale sank the three captured ships and formed a line of battle and bombarded the city of Kagoshima. The naval bombardment claimed five lives among the people of Satsuma. Captain Josling of the British flagship *Euryalus,* and his second-in-command Commander Wilmot, were killed. 500 wood-and-paper houses burned in Kagoshima (about 5% of Kagoshima's urban area), the Ryukyuan embassy was destroyed, and the three Satsuma steamships and five Ryukyuan junks destroyed. Satsuma however later negotiated and paid £25,000 but never turned over the responsible samurai.[15]

---

[12] Ibid at 13-14.

[13] Totman, Conrad. *The collapse of the Tokugawa Bakufu,* 1862-1868 University of Hawaii Press, Honolulu (1980) at 68-69.

[14] Rennie, David Field, *The British Arms in North China and Japan.* Originally published 1864. Facsimile by Adamant Media Corporation (2005) at382.

[15] Denney, John. *Respect and Consideration: Britain in Japan 1853 - 1868 and beyond.* Radiance Press (2011) at 191.

The conflict actually became the starting point of a close relationship between Satsuma and Britain, which became major allies in the ensuing Boshin War. From the start, the Satsuma province had generally been in favor of the opening and modernization of Japan. Although the Namamugi Incident was unfortunate, it was not characteristic of Satsuma's policy, and was rather abusively branded as an example of anti-foreign sonnō jōi sentiment, as a justification to a strong European show of force. Heihachiro Togo was manning one of the cannons used to defend the port, and this battle attributed to his future career as head and "father" of the Imperial Japanese Navy.

This incident again shows the importance of Mahan's third principle that a country with long stretches of coast but no Navy to protect it was strategically weak. In 1868 the shogunate system of government was overthrown and the Meiji Emperor was restored as a new Imperial Government of Japan. The Meiji Government saw naval power as paramount but domestic rebellions during the 1870s posed more immediate threats. Japan's strategic concepts in the 1870s rested on several assumptions in which the first was that Japan's vital interests were restricted to the home islands, and the existence and independence of the Japanese people, state and homeland. Due to the huge expense of a modern navy that was beyond Japan's ability to fund, the only defensive posture for Japan to take was a static defense comprising of coastal artillery, a standing army, and naval units that could impose unacceptable costs on an invasion force. Due to these assumptions the Army had the principal responsibility for Japanese security and this would limit funds for the Navy and begin an inter-service competition for those funds.[16]

A naval academy to train officers was established in 1869 on the waterfront at Tsukiji in Tokyo but in 1888 it was moved to Etajima on the Inland Sea, not far from Hiroshima. The four year course taught naval science, seamanship, navigation, gunnery as well as the traditional Japanese military values of loyalty, courtesy, valor, and simplicity. The officers that graduated from the academy were well disciplined, professional, and patriotic. Japan required more help to become a world naval power equal to the Western powers and turned to Great Britain and the United States. Her Navy and her officer corps would employ the Royal Navy as the model for the new Imperial Japanese Navy. The first steps in the creation of

[16] Evans, David C., Peattie, Mark R., *Kaigun: Strategy, Tactics, and Technology in the Imperial Japanese Navy 1887-1941* at 5-6.

the battle fleets that would take part in the largest naval war in human history had begun.[17]

[17] Ibid at 11.

CHAPTER 2: LINEAGE OF THE IMPERIAL JAPANESE NAVY

Yamamoto Gombei would become the most influential naval reformer for Japan at the turn of the century. He became Naval Minister in 1891. Mahan's work gave him the political argument to justify the importance of the Navy to Japan's strategic defense. With tremendous focus, political skill, and dedication to the goal of advancing the navy's ambitions, he was able to raise the political status of the Navy to near equal terms of that of the Army. He consistently gained more funds from the Diet. By doing so he also created an inter-service conflict that would continue to grow and become bitter as time went forward. The conflict's causes were professional hubris, jealousies from regional antagonisms, rivalry for public attention, and budgetary support, as well as differences in strategic thinking. Despite the conflict, Yamamoto was able to acquire the men and material for a true battle fleet.

Absolute power corrupts absolutely and Japan's government institutions did not have the checks and balances that the United States founding fathers placed in the United States constitution. In Japan the Emperor was the theoretical supreme head over all government institutions and agencies according to the Meiji Constitution of 1889. The authority of Emperor Mutsuhito (reigned 1867-1912) was sacred and unbreakable. His role in the day to day operations of the government was limited so that his practical role in the government was curbed. The civilian government and armed services operated just beneath the Emperor. Technically, Japan was a parliamentary state with a bilateral legislature called the Diet and a cabinet headed by a prime minister but did not operate with majority rule. A few senior statesmen either inside or outside the government could influence the collective will of the body

The two armed service ministers while in theory were responsible to the civilian government and the prime minister looked to their own services for direction since they were active military officers. Real power resided not in the service ministries but in the general staff of both armed services. The staffs were charged with the preparations of war plans, intelligence, and operations in the field and at sea and by doing so they created foreign policy. In performing these duties the authority of the Army and Navy remained immune to any interference by the civilian government. The military maintained this independence because the constitution gave the Emperor supreme command over the Army and Navy and in so doing the two ministers acting in the name of the Emperor held the right of supreme command. Since the throne did not normally interfere with the day to day mechanisms of the government, civilian or military, by exercising the right of supreme command meant that except for their annual budgets Japan's two armed services were essentially accountable to no one.[18] This led to the two armed services competing against each other for available funds.

From a social perspective naval officers held a very high status within Japanese society. By using the British Royal Navy as their model the officers were to regard themselves as gentlemen and officers were considered good husbands by Japanese women. Thousands of young men from all walks of life applied to Etajima and the Navy was a way to improve a family's social status and economic well-being. Naval officers were well paid with flag rank salaries at least the equivalent to those of college professors.[19] Therefore, many officers would place their loyalty to the Navy as an institution. This would lead to a failure in leadership that would directly lead to the war with the United States by placing the needs of the naval institution above the needs of the people and the nation.[20]

The first test of the young Japanese Navy came on September 17, 1894 during Sino-Japanese war and the Battle of the Yalu. The war was being fought for the control of Korea and Port Arthur. The Japanese Combined Fleet sank five Chinese ships and battered two Chinese battleships forcing them to retreat to Port Arthur losing no ships in return. The battle emphasized the line ahead formation, the naval gun, and tactical speed. This would heavily influence ship construction for the future.

Gombei would argue that the Navy had played the decisive role in the war through command of the seas and a vindication of Mahan's principles. Through the destruction of the Chinese fleet the army was allowed to land undisturbed and in total safety to later seize control of Port Arthur. Russia, Germany, and France, alarmed at the sudden change in the balance of power, intervened, forcing Japan

---

[18] Evans, David C., Peattie, Mark R., *Kaigun Strategy Tactics and Technology in the Imperial Japanese Navy 1887-1941* at 25-26.

[19] Marder, Arthur J., *Old Friends, New Enemies The Royal Navy and the Imperial Japanese Navy Strategic Illusions 1936-1941* at 265-266.

[20] Sadao, Asada, *From Alfred Thayer Mahan to Pearl Harbor* at 295-296.

to return the port and the peninsula back to China. Within three years Russia demanded and received a twenty-five year lease on Port Arthur and began to occupy Korea. This became a national humiliation for Japan and would set up the conditions for the Russo-Japanese War.

Japan began a naval expansion immediately so its fleet could challenge the strength of Russia's fleet. Great Britain would play a huge role in building and providing the ships to Japan as Japan's ability to build her own ships was still inadequate. By 1904 Japan possessed a modern battle fleet with the latest technology provided by the world's leader and most powerful navy. Funded by the First and Second Period Naval Extension Programs, the 6-6 Fleet established Japan as the premier naval power in the Far East. The battleship component of the plan included four new British-built ships which followed the example set by the *Fuji*s to form a homogeneous six-ship squadron. The fleet plan matched the strength of these battleships with the practicality of its armored cruisers, ships with few pretensions at a time when other navies were building cruisers that matched or exceeded battleship tonnage. But as with the Japanese battleships, the cruisers resembled one another despite their disparate origins, and they were melded into a coordinated team.

Russia's Navy was old though it still had the advantage in sheer numbers. There were two major fleet actions during the war. The Battle of the Yellow Sea on August 10, 1904 initially saw Admiral Toga of the Combined Fleet get outmaneuvered with the Russian fleet almost escaping. After a two hour chase, due to the Japanese ships having superior speed Admiral Toga finally was able to engage the rear elements of the Russian battle line. Initially it was the Japanese fleet that took the most damage but then the Russian flagship was hit, lost control, and the commanding Russian Admiral, Witgeft, was killed. The Russian fleet lost cohesion and became a disorderly rabble. The Russian fleet then retreated back to Port Arthur and Admiral Toga, fearing a destroyer torpedo attack on his own force as night fell, disengaged.

The battle was a strategic failure for Japan. The Combined Fleet held an opportunity to annihilate the Port Arthur fleet and missed it. In the end they would mine the harbor entrance and trap the Russian fleet inside the harbor and the Japanese Army would have to capture Port Arthur on its own. Russia decided to send its Baltic Fleet around the world to reinforce its beleaguered Pacific fleet and this would lead to the second major fleet action the Battle of Tsushima on May 27-28, 1905.

This was a massive running battle that lasted for two days as both battle lines blasted away at each other. Eventually the older Russian ships faltered and as their battle line fell apart the Japanese were able to isolate and destroy the separate elements. Of the thirty-eight warships that comprised the Russian fleet thirty-four were sunk, scuttled, captured, or interned at neutral ports. The Russians lost 4,830 killed and 5,917 captured including two admirals. In contrast the Japanese Combined Fleet had lost three torpedo boats sunk, three capital ships damaged and eight destroyer/torpedo boats damaged with 110 casualties. The Battle of Tsushima was a battle of annihilation un-paralleled in naval history. Corbett wrote:

> Tsushima was the most decisive and complete naval victory in history.[21]

This naval victory validated Mahan's principle of decisive battle, gave Japan sea control, and immediately made Japan the world's dominant naval power in the Pacific. This showed that Mahan's conviction that a strong battle fleet could create national greatness was well founded. It had been fifty-two years since Admiral Perry had anchored in Tokyo Bay when Japan had no navy, showing just how vulnerable Japan was to naval power. At the conclusion of this battle in 1905, Japan had become an Imperial power with territories beyond its home islands that all other world powers had to recognize.

Akiyama Saneyuki is known as the father of Japanese naval strategy and was a devoted disciple of Mahan. Under Navy Minister Gombei he was ordered to learn all he could of Western naval strategy. He met with Mahan himself in New York. He was able to sail with the American fleet during the Spanish-American War and observed Admiral William T. Sampson block the Spanish fleet at Santiago and destroy it. In 1902 he was appointed as the senior instructor at the Naval Staff College to teach tactics and strategy. He incorporated table top war games that he observed at the U.S. Navy War College and this provided the Japanese Navy a practical application of naval theory. It also created a mirror image between how the U.S. planned and prepared its war plans with that of Japan. In 1910 his strategic thoughts became the basis of the Naval Battle Instructions (*Kaisen yomurei*) which through five revisions would be the foundation of Japanese naval strategy leading up to WWII.[22]

Gombei continued his geopolitical goal of making the Navy the more important branch of national defense when he picked Sato Tetsutaro to further his naval first policy. Tetsutaro would become a leading naval theorist and propagandist. Yamagata Aritomo introduced the phrase *sotei tekikoku* (hypothetical enemy)

---

[21] Corbett, Julian, *Maritime Operations in the Russo-Japanese War,* 1904-5 at 333.

[22] Sadao, Asada, *From Alfred Thayer Mahan to Pearl Harbor,* at 31.

into the Meiji-era military lexicon in 1871. In "Preparedness for Naval War" 1897,[23] Mahan wrote:

> It is not the most probable of dangers, but the most formidable, that must be selected as measuring the degree of military precaution.[24]

In 1907, the country's leaders allowed the Navy to insert into the First Imperial National Defense Policy a hypothetical enemy and the Navy choose the United States. Why? What made the United States such a threat to Japan? Lt. Col. Tanaka Giichi led the work to create the First Imperial National Defense Policy and was a member of the Army General Staff. The Naval General Staff was represented by Captain Kawashima Reijiro and Commander Takarabe Takeshi.[25]

The operational thinking on blockade originates in the tack of a *"siege"* in land warfare. The word "blockade" is word derived from French and Dutch references to the "blockhouse", a small fort that protect against sieges in land warfare.[26] Thus, both the Imperial Japanese Army and Navy shared an operational and strategic perspective on blockade.

The United States developed war plans and gave them colors based on which country the United States was waging war with. Admiral George Dewey planned and directed the maneuvers in the Caribbean in 1902 for War Plan Black which was a war against Germany. In 1899, a basis of the Operation Plan III (Germany's war plans against the United States), had been revealed to the U. S. side after the publication of a book compiled by an officer who worked for the Imperial German Army General Staff.[27]

The objectives of a war under the Operation Plan III by Germany would be to solidify Germany's presence in the West Indies, to secure a free hand in South America and to defeat the Monroe Doctrine. To achieve these objectives, the Imperial German Navy was said to have planned to occupy Puerto Rico Island and Culebra Island, about thirty kilometers east of Puerto Rico, as bases for its fleets. It was also pointed out that the Imperial German Navy considered that the

---

[23] *Harper's Magazine*. March 1897.

[24] Asada, Sadao, *From Alfred Thayer Mahan to Pearl Harbor* at 35.

[25] Takahashi Fumio, The First War Plan Orange and the First Imperial Japanese Defense Policy: An Interpretation from the Geopolitical Strategic Perspective, NIDS Security Reports, No.5 (March 2004) at 70.

[26] Online Etymology Dictionary. "Blockade." http://www.etymonline.com/index.php?term=blockade

[27] Hagan Kenneth J, *This People's Navy: The Making of American Sea Power* (N.Y.: Free Press, 1991) at 237-238.

two islands separated the Atlantic from the Caribbean and was conveniently located to control the eastern exit of the Panama Canal when it was completed. The next step was thought to attack the east coastal cities in the United States from the two islands. Germany expected the U. S. Navy to wage the decisive fleet engagement after Germany occupied the two islands and believed it essential for its victory to defeat the U. S. Navy in the decisive fleet engagement because a blockade strategy could not lead to surrender of the United States which was rich in natural resources.

The Japanese Naval General Staff studied the U.S. Caribbean War maneuvers and developed a possible "Plan of Operations" on how the United States Navy would respond to such a situation. The Third Bureau of the Japanese Naval General Staff in 1902 described under the headings of "Hypothetical Situation," "Objective of War," "Goal of Operations" and "Courses of Action" as follows:

> United States Plan of Operations:
>
> Hypothetical Situation: A United States war against Germany to be triggered by the Venezuelan crisis.
>
> United States Objective of War: Protection of the Monroe Doctrine, the policy of the nation.[28]
>
> United States Goal of Operations: Recapture of Puerto Rico Island and Culebra Island.
>
> United States Courses of Action: Quick organization of United States Combined Fleet. Recapture of the two islands by United States Combined Fleet. Early detection of enemy fleets by means of thorough search. Destruction of the Imperial German Fleet through concentrated fire from United States Combined Fleet in a decisive naval engagement. Breakthrough of the enemy patrol line. Protection of transport convoy, and attack and destruction of enemy transport convoy.[29]

Tetsutaro adjusted this "hypothetical situation," an American war against Germany to be triggered by the Venezuelan crisis, to an American war against Japan to be triggered by a certain crisis. To develop his plan on just how the United States would wage a war against Japan he used a paper written by Commander Bradley A. Fiske published by the Army and Navy Journal (April 1, 1905).[30] In his

---

[28] The Monroe Doctrine was a U.S. foreign policy regarding European countries in 1823. It stated that further efforts by European nations to colonize land or interfere with states in North or South America would be viewed as acts of aggression, requiring U.S. intervention.

[29] Takahashi Fumio The First War Plan Orange and the First Imperial Japanese Defense Policy: An Interpretation from the Geopolitical Strategic Perspective, NIDS Security Reports, No.5 (March 2004) at 80.

[30] The Japanese Naval General Staff also included this paper in the "Kaigun Isan (Tsune) Dai-10-Gô (Compilation of the Information Materials on the Foreign Navy, Ordinary Edition, Vol. 10.)" compiled in September 1905.

paper, Commander Fiske wrote that the protection of the Monroe Doctrine was the most important duty of the U.S. Navy, and that the objective of the U.S. Navy lay in the implementation of U.S. policies as the will of the U.S. government, namely the expansion of national interest of the U.S. on the assumption that U.S. citizens would suffer great damage even if the U.S. was partially blockaded. Sato Tetsutaro used the protection of the Monroe Doctrine as the American Objective of the war.

Sato Tetsutaro added the occupation of the Philippines by the Japanese Imperial Army under the heading of Initial Situation. This corresponded to Germany capturing Puerto Rico Island and Culebra Island in the study of the Caribbean maneuvers. Rear Admiral George W. Melville, Director of the Engineering Bureau, Navy Department, said that the Philippines would be a place for a decisive battle and that Japan would likely win the battle thanks to geographical advantages.[31]

> "Goal of Operations" are changed from "recapture of Puerto Rico Island and Culebra Island" to "recapture of the Philippines."

On the premise of a war against the U. S., the Imperial Japanese Naval officers could easily imagine that the U. S. would temporarily renounce the Philippines and retreat its feeble Asiatic Fleet based in the Philippines to Guam or Hawaii, organize the United States Combined Fleet there and fight against the Imperial Japanese Naval Force to recapture the Philippines. On the basis of the aforementioned "Hypothetical Situation," "Objective of War" and "Initial Situation," "Courses of Action" to achieve "Goal of Operations" could be determined in accordance with "Plan of Operations" of the maneuvers in the Caribbean. And a draft of "War Planning of the U.S. Navy against Japan over the Acquisition of the Philippines" can be formulated as follows:

> War Planning of the U. S. Navy against Japan over the Acquisition of the Philippines.
>
> Hypothetical Situation: A war against Japan to be triggered by a certain crisis.
>
> Initial Situation: Occupation of the Philippines by the Imperial Japanese Army and Navy thanks to geographical advantages
>
> Objective of war: Protection of the Monroe Doctrine, the policy of the United States, and expansion of national interest.
>
> Goal of Operations: Recapture of the Philippines.

---

[31] The Third Bureau of the Japanese Naval General Staff carried this view under the title of "Gasshûkoku Kaigun-shô Kikan Kyokuchô George W. Melville Jyutu Kongo Jyûnenkan ni okeru Kaigun no Hattatsu (Development of the U.S. Navy for the Next Decade by George W. Melville, Director of the Engineering Bureau of the U.S. Navy Department)".

> Courses of Action: Escape of the feeble Asiatic Fleet in the Philippines from a patrol line of the Imperial Japanese Naval Fleet. Quick organization of the United States Combined Fleet (reinforcing fleet and Asiatic Fleet). Early detection of the Imperial Japanese Naval Fleet through large-scale search. Destruction of the Imperial Japanese Naval Fleet through concentrated fire in a decisive naval engagement. Recapture of the Philippines by the United States Combined Fleet. Attack on the Japanese transport vessels.[32]

This pointed out that Japan would be virtually subject to blockade if the first line of defense (which was the Imperial Japanese Navy) was destroyed. Tetsutaro went on to say that London would last less than five weeks if Britain, which depended on foreign countries for food, was blockaded, while Japan would hold only two months if Tokyo Bay, a route for food supply by the sea, was blockaded. He concluded that Japan had no choice but to surrender in starvation to an enemy.[33]

How did Tetsutaro come to the conclusion that the United States was capable of strategic level blockade against Japan? In the two most recent wars the United States and Japan had taken part in, the U. S. Navy blockaded Santiago Bay and Manila Bay during the Spanish-American War of 1898, and the Imperial Japanese Navy blockaded Port Arthur during the Sino-Japanese and Russo-Japanese Wars. Both are considered tactical blockades.

Tetsutaro had to go farther back to the U.S. Civil War of 1861-1865 and the "Anaconda Plan," which was the total blockade of the Southern Confederate States by the Northern Union of the United States. This demonstrated strategic level blockade could be accomplished. How would such a war end? Ulysses S. Grant recommended unconditional surrender in response to the offer of surrender from Fort Donelson in February 1862.[34] Unconditional and immediate surrender would result in a clash of culture. Americans were used to removing from power their leaders on a routine basis through elections. The Emperor of Japan was far more than a political leader. Within Japanese society *kokutai* was the most powerful belief. At its core value, plus the accretion of myths, faith, and customs, was the notion of Imperial Japan as a unique people by the virtue of its sacred Emperor. To Hirohito, *kokutai* meant the responsibility to his Imperial ancestors to pre-

---

[32] Takahashi Fumio, *The First War Plan Orange and the First Imperial Japanese Defense Policy: An Interpretation from the Geopolitical Strategic Perspective,* NIDS Security Reports, No.5 (March 2004) at 84.

[33] Ibid. at 85.

[34] Ulysses S. Grant, quoted from *Personal Memoirs of U. S. Grant, Vol. 1,* N. Y., The Century Co., 1917 at 255.

serve the unbroken Imperial line and for the Imperial Army and Navy it meant the preservation of the Imperial system, which became the repository for values and virtues of the military.[35] It was simply impossible within Japanese society that the Emperor be dethroned.

If the Imperial line ended then Japan itself ends and there was nothing that separated the Japanese people from any other Asian culture. For Japan, *kokutai* was worth unlimited sacrifice and any threat to *kokutai* would result in an unlimited war.

The United States developed War Plan Orange which detailed a war against Japan in 1906. The prototype of the War Plan Orange called for three phases.

> Phase-1 The Philippines is occupied by the Imperial Japanese armed forces. Feeble Asiatic Squadron retreats quickly at the first shoot by the Imperial Japanese armed forces.
>
> Phase-2 Reinforcing Fleet and troops are sent immediately from the Atlantic, and the Philippines are recaptured before the Imperial Japanese armed forces are poised for defense.
>
> Phase-3 Relentless blockade and destruction of ports, harbors and ships throws Japan into "final and complete commercial isolation," and drives it into "eventual impoverishment and exhaustion" and defeat.[36]

Tetsutaro through his study of Mathew Perry's intervention, the Namamugi Incident, and the Caribbean maneuvers had correctly outlined U.S. policy even before the U.S. developed War Plan Orange. The Naval General Staff armed with a plausible scenario of how the United States could destroy Japan through command of the seas and blockade could now justify the funds from the Deity to build the Imperial Japanese Navy.

> Only the Imperial Japanese Navy could protect the people of Japan from blockade by foreign powers and this in turn implied only the Imperial Japanese Navy could protect kokutai and the Emperor himself.

This was the most serious threat Japan had ever faced. Setting the United States as a hypothetical enemy would produce a perception of hostilities when both countries at the time were allies. Mahan's fear that two competing powers would

---

[35] Drea, Edward J., *In the Service of the Emperor* at 172.

[36] Edward S. Miller, *War Plan Orange: The U. S. Strategy to Defeat Japan, 1897-1945* at 389 -390.

be drawn into conflict had begun. The first domino toward war had fallen. Many years would pass before it came to pass, but the die was cast.

When dealing with an American adversary Sato Tetsutaro and Saneyuki conducted research at the Naval Staff College and came up that the Imperial Japanese Navy must comprise a 70% ratio in strength to the United States Navy in 1909. The basic rule was that an attacking fleet would need 50% superiority in firepower over a defending fleet in its territorial waters to be capable of defeating the defending fleet. Sato Tetsutaro determined that 70% was the minimum requirement and anything less would imperil Japanese security.[37]

Still, by the First World War Japan, Great Britain, and the United States were allies. Japan did not play a large role in the First World War. Japan did send a destroyer squadron to the Mediterranean and sent naval observers to Great Britain who were on board British ships during the Battle of Jutland, the largest battleship fleet encounter in history.

The horror of the First World War led many to demonize Mahan in both Great Britain and the United States. Many believed he was the devil, the mastermind of the naval arms race between Great Britain and Germany leading to the war itself: a philosopher of death. After the First World War had ended there was a genuine attempt to stop a future arms race and bring stability to the Pacific at the Washington Conference on November 12, 1921 which included Japan, Great Britain, and the United States. Though the intentions were well and good the results would only serve to damage relations between the U.S. and Japan. The Washington Treaty broke the Japanese-British alliance and separated all three powers. Japan insisted on the 70% ratio but Great Britain and the United States insisted on a 60% ratio. Kato Tomosaburo knew Japan was nearing national bankruptcy and that Japan's dream of naval expansion would never be realized so he decided to accept the 60% ratio to limit U.S. expansion. He fully understood that the United States could afford a Navy without equal and Japan could not hope to compete in an unlimited arms race. Kato Kanji was Kato Tomosaburo's chief naval adviser during the Washington Conference. He was adamant on the 70% ratio and when the 60% ratio was accepted he wrote in his diary on December 30, 1921:

[37] There is actually no data to support that an attacking fleet would need 50% more firepower over a defending fleet but the 70% ratio became an obsession within the Japanese Navy.

> "As far as I am concerned, war with America starts now. We'll get our revenge over this, by God!"[38]

Tomosaburo passed away August 25, 1923 and it was Kanji who would influence the Naval General Staff prior to World War II. The Washington Treaty saved Japan financially by allowing drastic cuts in its naval budget. National bankruptcy had been averted but within the Japanese naval establishment the treaty came has a huge shock. The National Defense Policy of 1923 which was drafted in February replaced Kato Tomosaburo's avoidance of war with the United States to Kato Kanji's ideology that war was inevitable. Now the hypothetical enemy was not only measured in capability but also intent and the economic war being waged was over China, the largest market in the world. This defense policy named the United States as the primary enemy of both the Navy and the Army. It also established certain principles one of which was "quick engagement, quick showdown."

Kato Kanji believed as a result of lessons learned from the Russo-Japanese War and World War One that any war with the United States had to be won quickly before U.S. industrial power could mobilize. He projected the Navy would complete the Philippine operation within a month and a decisive fleet encounter could be expected within forty-five days of opening hostilities. The General Plan called for offensive operations against the inferior Asiatic Fleet in the Far East and, in cooperation with the Army, destroy the U.S. naval bases at Luzon and Guam. As the U.S. main fleet came steaming to Far Eastern waters, the Imperial Japanese Navy would gradually reduce its strength en route with repeated attacks and at an appropriate moment the Japanese main battle fleet would annihilate the U.S. fleet. This concept meant that the Imperial Japanese Navy had a plan to defeat the United States Navy but did not have a plan for how to defeat the United States. This was a limited war strategy and the strategy ignored the concepts of total war.

The Japanese Army failed to devise a strategy for fighting the United States before the war and never developed one during the course of the war. The hypothetical enemy that the Army had focused on was the Soviet Union. After the Russo-Japanese War the Japanese General Staff feared that Russia would want revenge and would never accept Japanese presence in Manchuria or Korea. It was this war that the Imperial Army prepared for. As late as August 14, 1941—the date the Navy informed their Army counterparts that the schedule for preparations for war against the United States and Great Britain was to be completed by October 15, 1941—the Army was taken by surprise. They had not considered the

---

[38] Asada, Sadao, *From Alfred Thayer Mahan to Pearl Harbor* at 92.

United States a serious enemy so even on the eve of hostilities no comprehensive plan for a war had been established.[39]

Initially the Japanese Army considered offensive operations at the beginning of hostilities against Great Britain and the United States in terms of seizing the natural resources of Southeast Asia. This would provide Japan the raw materials to maintain her economy and become self-sufficient. However, no plans for how to conclude the war or what might be considered a Japanese victory were ever made. The Army assumed responsibility for the seizure of the Philippines, North Borneo, Malaya, Sumatra, and Java. The Navy would seize New Guinea, and the Bismarck Archipelago.

The Army argued for a protracted war and envisioned a war of attrition while the Navy proposed active offensive operations designed to produce Mahan's decisive battle. As aircraft matured and the range at which aircraft could operate increased, the plan was expanded in 1937 to include the occupation of Wake Island, Rabaul, the Gilberts and Ocean Islands. This defensive perimeter would act as a buffer and protect the Japanese home islands. The strategic planning which called on the heavy reliance on island outposts to act as defensive bases was flawed. Like Japan itself, each island had the same vulnerability identified in Mahan's third principle of sea power. The sea was an extension of each island's territory that could be seized just like an Army could take the high ground on land and place an objective under siege. An army cannot occupy this oceanic territory and therefore the island cannot be defended without a naval force capable of controlling the sea around it. The Japanese defensive perimeter was a house of cards for each island could be isolated and destroyed in detail. The great expansion of territory would only serve to over-extend the Imperial Japanese Navy.

---

[39] Drea, Edward J., *In The Service of the Emperor* at 26.

CHAPTER 3: THE BATTLE FLEET

Mahan's idea was that the purpose for construction of a battle fleet was to gain command of the sea. By doing so a nation can secure the seas as a great transportation highway and deny its use to others. The power that a battle fleet possessed could only be destroyed by another equally powerful battle fleet. If two nations processed a battle fleet and one was annihilated then the vanquished could no longer contest command of the seas, so the proper role of the battle fleet, in Mahan's eyes, was to seek out the enemy battle fleet and destroy it. On command of the sea, Corbett wrote that the only value the high seas had was the right of passage, and thus the seas were a means of communications. By denying an enemy this means of passage his national life at sea may be checked in the same way that armies check it on land by occupying territory.[40]

He continued by expressing that the object of naval warfare was to control communications and that control of the seas was the act of forbidding passage of public and private property upon the sea through its destruction.[41] The tool used to achieve this objective was the battle fleet. The primary purpose of battleships in particular was to secure control so that lesser ships could do their job without interference. Cruisers were constructed to exercise sea control due to their greater numbers. A nation could not exercise control through battleships alone because as these were expensive platforms there would never be enough to cover the territory required, while cruisers could exercise control without battleships if the enemy had no battleships to interfere with them.

This maxim demonstrated battleships need an opposing force of equal strength to remain relevant. If no one builds battleships then there is no need for battleships.

> ***With this said, there was no higher trump card to be played, no weapon or weapon system that could destroy a battle fleet.***

---

[40] Corbett, Julian S., *Principles of Maritime Strategy* at 89.

[41] Ibid at 91.

An individual battleship could be sunk by lesser ships but to stop a fleet of battleships and their supporting cruisers and destroyers required an equally powerful battle fleet. Thus, nations including Japan and the United States invested huge amounts of national treasure to construct this weapon system in order to command the sea. The result was an arms race between the two competing powers with the same ambition to control the Pacific Ocean.

Mahan's maxim that command of the sea depended on the battle fleet was perfectly sound if placed in proper context. The true function of the battleships was to protect cruisers and flotillas of smaller ships allowing them to do their jobs without interference. The best means to achieve this was to destroy the enemy's power of interference via the enemy battle fleet. Command of the sea depends on the battle fleet.[42] Battleships established tactical blockades around strategically significant waterways. These waterways could be entrances or exits to ports, straits, or the sea surrounding an island. This secured control of those waterways. To break that control one would have to commit to battle your own battle fleet that could occupy the geographical location being contested. This brought the battle fleets into conflict and brought about the decisive battle. In theory the war could be decided in a single afternoon.

Strategic level blockade would have to be maintained by lesser ships that were more numerous. In the age of sail this role belonged to cruisers but submarines and aircraft would assume this role of denying commerce in the more open water of the vast Pacific. The decisive battle required a willing partner and Corbett believed such battles would be rare as the weaker force would normally run. To set up conditions where one side could trap or prevent the escape of an enemy battle fleet would be difficult.

The Imperial Japanese Navy's battle fleet consisted of twelve battleships. Four were of the *Kongo* class and were originally battlecruisers. Two *Fuso* class, two *Ise* class, two *Nagato* class, and two *Yamato*-class battleships filled out the battle line.

---

[42] Ibid at 112-113.

Table 1. Japanese Battleships that Participated in World War II

Name	Program year	Project Name	Laid down	Launched	Completed
Kongo	1907	I GO Armored Cruiser	01-17 1911	5-18-1912	8-16-1913
Hiei	1904	BO GO Armored Cruiser	11-04 - 1911	11-21-1912	8-4-1914
Haruna	1903	No. 2 Armored Cruiser	3-16-1912	12-14-1913	4-19-1915
Kirishima	1903	No. 3 Armored Cruiser	3-17-1912	12-1-1913	4-19-1915
Fuso	1903	No. 3 Battleship	03-11 1912	3/28/1913	11/8/1915
Yamashiro	1913	No. 4 Battleship	11-20 -1913	11/3/1915	3/31/1917
Ise	1915	No. 5 Battleship	5/10/1915	11/12/1916	12/15/1917
Hyuga	1915	No. 6 Battleship	5/6/1915	1/27/1917	4/30/1918
Nagato	1916	No. 7 Battleship	8/28/1917	9/11/1919	11/25/1920
Mutsu	1917	No. 8 Battleship	6/1/1918	5/31/1920	10/24/1921
Yamato	1937	No. 1 Battleship	11/4/1937	8/8/1940	12/16/1941
Musashi	1937	No. 2 Battleship	3/29/1938	11/1/1940	8/5/1942

Ishibashi, Takao. *Nippon Teikoku Kaigun Zen-kansen 1868-1945: Senkan, Jun'yô-senkan [Illustrated Ships Data on Vessels of the Imperial Japanese Navy 1868-1945: Battleships, Battlecruisers],* Vol. 1. Namiki Shobo, 2007 at 208-382.

The Japanese had a policy that emphasized quality over quantity since they could not hope to out build the United States. Her ships were to have the largest guns and *Kongo* was the first ship to introduce the 14-inch gun caliber and *Nagato* introduced the 16.1-inch gun caliber. The *Yamato* would have the largest guns of all at 18.1-inch. The Japanese battleships were faster than their U.S. counterparts averaging 24-26 knots over the U.S. standards twenty-one knots. It was in their armor protection where the two nations differed in design details.

The Japanese ships were based on British design concepts. The *Kongo* was designed by British Architect Sir George Thurston and built by Vickers in England and Japan sent hundreds of Japanese architects to learn from the British so that

Kongo's three sisters could be built in Japan. This naturally produced designs similar to contemporary British designs of the day. Projectile performance influenced armor protection and the early projectiles performed more like high capacity projectiles then armor-piercing projectiles.

British and Japanese projectiles of this period of 1906-1916 used a very sensitive picric acid as an explosive filler. The Japanese called it *shimose.* It was extremely powerful and burned very hot making it excellent at starting fires. Fire was the leading cause of destroying the Russian fleet during the Russo/Japanese War and the Japanese liked this quality. The use of picric acid resulted in shells detonating prematurely. In addition the armor-piercing shells of this day had a non-delay fuse and a soft armor-piercing cap to protect the shell body's nose that only worked if the projectile struck within fifteen degrees of normal. Against face hardened armor if the cap failed the shell body would shatter reducing penetration and rendering the projectile ineffective. The result of the use of picric acid was that projectiles detonated on impact and acted as high-explosive shells without the advantage of a larger explosive charge.

In 1913 when *Kongo* was completed an armor-piercing projectile was only expected to punch a hole in the armor plate before it destroyed itself. Thin deck plates behind the main belt were placed to stop fragments. *Kongo* through *Nagato* were all designed with this fundamental protection scheme against this type of projectile performance. The armor protection is often referred to as an incremental system and was used by all the great powers in battleship design until the United States introduced a new armor scheme in 1916 with the completion of the *Nevada* class.[43]

At the Battle of Jutland in 1916 the German battleship projectiles introduced a delay fuse and they used a stable explosive filler that allowed an intact shell to penetrate the exterior armor and travel deep into the ship before the projectile detonated. The British lost three battlecruisers similar to *Kongo* from magazine explosions during the battle. After World War One the Washington Treaty stopped new battleship construction that would have replaced the older Japanese ships.

One of these cancelled battleships was *Tosa.* She would have been a member of the class after *Nagato* and represented the best design to that day. In 1924 *Tosa* was part of an experiment and a 16-inch projectile landing short of the hull by eighty-two feet and then dove underwater striking the ship twelve feet below the water-

---

[43] Friedman, Norman, *Battleships, Design and Development 1905-1945* at 55-63.

line near frame 288 and just below the main armor belt. This was between her two aft turrets in line with her main powder magazine. The projectile penetrated the outer compartments and detonated within the powder magazine which was empty. Flood water to the amount of 3,000 tons entered the ship and *Tosa* took a six degree list to port.[44]

Over the next seven years the Japanese would modify their projectiles to incorporate this underwater diving capability. In 1931 they introduced the Type 91 projectile. This shell had a hard armor-piercing cap with a cap head attached to it to protect the shell body nose for direct hits. Picric acid was abandoned for a more stable TNA explosive filler.[45] If the shell fell short the windscreen and a cap head came off leaving a flat nose. The shape of the nose allowed the projectile to stabilize its trajectory and run like a torpedo for about eighty meters underwater. This widened the danger space around a target. They hoped the shell would then either strike the target's side or detonate under the keel. To reach this point the projectile was given a long delay fuse of 0.4 seconds. The downside was that if a projectile hit thin plates such as in superstructure the projectile was likely to penetrate the entire structure without exploding.[46]

Fire control directors and rangefinders increased the accuracy of the main battery so hits at longer ranges became possible. Since the Washington Treaty had stopped new construction the older ships were modernized and gun elevations increased. Armor was added around the turrets, barbettes, and magazine spaces but typically the armor over machinery spaces was not modified. New engines, boilers, fire control, pagoda superstructure to carry the new directors, and more anti-aircraft guns transformed the ships during the 1920-1930s.

The Japanese battle line hoped to out-range their U.S. counterparts in a long range artillery duel. The Japanese battleships guns could elevate to forty-three degrees while the U.S. standard battleships could only elevate their guns to thirty degrees. The Japanese guns could fire projectiles out past 40,000 yards. If the salvo's of projectiles landed short their diving qualities would allow the projectiles to hit the target below the waterline. Type 91 projectiles were also made for 6" and

---

[44] Dulin, Robert O., Garzke, William H., *Battleships, United States Battleships in World War II* at 214.

[45] Japanese tri-nitro-aniso, designated as Type 91 *bakuyaku* (Model 1931 sive). Adopted on 25 July 1931, this was a methylated derivative of picric acid and a more stable burster than Shimose.

[46] Evans, David C., Peattie, Mark R, *Kaigun: Strategy, Tactics, and Technology in the Imperial Japanese Navy 1887-1941* at 260-266.

8" gun calibers. These projectile calibers widened the danger space fifteen meters for the 6" caliber and twenty meters for the 8" caliber over non-diving projectiles. By adopting an outranging policy it was hoped that they could inflict mortal damage on a superior fleet without receiving damage in return.

In addition they armed their cruisers and destroyers with long ranged oxygen fueled torpedoes known as the Type 93 Long Lance. These torpedoes had an incredible range of 40,000 yards, a speed of forty-eight knots and a huge 1,000-lb. warhead. The idea was to launch them by the hundreds to cripple and break up U.S. formations. The Japanese surface fleet trained heavily for night battles especially their destroyers and light cruisers.[47]

On December 7, 1941 the Imperial Japanese Navy surface forces consisted of twelve battleships supported by eighteen heavy cruisers, twenty light cruisers and one hundred and eleven destroyers. This was Japan's battle fleet, created in Mahan's vision to command the seas. During the course of the war six light cruisers and sixty-three destroyers would be added.

The basic war concepts were to destroy many with few since the Japanese Navy would be outnumbered. It was assumed that with the superior numbers of its battle fleet the U.S. would take the strategic initiative and launch an offensive across the Pacific. Submarines and aircraft were to wage a war of attrition and reduce the numerical advantage of the U.S. battle fleet. When the opportunity provided itself that the Japanese fleet had at least equal numbers if not superior numbers they would close and annihilate the American fleet. This was very similar to the strategy used in the Russo/Japanese war and was a limited war concept. While the navies will decide which nation will have command of the sea this strategy does not seek out the destruction of the United States. For Japan to achieve security her Navy must win and gain command of the seas. Failure opens Japan to blockade and invasion. This underscores the gravest flaw in the Japanese Navy's war plan. Even if it had succeeded with Tsushima-like one-sidedness, initiative remained with the enemy; Japan simply could not impose prohibitive conditions on the United States.

The American battle fleet was significantly larger than Japans but was divided between the Atlantic and Pacific fleets. On December 7, 1941 the United States had seventeen battleships with eight more under construction that would all participate in World War II. Many of the older battleships would have been replaced by the new construction but the opening of hostilities cancelled such ideas.

---

[47] Ibid at 266-271.

Table 2. U.S. Battleships that participated in World War II[48]

Name	Laid down	Launched	Completed
Arkansas	1/25/1910	1/11/1914	9/17/12
New York	9/11/1911	10/30/1912	4/15/14
Texas	4/17/1911	5/18/1912	3/12/1914
Nevada	11/4/1912	3/23/1914	3/11/1916
Oklahoma	10/26/12	3/23/1914	5/2/1916
Pennsylvania	10/27/1913	3/16/1915	6/12/1916
Arizona	3/16/1914	6/19/1915	10/17/1916
New Mexico	10/14/1915	4/23/1917	5/20/1918
Mississippi	4/5/1915	1/25/1917	12/18/1917
Idaho	1/20/1915	6/30/1917	3/24/1919
Tennessee	5/14/1917	4/30/1919	6/3/1920
California	10/25/1916	11/20/1919	8/10/1921
Maryland	4/24/1917	3/20/1920	7/21/1921
Colorado	5/29/1919	3/22/1921	8/30/1923
West Virginia	4/12/1920	11/19/1921	12/1/1923
North Caroli-na	10/27/1937	6/13/1940	4/9/1941
Washington	6/14/1938	6/1/1940	5/15/1941
South Dakota	7/5/1939	6/7/1941	3/20/1942
Indiana	11/20/1939	11/21/1941	4/30/1942
Massachusetts	7/20/1939	9/23/1941	5/12/1942
Alabama	2/1/1940	2/16/1942	8/16/1942
Iowa	6/27/1940	8/27/1942	2/22/1943
New Jersey	9/16/1940	12/7/1942	5/23/1943
Missouri	1/16/1941	1/29/1944	6/11/1944
Wisconsin	1/25/1941	12/7/1943	4/16/1944

The three oldest American battleships, *Arkansas, New York*, and *Texas* all had the same form of protection based on the theory of stopping fragments as their Japanese counterparts. Beginning with the *Nevada* class a new theory of armor protection was provided called "all or nothing." The theory was to provide sufficient thickness in armor and form an armored box to stop intact shells of a certain

[48] Whitley, M.J., *Battleships of World War II*, An International Encyclopedia at 242-306.

gun caliber within a given range for both side armor and deck armor and develop an immune zone. Any structure not vital to the ship was provided with no armor so in theory an armor-piercing shell would simply pass through without detonating. A ship with an immune zone could fight within this range and her armored citadel should remain intact. Therefore, in theory if her guns were superior she could fight within her immune zone and destroy any weaker adversary.[49]

With the improvement in projectiles after the First World War this form of armor protection was superior over the incremental system used in the older battleships. This meant the Washington Treaty that stopped battleship construction did not trap the U.S. with a fleet of ships with obsolete protection. The U.S. battleships were modernized with better fire control, new directors, radar, and more anti-aircraft guns during the 1920-1930's. The Americans actually were the last nation to adopt hard armor-piercing caps over the older soft caps and fell behind in developing a reliable delay fuse. It was not until 1936 when everything fell into place. The U.S. Navy also adopted a super-heavy projectile that was better at maintaining velocity down range and fell at a steeper angle of fall making them very good at penetrating deck armor.

This resulted in the U.S. Navy adopting a strategy of firing at long range where U.S. projectiles would defeat the relatively thin Japanese battleship's deck armor. Ironically, both the United States and Japan's strategy for a major fleet action mirrored each other in a long range artillery duel.

The new U.S. battleships beginning with the *North Carolina* class were fast making 27-28 knots and had gun elevations of 45 degrees. The Japanese range and speed advantage was largely eliminated. Four *South Dakota* class battleships to be followed by four *Iowa* class battleships capable of thirty-three knots would give the Americans ten modern battleships to Japan's two in *Yamato* and *Musashi*. None of the American battleships were as powerful as *Yamato* on an individual basis but numbers count and neither Japanese battleship was designed to take on five American battleships simultaneously.

These new ships were still under construction with the four *South Dakota* class ships being ready by 1942 and the four *Iowa* class being ready by 1943-44. The battleships assigned to the Pacific Fleet on December 7, 1941 were *Nevada, Oklahoma, Arizona, Pennsylvania, Tennessee, California, West Virginia Maryland*; *Colorado* was on the West Coast. In the Atlantic Fleet *Arkansas, New York, Texas, Idaho, New Mexico, Mississippi, North Carolina,* and *Washington* made up the U.S. battle

[49] Friedman, Norman, *Battleships, Design and Development 1905-1945* at 63-66.

line. To support the battleships the U.S. had eighteen heavy cruisers, nineteen light cruisers, and one hundred and eighty-one destroyers.

The U.S. Navy conceded that the Philippine Islands would be lost in a war with Japan in the early stages. The fleet in the South China Sea could fight a delaying action but ultimately would be forced to abandon this area to Japan. War Plan Orange called for an island-hopping campaign where the U.S. would seize the Mandated Islands (the Marshall, Caroline, and Mariana Island chains) and establish forward bases to take the next step back toward the Philippines. It was expected that the decisive battle with the Japanese battle fleet would occur around the Marianas and if the U.S. fleet was victorious it would move on to the Philippines. Once the Philippines were retaken the U.S. Navy would then establish a strategic blockade covering all of Japan and cutting off the oil from the South China Sea and blockade all ports.

CHAPTER 4: THE OPERATIONAL ART

How does an admiral develop an operation plan to achieve an objective? How does a collection of ships achieve national political goals? After the First World War the British theorist J.F.C. Fuller defined ten principles of war. These principles guide commanders in the planning and conduct of warfare. They provide a foundation for all military activity and a useful framework for understanding military history.

They are not absolute, immutable, or prescriptive. The relative importance of each must be taken with context, common sense, and proper judgement. Commanders must also consider the legitimacy of their actions based on legal, moral, political, diplomatic, and ethical propriety.

The ten principles as listed and defined below;

Selection and Maintenance of the Aim - A single, unambiguous aim is the keystone of successful military operations. Selection and maintenance of the aim is regarded as the master principle of war.

Maintenance of Morale - Morale is a positive state of mind derived from inspired political and military leadership, a shared sense of purpose and values, well-being, perceptions of worth and group cohesion.

Offensive Action - Offensive action is the practical way in which a commander seeks to gain advantage, sustain momentum and seize the initiative.

Security - Security is the provision and maintenance of an operating environment that affords the necessary freedom of action, when and where required, to achieve objectives.

Surprise - Surprise is the consequence of shock and confusion induced by the deliberate or incidental introduction of the unexpected.

Concentration of Force - Concentration of force involves the decisive, synchronized application of superior fighting power (conceptual, physical, and moral) to realize intended effects, when and where required.

Economy of Effort - Economy of effort is the judicious exploitation of manpower, materiel and time in relation to the achievement of objectives.

Flexibility — Flexibility is the ability to change readily to meet new circumstances – comprises agility, responsiveness, resilience, acuity and adaptability.

Cooperation - Cooperation entails the incorporation of teamwork and a sharing of dangers, burdens, risks and opportunities in every aspect of warfare.

Sustainability - To sustain a force is to generate the means by which its fighting power and freedom of action are maintained.[50]

The United States Armed Forces use the following nine principles of war:[51]

Objective – Direct every military operation toward a clearly defined, decisive and attainable objective. The ultimate military purpose of war is the destruction of the enemy's ability to fight and will to fight.

Offensive – Seize, retain, and exploit the initiative. Offensive action is the most effective and decisive way to attain a clearly defined common objective. Offensive operations are the means by which a military force seizes and holds the initiative while maintaining freedom of action and achieving decisive results. This is fundamentally true across all levels of war.

Mass – Mass the effects of overwhelming combat power at the decisive place and time. Synchronizing all the elements of combat power where they will have decisive effect on an enemy force in a short period of time is to achieve mass. Massing effects, rather than concentrating forces, can enable numerically inferior forces to achieve decisive results, while limiting exposure to enemy fire.

Economy of Force – Employ all combat power available in the most effective way possible; allocate minimum essential combat power to secondary efforts. Economy of force is the judicious employment and distribution of forces. No part of the force should ever be left without purpose. The allocation of available combat power to such tasks as limited attacks, defense, delays, deception, or even retrograde operations is measured in order to achieve mass elsewhere at the decisive point and time on the battlefield.

Maneuver – Place the enemy in a position of disadvantage through the flexible application of combat power. Maneuver is the movement of forces in relation to

---

[50] The 2011 edition of *British Defence Doctrine* (BDD) Joint Doctrine Publication 0-01 (JDP 0-01) (4th Edition) dated November 2011.

[51] *U.S. Army Field Manual FM 3–0.*

the enemy to gain positional advantage. Effective maneuver keeps the enemy off balance and protects the force. It is used to exploit successes, to preserve freedom of action, and to reduce vulnerability. It continually poses new problems for the enemy by rendering his actions ineffective, eventually leading to defeat....

Unity of Command – For every objective, seek unity of command and unity of effort. At all levels of war, employment of military forces in a manner that masses combat power toward a common objective requires unity of command and unity of effort. Unity of command means that all the forces are under one responsible commander with the requisite authority to direct all forces in pursuit of a unified purpose.

Security – Never permit the enemy to acquire unexpected advantage. Security enhances freedom of action by reducing vulnerability to hostile acts, influence, or surprise. Security results from the measures taken by a commander to protect his forces. Knowledge and understanding of enemy strategy, tactics, doctrine, and staff planning improve the detailed planning of adequate security measures.

Surprise – Strike the enemy at a time or place or in a manner for which he is unprepared. Surprise can decisively shift the balance of combat power. By seeking surprise, forces can achieve success well out of proportion to the effort expended. Surprise can be in tempo, size of force, direction or location of main effort, and timing. Deception can aid the probability of achieving surprise.

Simplicity – Prepare clear, uncomplicated plans and concise orders to ensure thorough understanding. Everything in war is very simple, but the simple thing is difficult. To the uninitiated, military operations are not difficult. Simplicity contributes to successful operations. Simple plans and clear, concise orders minimize misunderstanding and confusion. Other factors being equal, parsimony is to be preferred.

Officers in the U.S. military sometimes use the acronyms "MOSS COMES", "MOSS MOUSE", "MOOSE MUSS", "MOUSE MOSS", "MOM USE SOS", or "SUMO MOSES" to remember the first letters of these nine principles.

As this discussion illustrates centuries of study of war have produced similar distillations of wisdom. For the purpose of this book and the analysis of the naval battles the ten British principles will be applied. For naval warfare the tenth principle used by the British is paramount in establishing blockade.

In fact this single principle is the true measure of naval power. Without sustainability a Navy is unable to control the

seas which is the very essence of Mahan's and Corbett's philosophy.

On the subject of blockade, which was key for command of the sea, Corbett added that blockade was one of the weakest and least desirable forms of war but clarified this by saying he did not mean least effective but that to sustain operations was exhausting on both ships and men. He even recommended having two admirals available to relieve each other and one fifth of the blockading force would require refitting.[52]

The key element to an effective blockade was sustainability and this required a huge logistical support network. Blockade or control of the seas required forward deployment and the maintenance of the fleet at sea. This was extremely difficult on both men and ships but if done properly it could have a huge impact on the strategic outcome of the war. This form of offensive must be properly planned with ample reserves in place. Blockade can take the form of a naval blockade or a commercial blockade. A naval blockade focused its attention on the enemy's naval power and a commercial blockade focuses on exercising control of the seas and denying use of the oceans to the enemy's merchant shipping. Naval blockades can also be divided into "close" and "open." A close blockade prevents an enemy from putting to sea. It is a method of securing local and temporary command and its dominating purpose will usually be to prevent the enemy from acting in a certain area for a certain purpose.

An open blockade and commercial blockade are closely related. In an open blockade it is desirable for the enemy to put to sea. Closing of an enemy's commercial ports inflicts a high power of injury upon the enemy and can be fatal. The enemy can either submit or attempt to free himself by fighting. Therefore open blockade which will allow his forces to put to sea can help force the situation that would lead to decisive battle. Through decisive battle the war can be decided and the killing stopped.[53]

World War II in the Pacific would be dominated by amphibious operations. In defense of an enemy invasion it was not the battle fleet that should have been the primary target but the army while it was embarked on the transports and before it could reach its objective that was the primary objective.[54] However, naval com-

---

[52] Corbett, Julian S., *Principles of Maritime Strategy*, London, 1911 at 190.

[53] Ibid at 185-188.

[54] Ibid at 237.

manders, trained relentlessly to seek out decisive battle with the enemy's battle fleet, often interpreted their orders differently.

For joint operations elements of the battle fleet were always required to cover and support the transports that carried the Army or Marines and prevent their destruction at the hands of the defender. The attacker would normally sail the transports as a separate force and use evasion to avoid interference from a defending battle fleet. Command of the sea was vital for such operations. In defense of an invasion it was assumed that a defending battle fleet was present. If no defending fleet was present then command of the sea automatically shifted to the attacker. In an un-commanded sea where both sides have elements of their battle fleet available to secure command the attacker's position was extremely complex and he was at a disadvantage. This of course assumes the defending fleet was forward deployed and in-between the attacker and his objective to be invaded. In such cases the attacker needed to secure command of the sea through battle first before any attempt at invasion was possible.

What was the role of the battleships or battle fleet for such operations? The role envisioned was the battle fleet needed to be free to seek out the decisive battle and could not be tied to the invasion force as direct escorts. If the battle fleet was a direct escort then the defending battle fleet had both strategic targets available at once, the enemy battle fleet as well as the transports and enemy army. Due to the short range at which these battles were fought the transports needed to evade any hostile force. The job of escorting the army fell to the cruisers and destroyers. This required the invading battle fleet to weaken itself as it had to divide its forces for it also needed the cruisers and destroyers to successfully engage in a fleet action. The covering force had to keep itself between the hostile force and the transports.[55]

Evasion was the key for the army to reach its objective but by World War II with the inclusion of air power and the submarine the ability to evade detection and attack using these methods of a separate covering force and a smaller transport force would become problematic for both sides.[56] In the age of sail the great vastness of the ocean could hide two opposing forces far more easily than in the post-radio, post-airplane era of the 20th Century. Aircraft could search large stretches of ocean and the ability of aircraft to strike targets at long range allowed them to exercise open blockade even more efficiently than the cruisers did in the age of sail.

---

[55] Ibid at 242-243.

[56] Ibid at 288.

This ability was the chief advantage of airpower in the context of sea power and introduced strike warfare while admirals were developing operations based on tactics used during the age of sail. The principle of security would be instrumental in implementing naval power, including security from air power, and the side which most effectively upheld this principle would likely achieve victory.

The attack and defense of an oversea expeditions were probably the most complex form of operation the fleet could carry out. The paramount function of the covering squadron was to prevent interference with the actual combined operation–that is, the landing, support, and supply of the army. To do this it must achieve local command of the sea. Yet, at the same time it must be free to seek out and destroy any opposing battle fleet.[57]

The introduction of aircraft that could search large geographical areas in a short time span made evasion by separate transport and battle forces in an amphibious operation far more difficult and placed these forces at risk of being destroyed in detail. Securing the sea was the main responsibility of the battleship so that lesser ships could do their jobs. This would complicate their other role for seeking out the enemy battle fleet for a decisive battle. Thus combined operations increased the need for a willing partner in arranging a decisive battle. If one fleet was tied to a beachhead it would be unable to maneuver to intercept a nearby enemy battle fleet but would need the enemy to come to him, which would happen at a time of the enemy's choosing.

In addition the greater range of detection that aircraft provided also allowed one side to easily withdraw before it was trapped. This was true in dealing with both air and surface attack. Carrier operations during World War II were largely restricted to daylight hours and this allowed surface forces to either withdraw or advance at night depending on the tactical situation.

Since command of the sea implied the ability to deny passage to the enemy, the difficulty of night operations meant that airpower could not establish complete command of the sea on its own.

The great advantage in range became a liability at night and the inability to sustain operations at night allowed an enemy the use of passage during these time

[57] Corbett, Julian S., *Principles of Maritime Strategy*, London, 1911 at 285.

intervals. In addition aircraft had to expend energy to stay airborne and had a very limited time to do so. This also compromised the principle of sustainability and weather also impacted operations which could compromise it even further. While the battle fleet had the disadvantage in weapon range compared to aircraft it could establish command of the seas within this limited range twenty-four hours a day. Its reserve supply of fuel and ammunition could last several days to weeks depending on the operation. This allowed the battle fleet to implement sustained operations and this was the great advantage of the battle fleet.

Submarines operated by stealth and had a very limited supply of torpedoes, their primary weapon. They were slow and could not stay submerged indefinitely. They took time to travel the significant distances getting on station which also used up their ability to stay on station once they arrived. If located surface ships and aircraft could sink them. As a compliment to the battle fleet in establishing blockade they would prove more useful in open blockade vs close blockade but would require the support of the battle fleet and aircraft carriers to be truly successful.

CHAPTER 5: SUBMARINES AND COMMERCE WARFARE

The submarine as a naval weapon came into its own during the First World War with the German U-boat campaign in the Atlantic. Corbett believed in commerce raiding since one of the goals of sea power was to stop commerce. Corbett argued that a significant portion of the battle fleet should be assigned to commerce raiding. When he wrote his work the submarine was still unproven and his choice of ship type to do such work was the cruiser or the second tier of the battle fleet. The world's oceans were vast and to cover all the territory to establish sea control a navy needed numbers.[58]

Attack and defense of trade was the second method of exercising control of communications. Trade follows set routes and even when the open ocean portion of the route was varied, the destinations and the choke points do not vary. For this reason the concentration of defense was at the normal constriction of the trade routes. "Pelagic" commerce attack, as Corbett called attack on the open ocean, was a matter of "catch as catch can"' and was less profitable than concentration at the nodes of trade. Thus, defense of trade was easier than attack since the defensive force could wait at the nodes for the attacker. He also noted that when war on commerce was the object of the belligerent, it was usually because he was the weaker in naval power and did not wish to risk the decisive battle. Thus, the defensive force had the advantage.

Mahan viewed commerce raiding as a secondary goal for the battle fleet. He called it a great delusion because it required wide dissemination of force.

It was far more efficient to control the strategic centers of passage than to strike individual targets as the primary means of gaining command of the sea. [59] Mahan used Great Britain's merchant fleet as an example and with its large

[58] Ibid at 91.

[59] Mahan, Alfred T., *The Influence of Sea Power upon History* at 539-540.

number of resources the target was simply huge. Measuring in millions of tons of shipping such a large target could absorb a truly massive blow and it would not be fatal for the nation.

In World War One the British surface forces enforced a blockade of the Baltic Ocean cutting off all trade with German ports. The blockade was brutal and effective with approximately two million Germans starved to death. The German High Seas Fleet was not able to break the blockade. During the Battle of Jutland it was out-maneuvered by the British Grand Fleet twice but did manage to escape destruction.

Due to the effectiveness of the British blockade the Germans resorted to unrestricted submarine warfare, changing its primary strategic objective to commerce warfare, precisely as Corbett advised in this situation. His policy was being pursued by the weaker naval power since it could not defeat the Grand Fleet in decisive battle.

The submarine became a hated weapon because it struck without notice. When the passenger liner *Lusitania* was sunk this helped propel the United States to declare war. German U-boats sank 6,964 ships or 12,916,496 tons and damaged another 693 ships for 2,735,856 tons[60] during the First World War. This gave the German admirals an illusion of success. This success would lead Germany to repeat the experiment in World War II.

What was the illusion and why did Mahan refer to commerce warfare as a most dangerous delusion? Most scholars have claimed that Germany almost won the Battle of the Atlantic.[61] German U-boats sank 3,065 ships or 14,550,293 tons in the Second World War and damaged 408 ships for 2,745,923 tons.[62] Again, on the surface this would seem to reflect a very successful campaign. This was where Mahan's comments illuminate the nature of the delusion.

---

[60] Figures come from UBOAT.Net. *Allied warships hit.*

[61] Weir, Erin M.K., *German Submarine Blockade, Overseas Imports, and British Military Production in World War II*, page 2. Dan van der Vat's *The Atlantic Campaign* describes it as "a prolonged and desperate struggle that came closer than any other to deciding the war in Germany's favor." V. E. Tarrant, author of a history of Germany's submarine campaigns during the two World Wars, argues that "the U-Boats came close to being the single decisive factor in both wars." The Oxford Companion to World War II states, "U-Boats nearly brought the UK to its knees," and renowned military historian Basil Liddell-Hart agrees that "it is evident that Britain had herself narrowly escaped defeat." These quotes are from widely-cited and, with the exception of Liddell-Hart, recent academic books, and reflect the tone of most other scholarly and popular works on the subject.

[62] Figures come from UBOAT.Net. *Allied warships hit.*

Britain was an economic superpower with resources in India, Canada, New Zealand, and Australia. When the United States entered the war Germany was fighting two superpowers. Their wealth was spread out among tens of thousands of ships and even a blow as large as what the German's inflicted was not enough to inflict a fatal blow on Great Britain's economy much less the economy of the United States which in 1941 was 100% self-sufficient in all natural resources.

Commerce warfare is an attack on a nation's economy, and produces a war of attrition. It was not the number of ships being sunk that was truly important though that was a means to an end. It was how much of the cargo was getting through the U-Boat blockade to feed the British economy that was even more important. A surface fleet blockading a port can stop all traffic from entering or exiting this port. By taking command of the seas or denying passage, all traffic could be cut. Prime Minister Winston Churchill prioritized the destruction of the German surface fleet over the German U-boats for they had the potential of stopping traffic altogether from reaching a particular port either through a blockade or wiping out an entire convoy. However, the use of battleships as commerce raiders was not what battleships were built for. They would never be available in enough numbers to be effective which was why Corbett emphasized using cruisers for this type of mission in exercising command of the sea. The Axis powers in the European Theater during World War II misused their capital ships in a mission at which they could not succeed simply due to a lack of numbers. In fairness they also lacked sufficient numbers to defeat the Royal Navy in decisive battle. This resulted in the Kriegsmarine being used as Corbett's "fleet in being", which in turn resulted in the Royal Navy wasting resources guarding against its threat.[63]

The concept that commerce warfare was a delusion can further be explained by an economy adjusting to the needs of the country. One example of this was an iron ore mine in peace time may work one eight hour work shift but in a wartime economy it will work three eight hour shifts so it can operate twenty-four hours a day. This increased domestic production and this decreased the need for imports.

---

[63] Corbett, Julian S., *Principles of Maritime Strategy* at 211.

Table 3. Britain's Iron Ore Supplies, 1939-1945 (in thousands of tons). Imports Home Change in Stock Quantity Actual Production Reduction[64]

Year	Imports	Home production	Quantity available	Actual consumption
1939	5,200	14,486	19,686	?
1940	4,508	17,702	21,751	20,718
1941	2,241	18,974	21,176	19,911
1942	1,935	19,906	21,995	20,753
1943	1,924	18,494	20,157	19,001
1944	2,148	15,472	18,353	17,341
1945	4,191	14,175	18,322	17,691

What this chart shows was that Great Britain always had a surplus over consumption of iron ore needed to make steel largely due to increased domestic production. Britain was a major producer and exporter of steel immediately before World War II. It imported a large amount of iron ore, a significant amount of steel components (pig iron, scrap, and ferro-alloys) and a small amount of semi-finished steel, and exported a substantial quantity of finished steel. In other words, Britain profited by buying raw or partly processed material, manufacturing it, and then selling the finished steel.[65]

Britain's healthy iron and steel trade gave it much room to adjust for a decline in its imports of ferrous metals. It could increase the "net imports" derived from a given volume of imports simply by cutting exports. It could increase the value (in terms of finished steel) of a given tonnage of imports by importing lighter finished materials, rather than bulky raw materials. In 1939 and 1940, Britain reduced imports of ore, increased those of steel components and of semi-finished steel, and reduced its exports of finished steel. In 1941, Britain continued the shift from ore to steel components and semi-finished steel, and became a net importer of finished steel. It began to shift from steel components to semi-finished steel in 1942 and drove up its finished steel imports in 1943. It started to return to its peacetime position in 1944 and became a major iron ore importer and finished-steel exporter in 1945. Through these shifts Britain maintained (or even increased) the amount

---

[64] Weir, Erin M.K., *German Submarine Blockade, Overseas Imports, and British Military Production in World War II* at 10.

[65] Ibid. at 10.

of finished steel provided to the British economy, even though it imported fewer tons of ferrous metal.[66]

Austin Robinson, a Cambridge economist and wartime planner, identified "four main limits: materials, manpower, shipping, and capacity." "Shipping" more accurately refers to materials imported by ship, while "materials" refers to domestically produced resources. Likewise, "labor" and "(physical) capital" might be substituted for "manpower" and "capacity." Britain needed imported materials, but did it need them more than domestic materials, labor, or capital? Which of these factors was the operative constraint on output? Robinson argues that these various limits were effective in different degrees at different stages of the war. In 1940 and 1941 it was capacity that was the chief limiting factor. At important moments throughout the war, it was shipping. From the end of 1942 onwards the problems of manpower supply became paramount.[67]

In other words, imported materials were sometimes the operative constraint, but not for a sustained period of time. Labor was the effective limit for most of the war, although capital was more important early on.[68] This was just one example of how an economy can adjust and why Mahan did not favor commerce warfare as the main objective of the battle fleet. Overall, the German U-boat campaign was a failure in both World Wars, not a success as most scholars claim. Mahan's warning that it was a dangerous delusion held true in the Atlantic largely due to the fact it was being waged against two superpowers with immense resources.

In the Pacific War there were different factors that needed to be considered. For Japan, her economy was not of a superpower status like Great Britain and she was 100% dependent on imported oil. The oil embargo by the United States was the catalyst for Japan seizing the oil fields in the South China Sea. The raw materials to the south would allow Japan to become economically self-sufficient but these raw materials would need to be transported over thousands of miles across the sea. These lines of communication could be cut and the South China Sea was not the open Atlantic. The many islands which were the source of the oil also created many choke points that commerce would need to transit. These choke points were perfect traps for unrestricted submarine warfare.

---

[66] Ibid.

[67] Ibid.

[68] Ibid

Japan was fighting the world's largest economic superpower in the United States which was completely self-sufficient. A blockade of the West coast of the United States would have no impact since exports could be shipped from the Atlantic and the U.S. had no need for imports. For Japan, a war of attrition was impossible to win so it did not make any sense to wage one.

Japan's strategy was to use her submarines to attack the U.S. battle fleet. Japanese leaders also believed that U.S. naval strategy would mirror their own and the United States would not attack civilian targets. This was one of the primary reasons the United States had declared war on Germany in the First World War. So confident were the Japanese that the United States would not conduct unrestricted submarine warfare on civilian merchant ships that they ignored their defense and as the war approached actually reduced merchant ship construction. Anti-submarine warfare was also neglected and this would come to haunt Japan once the war began.

In the 1920's Admiral Suetsugu Nobumasa gave the submarine force its primary missions: surveillance of the enemy battle fleet in harbor, pursuit and shadowing of the enemy fleet once it left its base, and ambush and reduction in numbers prior to the decisive fleet action. Beginning in 1938 exercises began to show that this strategy had major flaws.[69]

First it was extremely difficult for submarines to remain undetected outside a heavily defended port. Enemy destroyers and aircraft often discovered the submarines and they were ruled sunk during the exercise. In 1939-40 maneuvers that created an invasion force and set the submarines the objective to acquire it, pursue it and then ambush it proved equally alarming. Submarines could barely maintain contact due to their surface speed being insufficient. It was difficult for them to get ahead of a surface fleet and lie in wait for a proper firing position. Once submerged they were virtually stationary and this also made them easy targets for destroyers. Firing on the surface against heavily armed surface ships was suicidal. They were easily detected by anti-submarine aircraft as well as screening destroyers. [70]

Another flaw in these operational maneuvers was the lesson that land-based bombers and sea planes with the additional support of submarines would be effective at defending an island outpost. Despite the maneuvers showing the major

---

[69] Evans, David C., Peattie, Mark R., *Kaigun, Strategy, Tactics, and Technology in the Imperial Japanese Navy, 1987-1941* at 428.

[70] Ibid at 428-429.

flaws in command and control Japanese admirals insisted that the command of submarines be shore-based.[71]

Maneuvers in October 1940 showed great success in commerce warfare around various straits close to the Japanese home islands. In this exercise 133 merchant ships were ruled sunk. Yet, the Japanese admirals did not take heed of this warning nor did they implement a new strategy. Commerce warfare was only to take place if it did not interfere with the primary objective of attacking the U.S. battle fleet.[72]

So fearful of being detected Japanese submarine commanders practiced total submerged shots or sound shots. The subs were equipped with the proper range-finders and could determine exact bearings but only on the surface. Commanders would make a final periscope reading to get range and bearings and then lower the periscope and make the final calculations on sound bearings. This technique was not unique as the Americans attempted it as well.[73]

These developments led to Japanese submarine commanders being very passive during the war. The strategy to attack major warships instead of commerce may have been the correct strategy for a short war. The only strategic target that Japan had assigned to end the war was the destruction of the U.S. Pacific Fleet. This would require the rest of the Imperial Japanese Navy to assume the strategic initiative and seek out the U.S. fleet and destroy it as a combined force. It was unrealistic to expect submarines alone to have success against this heavily defended target without the support of the other elements of the fleet.

Japanese strategy was to assume the strategic defensive and wait for the U.S. to advance across the Pacific. This would leave submarines on their own for much of the critical year of 1942 as an advanced way of waging a war of attrition on the U.S. combatants. After this year U.S. industrial would be at full capacity and the fleet that would emerge by the end of 1943 would overwhelm any defense Japan could offer. The U.S. economy could invest 41.7% of its total Gross National Product into the war effort. In comparison Japan's economy could only invest 3.5% of its total Gross National Product into the war effort.[74]

---

[71] Ibid at 430.

[72] Ibid at 432.

[73] Ibid at 433.

[74] Tully, Tony. *Why Japan lost the War*, Kaigin.com at 2.

While commerce warfare would give an illusion of success by sinking more merchant ships it would have no impact on the U.S. economy. A war of attrition with the United States was impossible to win. Simply put, if Japan did not achieve Mahan's battle of annihilation by the end of 1942 the outcome of the war would be preordained as a U.S. victory. On December 7, 1941 Japan's merchant shipping equaled 6,384,000 tons. In the month of December new construction would add 44,200 tons. U.S. submarines would sink three merchant ships for 9,963 tons, U.S. land-based air would sink one ship for 4,281 tons, Australian and Netherland forces would sink five ships for 29,352 tons, and three ships were lost in maritime accidents totaling 8,662 tons. Twelve ships for 52, 258 tons for a net loss of 8,058 tons for the month. On January 1st, 1942 Japan's merchant fleet stood at 6,375,942 tons.[75]

Similarly, the table below shows that the United States alone out produced by 17,505,847 tons of merchant shipping more than Germany could sink. Great Britain produced 12,823,942 million tons of additional shipping. This again reasserts Mahan's concept that commerce warfare against a superpower was delusional if used alone as the primary tool to enforce blockade.

Table 4. Merchant Ship Production in tons

Year	United States[76]	Japan[77]
1942	5,479,766	661,800
1943	11,448,360	1,067,100
1944	9,288,156	1,735,100
1945	5,839,858	465,000
Total	32,056,140	3,929,000

Prior to hostilities U.S. commanders had no plans to conduct unrestricted commerce warfare using submarines. Like Japanese submarines the U.S. boats were to be used to support the main battle fleet in the decisive fleet action. Commander Daniel E. Benere wrote that before the war the U.S. submarine

---

[75] *Joint Army-Navy Assessment Committee, Japanese Naval and Merchant Shipping Losses during World War II by All Causes.* (1947)

[76] Tully, Tony. *Why Japan lost the War*, Kaigin.com at 2.

[77] Ibid.

force had no real objective.[78] This resulted in many problems that would beset the force once hostilities commenced. As we recall from the discussion earlier, a single, unambiguous aim is the keystone of successful military operations. Selection and maintenance of the aim is regarded as the master principle of war.[79]

Without a clear objective Pacific submarines were a divided force and were used for missions that they were ill suited for. It would not be until the middle of 1943 that a clear doctrine would be established.[80] The U.S. submarine missions at the beginning of the war are stated below:

- Submarine concentrations to cut the enemy's supply lines to the target areas.
- Submarine photographic reconnaissance of beachheads marked for amphibious landings and enemy military or naval installations marked for future reference.
- Submarine lifeguarding during air strikes.
- Submarine scouting duty in the target area and off enemy bases to report enemy movements and intercept and attack enemy forces which sortied to oppose the attacking United States forces.
- Submarines stationed to intercept and attack fugitive shipping attempting to flee the target area.

Unrestricted submarine warfare against Japanese commerce did not really begin at the opening of hostilities. This was not to say if a target of opportunity presented itself that individual U.S. submarines would not attack; the same applied for Japanese submarines encountering Allied targets of opportunity. There was not a coordinated effort to enforce a submarine blockade and cut the lines of communications between the Dutch East Indies, Sumatra, Malaya, and Borneo where the oil fields were in the South China Sea to Japan.

In the early part of the war U.S. submarine commanders would face many obstacles similar to Japanese submarine commanders. Training to attack heavily defended fleet units led to extremely cautious tactics and U.S. commander's also

---

[78] Benere, Daniel, E. *A critical examination of the U.S. Navy's use of unrestricted submarine warfare in the Pacific Theater during WWII,* Naval War College at 2.

[79] The 2011 edition of British Defence Doctrine (BDD) *Joint Doctrine Publication 0-01 (JDP 0-01) (4th Edition)* dated November 2011.

[80] Clay Blair, Jr., *Silent Victory* (Philadelphia: J.B. Lippincott Company, 1975), v.1, at 335.

implemented sound attacks with no success. Poor torpedoes with many failure rates also hampered operations. Deployment to major Japanese ports that were heavily defended also led to extremely cautious tactics so in the very early stages of the Pacific War Japanese and American submarine campaigns did mirror each other. The full ramifications of these tactics will be discussed in future chapters.

CHAPTER 6: CARRIER OPERATIONS

Japanese carrier aviation was first organized in 1928 and the carriers were placed into divisions and added to the fleet organization. The first commander of the carrier divisions was Admiral Sankichi Takahashi who was succeeded by Takayoshi Kato, Koshiro Oikawa and Isoroku Yamamoto.[81]

Aircraft range in the late 1920's was only 60-70 miles and carrier tactics called for the first air strike to be launched from as far as possible. The first air strike would be aimed at carriers or battleships and subsequent air strike at battleships to support the main body in its decisive battle.

Normally the carriers would be close to the battleship groups on the non-engaged side to provide air cover to both the battleships and the carriers themselves. One concern in keeping the carriers close to the battleships was to prevent separation from the main body and then being attacked separately.

One disadvantage of these tactics was that the carriers restricted the movements of the battleships and this reduced the battleship's flexibility to seek out the decisive battle. In addition it increased the chance that the carriers would be discovered and in battle drills this led to the carriers being attacked 100% of the time. In addition providing air cover for both the battleships and carriers proved ineffective.

In 1934 new studies resulted in tactical changes. Carrier divisions would operate independently from the battleship group and attempt to encircle enemy carrier groups. Each carrier division was supported by cruisers and destroyers. Each carrier division was disposed so they would operate an equal distance from the enemy unless the situation dictated otherwise. Each carrier division would launch a simultaneous forestalling attack on the enemy carriers aiming to put them out of action. This would prevent friendly carriers from being attacked. To support the main body a carrier would be dispatched and operate separately.

---

[81] Ozawa, Jisaburo, *Outline Development of Tactics and Organization of Japanese Carrier Air Force, The Pacific War Papers*, Goldstein M. Donald and Dillon V. Katheryn, at 76-81.

Another tactic was to place a carrier closer to the enemy to act as bait and lure enemy attacks to it while the remaining carriers at a slightly greater distance would attack the enemy by surprise. This tactic was initiated by Capt. Kurio Toibana who later became a staff officer of Admiral Yamamoto. This use of separate divisions was reminiscent of Corbett's concepts for maneuver. Corbett believed that the use of divisions to maintain concealment and concentration made it easier for an enemy to locate friendly forces. He believed battles had to be won by taking risks and the risk of division would be the destruction of each task force in detail. However, the advantage would be for one or more elements to gain the principle of surprise through evasion.[82]

In contrast, Mahan's preference for concentration of force was based on unity of command. His major concern dealing with division was being able to coordinate widely separated forces. While division was useful the divided forces should be close enough for mutual support.[83]

Reconnaissance of the enemy and concealment of friendly forces were the principle elements for this strategy. Cooperation of land-based air, submarines, radio intelligence, and the interception of enemy aircraft and submarines were essential to maintain the element of surprise. Since this could not always be guaranteed reconnaissance fell to the float planes of the fleet so the carriers could maximize offensive capabilities. It was also determined to have the fleet formations well spread out while approaching the enemy both to reduce chances that all forces would be discovered and to encircle the enemy. Unless the enemy was close to their own land bases it was believed that this deployment strategy offered the greatest possibility to achieve surprise.

Up until 1936 the prevailing view was to launch the decisive battle using its battleships as the main fighting strength with carriers serving a secondary and supporting role. New aircraft were entering the fleet which increased the carriers overall power considerably. New Type 94 dive bombers had scored a 30% hit rate and aerial torpedo aircraft achieved a miraculous 100% hit rate. Carrier training and studies were made independently without a systematic approach. Minoru Genda commented on this development:[84]

---

[82] Corbett, Julian S. *Principles of Maritime Strategy*, at 131 and 134.

[83] Mahan, Alfred T., *Sea power in its relations to the war of 1812*, Volume 1 at 316.

[84] Genda, Minoru and Chihaya Masataka, *How the Japanese Task Force Idea Materialized, The Pearl Harbor Papers*, Goldstein M. Donald and Dillon V. Katheryn at 6.

> In view of a surprising big improvement in aerial torpedoes and bombs of late, won't they soon be more destructive than gun projectiles? .... With more accuracy as well as the unequalled long range of attacks, will they not soon deprive the leadership in a naval battle away from battleships gun power? ... Won't they make battleships useless in future sea battles?[85]

This new theory, a relatively radical one, that carrier aircraft would destroy everything afloat was slowly gaining a foothold within the Japanese high command that was a complete rejection of the battleship as the main arbiter of sea power. Genda made the following proposal:

> The main strength of a decisive battle should be air arms, while its auxiliary should be built mostly by submarines. Carriers and destroyers will be employed as screens of carrier groups, while battleships will be put out of commission and tied up.[86]

In 1940 when Admiral Isoroku Yamamoto became Commander in Chief of the Combined Fleet studies were made on the combined use of carriers and land-based air. In fleet maneuvers the 1st Carrier Division commander was ordered to take command of the 2nd Carrier Division and assume command of all carriers at that time.[87] The idea to concentrate carriers came from Minoru Genda who had seen a U.S. Navy newsreel showing two *Lexington* and two *Yorktown* class carriers in formation. He did not know if this was how U.S. carriers normally operated but it planted the idea on enabling the concentration of a large air force at sea.[88] Despite the increase in offensive power some defects of concentration were discovered. Determining the overall commander for the air wings, cohesion between the various squadrons, and lack of training and communication between the various squadrons were the main problems.

Ozawa then in command of the 1st Carrier Division recommended a permanent air fleet command.[89] Genda also agreed that this was necessary and unknown to Jisaburo Ozawa, Yamamoto had already intended to launch a concentrated at-

---

[85] Ibid.

[86] Ibid.

[87] Ozawa, Jisaburo, *Outline Development of Tactics and Organization of Japanese Carrier Air Force, The Pacific War Papers*, Goldstein M. Donald and Dillon V. Katheryn, at 76–81.

[88] Genda, Minoru and Chihaya Masataka, *How the Japanese Task Force Idea Materialized, The Pearl Harbor Papers*, Goldstein M. Donald and Dillon V. Katheryn, at 9-10.

[89] Jisaburo Ozawa Jisaburo, *Outline Development of Tactics and Organization of Japanese Carrier Air Force, The Pacific War Papers*, Goldstein M. Donald and Dillon V. Katheryn, pages 76–81

tack on Pearl Harbor.[90] 'However, Jisaburo Ozawa's recommendation was not accepted by then Commander in Chief Admiral Mineichi Koga on the grounds that as the 1st and 2nd Carrier Divisions would operate separately each fleet needed its own carrier division to provide fighter support. In order to concentrate all carriers for attack temporary authorization of command to the senior carrier commander would suffice.[91]

Jisaburo Ozawa countered that the carriers would bring about the decisive consequences for the naval battle and fighter support for the battle fleet could be provided when necessary.

Undaunted by the rejection he then sent his recommendation directly to the Chief of the General Staff and the Navy Minister.[92]

The General Staff accepted his idea and the 1st Air Fleet was organized in April 1941. Yamamoto scolded Ozawa for breaking the chain of command but said he was glad that the General Staff had agreed to his recommendation.[93] Initially the 1st Air Fleet was only supported by destroyers and it was not until the decision to use it for the Pearl Harbor attack that additional support ships were provided including two *Kongo* class battleships with a cruiser division of two *Tone* class cruisers.

The 1st Carrier Division consisted of the carriers *Akagi* and *Kaga*. These two ships were converted from a battlecruiser and battleship hull and had normal displacements of 41,300 and 42,541 tons. *Akagi* carried twenty-seven A6M2 "Zero" fighters, eighteen D3A "Val" dive bombers, and twenty-seven K5N "Kate" torpedo bombers. *Kaga* carried twenty-seven A6M2 fighters, twenty-seven D3A dive bombers, and twenty-seven K5N torpedo bombers. This totaled to one hundred and fifty-three aircraft for this carrier division.

The 2nd Carrier Division consisted of the carriers *Soryu* and the *Hiryu*. These two ships were smaller and had normal displacements of 18,800 and 20,250 tons. The *Soryu* carried twenty-seven A6M2 fighters, eighteen D3A dive bombers, and

---

[90] Genda, Minoru and Chihaya Masataka, *How the Japanese Task Force Idea Materialized, The Pearl Harbor Papers*, Goldstein M. Donald and Dillon V. Katheryn, page 10.

[91] Jisaburo Ozawa Jisaburo, *Outline Development of Tactics and Organization of Japanese Carrier Air Force, The Pacific War Papers*, Goldstein M. Donald and Dillon V. Katheryn, at 76-81.

[92] Ibid.

[93] Ibid.

eighteen K5N torpedo bombers. The *Hiryu* carried twenty-four A6M2 fighters, eighteen D3A dive bombers and eighteen K5N torpedo bombers. A total of one hundred and twenty-three aircraft comprised this carrier division.

The *Shokaku* and the *Zuikaku* made up the 5th Carrier Division. Both ships had a normal displacement of 29,800 tons. Each carrier had identical air wings which consisted of twenty-four A6M2 fighters, twenty-seven D3A dive bombers, and twenty-seven K5N torpedo bombers. This division had a total of one hundred and fifty-six aircraft. These three carrier divisions would be used in the Pearl Harbor attack and combined had four hundred and thirty-five aircraft. These six fleet carriers made up the majority of Japan's carrier strength.

In addition to the fleet carriers Japan had a total of six light carriers. The *Ryujo, Zuiho, Shoho, Ryuho, Taiyo,* and *Hosho.* These ships carried between twenty-seven and forty-eight aircraft.

CHAPTER 7: U.S. CARRIER DOCTRINE

In 1937 Captain Richmond K. Turner as a faculty member of the Naval War College gave a lecture entitled "The Strategic Employment of the Fleet." He said, echoing Mahan:

> The chief strategic function of the fleet is the creation of situations that will bring about decisive battle, and under conditions that will ensure the defeat of the enemy.[94]

How would carriers fit into this vision? Turner identified three areas in which carriers could be decisive. The first was to conduct raids and this was the foundation of strike warfare. The second was based on the principle of security. Carriers could gain important information on the enemy and prevent them from doing the same for friendly forces. The third was to carry a threat of permanency for future operations, so that an enemy would never feel safe in rear areas and would have to expend resources to defend these rear areas.

With carrier aircraft improving and the technology of aircraft maturing nothing behind the front lines was safe from raids or from observation. Command of the air was critical and the belief that enemy carriers had to be taken out first was key to their mission. In addition he felt naval aircraft had matured enough to be able to take out land-based air forces so these were included as necessary if a naval battle occurred within their range.[95]

However, not every problem on how to implement such a strategy had been fully worked out prior to hostilities. The principle of mass or concentration was still in question. How many carriers should operate together and would their combined air wings be enough to achieve the objective? Prior to hostilities U.S. carrier formations never operated more than two carriers in a single group. This

---

[94] Hone, Thomas C., *Replacing Battleships with Aircraft-Carriers in the Pacific in World War II*, Naval War College Review, winter 2013, Vol. 66, No. 1 at 1.

[95] Ibid.

would be how carrier groups would be formed early in the war. The limitations on mass also meant only so many missions could be accomplished at the same time so what would be required per mission had also an unknown factor.[96]

If the carriers were too spread out control of the air would become impossible so they had to be close enough for relative support of each other. Mass had to be translated into combat power through the use of proper scouting, bombing, and air-to-air combat tactics and this was still unknown because there was no combat experience. In carrier vs. carrier studies there didn't seem to be any location that was favorable that an enemy could not find and destroy friendly carriers. The ability to strike first became the foremost priority in conducting carrier operations. Protecting carriers became a real problem and how best to achieve this was still unanswered. This broke the principle of endurance which survivability was key to this principle.[97]

More fighters in a combat air patrol above friendly forces did not guarantee command of the air. Enemy aircraft in the exercises always made it past these fighters to attack the ships. Could aircraft truly gain command of the air on their own? If not then carriers needed another level of protection and this came from a screening force and their anti-aircraft guns.

This forced the battle fleet to give up their primary offensive duties for defensive duties to protect the carriers. The battle fleet required concentration so spreading out the fleet was in direct contradiction of what the battle fleet required. The battle fleet also needed to train together for the principle of cohesion. Spreading the fleet out also ruined this principle and this was extremely important to carry out a successful surface action.

The attrition rate on the air wing itself was still unknown. How long could carriers maintain operations and at what levels of air wing attrition did a carrier become combat-ineffective? How to operate carriers when their air wings were in flight was still not completely worked out. Typically, carriers sailed into the wind in a straight line so the air wing would know where the carriers where to return. However, in combat this may not be the best course and could lead the carriers into contact with surface forces or submarines.

Surface battle with carriers should be avoided at all costs especially at night. Their survivability depended on finding an enemy but not being found and in the

---

[96] Ibid.

[97] Ibid.

age of air power where aircraft could search vast areas of ocean this was particularly difficult.[98]

The level of logistical support required for carrier operations was still unknown. Without knowing the attrition rate on air wings in actual combat operations the replacement of aircraft and pilots could not be accounted for prior to hostilities. This too broke the principle of sustainability.

In April of 1939, Vice Admiral Ernest J. King, Commander Aircraft, Battle Force issued "Operations with Carriers." Their primary mission was to gain control of the air and mission requiring defensive operations militate against this assignment. Carriers were primarily offensive machines. While destroying enemy land bases was viewed as practical, carriers should avoid being tied to amphibious assaults due to a lack of strategic mobility. Direct support for an amphibious assault nailed one foot of the fleet to the operational area. This in turn made it easier for an enemy to locate friendly carriers and destroy them.

Carriers needed to roam so they could not be located and amphibious operations prevented the carriers from staying on the offensive.[99]

Both the Imperial Japanese Navy and the U.S. Navy developed strategies that focused on striking first. This was largely due to the perceived vulnerabilities of aircraft carriers themselves. Due to their armament of aircraft, aviation fuel, and munitions, they were essentially floating bombs and fire was a major hazard. They did have advantages in they were faster than most major surface combatants, and their aircraft could easily out-range any surface combatant, but they were extremely vulnerable to aircraft and submarines. Carriers would become their own worst enemy and their ability to survive strike warfare was still in question.[100]

Against enemy aircraft there would be four major forms of attack: level bombing, dive bombing, torpedo bombing, and glide bombing. Late in the war a fifth aerial threat in the form of kamikaze attack would be created by the Japanese against U.S. carriers. Level bombers usually attacked from high altitudes of 10,000

---

[98] Ibid.

[99] Hone, Thomas C., *Replacing Battleships with Aircraft-Carriers in the Pacific in World War II*, Naval War College Review, winter 2013, Vol. 66, No. 1 at 2-3.

[100] Heinz, Leonard, *Aircraft Carrier Defense in the Pacific War: The Carrier Battles of 1942* at 5.

feet or higher on an even level flight path dropping four to six bombs each. A formation would drop a salvo of bombs in hopes one or two would hit the target. The main level bombers attacking aircraft carriers in the first year of the Pacific War were, for the Americans, the B-17 "Flying Fortress," and, for the Japanese, the G3M "Nell" and the G4M "Betty." The B-17 was a large and sturdy four-engine bomber, built to pummel an enemy's industries and installations.[101]

The Japanese twin-engine G3Ms and G4Ms were operated by the navy, which meant that they were designed and operated with an emphasis on their anti-shipping role rather than strategic bombing. Their role was envisioned to inflict attrition on the larger U.S. fleet as it advanced toward the Philippines and thus reduce the size advantage the U.S. fleet processed prior to the main battle line engagement. Medium-altitude attacks by good-sized formations of aircraft, land-based IJN level bombers quickly emerged as a serious threat to Allied ships. These aircraft could also conduct torpedo attacks, which made them a more serious threat to surface ships.[102]

The Japanese B5N "Kate" could serve in a level bombing role in addition to serving both as a torpedo bomber and as the primary carrier-based search aircraft. The USN equivalents—the TBD "Devastator" and its successor the TBF "Avenger"—could also carry bombs for level bombing attacks in lieu of torpedoes.[103]

Dive bombing was first developed for supporting ground troops and then as an anti-ship tool. Dive bombers would typically start their dive at 10,000 feet or higher altitude and descend at an angle of 60 degrees or greater so that the pilot effectively became the bomb sight. The pilot would release the bomb between 1000-2000 feet and then pull out of its dive. Pre-war exercises showed this technique as highly accurate and difficult to counter.[104]

The D3A "Val" was the principle Japanese dive bomber at the start of the war. It was relatively lightly armed in that it carried two 7.7-mm machine guns forward and one 7.7-mm machine gun aft and could carry one 250-kg (551-lb.)

---

[101] Ibid.

[102] Ibid.

[103] Ibid.

[104] Ibid.

bomb. It was reasonably fast and long ranged but devoid of any armor or self-sealing fuel tanks.[105]

At the start of the war the standard U.S. dive bomber was the SBD "Dauntless." This plane could carry a 1,600-lb. bomb in overload condition and a 1000-lb. bomb for normal strike missions. It was also used as a scout and in this condition it normally carried a 500-lb. bomb to seek out targets of opportunity. The SBD was also armed with two forward-firing.50-in (12.7-mm) M2 Browning machine guns and either one or two rear flexible-mount.30-in (7.62-mm) AN/M2 machine guns and this made them effective against the lightly built Japanese fighters.[106]

The SBD also had armor and self-sealing fuel tanks. The latter were a relatively new technology, taking the form of a rubber bladder inside a metal tank. The idea was that the bladder would seal itself behind any bullet penetrating the metal tank, thus preventing a fuel leak and potential fire. Armor was heavy and self-sealing tanks cut down on the maximum potential fuel load that an aircraft could carry. This reduced speed and range but increased survivability. The Japanese aircraft engines were typically smaller than their U.S. counterparts so their aircraft stressed performance and range over protection. These decisions would have a major impact on the success and failure of strike warfare.[107]

Torpedo bombing would become the greatest threat to capital ships during the course of the war. The Japanese B5N "Kate" was fast and had excellent range and carried an excellent Type 91 aerial torpedo. This weapon permitted the B5Ns to make effective torpedo drops at airspeeds of up to 260 knots and altitudes of 1000 feet. These were far faster and higher drops than the USN aerial torpedo could handle. Once in the water, Type 91s ran at between 41 and 43 knots. Its gun armament was limited to a single flexible 7.7 mm machine gun firing to the rear. Like the D3A, the B5N completely lacked armor or fuel tank protection.[108]

At the beginning of the war the TBD *"Devastator"* was the standard torpedo bomber for the U.S. navy. The TBD was slower, had shorter range, and a lower ceiling than the B5N. It lacked the armor and self-sealing fuel tanks of the SBD. It only had a single.30 caliber machine gun firing though the propeller and another

---

[105] Ibid.

[106] Ibid.

[107] Ibid.

[108] Ibid.

in a flexible mount firing to the rear. The Mk 13 Mod 1 torpedo had failure rates up to 90%, required a drop as low as 50 feet or less at a slow 110 knots and only ran at a speed of 30.5-33.5 knots. These attributes made the TBD extremely vulnerable to enemy fighters.[109]

By June 1942 a new torpedo bomber entered the fleet, the TBF "Avenger." One.30-caliber machine gun was mounted in the nose, a.50-caliber (12.7-mm) gun was mounted right next to the turret gunner's head in a rear-facing electrically powered turret, and a single.30-caliber hand-fired machine gun mounted ventrally (under the tail), which was used to defend against enemy fighters attacking from below and to the rear. The Avenger had a large bomb bay, allowing for one Bliss-Leavitt Mark 13 torpedo, a single 2,000-pound (907-kg) bomb, or up to four 500-pound (227-kg) bombs. The aircraft had overall ruggedness and stability, and pilots say it flew like a truck, for better or worse. With a 30,000 ft. (10,000 m) ceiling and a fully loaded range of 1,000 mi (1,610 km), it was better than any previous American torpedo bomber, and better than its Japanese counterpart.[110]

Aircraft not equipped for dive bombing or air crews not trained for dive bombing could also perform a glide attack or a shallow form of dive bombing, normally from lower altitude. While this form of attack offered a bit more precision than level bombing it lacked the precision of true dive bombing. The G3M and TBF were capable of gliding attacks. While not the preferred method of attack certain tactical situations such as low cloud cover sometimes dictated its use.

Kamikaze or suicide tactics were developed in October 1944 during the Battle of Leyte Gulf. Vice Admiral Takijiro Onishi had planned some of the technical details for the Pearl Harbor attack under Yamamoto. He was against the attack on Pearl Harbor, fearing it would lead to a full scale war with a nation possessing unlimited natural resources, and his fears were being realized.

He was considered the foremost expert of aerial warfare and some believe he was the originator of the kamikaze tactic. In 1943, long before Leyte Gulf, this tactic had been discussed and was first recommended by Captain Eiichiro Jyo. [111]

---

[109] Ibid.

[110] Ibid.

[111] Captain Eiichiro Jyo is in command of the light carrier *Chiyoda* within Vice Admiral Jisaburo Ozawa's command.

Onishi felt such a tactic was pure heresy, was openly appalled and spoke against it. However, the discussion planted the seed of the tactic in his mind.[112]

The original concept was to use "A6M2 Zero" fighters carrying 500-lb. bombs and crash-dive onto the U.S. carrier flight decks in the hopes this would increase the accuracy by using a human guidance system and in effect made manned aircraft into guided missiles. As the war progressed all types of Japanese aircraft would conduct kamikaze attacks on all ship types. This form of attack was unique to the Japanese and their success and failure will be discussed later.

Protecting carriers was the principal duty of the combat air patrol and the ships fighter aircraft. Fighters made up a significant 25-33% of a carriers total aircraft compliment. Japanese fighter air groups varied between 18-27 fighters out of 54-72 total aircraft. The IJN main fighter at the beginning of the war was the A6M2 "Zero." Armed with two 7.7-mm machine guns and two short barreled 20-mm cannon it only carried enough ammunition for thirty seconds of fire for the machine guns and seven seconds of fire for the cannons. It was not provided any armor protection or self-sealing fuel tanks. Its small 950 horsepower engine also did not give it good performance at higher altitudes. At medium to low altitudes it was extremely agile and fast and depended on pilot skill for survivability.[113]

For the U.S. the F4F-3 "Wildcat" was the primary carrier-based fighter but the SBD could be pressed into combat air patrols for lower altitudes. The F4F-3 had a 1,200-horsepower engine with four.50-caliber machine guns capable of 30 seconds of fire. They were not initially equipped with armor or self-sealing fuel tanks but received both very early after hostilities had begun. By May of 1942 the F4F-3 were replaced by F4F-4 which were armed with six.50 caliber machine guns and folding wings that allowed the total number of fighters to be increased from eighteen to twenty-seven and then eventually thirty-six. These improvements however came at the cost of the aircraft having less range, speed, rate of climb, lower ceiling and only eighteen seconds of ammunition. Fighters for both the Japanese and U.S. were also assigned to escort strike missions with the belief they could effectively protect an air strike from enemy fighters.[114]

---

[112] Evans, David C. (Ed.). *The Japanese Navy in World War II.* Naval Institute Press, 1986. Inoguchi, Rikihei at 415 to 439 and Inoguchi, Rikihei, Nakajima Tadashi and Rodger Pineau, *The Divine Wind*, Bantam Books, 1958.

[113] Heinz, Leonard. *Aircraft Carrier Defense in the Pacific War: The Carrier Battles of 1942* at 26-27.

[114] Ibid.

In 1941 the U.S. Navy had six fleet carriers. The *Lexington, Saratoga, Yorktown, Enterprise, Hornet,* and the *Wasp.* The light carrier *Ranger* remained in the Atlantic theater for the entire war. The U.S. Navy's first carrier the *Langley* had been converted to a seaplane tender and was assigned to the Philippine Islands at Manila.

Initially the *Lexington* and *the Yorktown* class carriers carried thirty-seven fighters, thirty-seven dive bombers, and sixteen torpedo bombers for a total of ninety aircraft. The *Wasp* carried eighteen fighters, thirty-six dive bombers and eighteen torpedo bombers. On December 7, 1941 only the *Enterprise* and *Lexington* were assigned to Pearl Harbor and both were at sea so they avoided the attack. The *Saratoga* was on the West Coast at San Diego and the *Hornet, Yorktown,* and the *Wasp* were on the east coast. The *Hornet, Yorktown* and the *Wasp* would be transferred to the Pacific once hostilities commenced. The Japanese believed the *Lexington, Saratoga, Enterprise,* and the *Yorktown* were all assigned to Pearl Harbor and in the vicinity of Oahu on the morning of December 7, 1941.

CHAPTER 8: THE WAR BEGINS

There were four carrier vs. carrier battles within the first year of the war. They were the Battles of Coral Sea, Midway, Eastern Solomons, and Santa Cruz. There was also two major raids in the Pearl Harbor attack and the Indian Ocean raid. One very important land-based strike was the destruction of Force Z on December 10, 1941. Admiral Isoroku Yamamoto believed carrier aircraft could be decisive and wanted to avoid a war of attrition. His belief was primarily based on the tactical advantage aircraft had over battleships in range. Carriers or land-based aircraft could strike at a target much further than battleship guns.

In addition aircraft had matured to the point that they could carry weapons large enough to sink capital ships. The torpedo bomber would become the most effective weapon in sinking capital ships. The question however could carrier airpower deliver the strategic objective the Naval General Staff has issued for winning the war? Could it bring about Mahan's decisive battle and sweep an enemy battle fleet from the high seas in a battle of annihilation? This would in theory force the United States to the negotiation table and Japan could secure the natural resources it needed to become self-sufficient.

This foreign policy in hindsight was flawed however that was his political objective and how Japan's government believed they could win the war. So how did carrier airpower do?

Yamamoto did not want war with the United States and argued against the war but his ideas on how to fight such a war often went against the Naval General Staff's plans. He did not originate the idea of an air attack on Pearl Harbor. It had its origin in 1936 in a study made by the Naval Staff College. He also did not believe in the traditional war strategy. His choice of weapon was carrier-based aircraft. He was quoted as saying;

> The Naval General Staff is still devoted to the strategic thinking of the Meiji Era (1868-1912). War to be successful, must be of short duration, before the United States would fully mobilize its war potential. With the advent of aircraft, the battleship has become window dressing. The Navy is still trying to win a war with America by means of a decisive fleet encounter. But there is no way.[115]

[115] Asada, Sadao, *From Alfred Thayer Mahan to Pearl Harbor* at 279.

On January 7, 1941 in a letter to Oikawa he expressed his views:

> I don't think that throughout the whole period of the anticipated war there will be such things as all of the Combined Fleet closing in on an enemy force, deploying, engaging in a gunnery and torpedo duel, and finally charging into the enemy force in as gallant a way as possible.[116]
>
> The most important thing for us to do at the outset of the war with the U.S. I firmly believe, is to fiercely attack and destroy the U.S. main fleet at the outset of the war, so that morale of the U.S. Navy and the American people goes down to such an extent that it cannot recover.[117]

He borrowed from Kanji the idea that any war needed to be of short duration before the full industrial might of the United States could be realized. His major objection to traditional war strategy on how to achieve Mahan's decisive battle was the use of battleships as the main element of such a strategy. He believed battleships were obsolete and carriers could replace them.

The Naval General Staff was vehemently opposed to the Hawaii operation based on three objections. The first was it would divide the fleet. The second was it risked the entire first line carrier striking force on a single mission, one that might be futile if the harbor was empty. The third reason was Japan could not spare the ships from the southern operation which was the strategic objective of the Naval General Staff.

Yamamoto partially sold his idea that his attack would delay any American operations that might attack the Japanese flank during the southern operation. This would buy time for the southern expansion to take place without United States interference. Then the Japanese fleet would assume the strategic defensive and follow pre-war strategy. However, even this argument was not enough and he and his staff threatened resignation if the Hawaii operation was not pursued.

Osami Nagano, head of the Naval General Staff, was not convinced of the plan but could not see conducting the war without Yamamoto, so he allowed the operation to proceed. Because Yamamato's strategic plan was based on gaining an immediate advantage and negotiating a quick peace, he had stressed the sinking of battleships because he felt the American people would identify with these ships and their loss would break their morale. He believed that "Japan must seize the strategic initiative and pursue the U.S. fleet from the very beginning of hostilities.

---

[116] Yamamoto, Isoroku, *Letters from Yamamoto, The Pacific War Papers*, Goldstein M. Donald and Dillon V. Katheryn at 116.

[117] Ibid at 117.

Mahan would have agreed and believed offense was stronger than defense. This was the fundamental strategic concept of Mahan himself.

> If the true end [of the navy] is to preponderate over the enemy's navy and so control the sea, then the enemy's ships and fleets are the true objects to be assailed on all occasions. War once declared must be waged offensively, aggressively. The enemy must not be fended off, but smitten down.[118]

The Hawaii operation's success depended on achieving surprise. However, a declaration of war was supposed to be given to the U.S. Government thirty minutes prior to the attack. This was not accomplished and the United States did not receive the declaration of war until one hour after the attack had begun. This failure would have huge implications on the future conduct of the war and its outcome.

It was decided that the size of the task force was to remain small so that it would be more difficult to detect. Six carriers, two battleships, two heavy cruisers, one light cruiser, ten destroyers and eight tankers made up the task force. Twenty-three I-class submarines and five midget submarines were also included. The concentration of six carriers allowed the maximum strike capability and unity of effort through a single commander.

Vice Admiral Chuichi Nagumo's personality was described as placid, secure, and realistically optimistic. He was genuinely kind and good to his subordinates. He was against the Hawaii operation and argued against it to the last possible moment. He feared the safety of his carriers for they were extremely vulnerable to air attack. He was not on the best terms with Yamamoto on a personal level. In addition to commanding the entire First Air Fleet he was also in command of the First Carrier Division which included the carriers *Akagi* and *Kaga*.[119] From the perspective of economy of effort all hinged on the carrier pilots. The rest of the task force had little or no role in the offensive effort.

The carriers and surface ships had a combined 414 aircraft. The plan was that in the first wave fifty B5Ns (Kate) bombers would be used as high level bombers to attack battleships with modified 16-inch shells (in the event, one failed to launch). Forty B5Ns bombers would carry torpedoes and attack battleships and cruisers around Ford Island. Fifty-four D3As (Val) dive bombers would attack the airfields at Ford Island, Hickam, and Wheeler (three failed to launch). Forty-five

---

[118] Asada, Sadao, *From Alfred Thayer Mahan to Pearl Harbor* at 8.

[119] Goldstein, Donald M., Dillon, Katheryn V., *The Way it Was, Pearl Harbor* at 2-3.

A6Ms (Zero) fighters would gain command of the sky and attack the airfields of Hickam, Wheeler, Kaneohe, Bellows, and Ford Island (two failed to launch). There were a total of 183 aircraft in the first wave.

A second wave was to have eighty-one D3A Val dive bombers attacked cruisers and auxiliary ships but three failed to launch. Twenty-seven B5N Kates were to use high level bombing to attack the airfields of Kaneohe, Hickam, and Ford Island. Thirty-six A6M Zero fighters would control the air over Pearl Harbor and attack the airfields but one failed to launch. In the second wave a total of 171 planes made the attack.

Of the total force, 171 aircraft were to target ships within Pearl Harbor and 162 aircraft would attack the various bases. Fifty-four A6M Zero fighters would stay behind and protect the Japanese task force from possible counter-attack in three 18-plane patrols.

The five midget submarines would attempt to penetrate the harbor channel and once inside the harbor attack targets of opportunity. The twenty-three I-class submarines would establish patrol zones outside the harbor and attack ships attempting to escape.

There were 99 U.S. ships at Pearl Harbor at the time of the attack: eight battleships, two heavy cruisers, six light cruisers, thirty destroyers, and four submarines, with an additional forty-nine auxiliary ships. Between the Army and Navy 402 aircraft were spread out among the available airfields.

The carrier striking group would pass between Midway and the Aleutian Islands outside the range of patrol planes. Using screening destroyers ahead of a compact main body they would search for any contacts and if encountered divert the main body to avoid detection. Three submarines also sailed in advance of the main body to patrol ahead and give warning. The task force would maintain complete radio silence. This northern route was decided on because there was little chance of meeting commercial ships and being discovered. The risk of this route was poor weather and the need to refuel at sea. December 8 in Japan was decided as X-Day which was Sunday December 7, Hawaii Time. So as to allow maximum daylight for the operation the attack was to be launched at dawn. The attack should begin at 0800 Hawaii Time.

Searching for the enemy was left to Central Intelligence and submarine reconnaissance. Two float planes were assigned to the immediate front and the combat air patrol fighters were to serve as anti-submarine warfare patrols as well. No operational plans were made to maintain operations for several days. The operation was basically a hit and run raid. The only attempt at sea control was the twenty-three I-boats patrolling off the harbor entrance but submarines are very poor at establishing a blockade because they depend on stealth. There were no plans to bombard the base or attempt blockade through surface ships or keep the U.S. Pacific Fleet trapped within the harbor. The eight tankers were positioned well in the rear but no replacement planes, ammunition, or replacement pilots were planned for.

The results for the U.S. were severe: two battleships totally lost, two battleships sunk and recovered after lengthy delay, three battleships damaged, one battleship grounded that later sank but was recovered, two auxiliary ships sunk, three cruisers damaged, three destroyers damaged, three auxiliary ships damaged, 188 aircraft destroyed, 159 aircraft damaged, 2,403 killed 1,178 wounded.

Japanese losses were four midget submarines sunk, one midget submarine grounded, twenty-nine aircraft destroyed, seventy-four aircraft damaged, sixty-four killed, one captured. One I-class submarine did not return from the operation.

Analysis of Operation – Forward deployment in a time of peace by the U.S. Pacific Fleet was meant as a deterrent to war when it moved from the West coast to Pearl Harbor. This was not sound strategic thought for the aggressor always picks the time and place for hostilities to begin. By moving the fleet to Pearl Harbor the U.S. had simply placed its fleet within range of Japanese forces to attack it. The operation achieved the Naval General Staff's objective of delaying any American offensive during the first six months of the war.

As for implementing Mahan's decisive battle and destroying the U.S. Pacific Fleet it was a good first step but due to breaking the principle of sustainability the operation did not concentrate enough force or firepower to destroy an organism as large as 99 ships and a naval base. This would require multiple days to accomplish, some form of sea control to prevent the U.S. fleet from escaping the trap, and much more logistical support.

Despite achieving surprise they also broke this principle by giving the Americans time to recover. Sinking five U.S. battleships sounds well at first but, three were returned to service and would play important roles in the war. Only three ships out of the seventeen sunk or damaged ships were permanently out of the war. They were the battleships *Arizona*, *Oklahoma*, and the target ship *Utah*.

There were other signs that Yamamoto needed to heed. The attrition rate on Japanese aircraft was atrocious. Despite the twenty-nine aircraft shot down it was the seventy-four planes shot up and were no longer available for combat operations that mattered most. In the first two strikes the loss of aircraft had made the equivalent of two carriers combat-ineffective. With two U.S. carriers at sea and their position unknown Admiral Chuichi Nagumo would have to keep at least two carrier air wings' to protect his own task force and have even odds. He would have to keep all his aircraft to ensure an advantage. Thus, he decided a third strike would not pay dividends for the losses it would incur and choose to end the operation and withdraw. As measured against the principle of security he did not conduct aggressive searches for the U.S. carriers and did a poor job at reconnaissance. We know from hindsight that the two U.S. carriers were not close but he did not at the time.

Despite Yamamoto's belief that battleships were obsolete, aircraft by themselves had failed to deliver Mahan's decisive battle.

He had achieved surprise, destroyed the majority of U.S. aircraft and had gained command of the air, gained an advantage in capital ships, but needed the remainder of his battle fleet to finish the job by establishing sea control around Oahu, and blockade Pearl Harbor so as to prevent the U.S. Pacific Fleet from escaping. This was what Mahan's ideas demanded, but by leaving his battle fleet in home waters Yamamoto did not have the firepower using aircraft alone to finish the job.

In addition because the declaration of war was given one hour late all the U.S. casualties were listed as non-combatants as no war was in progress when the attack began. The attack broke international law. Later at the Potsdam Conference the men killed during the Pearl Harbor attack would be listed as murder victims and the Japanese leadership which included the Emperor had committed war crimes and would need to be held accountable. In regards to the political objective of keeping the war a limited war, the nature of the Pearl Harbor attack immediately made the war unlimited. This was a paradox for the only strategic objective given to him was the destruction of the U.S. Pacific Fleet. The political and strategic objectives contradicted each other Japan's leadership had failed to heed the warnings of Clausewitz that if the political objective was so vital to the enemy that it would result in the enemy exercising his full war making potential it is reasonable to reach the conclusion that the struggle would not be decided until his ability to make war was entirely crushed. If there was not a reasonable hope of being able to do this then it was poor policy to seek this political objective through the use of force.

The American people were enraged by the attack and this gave them the moral conviction that a democracy needed to embrace total war. For the United States this was now a fight to the finish and nothing short of unconditional surrender by Japan would end the war. ' Pearl Harbor had ended or at least dramatically reduced the prospects for a negotiated peace.

War is politics by another means and Japan's leadership had lost the war from a political standpoint on the very first day. To win they would now have to conquer the continental United States and occupy Washington D.C. On the other hand the United States with its massive industrial advantage in time could occupy Japan and Tokyo. Sworn to die to protect the Emperor and *kokutai* the only other option for the Japanese military was to make the war as bitter as possible and hope the U.S. public would not wish to endure the massive casualties that would result in such a war. Total war, where no quarter was asked for and none given.

CHAPTER 9: FORCE Z

Approximately one hour before the attack on Pearl Harbor Japanese troops landed at Kota Bharu, Malaya. The transports had a direct escort of one light cruiser and four destroyers. A second landing was made at Singora with troops embarking from eleven transports with an escort of four destroyers. By midnight all transports had unloaded and were heading back north. A third landing took place at Patani, Thailand. Five transports covered by two destroyers.

Additional landings were made at Prachuab, Jumbhorn, Nakhorn, and Bandon using a total of seven transports that had no escort. Once the transports had safely unloaded the screening destroyer escorts were free to join the covering force of Vice Admiral Nobutake Kondo.

Kondo's objective was to ensure the safety of the landings. Once the transports had reached their objectives Kondo was actually on the defensive, assigned to prevent any British interference with the landings.

War had not yet been declared on the morning of December 8. While tensions were high no British ships were at sea so as the Japanese fleet entered the Gulf of Siam control of these waters fell to the Japanese. Admiral Kondo was in command of both naval and air forces and was attempting to concentrate the combined power of both surface ships and airpower to overwhelm Force Z. At 'his command were two battleships, seven heavy cruisers, one light cruiser and fourteen destroyers. In addition Kondo had approximately one hundred G3M (Nell) and G4M Betty aircraft near Saigon and several submarines to help scout the seas around Malaya.

Admiral Thomas Phillips had the battleship *Prince of Wales*, battlecruiser *Repulse*, and four destroyers. His strategic objective was to protect Singapore, a crucial port, and, more immediately, to intercept the troop transports and stop the invasion. The Royal Air Force which was very weak to begin with in Malaya, could not provide him any support. The aircraft carrier he was supposed to have with him, *Indomitable,* had run aground en route at Kingston, Jamaica. She had not finished repairs and was unavailable.

On December 3, he had requested all four *Resolution* class battleships to sail to Singapore. In addition the heavy cruiser *Exeter* was en route and the cruisers *Achilles*, *Australia*, and *Hobart* left their bases on December 8 and were heading for Singapore. The cruiser *Java* would arrive on December 9.

Phillips set sail with Force Z on the same day he learned of the invasion. He did not wait for reinforcements to arrive. He had no resources other than his own float planes for scouting and was operating effectively blind. His objective was to attack the troop transports but with the invading forces already ashore and the transports departing this was futile. Corbett had emphasized the importance of placing your naval forces between the invading army and its objective before the army has reached it. '

Phillips was outnumbered in ships and aircraft breaking the principle of concentration of force. Without effective reconnaissance the principle of security was broken. The inability for cooperation with British land-based air units broke this principle and inhibits flexibility. Under these circumstances, it would be difficult to achieve surprise, and his ability to sustain operations would be limited by the difficulty of surviving outnumbered, without reconnaissance, and with limited fuel and ammunition.

Kondo wrote after the war:

> At 1700 of 9 December 1941, a warning message saying that two enemy battleships, accompanied by several destroyers, headed north at 1515 on that day, position so-and-so, was received on board the *Atago,* my flagship, from the submarine *I-58* which was patrolling the area between Singapore and the Japanese landing beaches. What impressed me instinctively and concerned me most, receiving that warning, was whether or not the enemy main fleet aimed to divert our fleet in the South China Sea so as to make an attack with their light vessel group upon our landing forces then under the landing operation. According to the scheduled plan, our army landing operations on Malaya would take three or four days after the first step of the landing was set at about 0130 of 8 December, 1941.
>
> Against this sighted British Fleet, I decided to decoy them north in the area within the reach of our land-based air forces in French Indochina, in order to launch a decisive blow upon them with all of our air and surface forces. The submarine force was assigned to continue their original missions at their present positions.
>
> My conduct of the operation; its principle was all convoys would immediately stop their landing operations and head north into Siam Bay as far as possible. The 22nd Air Sqd. Would make searching attacks upon the suspected enemy fleet with all its force from dawn of 10 December.
>
> The 1st Southern Expeditionary Fleet, including the 7th CA Sqd. And the 3rd Des. Sqd. Temporarily assigned under its control, would join in the covering forces under my direct control. Meanwhile, radio activities would frequently be discharged so as to divert enemy attention to us.
>
> At that time, the 3rd Des. Sqd. that was directly covering the landing operation, needed refueling, so they were being refueled one by one from an oiler which had previously been at Poulo Condore Island. In consequence, those ships of the 3rd Des. Sqd. Were under such circumstances that they could not but join the fleet one after another.

> This problem of refueling the 3rd Des. Sqd. Was one of the factors which made me give up a night engagement, together with the fact that those of the 1st Expeditionary Fleet lacked enough training in night engagements and also that there was little hope of making contact with the enemy fleet by midnight, even if the enemy fleet had continued north at the speed observed in that afternoon, so that we would not have enough time to make a systematized night attack against the enemy. Therefore, I gave up a night attack and attempted a day attack after dawn of 10 December.
>
> In order to achieve this aim, I fixed our rendezvous point at about 40 miles southwest of Poulo Condore Island at 1000 on 10 December. At 0400 on 10 December all forces except destroyers of the 3rd Des. Sqd. Rendezvoused as scheduled at the designation point, thence we headed south. However, having received a message radioed at about 1300 from submarine *I-58* saying that the enemy fleet was heading south at high speed, I ordered the fleet to increase speed and at the same time ordered the air force to make every effort to catch the enemy fleet.[120]

Phillips sailed his small force so that he would pass to the east of Anambas Island. At 0400 on December 9 he turned north. At 0559 he knew he had been sighted for one of his destroyers, HMS *Vampire* reported seeing a reconnaissance plane. He continued north until he was 150 miles south of French Indochina and 250 miles east of Malaya. At 1740 another Japanese plane was sighted. At 1805 the destroyer *Tenedos* was ordered back to Singapore reducing his screen to three destroyers. The remainder of Force Z headed for Singora but then at 2330 he received a false report that Japanese troops were landing at Kuantan to his south so he decided to head there at full speed. This new course took him away Kondo's surface fleet to his northeast.

At 0800 10 December he arrived off Kuantan to find nothing. He turned his ships to head back north and then to the east. At 1120 he was sighted by Japanese planes who reported his position. At 1148, eighty-four Japanese aircraft attacked Force Z.

Battle results – At 1148 December 10, 1941 eighty-four planes attacked Force Z and sank both *Prince of Wales* and *Repulse* at the loss of three planes and twenty-eight planes damaged. 513 men were lost on *Repulse* and 327 men were lost on *Prince of Wales.*

Not much has changed in fleet dispositions since the age of sail. The Japanese were using separate transport groups to transport the army to their objective and separate covering forces to be free and attack any British fleet which wanted to

---

[120] Goldstein, Donald M., Dillon, Katheryn V. *The Pacific War Papers* at 304-317.

interfere with the landings. Since war had yet to be declared the Japanese forces were able to choose the time and place for their attack and held all of the advantages. No British ships were at sea and most of the landings were unopposed. While the British may not have been shocked at the attack they were still caught unprepared so the Japanese still gained the element of surprise.

However, the loss of two capital ships at sea by airpower alone for the first time in naval warfare had a huge impact. Many people viewed this as the end of the battleship era. Captain Hashimoto Shozo, Chief of the 1st Section of the Mobilization Bureau in the Navy Ministry commented after Pearl Harbor;

> Still too early to verify the power of naval air. Chuichi Nagumo succeeded only by a surprise attack.[121]

After the battle of Malaya he came into Yamamoto's office and said:

> Isoroku Yamamoto, now you have won. I will do my best at naval Affairs Bureau to comply with the requests of the Naval Aviation Department. [122]

The Naval Minister Admiral Shimada suggested that the construction of the giant battleship *Musashi* be stopped. Vice Admiral Matome Ukagi who was Isoroku Yamamoto's chief of staff is quoted as saying,

> The battleship, which had participated in the operation that led to the destruction of the German battleship Bismarck, proved unexpectedly vulnerable in her AA defenses. Through the results of this battle the no more battleship doctrine and the doctrine of the omnipotence of air power will be more vigorously advocated.[123]

Vice Admiral Nobutake Kondo's expression did not change when informed that both ships had been sunk as the crew on the bridge of *Atago* celebrated. The action meant he could now act freely for he had secured communications and control of the seas off Malaya. After the war he gave this account;

> The success of this operation, I believe, can be attributed to the following factors:
>
> We were favored by such good luck as to catch the enemy in sight through the slit in the clouds.
>
> Crews of the naval air forces were fired up with fierce fighting spirit and firm confidence in the battle. It would deserve to be cited as one of good examples that some planes showed no hesitation in making attacks

---

[121] Marder, Arthur J., *Old Friends New Enemies* at 518.

[122] Ibid.

[123] Ugaki, Matome, *Fading Victory* at 49.

> upon the enemy, even at the moment when so doing would have caused a shortage of fuel necessary to return to their base.
>
> Good conduct of the leaders of the air force.
>
> Japanese air forces did not meet any enemy interceptors.
>
> The enemy fleet not only lacked sufficient screen but did not make an efficient avoiding movement.[124]

In the operation's room at Combined Fleet Headquarters while waiting to hear the results of the battle Admiral Isoroku Yamamoto made a bet with Captain Miwa Yoshitake for ten beers that *Prince of Wales* would survive but *Repulse* would be sunk. Captain Yoshitake said both ships will be sunk. Word came:

They had won! They had won! Won superbly! Aircraft had defeated battleships.[125]

Admiral Isoroku Yamamoto was smiling with both cheeks flush and he was full of joy. He said to Captain Yoshitake;

> You may take ten dozen, nay even 50 dozen, or as much as you like.[126]

Later, while playing chess with Lieutenant Commander Yasuji Watanabe in a more quiet and thoughtful time after the news had really sunk in, he expressed his thoughts:

> Our success cannot possibly continue for more than a year. I feel great sympathy for the British commander who apparently went down with the *Prince of Wales*. The same thing may happen to me someday in the not-too-distant future.[127]

The Imperial Navy began to increase aircraft production as a result. For the leading Japanese decision maker's aircraft had now superseded the battleship. Many authors in their books and writings still claimed that the Japanese were battleship-minded but I disagree completely. All pre-war planning simply was thrown out the window and the war would be fought by the Japanese almost exclusively through the use of airpower.

There were however important questions that needed to be asked. Mahan's concepts were based on control of the seas. Corbett said the only thing useful about the seas was it could be used as a transportation highway. There were two

---

[124] Goldstein, Donald M., Dillon, Katheryn V. *The Pacific War Papers* at 304-317.

[125] Marder, Arthur J., *Old Friends New Enemies* at 510-511.

[126] Ibid.

[127] Ibid.

purposes for Mahan's battle fleet. One was to establish blockade and deny the use of that highway to any adversary. The second was to destroy any adversary's combat ships that might interfere with the blockade or break an opposing blockade to gain use of the transportation highway. The destruction of Force Z gave the Japanese the advantage in surface combatants that could now establish control of the Gulf of Siam so supplies, troops, and equipment could be transported from French Indochina to Malaya. The presence of *Kongo* and *Haruna* now complicated any attacker's ability to break that control for the most powerful surface combatants available to the Allies were heavy cruisers and they would be outgunned.

British airpower was being destroyed by overwhelming numbers of Japanese aircraft, which at this time were superior in quality and had better pilots. There was little hope British airpower could mass enough strength to break Japanese control or return the favor and destroy Japanese capital ships. Could air power on its own establish control of the sea? How much mass would this require? At this time night operations were extremely rare and almost impossible to conduct a strike on a fleet during the night. This limited air power's use to daylight hours. So aircraft technology had not yet matured into a twenty-four hour a day weapon and was largely restricted to half a day.

Yamamoto through his Pearl Harbor attack and the success off Malaya had shown strike warfare could prove tactically decisive due to its inherent greater range over surface ships. He had yet to show it could replace surface ships which can occupy geographical locations. And he had yet to carry out the political policy by which his government believed it could force the United States into a negotiated peace. Three days into the war, he had no idea that this goal had already been made impossible to achieve.

CHAPTER 10: EARLY RAIDS

On December 10, 1941 Admiral Husband Kimmel, Commander U.S. Pacific Fleet issued a campaign plan stating the following;

> Information. (a) The campaign for which this this is the plan comprise the operations which will be undertaken until Fleet 1 is strong enough to conduct strategically offensive operations.
>
> b) Motivating Considerations.
>
> The basic Rainbow Five Plan has been modified to take into account of the present reduced strength of the Pacific Fleet. The only strategically offensive task remaining in the Plan is to raid Japanese communications. The remaining assigned tasks require protection of the territory and communications of the associated powers of the Pacific Area. (The definition of the Pacific Area remains the same as in the Rainbow Five Plan.) Wake is to be defended as category C—all other territory in general Hawaiian Area, in category D. It is considered by the Commander in Chief that Oahu group of islands must be made secure at all costs. He expects great quantities of men and material to augment the present defending forces, and will prosecute a vigorous offensive against any threatening forces. The line of communications to the West Coast is of course vital. That of Samoa and beyond to Australia must be kept open. Our outlaying islands must be protected and supplied.
>
> With the losses we have sustained, it is necessary to revise completely our strategy of a Pacific War. The loss of battleships commits us to the strategic defensive until our forces can again be built up. However, a very powerful striking force of carriers, cruisers, and destroyers survive. These forces must be operated boldly and vigorously on the tactical offensive in order to retrieve our initial disaster.[128]

Ironically, the two opposing fleets would mirror each other at the beginning of the war.

Yamamoto by his successful raid on Pearl Harbor and the destruction of Force Z had gained a decisive edge in capital ships but made no operational plans to seize this advantage.

---

[128] Kimmel, Husband E., *Chester Nimitz Gray Book* Vol. 1 at 11.

This decision by the Japanese was by choice. For the American admirals it was forced upon them. Kimmel however was soon replaced by Nimitz. He did not give up on the battleship. In fact, they would hold an important role in offensive planning when he launched his counter offensive in September 1943.

Nimitz sent out Halsey to raid the Gilberts and Marshals on January 31, 1942 (February 1, local time). Morale at Pearl Harbor as well as within the U.S. public at home was falling and these early raids lifted morale that the U.S. Navy was indeed fighting back. About 1:40 PM on 1 February 1942 while operating in the northeastern Marshalls, *Enterprise* was approached on the starboard bow by five Japanese G3M bombers flying at 10,000 feet. While in a shallow power dive to about 3,500 feet, each plane released three bombs. There were seven F4F and six SBD above the carrier in a combat air patrol. It is seen about 15 miles from *Enterprise* and the F4F intercepted at 10,000 feet. The G3M bombers started a glide bomb attack and nosed down to 6,000 feet. The F4F pilots reported their guns jammed and anti-aircraft fire engaged the Japanese aircraft. All five were able to drop their bombs at 3,500 feet and recovered at 1,500 feet but no bombs scored a hit. One G3M was destroyed by anti-aircraft fire after it dropped its bombs.[129]

The *Enterprise* was maneuvered at high speed and all bombs fell beyond the ship, the nearest about 50 feet off the port quarter at frame 130. The bombs were estimated by the ship to be general purpose with instantaneous fuses, weight between 100 and 200 pounds. Splashes were 100 to 125 feet high. Slight shock was felt throughout the ship, similar to that caused by firing the ship's guns. Fragments from the attack opened four 1/2-inch holes in the 1/4-inch medium steel plating of the port hangar bulkhead between frames 130 and 133 and six holes in the hangar roller curtain. The externally fitted 2- to 2 1/2-inch gasoline line was pierced by fragments in nine places between frames 119 and 135. The M-1, M-2 and M-6 coils of the externally fitted degaussing cable at frame 126, and fifteen minor electrical cables were pierced or severed by fragments or destroyed in the gasoline fire.[130]

Gasoline from the pierced gasoline line caught fire either from hot fragments or electrical short circuits and the fire spread over the port gallery walkway and the boat pocket between frames 130 and 144. Flames from the gasoline fire consumed canvas covers, splinter mats, airplane fueling hose, rubber deck matting, life jackets and paint on the deck and bulkheads. Although the fire seemed very

---

[129] U.S.S. *Enterprise* Action Report February 1, 1942.

[130] U.S.S. *Enterprise* Action Report February 1, 1942.

threatening, it was soon extinguished with chemical foam from pressure-operated foam generators. By quick and effective use of the available firefighting apparatus, the *Enterprise* repair parties successfully passed their first real test.

Although the gasoline fire developed as a result of penetration of the exposed portion of the gasoline piping by fragments, no change in its location was seriously considered. It would have been impracticable to give adequate protection to this main, and a fire on the gallery walkway was obviously preferable to one in the hangar. Although internal fitting of degaussing cables had become standard practice, *Enterprise* could not be so fitted until her extensive 1943 overhaul.[131]

A second raid appeared two hours later when two G3M bombers approached and were detected at twenty-five miles. Nine F4F fighters failed to engage the bombers and both made a level attack at 14,000 feet with no hits. One bomber was shot down by a F4F after it attacked and during withdraw. This was not a good start for either the combat air patrol or anti-aircraft fire. The only reason *Enterprise* was not hit was because she was well maneuvered. The combat air patrol had failed to gain command of the air allowing every attacking plane to make an attack.[132]

As the war in the South China Sea progressed and Allied positions fell one after another. Admiral Ernest J. King Commander in Chief, United States Fleet (COMINCH) and Chief of Naval Operations urged Nimitz to take more aggressive action including using the older battleships to raid the Marshall Islands. Ernest J King was hoping such action may divert Japanese forces away from the Southwest Pacific.

Nimitz responded:

> Pacific Fleet markedly inferior in all types to enemy. Cannot conduct aggressive action Pacific except raids of hit and run character which are unlikely to relieve pressure Southwest Pacific. Logistic problems far surpass peacetime conception and always precarious due to fueling at sea and dependence on weather. Offensive employment battleships does not fit in with hit and run operations, and their independent or supporting use considered inadvisable at present. Continued operation of one or more Pacific Fleet forces in ANZAC area will involve dependence upon logistic support from Australia and New Zealand, which support appears limited. Unless this fleet is strengthened by strong additions, par-

---

[131] U.S.S. *Enterprise* Action Report February 1, 1942.

[132] Heinz, Leonard, *Aircraft Carrier Defense in the Pacific War: The Carrier Battles of 1942* at 30-32.

> ticularly in aircraft, light forces, carriers, and fast fleet tankers, its effectiveness for offensive action is limited.[133]

King however was determined to increase pressure on the Japanese. His response on February 9 shocked Admiral Nimitz and his staff. It read:

> Pacific Fleet not, repeat not, markedly inferior in all types to forces enemy can bring to bear within operating radius of Hawaii while he is committed to extensive operations in Southwest pacific. Your forces will however be markedly inferior from Australia to Alaska when enemy has gained objectives in Southwest Pacific unless every effort is continuously made to damage his ships and bases. Action by you towards and in the Mandates will of itself cover and protect Midway-Hawaii line while affording badly needed relief of pressure in Southwest Pacific. Review situation in above premises and consider active operations against Mandates and Wake from Northward and eastward or otherwise vary pattern of operation.[134]

Nimitz conferred with Halsey and decided to send the *Enterprise* and the *Yorktown* to raid Wake and Marcus Islands. The *Lexington* with Admiral Wilson Brown would raid Rabaul. Nimitz refused to use the battleships without a proper escort and he simply did not have the ships available to protect both carriers and battleships. In addition the old battleships were too slow to operate with the carriers. He argued that without proper support any offensive operations were not sustainable. He also noted that no troops were ready to seize advanced bases. Plans for raids on Truk and Saipan were made but such deep raids into enemy territory Nimitz considered unadvisable.[135] He did not believe any of these actions would relieve the ABDA (American, British, Dutch, and Australian Command) forces in the Dutch East Indies and this was not the time to seek a decisive battle relying on battleships alone.[136]

Halsey raided Wake on February 24, and Marcus on March 4, 1942 but the results were insignificant. Admiral Wilson Brown on February 20, was detected and attacked by land-based planes. No damage was inflicted on his ships but with surprise lost Brown decided to withdraw so no raid was carried out on Rabaul.

---

[133] Nimitz, Chester, *Chester Nimitz Gray Book* Vol. 1 at 214.

[134] Potter, E.B. *Chester Nimitz* at 41.

[135] Nimitz, Chester, *Chester Nimitz Gray Book* Vol. 1 at 243.

[136] The principles of sustainability and seizing command of the sea implied that it would be important capturing advanced bases to stay forward deployed, but this early in the war the logistical support for such operations deep in Japanese areas was not ready. These principles are key to battleship operations, but are not as essential as for hit and run carrier raids so he felt he could carry out such raids at this time without compromising fundamental principles of sea power.

On February 20, 1942 the *Lexington* attempted to raid the newly captured Japanese base at Rabaul. The raid was called off when the task force was spotted by a Japanese reconnaissance aircraft well short of its destination, but not before the IJN was able to send out a strike of seventeen bomb-carrying G4Ms to strike the task force. The strike split into two groups. [137]

The first Japanese attack group of nine G4Ms were detected seventy-five miles out by radar. The sighting occurred when six F4F-3 fighters were about to launch and six low on fuel were about to land. All twelve fighters headed out to intercept. Nineteen minutes after the first radar sighting and now only ten miles out ten of the F4Fs engaged the bombers and shot down five. Four made a level bombing attack with no hits scored. Again one G4M badly damaged attempted to crash into the *Lexington* but was destroyed by her anti-aircraft guns.[138]

The *Lexington* launched four more fighters and two of these plus two from the original twelve engaged the final four G4Ms. Two F4F fighters were shot down by the G4Ms tail gunners but three G4Ms were also shot down and the last G4M was brought down by a SBD dive bomber. [139]

The second wave of eight G4Ms was picked up on radar at thirty miles but was identified as part of the combat air patrol. A screening destroyer identified the second wave as enemy seven minutes after the radar sighting. Two unengaged F4Fs raced to intercept. One F4F had its guns jam but the second F4F shot down two, forced two to abort, and damaged two others. Four planes were able to attack *Lexington* but with no results. A damaged G4M attempt to crash into the *Lexington* but was shot down before it could hit by the ships guns. The combat air patrol shot down one more as they withdrew and two damaged G4Ms ditched with only two making it back to Rabaul.[140]

This engagement was much better but once again the combat air patrol could not gain command of the air as four attacking planes were successful in making an attack. Overall, fifteen G4Ms were shot down and two F4Fs lost. For the Japanese the attrition rate was horrible for absolutely no results. An ominous warning of what was to come. Still, questions remained. The attacks were made with rela-

---

[137] Heinz, Leonard, *Aircraft Carrier Defense in the Pacific War: The Carrier Battles of 1942* at 30-32.

[138] Ibid.

[139] Ibid.

[140] Ibid.

tively small forces. How would the carriers defend themselves against a full carrier air wing of fifty-four bombers and escorting fighters?[141]

[141] Heinz, Leonard, *Aircraft Carrier Defense in the Pacific War: The Carrier Battles of 1942* at 32-36.

CHAPTER 11: THE BATTLE OF JAVA SEA

Admiral Karel Doorman in command of the Allied ABDA forces first attempted to resist the Japanese invasions at Makassar Strait on the southern tip of Celebes, Island. On February 4 his forces came under air attack. The American heavy cruiser *Houston* lost her aft turret to a bomb with forty-eight men killed and over fifty wounded. The light cruiser *Marblehead* was damaged and lost steering control temporarily. Doorman decided to withdraw and Japanese forces took Makassar on February 8.[142] Singapore surrendered on February 15, 1942 and on this same day Nagumo sailed with his six carriers to make a raid on Port Darwin, Australia. On February 19, 188 aircraft attacked the port sinking eight ships and damaging nine others. Most of the ships were either transports or auxiliary ships only one combatant the destroyer *Peary* was sunk. Eighteen Allied planes were destroyed. The Japanese lost two planes in the raid.[143]

On February 19, Doorman attempted to stop the invasion of Bali but his forces were scattered and in three groups which arrived at different times. The battle that resulted was disorganized and neither side really distinguished themselves. Doorman managed to severely damage a single Japanese destroyer, lightly damage two more and two transports were damaged at a cost of the light cruiser *Tromp* being badly damaged and the destroyer *Piet Hein* sunk. The invasion went ahead as planned and Bali and Lombok fell later in the day on February 19.[144]

The Battle of Java Sea took place on February 27-1 March which shattered the ABDA forces leaving Japan in total control of the South China Sea. Doorman's objective was to destroy the invasion transports. Rear Admiral Takeo Takagi covered the invasion fleet. Morale was high for both sides. Doorman was informed that at 1155 (Java Time, Zone -7½) an enemy force consisting of thirty transports protected by two cruisers and four destroyers was at position 04°50' S., 114°20'

---

[142] Dull, Paul S., *The Battle History of The Imperial Japanese Navy* at 53.

[143] Ibid at 64.

[144] Ibid at 64-66.

E., course 240° T., speed 10 knots. He was directed to proceed to sea, attack after dark then retire toward Tandjong Priok. Admiral Karel Doorman was in the offensive role and the Japanese covering force was in the defensive'.[145] Reconnaissance was mainly supplied by land-based ship float planes for both sides. Neither side was surprised. Both received reports from their own aircraft as to each other's location.

Doorman's striking force consisted of the Dutch light cruisers *De Ruyter* (his flag) and *Java*, the American heavy cruiser *Houston*, British heavy *Exeter* and Australian light *Perth*. These were supported by Dutch destroyers *Kortenaer* and *Witte de with*, British *Jupiter*, *Electra* and the *Encounter*, and five American destroyers, *J. D. Edwards*, *Alden*, *Ford Pope* and *Paul Jones*.

The Japanese force consisted of the heavy cruisers *Nachi* and *Haguro* and he light cruisers *Naka* and *Jintsu*. The remainder of the screen was made up of fourteen destroyers, *Minegumo, Asagumo, Murasame, Samidare, Harukaze, Yudachi, Ushio, Sazanami, Yamakaze, Kawakaze, Yukikaze, Tokitsukaze, Amatsukaze*, and *Hatsukaze*.

If successful Doorman could still engage the transports while troops remain embarked, so his strategic objective remained valid. The two fleets sighted each other at 16:00 on February 27, and opened fire at long range at 16:16. The battle raged from mid-afternoon to midnight with Doorman attempting to get to the transports and each time being repulsed. Initial gunnery and torpedo attacks were poor for both sides.

The Allies had local air superiority during the daylight hours, because Japanese air power could not reach the fleet in the bad weather. The weather also hindered communications, making cooperation between the many Allied parties involved—in reconnaissance, air cover and fleet headquarters—even worse than it already was. The Japanese also jammed the radio frequencies. *Exeter* was the only ship in the battle equipped with radar, an emerging technology at the time.

Exeter was critically damaged by a hit in the boiler room from an 8-inch shell. The ship withdrew to Surabaya, escorted by *Witte de with*. The Japanese launched two huge torpedo salvos, 92 in all, but scored only one hit, on *Kortenaer* which broke in two and sank rapidly after the hit.

Electra while attempting to cover *Exeter*, engaged *Jintsu* and *Asagumo*, scoring several hits but suffering severe damage in return. A serious fire started on *Electra*

[145] The Office of Naval Intelligence, *The Battle of Java Sea February 27* at 50-77.

and eventually abandon ship was ordered. *Asagumo* was forced to retire because of damage.

Karel Doorman's force broke off and turned away around 18:00, covered by a smoke screen laid by the four U.S. destroyers. They also launched a torpedo attack but at too long a range to be effective. Doorman's force turned south toward the Java coast, then west and north as night fell in an attempt to evade the Japanese escort group and fall on the convoy. It was at this point that the ships of U.S. destroyers—their torpedoes expended—left on their own initiative to return to Surabaya.

Shortly after, at 21:25 *Jupiter* ran onto a mine and was sunk, while about 20 minutes later, the fleet passed where *Kortenaer* had sunk earlier, and *Encounter* was detached to pick up survivors. Doorman's command, now reduced to four cruisers, again encountered the Japanese escort group at 2300 and both columns exchanged fire in the darkness at long range, until *De Ruyter* and *Java* were sunk by one devastating torpedo salvo. Doorman and most of his crew went down with *De Ruyter*; only 111 were saved from both ships.

Now only the cruisers *Perth* and *Houston* remained; low on fuel and ammunition, and following Doorman's last instructions, the two ships retired, arriving at Tanjung Priok on February 28. Although the Allied fleet did not reach the invasion fleet, the battle did give the defenders of Java a one-day respite.

Perth and *Houston* were at Tanjung Priok on 28 February when they received orders to sail through Sunda Strait to Tjilatjap. Material was running short in Java, and neither was able to rearm or fully refuel. Departing at 2100 on February 28 for the Sunda Strait, by chance they encountered the main Japanese invasion fleet for West Java in Bantam Bay. The Allied ships were engaged by at least three cruisers and several destroyers. In a ferocious night action that ended after midnight on March 1, *Perth* and *Houston* were sunk. A Japanese minesweeper and a troop transport were sunk by friendly fire, while three other transports were damaged and had to be beached.

After emergency repairs the badly-damaged *Exeter* left Surabaya for Ceylon; she departed at dusk on February 28 and limped toward Sunda Strait, escorted by the destroyers *Encounter* and *Pope*. However, all three ships were intercepted by the Japanese heavy cruisers *Nachi, Haguro, Myoko* and *Ashigara*—and their attendant destroyers—on the morning of March 1. *Exeter* and *Encounter* were sunk together around noon, while *Pope* escaped only to be sunk several hours later by aerial attack. The four U.S destroyers *John D. Edwards, John D. Ford Alden* and *Paul Jones* were also at Surabaya; they left for Australia at nightfall on 28 February.

After a brief encounter with a Japanese destroyer in the Bali Strait, which they were able to evade, they reached Fremantle safely on March 4.

Doorman's striking force was composed of ships of four nations which had little opportunity of joint training or of working out common tactical doctrines. There was no opportunity to promulgate a well-considered plan of battle. Communication was inadequate and broke down completely during the battle. It was carried on by flashing light in plain English or by Dutch high-frequency radio to *Houston*, which relayed to the destroyers. There were no common flag signals or signal books available, nor were there any tactical plans save of a most rudimentary nature. The Japanese forces had the ability to sustain operations for multiple days at sea and this allowed them to maintain pressure on the ABDA forces until their destruction. The ABDA forces were close to friendly ports but could not stay at sea as long as the Japanese, and forces were not provided or immediately available to replenish at sea.

The Battle of Java Sea was the first strategic victory by Japan because it annihilated the Allied naval forces in the South China Sea.

The Army was free to move without interference from this point forward. On March 8 the Netherland East Indies surrendered and by March 28 the Japanese occupied all of Sumatra. Japan gained ultimate control over the resources of the fourth largest oil producer in the world in 1940. With the South China Sea in total Japanese hands the U.S. forces in the Philippines were now isolated and cut off completely. MacArthur escaped Corregidor on the night of March 11, 1942 in *PT-41* bound for Australia 4,000 km away through Japanese controlled waters. 76,000 starving and sick American and Filipino defenders in Bataan surrendered to the Japanese on April 9, 1942. The 13,000 survivors on Corregidor surrendered on May 6, 1942.

Naval General Staff had accomplished their primary strategic goal for opening hostilities. Japan now had enough raw oil to supply her economy despite the U.S. embargo. The Battle of Java Sea was a surface action and it fit Mahan's decisive battle concept. The forces involved were at the tier two and three levels of the battle fleet so even though the Japanese had an advantage in capital ships they failed to take advantage of it (and due to the absence of Allied battleships in the area, did not need to). With superior endurance Japanese surface forces maintained pressure on the Allied fleet until it broke and then isolated individual groups and destroyed them in detail. The Allied forces lacked cohesion and the results of the battle shows just how important it is for a surface fleet needs to train and operate together to maximize its fighting power. A collection of ships with roughly equal mass may look good on paper but without cohesion it does not translate into true fighting power. The Allied ships fought bravely but their formations broke down multiple times and the Japanese were able to take advantage of it.

Airpower contributed in a supporting role but was not the decisive factor in the outcome of the battle. Not much had changed since the age of sail concerning a surface action. The battle occurred because both sides were willing to engage each other, pointing out Corbett's philosophy that a decisive battle required a willing partner.

The Japanese surface fleet still validated Mahan's basic principle that if you destroy an opposing fleet so they can no longer offer resistance, the highway that is the sea is under your control to use freely. Allied submarines were all that could still offer some resistance but they would have to overcome huge obstacles.

CHAPTER 12: INDIAN OCEAN RAID

Yamamoto believed negotiations for peace with Great Britain should begin after the fall of Singapore. He told fellow officers that Japan should seek peace even if it meant returning territories already conquered.[146]

Japan's government did not know how to get out of the war and the early success boosted their leadership into over-confidence into what historians have now called, "Victory Fever." His views that this was the time to begin negotiations went nowhere in Tokyo. Yamamoto was left with no choice but to destroy both the British fleet in the Indian Ocean and the remaining U.S. Pacific fleet, which were each considerably larger than the ABDA forces. Yamamoto would turn his attention to the British fleet first.

The Naval General Staff wanted to launch the second phase of their offensive into the South Pacific and cut off the lines of communication to Australia. Admiral Isoroku Yamamoto proposed to attack the British fleet in the Indian Ocean and effect the capture of Ceylon. This would require five divisions from the Japanese Army who were shocked at the proposal. The Army rejected the idea but Yamamoto ordered Nagumo to conduct a Pearl Harbor style raid on the British ports of Colombo and Trincomalee. While this was being undertaken a Japanese raiding force would attack British shipping in the Bay of Bengal.[147]

Yamamoto's strategic aim was to fight Mahan's decisive battle using carrier-based aircraft and destroy the British naval forces in the Indian Ocean.

The official orders were as follows to protect the Japanese military sea transport route from flank attack by units of the British Army; to sweep the Bay of Bengal clear of British naval units in preparation for the occupation of the

---

[146] Stille, Mark, *Yamamoto Isoroku* at 28.

[147] Stille, Mark, *Yamamoto Isoroku*, pages 28-29.

Nicobar and Andaman Islands; and to deny the sea route along the east coast of India to the British.[148]

Admiral James Somerville was on the strategic defensive with the objectives of denying the Indian Ocean to the Japanese, protecting the ports Colombo and Trincomalee, and inflicting as many losses as he could on the Japanese Imperial Navy. On March 28, he received a report which indicated the Japanese were to attack Ceylon on April 1. The report estimated two or more carriers, several cruisers and a large force consisting of *Kongo* class battleships. James Somerville expected the Japanese to attack at night due to a full moon on April 1 and then return to their carriers at dawn. He had two carriers, *Indomitable* and *Formidable,* with the battleship *Warspite.*[149]

He maneuvered his fleet on March 31, so that it was eighty miles south of Dondra. He wished to stay out of range of Japanese land-based search aircraft during the day and then would close at night to be in position to attack. By the evening of April 2, nothing had been sighted. So he returned to Addu Atoll to refuel and take on fresh water. On April 3, he sent the cruisers *Dorsetshire* and *Cornwall* to Colombo. He sent the carrier *Hermes* and the destroyer *Vampire* to Trincomalee. At 1605 on April 4, the Japanese task force was sighted but before the search plane could report the strength of the Japanese task force it was shot down.[150]

Nagumo was on the offensive and scheduled his raid like at Pearl Harbor for Sunday April 5, which was Easter Sunday. Just before 0800 his planes attacked, 315 in all. Forty-two British aircraft were engaged and two Catalina' flying boats, four Fulmer fighters, fifteen Hurricane land-based fighters, and six Swordfish torpedo attack planes were shot down. The Japanese lost seven aircraft by fighters.[151] The destroyer *Tenedos* was sunk. The armed merchant ship *Hector* was set on fire and eventually sunk. The submarine depot ship *Lucia* was damaged and one merchant ship damaged.[152]

---

[148] Ministry of Defense, *War with Japan* at 123-131.

[149] Ibid.

[150] Ibid.

[151] Dull, Paul S., *The Battle History of The Imperial Japanese Navy* at 104-111.

[152] Ibid.

At approximately 1300 *Dorsetshire* and *Cornwall* were sighted and Admiral Nagumo sent eighty aircraft to attack the two cruisers. *Dorsetshire* was sunk in seven to eight minutes and *Cornwall* five minutes after the *Dorsetshire* went down.[153]

On April 9, Nagumo launched an attack on the port of Trincomalee. Eighty-five planes hit the port at 0725 but the port was empty of ships so the Japanese attacked the naval installations. Japanese fighters shot down eight Hurricanes and one Fulmer fighter. During this raid the carrier *Hermes*, destroyer *Vampire*, the oiler *British Sergent*, the corvette *Hollyhock*, and the destroyer depot ship *Athelsane* were spotted sixty-five miles south of Trincomalee. Believing the air raid was over they began to return to Trincomalee. Nagumo sent ninety aircraft to attack them. At 1035 the ships of this small task force were assaulted. None survived.[154]

For the first four months of the Pacific War Japanese carriers had not seen a single enemy aircraft. At 1025 nine Blenheim bombers of the Royal Air Force (RAF) surprised the IJN carriers with a level bombing raid. They were unable to score any hits but the combat air patrol had completely missed their approach. After they had released their bombs at the carrier *Akagi* the fighters engaged shooting down five. They scored no hits but did achieve three near misses. This was not an encouraging start for the Japanese carrier defense. Once again fighter aircraft had not gained command of the air. [155]

Rear Admiral Takeo Kurita had taken the carrier *Ryujo* and the cruisers *Chokai, Atago, Takao, Maya, Suzuya*, and *Kumano* with the light cruiser *Yura* and four destroyers *Yugiri, Asagiri, Amagiri*, and *Shirakumo* to raid the Bay of Bengal. From March 31 to April 6 he sank eighteen merchant ships. The Japanese also ran supplies up to Rangoon. Admiral James Somerville decided to abandon the Indian Ocean. He felt it was important to maintain a "fleet in being" to act as a deterrent to future Japanese incursion. He headed to Bombay and sent his remaining forces to Kilindini.[156]

Nagumo had won a strategic victory with the British withdrawal but Yamamoto had no plans to take advantage of the situation and Nagumo returned to Singapore allowing the British to regroup and recover. The Japanese in effect abandoned the Indian Ocean just as they gained command of the sea. Without the

---

[153] Ministry of Defense, *War with Japan* at 123-131.

[154] Ibid.

[155] Heinz, Leonard, *Aircraft Carrier Defense in the Pacific War: The Carrier Battles of 1942* at 32-36.

[156] Ministry of Defense, *War with Japan* at 123-131.

participation of the Japanese Army, sustained operations in the Indian Ocean were impossible.

CHAPTER 13: THE BATTLE OF THE CORAL SEA

Japanese leaders wanted to expand their gains by pushing south and eventually cutting the lines of communication between the United States and Australia. They planned to capture New Guinea, New Britain, the Fijis, and Samoa. They also wanted to push east by taking Midway and islands in the Aleutians in the North. The Naval General Staff also included parts of Australia in their target list but the Army rejected the idea.[157]

The Naval General Staff wanted to push south first. On March 8, Lae and Salamaua on the eastern edge of New Guinea was captured. On March 13, U.S. carrier aircraft from *Lexington* struck the invasion force causing considerable damage. This stopped plans until the Japanese naval forces could be allocated to cover the advance.[158]

On April 18, 1942 sixteen B-25 bombers took off the carrier *Hornet* with the carrier *Enterprise* in escort to raid Tokyo. The idea originated with President Roosevelt who wanted Japan bombed to boost U.S. morale and to show that the Japanese home islands were not safe. The raid caused insignificant damage but succeeded in shocking the Japanese military sworn to protect the Emperor and *kokutai*. This raid had a significant impact on Yamamoto and how the war would proceed. Yamamoto felt that the eastern edge of the Japanese defenses (now Wake Island) must be strengthened by taking the island of Midway. In the process he hoped to lure the rest of the American Navy into a major fleet action and destroy it.

By the end of April the Army and the Naval General Staff wanted to strengthen the southern edge of their defensive sphere by taking Port Moresby on New Guinea and establish an airstrip on Guadalcanal and a seaplane base on Tulagi at the very southern edge of the Solomon Island chain for future advances on New Caledonia. This would begin to cut the lines of communication with Australia. However, Yamamoto wanted to push east and take Midway so he was at odds

---

[157] Dull, Paul S., *The Battle History of The Imperial Japanese Navy* at 115-131.

[158] Ibid.

with the Naval General Staff yet again. The major disagreement between Yamamoto and his superiors was the question of how to keep Midway supplied if it were captured, with its location so close to the home base of the U.S. Pacific Fleet in Oahu. Midway lacked a port to base defense forces and its lines of communication could be easily cut. Nevertheless Yamamoto was convinced this was the place for the decisive battle.[159]

Yamamoto once again threatened resignation and eventually got his way. In exchange for permission to conduct the Midway operation he agreed to send the 5th Carrier Division to support the capture of Port Moresby on New Guinea and capture Guadalcanal and Tulagi in early May. He also agreed to capture parts of the Aleutians to be included in his Midway operation. Operation MO was the code name for the Port Moresby operation and this would lead to the first carrier vs. carrier battle in history.[160]

The MO operation first objective was to capture Tulagi and use this base for seaplanes that would enable the Japanese to scout further south. Tulagi is across from the larger island of Guadalcanal and it would be seized for an airfield. The Tulagi invasion force was commanded by Rear Admiral Kiyohide Shima. The destroyers *Kikuzuki* and *Yuzuki* with the minelayers *Okinoshima* and *Koei Maru*, escorted one transport and several gunboats. They left Rabaul at 0830 on April 30. May 4th was the scheduled occupation date. Once this base was secured the same troops would occupy Nauru and Ocean Islands.[161]

The Port Moresby invasion force was commanded by Rear Admiral Kosa Abe and comprised twelve transports plus the minelayer *Tsugaru*. This force left Rabaul on May 4 and would be joined by Rear Admiral Sadamichi Kajioka's Attack Force which included the light cruiser *Yubari*, destroyers *Oite*, *Asanagi*, *Mutsuki*, *Mochizuki*, and *Yayoi*. Its route would take it through Jomard Passage and east of Milne Bay at the southern tip of New Guinea.[162]

A support force under command of Rear Admiral Aritomo Goto, 'whose orders required him to cover both the Port Moresby Invasion Force and the Tulagi Invasion Force, left Truk on April 28 and stayed just south of New Georgia Island. At his disposal were the light carrier *Shoho*, heavy cruisers *Aoba*, *Kako*, *Kinu-*

---

[159] Ibid.

[160] Ibid.

[161] Ibid.

[162] Ibid.

gasa, Furutaka, and the destroyer *Sazanami.* The *Shoho*'s orders were to conduct reconnaissance and anti-submarine warfare. The planners of the operation did not believe U.S. carriers would show up at the end of the operation after the Army had already reached its objective.[163]

A light support force under the command of Rear Admiral Kuninori Marumo was sixty miles west of Tulagi having left Rabaul on April 29. His force consisted of the light cruisers *Tenryu, Tatsuta,* the seaplane tender *Kamikawa Maru* and three gunboats.[164] This left the main body under the command of Takagi, the victorious admiral during the Battle of Java Sea. He had the 5th Carrier Division which included the carriers *Shokaku* and *Zuikaku* with the heavy cruisers *Myoko* and *Haguro* and the destroyers *Ariake, Yugure, Shigure, Shiratsuyu, Ushio,* and *Akebono.*[165] The *Shokaku* air group consisted of eighteen A6Ms, twenty D3As, and nineteen B5Ns. The *Zuikaku* air group consisted of twenty A6Ms, twenty-two D3As, and twenty-two B5Ns. The Japanese were using Corbett's philosophy of division to hide the various task forces and several separate covering forces to protect the invasion forces. By using separate forces it was hoped that the troop transports could evade detection and attack. Not much had changed with this approach to disposition of forces since the age of sail.

What had changed in the circumstances was that now aircraft could search quickly large geographical areas and attack aircraft could strike over hundreds of miles. Under these circumstances, division became more problematic. The Japanese plan was very inflexible. The widely separated force would have to keep a strict time table for all to go smoothly. This was one reason Mahan preferred concentration over division in that it made command of subordinates easier and the entire force would have less disunity of effort. The inflexibility broke one of the operational principles that it was usually better to keep operational plans simple and not so complex.

U.S. forces deployed in the area consisted of Task Forces Baker and Fox of TG 17.5. Rear Admiral Frank J. Fletcher, commander of Task Force Fox, had been given command of the combined forces. Rear Admiral Aubrey Fitch was in command of Task Force Baker. The two task forces joined on May 1, 1942. Fletcher had at his command the carriers *Lexington* and *Yorktown*; five heavy cruisers, the *Minneapolis, New Orleans, Astoria, Chester,* and *Portland*; nine destroyers,

---

[163] Ibid.

[164] Ibid.

[165] Ibid.

the *Morris, Anderson, Hammann, Russell, Phelps, Dewey, Aylwin,* and *Monahan.* TG 17.9 consisted of the seaplane tender *Tangier.* TG 17.6 with the tankers *Neosho* and *Tippecanoe* with an escort of two destroyers, *Sims* and *Worden,* filled out Fletchers command.[166] MacArthur was in command of ANZAC force in Australia. TG 17.3 was commanded by British Admiral J. G. Crace and consisted of *Australia, Hobart, Chicago, Perkins, Farragut* and *Walke.*[167]

Japanese strategic aims included seizing Port Moresby, seizing Tulagi Island, and, in addition, drawing out the U.S. forces and annihilating them. These aims were confusing and potentially self-contradictory.

The Americans had an advantage in security in that the Japanese JN-25 codes had been broken and the U.S. was aware of Japanese planning. The successful implementation of the principle of security by the breaking of the JN-25 codes allowed the U.S. forces to implement an ambush strategy and prevent an invasion. This was exactly the kind of mission that was envisioned for carriers before the advent of hostilities. With the advantage in security it was hoped that the Americans could achieve surprise and due to this morale was very high. Corbett taught that to prevent invasion it was absolutely critical to have your forces at sea prior to the enemy army reaching its objective. On May 1st Fletcher had concentrated his forces making command decisions much easier to control. Each carrier however would operate with its own screen but within close proximity to each other. The tankers gave them enough logistics to sustain operations for several days.

Only one operational principle was broken for this naval battle on the Allied side and that was cooperation between Fletcher's forces and MacArthur's forces. The responsibility for air operations in the Coral Sea area had been allotted to MacArthur, but he did not have enough long range planes to make a thorough search of the Coral Sea area. Nimitz was forbidden, by the terms of the official division of air operations set up by the Joint Chiefs of Staff, to intrude into Douglas MacArthur's zone. The dividing line was a 45 degree angle from latitude 10 degrees and longitude 165 degrees. This left areas that could not be searched.[168]

---

[166] Ibid.

[167] Ibid.

[168] Ibid.

Task Force Baker refueled from *Tippecanoe* on May 1st. Task Force Fox refueled from *Neosho* on May 2. Fletcher wanted to concentrate all forces so he gave British Admiral J. G. Crace of TG 17.3 a rendezvous for May 4th, at latitude 15°00' S., longitude 157°00' E. Task Force Baker was to join up at the same coordinates at daylight May 4. At 1900 on May 3rd Fletcher received intelligence reports from Commander Southwest Pacific Forces indicating that the Japanese had begun to occupy Florida Island in the Solomons, going ashore from transports in Tulagi Harbor.

By 0700 on May 4th Task Force Fox had reached a point about 100 miles southwest of Guadalcanal Island. Weather conditions were unfavorable for flying. A frontal zone extending east and west covered Guadalcanal and the area to the south for a distance of seventy miles. Showers from cumulonimbus and stratocumulus clouds were encountered in the morning and scattered squalls in the afternoon, so that visibility was limited between the carrier and Guadalcanal. Wind gusts varying in forces from seventeen to thirty-five knots somewhat hampered the planes.[169]

By 0701 the cruisers had launched an inner air patrol and the *Yorktown* began launching a combat air patrol of six fighters F4F, followed by the attack group. A combat air patrol of six planes, working in three shifts, was maintained throughout the day. Lt. Comdr. Oscar Pederson was commander of the *Yorktown* air group. The attack group was composed as follows: twelve TBD torpedo planes thirteen SBD scout planes, and fifteen SBD bombers. All torpedo planes were armed with Mark 13 torpedoes, the depth setting ten feet, and all scout planes and bombers with Mark 13 1,000-pound bombs.[170]

At Tulagi *Kikuzuki, Yuzuki,* and *Okinoshima* had formed a protective cordon around the harbor entrance. Approximately 0820-0845 the thirteen SBD dive bombers of Scouting Five attacked *Kikuzuki* scoring one direct hit that penetrated her engine room. She was beached on nearby Gavutu Island but later sank. *Okinoshima* was also damaged. The twelve torpedo planes and the fifteen SBDs attacked at 0850 and 0900 respectively but did no further damage.[171]

When the strike returned to *Yorktown* it was immediately re-fueled and re-armed for a second strike. This was launched at 1106 consisting of twenty-seven

---

[169] Ibid.

[170] Office of Naval Intelligence: *The Battle of the Coral Sea* at 5.

[171] Dull, Paul S., *The Battle History of The Imperial Japanese Navy* at 115-131.

SBDs and eleven TBDs. They arrived over Tulagi at 1210 and sank two gunboats and damaged the transport *Tama Maru*. The destroyer *Yuzuki* was strafed and her captain killed along with nine others and twenty wounded. A third strike arrived at 1500 consisting of twelve SBDs which damaged a transport, destroyer, and a minelayer. The U.S. lost two F4F and one TBD. The Japanese however had succeeded in landing their troops and capturing their first objective of Operation MO. Strike warfare had resulted in heavy casualties but had not stopped the Japanese from using the ocean to transport their men to Tulagi.[172]

The sighting of U.S. carrier planes surprised the Japanese who were not expecting U.S. carriers to be in the area. Inouye sent out float planes in search and when one did not return they knew American carriers were in the Coral Sea but their exact location could not be determined. Most of his G3M and G4M were bombing Port Moresby. Takagi also only used his float planes for reconnaissance. The result was for two days he could not find the U.S. ships. For the Americans "Murphy's Law"[173] was in effect as the Japanese were located in an area not covered due to the lack of cooperation between Douglas MacArthur's search aircraft and Nimitz's search aircraft. *Neosho* and *Sims* separated from Task Force Fox to operate southeast of the carrier group. *Tippecanoe* and *Worden* had been ordered back to Efate Island.[174] Admiral Fletcher at 0600 May 7, ordered his support force under the command of Admiral J. G. Crace to proceed to Jonard Passage where a group of transports had been sighted. This force would block the use of Jonard Passage and with this tactical blockade in place deny the Japanese access to Port Moresby.[175]

At 0700 Takagi ordered Abe not to take his transports through Jonard Passage but to retire northward. Kajioka's attack force was now escorting Admiral Abe's transports. Goto's cruisers were with *Shoho*. He ordered four fighters and one attack plane from *Shoho* to provide combat air patrol over the invasion fleet.[176]

At 0840 Crace was informed three Japanese planes were shadowing the task group; identified as twin-engine monoplanes they were either G3Ms or G4Ms from Rabaul. At 1427 ten or twelve single engine planes were sighted. At this

---

[172] Office of Naval Intelligence, *The Battle of the Coral Sea* at 5-8 and Dull, Paul S., *The Battle History of The Imperial Japanese Navy* at 121.

[173] Murphy's Law is that anything that can go wrong will go wrong.

[174] Office of Naval Intelligence, *The Battle of the Coral Sea* at 9-10

[175] Ibid at 11-13.

[176] Dull, Paul S., *The Battle History of The Imperial Japanese Navy* at 115-131.

time the support force was in latitude 12°00' S., longitude 151°31' E., in formation "Victor." The planes passed within about 6,000 yards of *Farragut*, which was on station bearing approximately 300° from the guide ship, *Australia*. Several ships opened fire briefly but no hits were made, and the planes passed rapidly ahead and out of sight.[177]

Crace's force would not be ignored for very long for at 1505 ten to fourteen G4Ms attacked with torpedoes. Fire was opened by the leading ships in the formation at a range of about 6,500 yards, and as nearly as can be determined two enemy planes, including the formation leader, were shot down almost immediately, whereupon the planes broke their tight V formation and came on in smaller groups from both port and starboard of *Perkins*. Only five torpedo tracks were observed, and of these two were seen passing by *Australia* and three by *Chicago*. All torpedoes were avoided. The planes strafed *Chicago* wounding seven men, two of whom later died. Two more aircraft were seen to fall as they withdrew. During the attack additional planes were picked up on radar. Six G3Ms made a level bombing attack at 14,000 feet and a salvo of bombs landed near *Australia* without damaging the cruiser. Only a few minutes after this attack three friendly B-26s or B-17s dropped a salvo of bombs near the destroyer *Farragut* but luckily no damage was sustained.[178]

On May 7, at 0730 Takagi received a report of a sighting of one carrier and one destroyer and he launched an all-out attack. In reality what he found was the tanker *Neosho* and her escorting destroyer *Sims* and both ships were sunk. Fletcher received word they were under attack but it did not specify if the attacking aircraft were carrier-based aircraft. Upon being detached from Task Force Fox on May 6th, *Neosho*, with *Sims* as escort, proceeded southward in accordance with fueling arrangements. The ships had reached a position at latitude 16°01' S., longitude 158°01' E. by about 0800 of the 7th, when planes began to be contacted both by radar and visually. For a time it was thought possible that the planes were American. However, at 0929 *Sims*, then moving ahead of *Neosho* as antisubmarine screen, was attacked by a single reconnaissance type plane which dropped one bomb about 100 yards off the destroyer's starboard quarter. According to *Sims* survivors, the plane, which came over at an altitude of about 15,000 feet, was not seen before the bomb fell.

---

[177] Office of Naval Intelligence. *The Battle of the Coral Sea* at 13.

[178] Office of Naval Intelligence. *The Battle of the Coral Sea* at 48.

Both American ships at this point sounded general quarters and built up speed to eighteen knots. After one or more false alarms occasioned by radar contacts, fifteen aircraft were clearly sighted bearing 025° true from *Neosho* at a high altitude. They flew past on the port side and then disappeared to the northeastward without making any attempt to attack. *Sims* fired on the aircraft without visible effect. A few minutes later seven more planes were observed approaching from 010° true. These likewise flew parallel to the American ships for a time but made no attacks. Both *Neosho* and *Sims* fired on them as they passed to port. At 1033 still another group of planes, ten in number, approached from 140° true. Three of them, all twin-engine bombers, made a horizontal run on *Neosho*, dropping three bombs from a high altitude. All fell to starboard, two within twenty-five yards. Both ships fired on the attacking planes, but apparently no hits were made and the enemy flew off to the northeastward.

Planes continued to show on the radar screen, but no more appeared until 1201, when approximately twenty-four enemy dive bombers were sighted at a considerable altitude, apparently maneuvering into position to attack. The *Sims* thereupon moved back to take up position on *Neosho*'s port quarter. Both ships were attacked heavily during the ensuing fifteen or more minutes. The enemy planes dived from all directions and the sequence of events was lost in the confusion and destruction which followed.

Only thirteen enlisted men survived of *Sims* entire complement. It was apparent that the destroyer took at least three direct hits from bombs estimated to weigh 500 pounds. As near as can be determined, four enemy planes dove extremely low on *Sims*. People aboard*Neosho* said afterward that none of the four survived their dives, being either shot down or destroyed by the blast of their own bombs. Nevertheless, bombs exploded in both the forward and after engine rooms and wrecked *Sims*. *Neosho* was also sunk in the same attack.

At 0815 scouts from *Yorktown* reported spotting two carriers and four cruisers. They had spotted *Shoho* not Takagi's main body but Fletcher launched everything he had. *Lexington* started launching planes at 0850 and *Yorktown* at 0900. This would be the first time a Japanese combat air patrol would engage an American strike force. The *Shoho* was a light carrier not a fleet carrier and she was engaged in anti-submarine patrol. At the time, *Shoho* had two A5Ms and one A6M aloft as combat air patrol (CAP) and was just landing four A6Ms and a B5N that had been patrolling over a nearby convoy. The IJN sighting gave the CAP about twenty minutes to intercept the U.S. formation before the strike began its attacks. In that time, the airborne CAP climbed to intercept the dive bombers while the *Shoho* prepared to launch three more A6Ms.[179]

At 0950 the *Lexington*'s strike group sighted the *Shoho*. Her strike consisted of twenty-eight SBDs, twelve TBDs and ten F4Fs. The fighters split up with four escorting the SBD dive bombers and four escorting the TBD torpedo bombers and two escorting three command SBDs. At 1000 *Shoho* sighted the American planes.[180] *Shoho*'s total compliment of fighters were eight A6Ms and four A5Ms. The A5M was armed with two 7.7 mm machine guns and outclassed by the F4F fighters. The three command SBDs were the first to dive but no hits were scored. The Japanese fighters failed to intercept these three planes. The Japanese fighters engaged the ten SBDs to no effect but the ten SBDs all missed *Shoho* which was maneuvering violently. *Shoho* at this time was able to launch the three fighters on deck. Then *Lexington*'s remaining fifteen SBD dive bombers attacked and they scored two 1,000-lb. bomb hits. Fires ignited in the ships hanger deck. Twelve TBDs from *Lexington* attacked next in an anvil attack. Two A5Ms attempted to intervene but the close escort of F4Fs drove them off. They descended from 4,000 feet and scored five hits.[181]

Then *Yorktown*'s twenty-five SBDs, ten TBDs, with three F4Fs escorting the SBDs and five escorting the TBDs arrived over the *Shoho*. Twenty-four SBDs dived on the *Shoho* scoring five to eleven hits. The *Shoho* steering gear jammed. Then the ten TBDs attacked scoring two more hits. They shot down two A6M and one A5M with no losses to themselves. The last SBD attacked one of Goto's cruisers but missed. *Shoho* was doomed and sank at 1035. Only 255 men out of a crew of 800 were rescued. Goto's four cruisers headed northeast to join the *Kamikawa Maru* near Deboyne Island.[182]

The *Shoho* was clearly finished after the *Lexington* air group had attacked, but only one plane from the *Yorktown* group switched to another target on the pilot's own initiative. There were four heavy cruisers in company with *Shoho*. To achieve Mahan's vision of a battle of annihilation aircraft needed to target more than one ship. *Shoho*'s combat air patrol was ineffective and did not score any kills. Once again the fighters could not gain or maintain control of the air. Ship han-

---

[179] Heinz, Leonard, *Aircraft Carrier Defense in the Pacific War: The Carrier Battles of 1942* at 35-48.

[180] Ibid.

[181] Ibid.

[182] Dull, Paul S. *The Battle History of The Imperial Japanese Navy* at 115-131.

dling prolonged *Shoho*'s life, but only by a few minutes showing again that maneuvering could be overcome with sheer numbers. [183]

The combat air patrol for Task Force Fox received its first test on May 7th. It was in the evening with the sun setting and the sky was overcast. The strike was spotted forty-eight miles out. The strike consisted of a dozen D3As and fifteen B5Ns. combat air patrol at the time of sighting was twelve F4Fs, all low on fuel. Four of the airborne F4Fs were sent to attack the strike while another seven F4Fs were scrambled for an intercept. Four of the F4Fs low on fuel were sent to attack the incoming raid. Seven more were launched from the carriers. The first interception took place about seventeen minutes after the first sighting. The first four F4Fs found the B5Ns, shooting five down and seriously damaging another. One of the F4Fs was lost when its target exploded.[184]

Of the F4Fs scrambled to intercept, two found another B5N formation, downing two of the planes and damaging a third. One F4F was lost, either to defensive fire or to navigational difficulties. The other five scrambled F4Fs bounced the D3As, killing one before the formation broke apart. Scattered and hurt, the IJN strike aircraft jettisoned their ordnance and headed back to their carriers. Only then did some of them spot the USN ships. One final F4F was lost when it could not find its way back to the USN task force.[185] The performance of the combat air patrol was excellent. All the fighters were able to engage enemy aircraft. No enemy aircraft attacked the ships. The U.S. lost three F4Fs while the Japanese lost seven B5Ns and one D3A outright, with two more B5Ns damaged and one of those ditching on return to its carrier. A job well done by combat air patrol.[186]

Task Force Fox continued to the southwestward during the night of the 7th and by 0800 of the 8th was at latitude 14°25' S., longitude 154°31' E., on course 125° true. Takagi's main body was at latitude 11°51' S., longitude 156°04' E. Both Fletcher and Takagi would discover each other and launch simultaneous attacks on each other. The *Lexington* and the *Yorktown* were still concentrated. The number of aircraft launched by the 5th Carrier Division was sixty-nine aircraft strong: eighteen A6M escorting eighteen B5N and thirty-three D3A. Eight F4F and eighteen SBDs made up the combat air patrol. *Lexington* launched five more

---

[183] Heinz, Leonard, *Aircraft Carrier Defense in the Pacific War: The Carrier Battles of 1942* at 35-48.

[184] Ibid.

[185] Ibid.

[186] Ibid.

F4Fs and five more SBDs with five minutes of sighting the raid. *Yorktown* launched four more F4Fs.[187]

The Japanese D3As came in at 14,000 feet and the B5Ns came in at 10,000 feet but used a slow descent to 4,000 feet. The F4Fs had a difficult time reaching altitude or the Fighter Direction Office was thrown off by the B5Ns beginning at a higher altitude. Three F4Fs were sent after the D3As and six after the B5Ns but the six fighters that were supposed to engage the B5Ns missed them entirely. The three F4Fs were still too low at 10,000 feet to make an interception of the D3As but one fighter peeled off and attacked the B5Ns shooting down one before the escorting A6Ms chased him away. Twenty-one minutes had elapsed since the raid was first sighted. [188]

The Japanese fighters then engaged the low altitude SBDs, which were too low to intercept the B5Ns. The A6Ms shot down four SBDs. *Lexington*'s SBDs did engage the B5Ns shooting down two and damaging a third that was later shot down by ship anti-aircraft guns. Twenty-six minutes had passed from the first sighting and time had run out. One F4F engaged the D3As but was shot down in the attempt. *Yorktown* was the first ship to be attacked and four B5Ns dropped their torpedoes but *Yorktown* was able to avoid them and shot down two. Nine B5Ns attacked the *Lexington* in an anvil attack. This was when the one B5N that the damaged was shot down. Eight torpedoes were dropped and two hit the ship. Two B5Ns attacked a heavy cruiser but the cruiser avoided the torpedoes. Out of eighteen torpedo bombers fourteen had been able to drop their torpedoes. Next came the D3As in which all thirty-three attacked. They split up so seventeen attacked *Lexington* and sixteen attacked *Yorktown*.[189]

Some of the F4Fs engaged even as the dive bombers were in their dives and were able to shoot one down before the plane had dropped its bomb and one after. Another D3A was destroyed by anti-aircraft fire. Two direct hits were scored on *Lexington* and another landing next to the carrier damaged her side. *Yorktown* suffered one direct hit and two along her side that caused damage. The bomb which struck the *Yorktown*'s flight deck penetrated a vertical distance of fifty feet

---

[187] Office of Naval Intelligence. *The Battle of the Coral Sea* at 17.

[188] Heinz, Leonard, *Aircraft Carrier Defense in the Pacific War: The Carrier Battles of 1942* at 35-48.

[189] Ibid.

from the point of impact to the point of detonation, piercing a total thickness of 1.68 inches of steel deck plating.[190]

The hole in the flight deck was clean. The holes in the hangar and second decks were jagged and somewhat larger. The ship's shell was not punctured. The flight and galley decks were not harmed, but the hangar deck was bulged across its entire breadth from frame No.100 to frame No.115. A hole four feet in diameter was blown up through the second deck eight feet inboard of the bomb impact hole, and the entire deck in the Marine living compartment was bulged upward. Also, the transverse bulkheads of this compartment were badly bulged forward and aft. However, they did not rupture, and all doors remained secure, though severely warped. When the bomb hit the second deck it pierced the general lighting and battle light and power circuits for the damaged area, causing short circuits. Several people in the fire parties were shocked, one seriously.[191]

A hole six feet in diameter was blown out of the third deck, with the deck turned and peeled back over an area of thirty-five square feet. The entire deck in compartment C-301-1L was bulged upward, and the ship's service store and office, soda fountain, engineer's office, and laundry issue room were wrecked. The fourth deck was not ruptured but was dished downward over an area of forty square feet. The inboard bulkhead of the forward engine room access truck, and the after bulkhead of the laundry storeroom, were shattered. Two watertight doors were severely damaged and a large hatch cover was thrown about fifteen feet up into the No. 2 elevator pit. The transverse bulkheads and doors joining four compartments were blown out. Minor fires broke out in the aviation storeroom, and the flash of the explosion passed up to the hangar overhead, causing a small paint fire directly above the bomb impact hole. A minor fire also broke out in the Marine living compartment. The explosion was responsible for thirty-seven of the forty deaths aboard *Yorktown* and for many of the twenty-six serious injuries.[192]

Hoses attached to fireplugs in the hangar were led to the bomb hole and No. 2 elevator pit and used to extinguish the fires on the three decks below. By chance, a shorted power circuit in the aviation storeroom started the sprinkling system, and this aided the fire parties materially. The fire and repair parties performed excellently. Noteworthy was the action of Lt Milton E. Ricketts, officer in charge of

---

[190] Office of Naval Intelligence. *The Battle of the Coral Sea* at 31.

[191] Ibid.

[192] Ibid.

repair No. 5. His men all killed, wounded, or stunned by the bomb blast immediately below his station, and himself mortally wounded, Lieutenant Ricketts opened the valve of a fireplug, partially led out the hose and directed a stream of water into the fire before dropping dead. This was the first hose put on the fire. Only two near misses caused perceptible damage, and this was restricted to piercings of the hull above the water line.[193]

Now the Japanese planes attempted to withdraw. Three F4Fs were shot down by the A6Ms while one A6M was damaged and later ditched attempting to get back to his carrier. One F4F shot down one D3A. The SBDs shot down two B5Ns and two D3As but lost two SBDs in return, one to friendly anti-aircraft gunfire.[194] The *Lexington* suffered one bomb hit that penetrated the flight deck and exploded in her hanger causing a fire. The bombs that detonated along her sides opened up fuel bunkers. One bomb hit wiped out an entire 5-inch gun crew and the other hit her stack which killed many of her anti-aircraft crew on *Lexington*. The bomb that detonated along her side opened fuel bunkers. One torpedo hit along her boiler rooms forcing three to shut down and the second torpedo jammed her elevators in place and fractured her aviation fuel lines. Fumes from these lines began to build up and later exploded. The explosions lasted for five hours, and eight hours after the strike, she was ordered abandoned and scuttled.[195]

The Japanese fighter escort did well. They showed flexibility and cooperated well with both the B5Ns and D3As. The escorts however were less effective during withdrawal having used up the ammunition for their 20-mm cannons. The 7.7-mm guns required longer engagements to bring down the sturdy American planes. In addition the lightly built Japanese planes were mostly brought down by SBDs and their firepower was far less than F4Fs. Over-claiming by the Japanese fliers which reported ten bomb hits on *Lexington* and eight to ten hits on *Yorktown* led the Japanese to believe that they had inflicted far more severe bomb damage. This had a major impact on future operations.[196]

Overall the U.S. combat air patrol was a failure. Only three F4Fs out of seventeen engaged the enemy due to the low altitude of the attackers. The low altitude forced the F4Fs to engage the escort A6Ms and they were unable to dive passed

---

[193] Ibid.

[194] Heinz, Leonard, *Aircraft Carrier Defense in the Pacific War: The Carrier Battles of 1942* at 35-48.

[195] Ibid.

[196] Ibid.

the escort and into the strike aircraft. They lost two F4Fs to one A6M. Only fifteen of the SBDs out of twenty-three engaged the enemy. They lost six of their number but these twenty-three planes being kept back for a combat air patrol meant they were not available to strike the Japanese carriers. The SBDs shot down four B5Ns but only two before they made their attack and one D3A before it attacked and one after. [197]

Anti-aircraft fire was also ineffective only shooting down two B5Ns and one D3A with a third B5N being shared with a SBD. The F4Fs shot down one D3A before it attacked one after it attacked and one A6M during the Japanese withdraw. Concentration of the two carriers led to concentration of the combat air patrol and the anti-aircraft batteries. The *Yorktown*'s armored deck stopped the D3A's 500lb. bomb and the small payload of the D3A would be a weakness for the Japanese. Both U.S. carriers should have survived the damage inflicted but *Lexington*'s aviation fuel lines proved vulnerable to shock effects. Had the carriers been separated it is likely one carrier would have been sunk none-the-less. Maneuver of the carriers saved them from further damage and in the very early stages of ship vs. aircraft this seemed to be the best defense. In total the Japanese lost two A6M, ten B5Ns, and seven D3As. The Americans lost four F4Fs and six SBDs. When we add the losses from May 7, the Japanese had lost eighteen B5Ns and eleven D3As. The U.S. had lost an additional F4F for a total of five for the two Japanese air strikes against U.S. forces.[198]

On May 8 the carriers *Shokaku* and *Zuikaku* were sailing with a concentrated force in an overcast day with rain squalls and overcast. The *Yorktown* strike was made up of thirty-four SBDs and nine TBDs, with four F4Fs escorting the TBDs. Two F4Fs had set out with the SBDs, but became separated in the heavy weather and proceeded to the IJN task force separately. On combat air patrol were five A6Ms high over the IJN task force, five more A6Ms low over the ships, and another six poised for take-off.[199] The SBDs had sighted the Japanese force at 1032. At 1055 the TBDs radioed they had sighted the Japanese task force. The SBDs began an attack run on *Shokaku* at 1057. This was slightly too early as the SBDs would attack alone and the TBDs would attack separately ten minutes after the SBDs. [200] The SBDs split into two seventeen plane squadrons.

---

[197] Ibid.

[198] Ibid.

[199] Ibid.

[200] Ibid.

Three A6Ms attacked the first wave of SBD dive bombers without effect. The first seventeen dive bomber were all able to make drops on *Shokaku* but all missed the carrier partly due to windscreens and bomb sights fogging up due to high humidity. Four A6Ms pursued them as they withdrew but again without results. The second squadron of seventeen SBDs was intercepted by two A6Ms and the fighters shot down two SBDs but all seventeen were able to release their bombs scoring two hits.[201]

Now the nine TBDs made their attack run. Five A6Ms engaged the four F4Fs escort and lost two A6Ms and a third badly damaged. The TBDs scored no hits and one was heavily damaged due to anti-aircraft fire. The score from *Yorktown* strike was two SBDs lost and a TBD seriously damaged. Two A6Ms lost and one seriously damaged. The two hits scored on *Shokaku* were not fatal but did hamper her ability to continue air operations: one hit on the carrier's port bow which caused local flooding of the bow, and one to starboard at the forward end of the flight deck.[202] *Shokaku*'s anti-aircraft guns were ineffective against the dive bombers.

The *Lexington* strike arrived at 1130 with nineteen SBDs and eleven TBDs, with an escort of six F4Fs. The *Lexington* strike faced thirteen A6Ms on combat air patrol: six high and seven low. Four A6Ms attacked the F4F escort, downing two. The bad weather allowed the Japanese task force to hide and fifteen SBDs failed to spot the Japanese and turned back low on fuel. Four SBDs did find the Japanese carriers, although the low cloud ceiling forced them into a less accurate low-level glide-bombing attack. Four SBDs split up and two attacked *Shokaku* and two attacked *Zuikaku*. One hit was scored just abaft the island on *Shokaku*. With her flight deck heavily damaged and 223 of her crew killed or wounded, *Shokaku* was unable to conduct further aircraft operations. Her captain, Takatsugu Jōjima, requested permission from Takagi to withdraw from the battle, to which Takagi agreed.[203]

No hits were scored on *Zuikaku*. The SBDs were not engaged by the combat air patrol until after they had released their bombs. One SBD soon discovered his bomb had not released; the pilot returned to the enemy task force but he was never seen again. Two A6Ms engaged with the result of one A6M being badly damaged and one SBD being badly damaged. Three A6M engaged the escort

[201] Ibid.

[202] Ibid.

[203] Office of Naval Intelligence, *The Battle of the Coral Sea*.

F4Fs and one F4F was shot down.[204] Four A6Ms fought the escort for the TBDs, downing two F4Fs. Three attacked the TBDs before they could drop their torpedoes, but the TBDs all survived. They began their attack on *Shokaku* a couple of minutes after the SBDs, scoring no hits for eleven drops. By the time that the Japanese strike returned, *Shokaku* was out of business as a carrier. Twenty-two Japanese aircraft went missing or ditched due to battle damage or lack of fuel.[205]

Defensively, the Japanese tactic of out-ranging was not effective. Both forces were in range of each other. While in theory out-ranging sounds clever, in actual combat conditions it was difficult to position your ships to take advantage of this technique. Bad weather over the Japanese task force helped. The SBD underfueling mistake did contribute to a quarter of the U.S. dive bombers failing to attack. Concentration was a net help to the Japanese, as the A6Ms from both carriers formed the combat air patrol while the weather hid one carrier from view. In essence, the weather gave the Japanese the best of both worlds: the carriers could pool their fighter assets while not being in view of the same attackers. Japanese armor and damage control were effective, keeping the 1,000 pound bomb blasts from *Shokaku*'s vitals and controlling the fires that the bomb blasts started. [206]

Combat air performance and anti-aircraft gunnery were another matter. *Shokaku* had more than five times the light anti-aircraft weapons as *Shoho,* but could manage only to damage one relatively vulnerable TBD. It was a performance that made the three and one half victories credited to the U.S. anti-aircraft batteries look good. However, the fact that twenty-two Japanese aircraft did not make it back to their carriers was an indication that allied anti-aircraft firepower may have contributed to more than the three confirmed kills.[207] Total loses for the Japanese 5th carrier division was nineteen A6Ms, nineteen D3As, and thirty-one B5Ns.[208] The Japanese were able to put more fighters on the SBDs as they dove than the U.S. were able to against the D3As with clearer skies and radar. The real difference in combat air patrol performance came in aircraft downed, not in interceptions made. This would have been hard for the Japanese to see, given the usual

---

[204] Heinz, Leonard, *Aircraft Carrier Defense in the Pacific War: The Carrier Battles of 1942* at 35-48.

[205] Ibid.

[206] Ibid.

[207] Ibid.

[208] Lundstrom, *Guadalcanal Campaign* at 92.

tendency to make exaggerated claims for aerial victories, but dive bombers were hard to handle, even with the advantage of radar.[209]

From a Mahanist perspective view the Battle of the Coral Sea was a failure. Naval forces were supposed to create conditions for a battle of annihilation. Yamamoto did order Takagi to take *Zuikaku* back and annihilate the enemy near dusk on May 8, but this order was later cancelled.

What this first carrier battle showed was that carrier battles were characterized by attrition.

When two forces attacked at long range, it became easy for one or both sides to withdraw and escape destruction. The attrition rate on aircraft was much higher than pre-war expectations. After four days combat the Japanese had lost 87 out of 127 aircraft or 69%. The U.S. lost 66 aircraft including thirty-five aircraft going down when *Lexington* foundered out of 128 aircraft or 53%. Casualties were estimated at 966 Japanese sailors killed and 709 U.S. sailors killed.[210]

This was extremely bad news for the Japanese who could not afford to fight a war of attrition. The number of aircraft that bypassed the combat air patrol and reached their targets was significant and should have been alarming for both sides. On military terms the Battle of Coral Sea was a tactical Japanese victory. It achieved one half of its strategic goal by taking Tulagi and drawing out the U.S. fleet. The U.S. lost one fleet carrier to the Japanese losing one light carrier. Each had one fleet carrier damaged in the battle and both lost heavily in planes. Two out of three Japanese objectives were met: capturing Tulagi and inflicting heavier losses on the enemy.

On a larger strategic level it could be considered that stopping the main element of Operation MO, which was the Port Moresby invasion, was a U.S. victory. Breaking the Japanese codes allowed the U.S. to get between the Japanese transports while their Army was embarked and their objective Port Moresby. This was a classic defense against invasion as Corbett had observed. The Japanese air attacks on Crace's Task Group were ineffective and this force blocked any attempt to pass through Jonard Passage either by day or night. The U.S. carriers inflicted enough damage on the Japanese main body which was covering the transports,

---

[209] Ibid.

[210] Office of Naval Intelligence. *The Battle of the Coral Sea at* 47.

Takagi to postpone the operation, so Admiral Fletcher's mission prevented the Japanese from achieving one of their three strategic objectives.

Nimitz was concerned with the results once he learned *Lexington* was lost. In a memo to King dated May 10;

> 10 0237 CINCPAC to COMINCH
>
> Loss of Lexington represents one fifth our carrier strength in Pacific. Japanese loss one large carrier with temporary serious damage to another carrier approximates one fifth enemy carrier strength. At present stage of our carrier building program we cannot afford to swap losses with this ratio. Japanese success to date due primarily to decisive air superiority and possession of many mutually supporting air bases. Our aircraft staging points between west coast and x-ray too widely separated to be mutually supporting to same degree and each is vulnerable to determined major attack due to lack sufficient air strength. Each point must be given sufficient air strength to force enemy accept large risk in capture attempts while in meantime we build up our general air strength. Importance Pacific Area to our national interest requires resurvey of distribution of American plane output with larger allocation planes to Pacific areas. Particularly needed carrier type planes with maximum military characteristics. Also needed are long range naval landplane bombers to afford relatively safe and efficient patrolling and scouting in the face of the enemy and provide strong striking force."[211]

King followed with a question for Nimitz on using surface forces to attack the Japanese fleet May 15:

> 150825 COMINCH to CINCPAC
>
> While not familiar with all the circumstances attending operations last week I feel I must express my feeling that destroyers might have been used in night attacks on enemy especially since Junction of Task Force 11 and 17 made large number of destroyers available.[212]

Admiral Fletcher responded with this memo to Nimitz;

> COMTASKFORCE 17 to CINCPAC your 150825.
>
> Task Force 17 was organized with an attack group of cruisers and destroyers for the purpose of making night and day attacks on enemy surface craft and support group of cruisers and destroyers to protect carriers or attack surface craft. On the morning of 7 May the support group 3 cruisers and 3 destroyers were directed to destroy transports reported moving through Jomard Pass toward Moresby. After the attack of ships off Hisma Island the only surface ships known to be in range of a surface attack force were those which the support group had been ordered to destroy. When Task Force 17 was attacked by carrier planes at sunset May 7th it was realized that carrier groups were in the vicinity but their

---

[211] Nimitz, Chester, *Chester Nimitz Gray Book*, Vol 1 at 463.

[212] King, Ernest J., *Chester Nimitz Gray Book*, Vol 1 at 468.

> location was indefinite. At that time 5 cruisers and 7 destroyers were with my carriers and it was not considered that the attack group was large enough. After carrier action on May 8th serious consideration was given to sending the attack group in for surface attack that night but plan was rejected for the following reasons. It was reported that one of the enemy carriers was undamaged and the Lexington reported that radio information indicated a 3rd carrier had joined the enemy the attack group would therefore have had to search for an enemy whose location was known only generally to be 135 miles to northward in the afternoon. If started immediately the element of surprise would be lost while approaching in daylight subject to enemy air attack. Both of my carriers were damaged. Operating planes were greatly reduced in numbers and presence of the attack group was needed for carrier defense. Destroyer's fuel reduced to 50% fuel precluding high speed operations for any extensive time. After sinking of Lexington at nightfall surface ships were crowded with survivors up to 300% of complement in some cases greatly reducing military efficiency. Acting in best judgement on the spot no opportunity could be found to use destroyers in night attacks on the enemy except the attack by support group which I ordered.[213]

Nimitz could accept a war of attrition but he needed time to allow the U.S. economy to fully mobilize. Swapping carrier for carrier in 1942 was dangerous as the first *Essex* class carrier was not expected until 1943. In addition plane production would need to be increased as the loss rates were considerable. Island airfields also needed to be strengthened. Nimitz needed his own search planes if MacArthur's command was not going to cooperate. Other tactical concerns had revealed themselves. Carriers were incapable of operating alone. As a platform they were not highly survivable, and they needed protection. That protection could only come from the battle fleet. This robbed the battle fleet of its primary offensive role in seeking out the enemy fleet. Nimitz needed to resolve this problem so that he could achieve Mahan's decisive battle of annihilation.

[213] Fletcher, Frank J. *Chester Nimitz Gray Book*, Vol 1 at 469.

CHAPTER 14: THE BATTLE OF MIDWAY

Despite the setback of Operation MO and the postponement of the Port Moresby invasion Yamamoto was now ready to begin operation MI. His primary objective was to draw out the U.S. Pacific Fleet and with superior numbers inflict upon it Mahan's vision for a battle of annihilation. The Naval General Staff wanted to expand the line of defense to the south and north. The initial plan was for Operation FS or the occupation of New Caledonia, Samoa, and the Fijis Islands to be the next step but Yamamoto wanted operation MI to take priority. He had threatened resignation again and the Naval General Staff caved in but on the condition that he support Operation MO and he include in his operation MI plans for seizing Attu and Kiska Islands in the Aleutian chain to secure the northern defensive sphere.

Upon their return to home ports on 22 and 23 April, after the Indian Ocean raid the four carriers *Akagi, Kaga, Hiryu*, and *Soryu* immediately underwent repair and maintenance operations. From the latter part of April, the carrier planes engaged in training at Kagoshima. Float plane training was conducted at Kagoshima from 6 May. There had been considerable turn-over since the Pearl Harbor attack. Inexperienced fliers barely got to the point where they could make daytime landings on carriers. No opportunity was available to carry out joint training, which, of course made impossible any coordinated action between contact units, illumination units, and attack units. The likelihood of obtaining any satisfactory results from night attacks, therefore, was practically nil.[214]

During the middle part of May, mock torpedo attacks were carried out, with judges from the Yokosuka Air Group acting as referees. The records during these tests were very disappointing. On 18 May, actual tests were made against CruDiv 8 traveling at high speed. In spite of the fact that the speed was thirty knots with

[214] Supplement to First Air Fleet secret file #37 of 6. Mobile Force Detailed Action Report #6, First Air Fleet Detailed Action Report #6, Occupation of Midway Operations, May 27-June 6. Office of Naval Intelligence, *The Battle of Midway*, Japanese Experience.

only 45-degree turns, the records made by the fliers were again exceedingly poor. With water depth at 40 to 50 meters, about a third of the torpedoes were lost. [215]

Bomber leaders were concentrated at Iwakuni and practiced level bombing using the target ship *Settsu*. The men attained a fair degree of skill, but they had no opportunity to participate in any formation bombing drills. Since *Settsu* was limited to the waters in the vicinity of Naikai Seibu (Western Inland Sea) valuable time was wasted by the fliers in coming and going. The men could not participate in more than one dive bombing drill a day without seriously interfering with their basic training. Even this minimum practice could not be conducted satisfactorily because the men were kept busy with maintenance work.[216]

For air combat the pilots engaged in this phase were able to get no further than to actual firing and basic training for lone air combat operations. The more experienced were employed in formation air combat tactics, but even they were limited to about a three-plane formation. Since the carriers were undergoing repair and maintenance operations, the only available ship for take-off and landing drills was *Kaga*. She was kept busy from early morning to nightfall but even at that the young fliers barely were able to learn the rudiments of carrier landings. The more seasoned fliers were given about one chance each to make dusk landings.[217]

Insofar as the weather permitted, night flying tactics were trained every day. Due to maintenance needs and because of the limited time, only the very fundamentals were learned by the inexperienced fliers. Because of the need for replacements and transfers of personnel, the combat efficiency of each ship had been greatly lowered. Moreover, since most of the ships were undergoing maintenance and repair work until only a few days before departure, the men's efficiency suffered greatly.[218]

As the operation began, Japanese had practically no accurate intelligence concerning U.S. forces. On 24 May aircraft were taken aboard and on the 26th operation plans were agreed upon. At 0600 27 May the Japanese carrier force departed for its operations area.[219]

---

[215] Ibid.

[216] Ibid.

[217] Ibid.

[218] Ibid.

[219] Ibid.

The Japanese estimated of Midway's defenses taken from their detailed action reports:

> Midway acts as a sentry for Hawaii. Its importance was further enhanced after the loss of Wake and it was apparent that the enemy was expediting the reinforcing of its defensive installations, its air base facilities, and other military installations as well as the personnel.
>
> Estimate of existing conditions there were as follows:
>
> a. Air strength: 1 Reconnaissance. Flying Boats 2 squadrons.
>
> Army Bombers 1 squadron.
>
> Fighters 1 squadron.
>
> b. The above estimated strength could be doubled in an emergency.
>
> c. Strict Air Patrols were maintained both day and night to the West to a distance of about 600 miles. About three fighters covered the Island at all times.
>
> d. Some surface vessels patrolled the area and some submarines were active to the West.
>
> e. Of the enemy's carriers, the Ranger was apparently in the Atlantic. According to some prisoners' statements, the Lexington had been sunk. There were others, however, who claimed that she was under repair on the West Coast.
>
> f. The Enterprise and the Hornet were definitely placed in the Pacific, but we could get no reliable information as to the whereabouts of the Wasp.
>
> g. About six auxiliary carriers had been completed and there were indications that about half of this number were in the Pacific. However, they were known to be inferior in speed and could not be effectively employed for positive action.
>
> g. Air strength in the Hawaii area was estimated to be as follows:
>
> Flying Boats about 60.
>
> Bombers about 100.
>
> Fighters about 200.
>
> h. These could be used for the speedy reinforcement of Midway.
>
> I. Enemy surface units in the Hawaii area were estimated to be in about the strength noted below. It was likely that these units would sortie in the event of an attack on Midway.
>
> Aircraft Carriers 2 to 3.
>
> Special Carriers 2 to 3.
>
> Battleships 2.
>
> Type A Cruisers 4 to 5.
>
> Type B Cruisers 3 to 4.
>
> Light Cruisers 4.
>
> Destroyers about 30.
>
> Submarines 25.
>
> j. Shore Defense Installations on Midway.
>
> Large numbers of various types of level and high angle large caliber guns as well as high angle machine guns had been installed. Marines had also been landed and all in all, the island was very strongly defended.
>
> 4. Mobile Force Commander's Estimate of the Situation
>
> g. Although the enemy lacks the will to fight, it is likely that he will counter-attack if our occupation operations progress satisfactorily.

h. The enemy conducts air reconnaissance mainly to the West and to the South but does not maintain a strict vigil to the Northwest or to the North.

I. The enemy's patrol radius is about 500 miles.

j. The enemy is not aware of our plans.

k. It is not believed that the enemy has any powerful unit, with carriers as its nucleus, in the vicinity.

l. After attacking Midway by air and destroying the enemy's shore-based air strength to facilitate our landing operations, we would still be able to destroy any enemy task force which may choose to counterattack.

m. The enemy's attempt to counterattack with use of shore-based aircraft could be neutralized by our cover fighters and AA fire.[220]

Of these assumption "j" was by far the most crucial for the belief the United States was not aware of Japanese intentions. While the Japanese admirals were making their plans, code breakers at Pearl Harbor were briefing Nimitz on Japanese intentions. Since the war began it was a duel of carriers and *Saratoga* had been torpedoed by submarine *I-6* on January 11, 1942 and was believed sunk.[221] Their intelligence at the time also believed *Lexington* and *Yorktown* were sunk at Coral Sea. If *Wasp* and *Ranger* were still in the Atlantic then the U.S. Pacific Fleet had only two remaining carriers, *Hornet* and *Enterprise.* Admiral Yamamoto with his four undamaged fleet carriers *Akagi, Kaga, Soryu,* and *Hiryu* would have a two-one advantage so the loss of *Shokaku* and *Zuikaku* for operation MI was not at the time immediately recognized as critical. The estimated defenses at Midway were not much higher than their pre-war estimates of the defenses of Wake Island, which had fallen after a sharp but short defense. However, Midway Island was only an excuse to draw out the U.S. Fleet. Yamamoto needed Corbett's willing partner for a Mahanian decisive battle.

His plan was to secure the sea around Midway and cut off the lines of communication with Pearl Harbor. This was a seaway that he felt the U.S. must fight for. When the U.S. Pacific Fleet reacted to the occupation of Midway the Imperial Japanese Navy with superior numbers would annihilate it. Then public morale in the U.S. would falter, the Emperor could negotiate a treaty from a position of strength, and the killing could stop. The plan again used Corbett's philosophy of

---

[220] Supplement to First Air Fleet secret file #37 of 6. Mobile Force Detailed Action Report #6, First Air Fleet Detailed Action Report #6, Occupation of Midway Operations, May 27-June 6. Office of Naval Intelligence, *the Battle of Midway*, Japanese Experience.

[221] Repairs had just been completed and the *Saratoga* left the west coast for Pearl Harbor on May 31.

division. Widely separated forces would have to act in unison and this broke the principle of flexibility. The order of battle was complex.

1. The Main Body would be commanded by Admiral Yamamoto.
   a. Battleships: *Yamato, Nagato, Mutsu*
   b. Carrier: *Hosho* (8 x D3A aircraft)
   c. Light cruiser: *Sendai*
   d. Nine destroyers
2. First Carrier Striking Force was commanded by Vice Admiral Chuichi Nagumo.
   a. Carriers: *Akagi, Kaga, Soryu, Hiryu*
   b. Battleships: *Haruna, Kirishima*
   c. *Light cruiser: Nagara*
   d. Eleven destroyers
   e. 1st Carrier division air wing (42 A6M, 42 D3A, 51 B5N)
   f. 2nd Carrier division air wing (42 A6M, 42 D3A, 42 B5N.
3. Midway Invasion Force was commanded by Vice Admiral Nobutake Kondo.
   a. Battleships *Hiei, Kongo*
   b. Carrier *Zuiho* (12 A6M, 12 B5N)
   c. Heavy cruisers *Atago, Chokai, Myoko, Haguro*
   d. Light cruiser *Yura*
   e. Eight destroyers
4. Close support group was commanded by Vice Admiral Takeo Kurita.
   a. Heavy cruisers *Kumano, Suzuya, Mikuma, Mogami*
   b. Two destroyers.
5. Transport Group was commanded by Rear Admiral Raizo Tanaka.
   a. Twelve transports with 5,000 men.
   b. Ten destroyers.
6. Seaplane Tender Group was commanded by Rear Admiral Ruitaro Fujita.

   a. Seaplane carrier *Chitose* (16 float fighters, 4 float scouts).
   b. Seaplane carrier *Kamikawa Maru* (8 float fighters, 4 float scouts).
   c. One destroyer.
   d. One patrol boat.

7. Northern Aleutians Force Main Body was commanded by Vice Admiral Moshiro Hosogaya.
   a. Heavy cruiser *Nachi.*
   b. Two destroyers.
8. Second Carrier Striking Force was commanded by Rear Admiral Kakuji Kakuta.
   a. Carrier *Ryujo* (16 A6M, 21 B5N).
   b. Carrier *Junyo* (24 A6M, 21 D3A).
   c. Heavy cruisers *Maya* and *Takao.*
   d. Three destroyers.
9. Attu Invasion Force was commanded by Rear Admiral Sentaro Omori.
   a. Light cruiser *Abukuma.*
   b. Four destroyers.
   c. One transport with 1,200 men.
10. Kiska Invasion Force was in command of Captain Takeji Ono.
    a. Light cruiser *Kiso* and *Tama.*
    b. Auxiliary Cruiser *Asaka Maru.*
    c. Three destroyers.
    d. Two Transports with 1,250 men.

Why would Admiral Yamamoto divide his forces into so many separate parts? Corbett believed division would enhance a fleet's ability to stay undetected. This would best enable the commander to achieve the sea power principle of security. Similarly, while one part of the force may be detected, the remaining ones may go undetected, thus gaining the advantage of surprise. This tactic does bear with it the risk of each force being destroyed in detail by a stronger or equal force. In addition, there was an intrinsic contradiction. For divided forces to operate effectively together, good and immediate communications between the various forces would be needed, but in war radio silence will be the normal for operations. In the age of sail such communication was carried out by picket frigates and sloops using semaphore, but in the modern era radio communications were intrinsically faster, especially over the horizon, at night, and under inclement conditions or enemy interference. Corbett also believed that decisive battles would be very rare because the weaker fleet would typically run and this was why he favored division over Mahan's view of concentration. Yamamoto needed the Americans to stand and fight but feared if a force as large as his was discovered early the Americans would simply withdraw. While carriers did have the ability to out-range battleship guns this was also a double–edged sword. The long distances made it easy for one side to escape.

Mahan preferred concentration mainly for unity of command. Once these widely separated forces were on their own it was difficult for a single commander to yield them as a coordinated weapon. This created disunity of effort. Moreover, the principles of cooperation and flexibility are broken if the forces are too widely separated for mutual support.

The number of ships going to sea for the Midway operation would use up a tremendous amount of fuel. A significant logistical supply train must be established, and each division must be supplied separately. And, once these islands are captured how are they to be re-supplied?

Finally, Yamamoto and the Naval General Staff were breaking the principle of economy of effort because Japan will gain very little for seizing Midway, Attu, and Kiska Islands when the real chief aim of the entire operation was the destruction of the U.S. Pacific Fleet.

How did Admiral Nimitz respond? What follows are copies of the actual primary documents. Few people other than researchers get to read. The purpose of using lengthy quotations is so that the reader can see what the admirals in question wrote in their own hand. These detailed remarks provide insight into political objectives and the way the admirals used the tools at hand. The level of detail of Nimitz's plan contrasts with Yamamoto's plan and the level of intelligence Nimitz had showing how important the principle of security was to planning a military operation. [222]

---

[222] Nimitz, Chester, *Chester Nimitz Gray Book* at 506-521.

SECRET

May 26, 1942

ESTIMATE OF THE SITUATION

ATTACK ON HAWAIIAN AND ALASKAN BASES

PART I - MISSION

The Problem

1. There are indications that the enemy will make a strong simultaneous effort, commencing after May 26, 1942, to -

(a) Capture MIDWAY for possible subsequent operations against OAHU, and

(b) Capture an advanced position in the ALEUTIAN ISLANDS.

The problem here considered is how to deal with that enemy effort, while continuing to carry out tasks assigned but not directly related to this problem.

The Situation

2. The basic task of the Commander-in-Chief, U.S. Pacific Fleet, which applies is:

"covering and holding the line HAWAII-MIDWAY and maintaining tis communications with West Coast".

The Commander-in-Chief, Pacific Ocean Areas, is assigned, among others, the following supplementary tasks:

"(a) Hold island positions between the United States and Southwest Pacific Area necessary for security of the line of communications between these regions and for supporting naval, air, and amphibious operations against Japanese."

"(d) Support defense of the continent of North America."

"(e) Protect essential sea and air communications." 506

I-1-

3. The following is quoted from a message from COMINCH: "I consider that our appropriate strategy is to make strong concentration HAWAIIAN AREA and ---- to employ strong attrition tactics and not allow our forces to accept such decisive action as would be likely to incur heavy losses in our carriers and cruisers.

"Create for the defense of ALASKA the North Pacific Force comprising northwest and frontier forces plus such western sea frontier forces as you elect to include sound school destroyers and submarines plus such Fleet units as you can make available all preferably to be concentrated initially at KODIAK and/or COLD BAY."

4. The Commander-in-Chief, U.S. Pacific Fleet will employ the major part of his forces to repel these attacks. He will expect full cooperation from Army forces stationed in ALASKA.

PART II - SURVEY OF OPPOSING STRENGTHS

1. (a) The Japanese have just experienced a setback in the NEW BRITAIN - NEW GUINEA Area. In spite of this, their morale is high.

(b) It is to be expected that the planning for this campaign will be excellent and the preparations complete. They are indicated having a rehearsal for parts of the campaign.

(c) Their planes, are generally speaking, of greater range than ours. Their fighters out-perform ours.

(d) Theyhave amply demonstrated their ability to use their carrier air with great ability. We can no longer underestimate their naval air efficiency.

(e) On the other hand, our men are just as brave, and those who have been properly trained are believed to be better than their opposite Jap number. Our Army is untried except in Bataan. The Army air has not demonstrated that it has the ability to coordinate with surface forces, and they are not very successful in hitting mobile targets with their high altitude bombers.

(f) Our submarines have demonstrated considerable superiority. Division tactics have not been tried out against the enemy.

2. Character of the Theater.

(a) Hydrography, topography. The Hawaiian Sea Frontier presents no problem. Ships up to the size of CAs can enter and berth at MIDWAY, but must exercise extreme caution.

In the ALASKAN Sector navigation is difficult because of fog. Charts are only fairly accurate. Harbors are generally poor from the viewpoint of the fair weather sailor. The best anchorage for a Fleet is at COLD HARBOR, ubt it has no resources. The islands are rugged and very thinly populated and will not support troops.

(b) The Weather. The normal trades are expected in the Hawaiian Islands Area, while in the Aleutians south of the chain overcast weather with fog and occasional rain will be an average condition. North of the Aleutian chain there will be a somewhat higher percentage of good flying weather.

(c) Daylight will be from about 0341 to 2014 in Latitude 25°N on June 1st. In Latitude 50°N it will be from about 0023 to 2342.

There will be a full moon on June 1st.

(d) The following distances are pertinent:

PEARL	to MIDWAY	1149 mi.
PEARL	to SAN DIEGO	2200 mi.
PEARL	to DUTCH HARBOR	2046 mi.
MIDWAY	to SAIPAN	2300 mi.
MIDWAY	to DUTCH HARBOR	1653 mi.
DUTCH HARBOR	to COLD BAY	200 mi.
DUTCH HARBOR	to KODIAK	600 mi.

2. (Continued)

SAIPAN	to TOKYO	1343 mi.
SAIPAN	to TRUK	570 mi.
WOTJE	to PEARL	1986 mi.

3. Information.

(a) Our sole source of information for this problem is RI and CI. The enemy may be deceiving us.

(b) We may expect the enemy to have had full information prior to December 7, 1941. Since that time he has not had such good opportunities. Nevertheless he spotted the return of Task Force 16 in April due to our radio carelessness.

(c) Communication facilities are considered equal, with the exception of our ECM.

4. Enemy Forces.

(a) Ultimate Japanese strength which will be employed in each sector cannot be accurately determined at this time.

In the Hawaiian sector he may employ:

Cominch estimate		CinCPac estimate	
Fast BBs	4	BBs	2-4
Crudivs 4 and 8	?	CVs	4
Cardivs 1 & 2 plus 1	5	CAs	8-9
At least 2 Desrons	?	DDs	15-20
A landing force	?	SS	2 surbrons
		A landing force.	

II-3- 510

6. (Continued)

(b) Carrier Task Forces.

(1) Task Force SIXTEEN should arrive in the OAHU area about May 26th. Departing OAHU 28 May it can arrive off MIDWAY, fueled, about 1 June.

(2) Task Force SEVENTEEN will arrive Pearl about May 28th. The YORKTOWN is damaged and must receive plane replacements. It is possible that she can be placed in service four days after arrival Pearl. If she cannot be given adequate temporary repairs in that time she will be sent to BREMERTON at once.

(3) The SARATOGA will be ready at San Diego June 5th. She could arrive in the critical area of the Central Pacific only if the Japs are considerably later than now expected.

(4) The WASP will not arrive in time to be considered.

(5) The LONG ISLAND is not suitable as a Carrier Task Force nucleus for present operations but might be used after June 15th.

(c) North Pacific Force.

This force is being formed at the direction of the Commander-in-Chief, U.S. Fleet. It comprises all of the forces which can reach Alaskan waters during the first week in June.

II-8- 512

4. (Continued)

In the Alaskan Sector he may employ:

Cardiv Three (RYUJO and 1 XCV)	2 CV
NACHI (Flag CinC 5th Fleet)	1 CA
One section of Crudiv 4	2 CA
One old cruiser of TAMA type	1 OCL
Desron ONE, less 1 Desdiv, and Desdiv TWO	16 DD
Subron ONE	8-10 SS

This force will escort and cover auxiliary types consisting of transports, landing boat carriers, cargo vessels, and tankers.

(b) Shore based air can only be employed by some refueling method such as fueling seaplanes from submarines and/or tankers, and using CVs to act as staging points.

5. Bases.

The nearest bases are too far distant for consideration. He will be well over 2000 miles from any good base support.

6. Own Forces.

(a) Battleships.

We have seven battleships on the Pacific Coast. All of them can be moved westward, but because of entire lack of air support and inadequacy of screening vessels they will be kept where they are at the present. They could hardly be secure at Pearl during the period of this estimate because of the strong probability of an air raid.

- II-4 -

511

6. (c) (Continued)

As Task Force EIGHT, this will eventually comprise: 2 CA, 3 CL, 12 DD, PG, 1 AVP, 1 AM, 14 YP, 4 AMC, 15 CG, 6 SS, 20 PBY-5A, 9 VSO and all Army aircraft that can be made available.

The major part of this task force can rendezvous at COLD BAY or KODIAK about June 5th.

Being opposed to a force containing carriers, it must depend very heavily on land based air.

(d) Escorts.

All of the remaining surface forces are assigned to escort duty.

(e) Submarines.

At daylight May 26th submarines will be disposed off MIDWAY as follows:

1 - 50 miles NW of MIDWAY.
1 - 50 miles NNW of MIDWAY.
3 - in the arc 215-315 from MIDWAY distant 175 miles.

Eight more submarines will be ready at Pearl between May 24 - 30 to take up offensive patrol in the MIDWAY - OAHU Area.

Other submarines of the Pacific Fleet not under overhaul are on patrol in enemy waters.

(f) Oilers.

(1) The COMET with ten days oil for Task Force EIGHT is being sent to KODIAK for orders. The SABINE is available for that force also.

II-6- 513

6. (f) (Continued)

(2) Other oilers will be used as necessary in the Hawaiian Sea Frontier.

(g) Aircraft.

ARMY

NUMBER	TYPE	REMARKS
50	Heavy bombers (B-17)	30 of these are already here. The remaining 20 are due within the next few days, to stay here until further orders.
26	Medium bombers (B-26)	Due within next few days, to remain here until further orders.
17	Medium bombers (B-18)	These are obsolescent.
180	Pursuit (P-39, P-40)	
7	Attack (A-20)	

NAVY

96	Patrol	Does not include 18 planes at NOUMEA. Does include 16 at or enroute MIDWAY. Total actually based OAHU and KAUAI: 80. 11 more due within a few weeks.
43	Fighters	SARATOGA Squadron (22) and Marines (21). 27 more in reserve as CV replacements.
29	Scout Bombers	SARATOGA Squadron (18) and Marines (11). 16 more in reserve as CV replacements.
13	Torpedo planes	SARATOGA Squadron. 3 more in reserve as CV replacements.
15	VO/VS	
12	VJ (large)	
26	VJ (small)	

6. (Continued)

(h) Bases.

(1) Pearl Harbor is being cleared of shipping as far as possible.

(2) Midway can be used as a staging point for Army bombers.

(3) Alaskan bases are shown in Annex "A" to Task Force EIGHT Operation Plan No. 28-42.

(i) i. Defense troops at:

OAHU (Army)	64,843 total	
MIDWAY (Marines)	Officers	Men
Defense Battalion	71	1828
2 Raider Companies	9	270

ii. ALASKA (Army) troops 23,518 total

iii. Note: The above does not include air personnel at MIDWAY who are sufficient to handle the 16 PBY (Navy) and the 54 Marine planes, but do include some air personnel in ALASKA.

7. Logistics.

The enemy will have a difficult logistic problem. Because of this the time spent by their combatant types east of 180° will be strictly limited. Should they establish themselves in Alaska or Hawaii their logistic supply will be an immediate objective of the Pacific Fleet forces.

II-8 -

7. (Continued)

Own logistic supply will mainly be from Pearl. Small Navy tankers and supply ships now assigned to Alaska cannot be diverted to supply Task Force EIGHT.

8. Summary of Strength and Weakness Factors.

Strength

Own	Enemy
1. Fairly good idea of enemy intentions.	1. Superior CV and BB strength.
2. Present ability to detect changes in enemy intentions.	2. Sufficient and seasoned amphibious troops and transports.
3. Fairly strong shore based air.	3. Training and experience in amphibious warfare.
4. Strength inherent in defense of strong positions.	4. Possible carrier VF superiority.
5. Reinforcement of MIDWAY.	5. Larger range of CV aircraft.
6. Submarines available in probable area.	6. Efficient air weapons.
7. A strong base at PEARL.	7. Initiative due to superior strength.
8. Adequate logistics.	

Weakness

Own	Enemy
1. We are forced to employ attrition.	1. Operation projected at long distance from own bases.
2. The YORKTOWN may have to go to Bremerton at once.	2. Must establish new bases.
	3. Difficult logistic problem.

II-9 -

516

8. (Continued)

Weakness (Cont'd)

Own	**Enemy**
3. We have no adequate air or submarine protection for our BBs.	4. Inability to adapt themselves to forced change of plan.
4. Army air is of uncertain value.	5. Striking forces will be hampered by train.
5. Our submarines have not operated as a division against the enemy.	
6. Coordination with the Army in Alaska will be difficult.	

PART III - ENEMY COURSES OF ACTION

1. The enemy knows our building program - and that in time - our forces will be sufficiently strong to take the offensive. He further knows our defenses are inadequate now - but gradually being strengthened. Hence, from the time factor alone, such operation should be conducted at the earliest possible time. While he is "extended", he is able to assemble a considerable force - as most of the occupied territory is unable to make any real effort. He knows that AUSTRALIA is being heavily reinforced from the United States and would undoubtedly desire to cut that supply line. But he may also consider MIDWAY to be just another WAKE and ALASKA undefended. Regardless of our ideas of his strategic possibilities, the purpose here is to discuss immediate possibilities.

2. To hamstring our efforts to build up facilities for the offensive we conclude that he will:

(a) Attempt to capture MIDWAY.

(b) Raid OAHU.

(c) Attempt to secure an advance position in the ALEUTIAN Islands.

3. It is believed that his forces will depart for the ALEUTIANS from a point in northern Japan on May 25 or 26; and that the Hawaiian forces will depart from the SAIPAN Area a bit later. If these beliefs are accepted our opposing forces should be in initial positions in the ALASKAN Sector by June 1st and in the MIDWAY - OAHU Sector June 3rd.

III-1 -

518

PART IV - OWN COURSES OF ACTION

1. We have decided:

(a) To retain the battleships on the West Coast.

(b) To employ Task Force SIXTEEN to the northeast of MIDWAY initially as soon as possible.

(c) To employ Task Force EIGHT in the ALEUTIANS.

(d) To initially employ a submarine screen of 6 fleet submarines off MIDWAY.

(e) To employ Task Force SEVENTEEN in the MIDWAY - OAHU Area if temporary repairs can be made at Pearl. Otherwise the YORKTOWN will be sent to Bremerton.

(f) To expedite the arrival of the SARATOGA in the HAWAIIAN Area.

(g) To reinforce the submarine screen with 6 fleet submarines at Pearl as soon as possible.

(h) To reinforce MIDWAY with PBYs, AA, and a small Raider Group.

(i) To alert forces in the HAWAIIAN Area.

(j) To clear Pearl Harbor of ships as much as is possible.

(k) To hold Army bombers enroute to AUSTRALIA at OAHU during the present emergency.

(l) To use MIDWAY to stage Army bombers to enemy carriers.

IV-1

519

2. Danger from submarines and other raiders along the Pacific lines of communications requires the continued use of convoys and escorts.

3. Not only our directive from Commander-in-Chief, U.S. Fleet, but also common sense dictates that we cannot now afford to slug it out with the probably superior approaching Japanese forces. We must endeavor to reduce his forces by attrition - submarine attacks, air bombing, attack on isolated units. The principle of calculated chance is indicated, as set forth in a letter of instructions to Task Force EIGHT. If attrition is successful the enemy must accept the failure of his venture or risk battle on disadvantageous terms for him.

4. There is the suggestion that the enemy will attempt to trap our surface forces. Our air umbrella will assist in preventing that.

5. While the difficulty of placing our submarines within reach of the enemy is extremely great, and dependent to a large extent on chance, the risk to them is no more than normal and we only do it at the expense of ultimate reduction in offensive patrol in close to the enemy homeland. The placing of submarine leaving Pearl May 28-30 will depend somewhat on the RI and CI information.

IV-8

520

PART V - DISPOSITIONS AND FUTURE DECISIONS

1. More information of the enemy is expected. On present information the following, not indicated in Part IV, is planned:

(a) All submarines available in the Hawaiian Area will be placed on a scouting line to the westward of Midway. They are assigned patrol sectors until contact. On contact they will close in for attack without regard to the assigned sectors.

(b) The SARATOGA will be the carrier of a new task force which will be assigned to the Striking Forces operating in the critical area.

(c) Key personnel under orders to other stations will be retained in present duties until further orders.

(d) Leave and liberty for officers and men will be cancelled until further orders.

(e) Extreme care will be used to prevent the enemy from gaining information of own deployment by radio or otherwise.

(f) The Amphibious Force at San Diego will be put on 48 hours notice in order that it may load and retake any positions captured by the enemy.

(g) Part of a marine Raider Battalion will be retained at Pearl for use in eventualities.

2. The disposition of the YORKTOWN should be determined by May 28th.

3. An Operation Plan for MIDWAY Area will be issued to all concerned prior to the departure of major forces.

Nimitz's strategic objective was simple and that was to hit the Imperial Japanese Navy hard but not attempt to annihilate the entire Japanese Navy at this time in a major fleet engagement. He was not the true willing partner that Yamamoto was hoping for. He was concentrating his carriers but not his battleships. He was still on the strategic defensive and he understood he was in a war of attrition. For now his plan to whittle away Japan's carrier air strength and protect the Midway-Oahu line of communication. This was fundamentally an ambush to which carrier tactics were better suited then committing a blockade of Midway to prevent access to Midway. Morale was quite high for the men on the ships and the pilots, but with the exception of *Yorktown*'s pilots the majority of the U.S. pilots were inexperienced in actual combat. Nimitz was hoping to gain a countervailing advantage by securing the element of surprise.

His three carriers would not operate as one task force but as two which was consistent with pre-war concepts. *Enterprise* and *Hornet* were within the same task force but *Yorktown* would be in a second. They were to operate close enough so that they could mutually support each other. This incorporates the principles of cooperation and flexibility while using divided forces. U.S. forces were close to their own bases so they could sustain operations longer and *Saratoga's* carrier division was sailing to Pearl Harbor as a reinforcement. Nimitz was deploying search aircraft in significant numbers and he was deploying submarines as scouts to provide security in terms of awareness of the surrounding seas.

All ten principles of the operational art were followed. There was one caveat, and this was with sustainability. Survivability was just as important as initial logistics. Carriers were their own worst enemy and the American admirals knew that the side that could strike first usually won. It was not only the survivability of the ship but also its air wing that is important to consider if operations can be sustained. No matter how well you establish a military operation, mistakes can happen that can lead to defeat.

Nimitz was very much in a defensive role and by placing his fleet where it could interfere with the Japanese operations before the Japanese Army reached its objective he was also implementing the proper role in defense against invasion. Without a naval force to support the island Midway cannot be defended if the Japanese establish command of the sea around it. Even if Midway was captured it would be relatively easy for the U.S. to recapture and extremely difficult for Japan to defend.

The West Coast battleships included *Colorado, Maryland, Tennessee, New Mexico, Idaho,* and *Mississippi.*[223] *Pennsylvania* was the seventh operational battleship capable of deployment. *Washington* and *North Carolina* were to be transferred to the Pacific soon. Yamamoto's advantage in capital ships gained at Pearl Harbor had already evaporated. This was one reason why Mahan stressed that once a navy is unleashed it must maintain pressure on the enemy until it is destroyed and never given time to recover. However, carriers and battleships fight two very different kinds of war and Nimitz was not ready to use the battleship tool.

Table 5. Status of US battleships prior to Midway.

Battleships in port before the war	Damages sustained during Battle of Hawaii	Subsequent movements in 1942	Destination
Pennsylvania	Medium	Departed in February	Seattle
Nevada	Sunk	Refloated and departed in May	Seattle
West Virginia	Sunk	Refloated and departed in May	Seattle
California	Sunk	Refloated and departed in May	Seattle
Arizona	Total Loss	N/A	N/A
Oklahoma	Total Loss	N/A	N/A

Task Force 16 was commanded by Rear Admiral Raymond A. Spruance.

Carriers: *Enterprise* (25 F4F, 33 SBD, 14 TBD) *Hornet* (27-F4F, 34-SBD, 12-TBD)

Heavy cruisers: *Pensacola, New Orleans, Northampton, Minneapolis, Vincennes*

Light cruisers: *Atlanta*

Destroyers: *Phelps, Worden, Monaghan, Aylwin, Balch, Conyngham, Benham, Ellet, Maury*

Task Group 16.6 (Fueling Group)

Destroyers: *Dewey, Monssen*

Fleet Oilers: *Cimarron, Platte*

Task Group 17 was commanded by Rear Admiral Frank J. Fletcher.

Carrier, *Yorktown* (25-F4F, 36-SBD, 15-TBD)

---

223 Office of Naval Intelligence: *The Battle of Midway* Japanese Account at 72.

Heavy cruisers: *Astoria, Portland*

Destroyers: *Morris, Hughes, Anderson, Hammann, Russell*

Midway Air Station was commanded by Captain Cyril T. Simard.

Aircraft (30 PBY's[224], 20-F2A[225], 6 –F4F, 18-SBD, 17-SB2U[226], 6-TBF[227], 21-B-17, 4-B-26.)[228]

This battle was not fought entirely by airpower. The Japanese underestimated the amount of firepower the Americans had at Midway. Nagumo's First Striking Force came under eight separate attacks by airpower and Task Group 17 came under two separate attacks by airpower. Submarines also played a role. The *Yorktown* was attacked by a submarine *I-168* and *Kaga* was attacked by the submarine *Nautilus*.

Nagumo gave the follow operation plan on June 5.[229]

> '1. For three hours and 30 minutes following the first wave's take-off, the fleet will proceed on course 135 degrees, speed, and 24 knots. Thereafter, if the prevailing winds are from the east, course will be 45 degrees, speed 20; if west winds prevail, course will be 270 degrees, speed, and 20 knots.
>
> 2. Change in plans may be necessitated by enemy actions. Bear this in mind in making preparations for assembling and taking aboard the air control units.
>
> 3. Unless otherwise specified, the search units will take off at the same time as the attack units.[230]

The Battle of Midway has been covered by many scholars so the focus of this chapter will be on carrier defense of both American and Japanese carrier groups. At 0705 *Akagi* sighted nine enemy planes bearing 150 degrees, distance 25,000 meters, elevation 0.5 degrees. She assumed battle speed #5, heading into the above mentioned planes.[231] At the same time *Tone* sighted ten enemy aircraft bearing 35 degrees to port, elevation 15 degrees. The first American aircraft to reach the Japanese fleet were four B-26s medium bombers and six TBF torpedo planes

---

[224] The PBY float aircraft that was mainly used on search missions.

[225] F2A Buffalo fighter was a predecessor to the F4F fighter.

[226] The SB2U was a predecessor to the SBD in USN scout bomber service.

[227] This would be the first time the TBF was used in combat.

[228] The B-26 was a twin engine medium level bomber.

[229] Japanese dates and times reflect Tokyo time not local time.

[230] Mobile Force's Detailed Battle Report #6, First Air Fleet's Detailed Battle Report #6, Office of Naval Intelligence: *The Battle of the Midway Japanese Account* at 6-68.

[231] Mobile Force's Detailed Battle Report #6, First Air Fleet's Detailed Battle Report #6.

from Midway Island. Japanese had underestimated the amount of firepower the Americans had at Midway, although it did not prove to be very effective.

At 0707 *Akagi* commenced firing with her starboard AA guns and *Tone* commenced firing her main guns to get the attention of the combat air patrol. In the absence of effective fighter direction by radio, this was a standard IJN practice for getting the combat air patrol onto incoming raids. About ten A6M fighters headed for the enemy at 0708. At 0710 three A6M fighters took off from *Akagi*. The TBF torpedo planes divided into two groups. The A6Ms shot down two B-26s and three TBFs before they can launch their weapons. Three TBFs attacked *Akagi* one to her starboard side and two to her port side at 0712. *Akagi* noted that all three enemy planes dropped their torpedoes. The TBFs strafed *Akagi* as they passed her and seriously injured two men manning the #3 AA gun. The revolving mechanism of this gun was damaged (repaired about half an hour later). Both transmitting antennae cut. The *Akagi* made a full turn to evade, successfully, the torpedo to starboard, and another full turn to evade another to port. She noted one torpedo to starboard, two to port (of which one exploded automatically) on parallel courses, and other which crossed astern. Two more TBFs were shot down by AA guns after they made their attack. The A6Ms killed one more B-26 which attempted unsuccessfully to crash *Akagi*.[232] By 0713 the first air battle was over. Only one TBF and one B-26 returned from the strike to Midway.

At 0754 message from *Haruna* to Mobile Force: "*Sight enemy plane bearing 100 degrees.*"[233] The second raid was a combined raid of sixteen Marine SBDs and fifteen Army B-17s quickly followed by eleven Marine SB2Us. The combat air patrol at this time was nine A6Ms and all engaged the SBDs. They shot down six SBDs and one A6M was shot down in return. At 0755 ten SBDs attempted to bomb *Hiryu* through a glide-bombing attack but scored no hits. Japanese anti-aircraft fire shot down six and two more were badly damaged and did not make it back to Midway. A message from Comdr. aboard *Soryu* to Mobile Force: "*14 enemy twin-engine planes flew over us at 270 degrees, altitude 30,000 meters.*"[234] These were the B-17 bombers *Soryu* noted that *Akagi* and *Hiryu* were being subjected to bombings but no hits were scored. The fifteen B-17s dropped bombs over twenty minutes were engaged by twelve A6Ms but none of the heavy bombers were shot down nor were any Japanese fighters shot down in return. At 0830 eleven Marine

---

[232] Heinz, Leonard, *Aircraft Carrier Defense in the Pacific War: The Carrier Battles of 1942* at 48-66.

[233] Mobile Force's Detailed Battle Report #6, First Air Fleet's Detailed Battle Report #6.

[234] Ibid.

SB2Us came in next and attacked the battleship *Haruna*. Eleven A6M fighters engaged the SB2Us in air combat. All the dive bombers were able to release their bombs but none scored. Two fell within sight of the Japanese fleet and two more did not return to Midway.

The third attack was by *Hornet*'s fifteen TBDs torpedo bombers. They had become separated from the rest of the *Hornet* strike and without any support drove into the Japanese fleet. The bombers were sighted twenty miles out and eighteen A6Ms followed by eleven more that had just been launched intercepted the TBDs. A total of nine TBDs were shot down before they could launch their torpedoes. One made an unsuccessful attack on *Soryu,* and five made an unsuccessful attack on *Kaga*. All six were shot down attempting to withdraw with one A6M being shot down in return.[235]

The *Enterprise*'s fifteen TBDs arrived next and they too went in without any support. They were jumped by thirty-nine A6Ms but low on 20 mm cannon ammunition after shooting down the *Hornet*'s torpedo squadron it took the Japanese longer to shoot down the *Enterprise*'s bombers. Nine TBDs fell before they could launch their torpedoes one aborted and crashed, and five attacked *Kaga* who avoided all of the torpedoes. The last five were able to get away and return to the *Enterprise*.[236] Now the battle reached its peak and fifteen SBDs from the *Enterprise* and seventeen SBDs twelve TBDs and six F4Fs from *Yorktown* made the first coordinated attack by the Americans. However, only thirteen of *Yorktown*'s SBDs had bombs due to a faulty arming mechanism which caused five aircraft to lose their bombs in flight. The pilots without bombs still made dives hoping to divert anti-aircraft fire away from those planes that did. The *Akagi* was the first to sight the incoming TBDs. Approximately thirty-six A6Ms were in the air but probably about half were chasing *Enterprise*'s last five TBDs.[237]

At 0110 the heavy cruiser *Chikuma* fired her main battery at the *Yorktown* TBDs, now about fourteen miles out, to attract the attention of the combat air patrol. A number of A6Ms engaged the six F4F escort. In a fight that stretched over twenty-five minutes, the F4Fs downed four A6Ms while the A6Ms killed an F4F and damaged two others. Fifteen to twenty A6Ms engaged the TBDs shooting down seven and five were able to make an attack on *Hiryu* but no hits were

---

[235] Heinz, Leonard, *Aircraft Carrier Defense in the Pacific War: The Carrier Battles of 1942* at 48-66.

[236] Ibid.

[237] Ibid.

scored. Four of the remaining five TBDs were shot down as they attempted to withdraw.[238]

The SBDs were not spotted until they began to make their dives. Twenty-eight attacked *Kaga* scoring five hits. Thirteen attacked *Soryu* scoring three hits, and *Akagi* was attacked by three SBDs scoring one direct hit and two hits alongside her that resulted in significant damage to her steering gear. The *Yorktown*'s SBDs were not intercepted. The *Enterprise*'s SBDs were not intercepted until after they made their attack lost three to A6Ms but also shot down one A6M.[239] All three Japanese carriers were unable to gain control of the fires. Secondary explosions from their own planes and ammunition subsequently finished the job the American planes had started. Nagumo's fear of the vulnerability of his carriers had come true. Concentration, while it maximized the combat air patrol by the fighters, had not been enough to gain command of the air. Maneuver had worked for a small period of time but was eventually overwhelmed. Anti-aircraft fire was insufficient especially against dive bombers which were very difficult to engage. The *Hiryu* would have to fight alone.

At 1430 the *Hiryu*'s first strike of eighteen D3As and six A6Ms were picked up on *Yorktown*'s radar thirty-two miles out. Five minutes later the strike found *Yorktown* twenty-five miles out. Two A6Ms suffered damage when they intercepted some SBDs while they were withdrawing from their own strike on the Japanese fleet. This left four A6Ms as escort. *Yorktown* launched twelve F4Fs when the strike was detected. *Hornet* and *Enterprise* about thirty miles away had nineteen F4Fs as a combat air patrol. The fighter direction officer directed eight F4Fs to help *Yorktown* but only six responded to the order. The fighter director had correctly determined that the Japanese strike was made up of dive bombers and directed the F4Fs to climb for altitude. The six planes coming from Task Group 16 were already at 20,000 feet but they had thirty miles to close. Ten to fifteen miles out *Yorktown*'s F4Fs intercepted the incoming strike, breaking its formation. As the Japanese D3As tried to reform the remaining F4Fs climbed for altitude; for an F4F to reach 20,000 feet took 12 to 13 minutes. One D3A was shot down by the initial interception. Seven more F4Fs shot down eight D3As and one A6M. Two D3As jettison their bombs to get away from the fighters. Task Group 16's F4Fs shot down one D3A. Seven D3As made an attack on the *Yorktown* scoring three hits.

---

[238] Ibid.

[239] Heinz, Leonard, *Aircraft Carrier Defense in the Pacific War: The Carrier Battles of 1942* at 48-66.

The *Hiryu*'s second attack now approached. At 1427 *Pensacola*, which had assumed radar guard after *Yorktown* was damaged, picked up enemy planes bearing 340°, distance 33 miles. The ten B5Ns split up so they could make an anvil attack. They came in at 13,500 feet and started to descend but the fighter direction officer mistook the planes as dive bombers. TF 16's CAP amounted to fifteen F4Fs, of which eight were committed to help *Yorktown,* but the distance from Task Group 16 was now forty miles. *Yorktown* did not launch her on-deck F4Fs until one minute before the B5Ns dropped their torpedoes. The first group (of four B5Ns) arrived before the second, to be greeted by four just-launched F4Fs. Two F4Fs each downed a B5N, while the third probably shared its B5N victory with AA fire. Of the three B5Ns downed, two went down after completing their attacks. Thus, the first group dropped three torpedoes on *Yorktown*. She managed to evade all three. In the mêlée, the four F4Fs that initially overflew the Japanese strike returned, killing two A6Ms and causing a third A6M to abort. The single B5N from the first group of torpedo bombers to escape survived only long enough to meet three F4Fs from the TF 16, which shot it into the sea.[240]

The second wave of six B5Ns had much more success. The last four of the eight F4Fs launched by *Yorktown* made much less of an impact, with one F4F downed by friendly AA fire and another by an A6M. The first group of just-launched F4Fs was too low and slow to set up on the second wave of B5Ns. The result was no losses for the torpedo bombers and two hits on *Yorktown* from the six torpedoes dropped. Both hitting on the same side, the torpedoes flooded many of her fire rooms while the concussion from their blasts shut down *Yorktown*'s boilers and caused her to lose all power. She quickly took on a serious list from flooding. The entire second wave escaped both the combat air patrol and anti-aircraft fire.[241]

By 1447 firing ceased. *Yorktown,* listing heavily to port, was losing speed and turning in a small circle to port. She stopped and white smoke poured from her stacks. The screening vessels began to circle. Inside *Yorktown* all lights had gone out. The diesel generators were cut in, but the circuit breakers would not hold and the ship remained in darkness. The list gradually increased to 26°. Without power nothing could be done to correct it. Captain Buckmaster and the Damage Control Officer thought it probable that the ship would capsize in a few minutes, and at 1455 orders were given to abandon ship. Inside, men clambered over

---

[240] Ibid.

[241] Ibid.

steeply sloping decks in total darkness to remove the wounded. After an inspection on which no living personnel were found, Captain Buckmaster left the ship.

At 1701 *Chikuma* sighted twenty-four SBDs from *Enterprise*. Fourteen A6Ms engaged, which shot down three SBDs before they could attack but twenty-one made it past the Japanese fighters scoring four hits on *Hiryu*. Then fifteen minutes later sixteen SBDs from *Hornet* arrived and they attacked the cruiser *Tone* and *Haruna* but with no hits scored. They were not intercepted by any Japanese fighters.[242] *Hiryu*'s fires went out of control and she later sank. A dozen B-17 bomb attacked without result: six flying from Midway and another six from Hawaii, but both groups arrived coincidentally at the same time. No B-17s or CAP fighters were lost. They attacked *Chikuma* and *Tone*.[243] This ended the carrier battle for Midway.

Yamamoto ordered Vice Admiral Takeo Kurita with his four heavy cruisers to bombard Midway during the night of June 5. He was hoping to engage the American carriers in a night battle with his battleships while Kurita neutralized Midway through bombardment. Then at 0015 he cancelled Operation MI. Kurita did not receive the message until 0210. When his staff suggested the use of the battleships to neutralize Midway Yamamoto responded:

> You ought to know that of all naval tactics, firing one's guns at an island is considered the most stupid.[244]

This was an interesting statement by Yamamoto. It implies that he believed Midway was an unsinkable aircraft carrier that guns could not sink. One can only speculate what his actual thoughts were but his available forces were sufficient to cut the lines of communication around Midway if he chose to do so. He probably did have the forces to take Midway but the true objective for Operation MI was to fight a decisive battle and Midway was simply an excuse to draw out the American fleet so he had a willing partner. Spruance followed American carrier doctrine never to allow a carrier force to be caught in a surface action and fell back to the east so he would stay out of range of the Japanese battleships during the night. Spruance was fighting a war of attrition in this battle and was not a willing partner for a fleet engagement.

During the night the submarine *Tamber* was spotted by the heavy cruiser *Kumano*. Kurita ordered a turn of forty-five degrees in case the submarine launched

---

[242] Ibid.

[243] Ibid.

[244] Stille, Mark, *Yamamoto Isoroku* at 39.

torpedoes but *Mikuma* made a ninety degree turn which resulted in her colliding with *Mogami*, whose bow caved in causing severe damage. *Mikuma*'s portside oil tanks ruptured and she began to spill oil, but otherwise her damage was slight. Kurita now withdrawing ordered the destroyers *Arashio* and *Asashio* to give the two damaged cruisers escort.[245]

Once the sun rose they were attacked by thirty-one SBD Dauntless dive bombers from *Enterprise* and *Hornet*. *Mogami* was hit by six bombs. *Mikuma* was hit by at least five bombs in the forecastle, bridge area and amidships and set afire. The hit on the forecastle put the forward guns out of commission. The hit near the bridge area set off some AA shells and caused considerable damage to the bridge and personnel. The hit amidships set off several torpedoes and the resultant explosions destroyed the ship. Captain Sakiyama was severely wounded. *Mikuma* turned on her port side and sank at 29°20′N 173°30′E.

How well *Enterprise* and *Hornet* could sustain operations can be shown in the losses to their air wings. The American carriers had been reduced to fifty-five F4F fighters, fifty-six SBD dive bombers, and only five TBD torpedo planes. The SBDs were proving themselves to be a very sturdy aircraft and the investment in armor and self-sealing fuel tanks was well worth the cost. The TBD torpedo bombers however had almost been completely annihilated after one strike. This was largely due to attacking unsupported. Later American tactics would attempt to reduce an enemy ship's AA firepower through dive bombers and fighter planes prior to torpedo bombers making an attack run. *Hiryu*'s air wing had been effectively destroyed after the two separate strikes she was able to conduct. The lack of aircraft armor was proving to be disastrous.

---

[245] Office of Naval Intelligence: *The Battle of the Midway*.

Table 6. Loss of Carrier Type Aircraft[246]

Ship	Aircraft	Type	Losses in combat	Losses due to damage	Total	% lost	Survived combat
Enterprise	25	F4F	1	0	1	4%	24
Enterprise	33	SBD	17	6	22	66%	11
Enterprise	14	TBD	9	0	9	63%	5
Hornet	27	F4F	6	5	11	41%	16
Hornet	34	SBD	6	1	7	20%	27
Hornet	12	TBD	12	0	12	100%	0
Yorktown	25	F4F	7	3	10	40%	15
Yorktown	26	SBD	4	4 (ship sank)	8	30%	18
Yorktown	12	TBD	11	1 (ship sank)	12	100%	0
Midway Island	6	TBF	5	0	5	80%	1
Hiryu[247]	4	A6M	3	Unknown	3	75%	1
Hiryu	21	D3A	16 total 3 in Midway strike	Unknown	16	75%	5
Hiryu	10	B5N	4	Unknown	4	40%	6

Midway also had a profound effect on the Japanese battle fleet. *Fuso* and *Yamashiro* were to be decommissioned and used as training ships in the Inland Sea. The Japanese wanted to convert *Ise* and *Hyuga* into full carriers but the demands of war resulted into hybrid carriers. *Hyuga* and *Ise* maintained two thirds of the main armament and were to operate seaplanes, which had to be catapulted but could not land on the ships. The Japanese designers were forced to accept this unsatisfactory compromise to realize the conversion in the shortest possible time, In the end, the conversion came out as waste of material, personnel, and time and instead of reinforcing the fighting power of the fleet it was weakened.[248] By the stroke of a pen

[246] USN Overseas *Aircraft Loss List* June 1942.

[247] Chart represents *Hiryu*'s airstrikes only. A total of 261 Japanese aircraft were lost when all four Japanese carriers sank.

[248] Lengerer, Hans, *Contributions to the History of Imperial Japanese Warships* at 6.

the Japanese had eliminated one third of their battle line instead of developing a strategy to combine their firepower with that of carriers in the most critical year of the war.

The attrition rate of aircraft was much higher than for ships and large percentages of the combat power of the carriers was used up even after a single strike. Neither Japanese nor American combat air patrols could establish true command of the skies and dive bombers and torpedo bombers all made it past the fighters making their attacks. Anti-aircraft fire was not very good for either side though some of the aircraft that made it back but were complete write-offs due to the damage they had absorbed may have come from anti-aircraft fire. Attacking first did pay off and this would remain a tactical objective for the future carrier operations.

Concentration of carriers in this battle did not work. The four Japanese carriers were able to mass their fighter strength and the fact that they were unable to command the skies while concentrated resulted in all four being discovered and sunk. Out-ranging the enemy also did not work very well. Many U.S. planes were at the extreme edge of their range and some did not find the Japanese fleet or make it back to their carriers. *Hiryu* stayed within range of the U.S. aircraft and made a stand and fought when maybe a tactical retreat to take advantage of her aircraft's greater range may have paid some dividends.

Division of carrier task groups for the U.S. formations did work for *Hornet* and *Enterprise* were not attacked. They were however close enough to offer mutual assistance. *Yorktown* by herself was not crippled until the two torpedo hits. By the end of this strike *Hiryu* was combat-ineffective as her attack air wings had been reduced to just a hand-full of planes. This demonstrated a major problem especially for Japan. Carriers and strike warfare were not bringing about the destruction of an entire fleet or task group but were largely cancelling one another out. After one strike their fighting power was exhausted.

The goal of any war should be to achieve your military objective quickly so the killing can stop. This aerial warfare was not efficient and like the German U-boat campaign a war of attrition was the result. For the United States with a superpower economy and 100% self-sufficient in natural resources, a war of attrition could be accepted if the citizens were willing to pay the price in blood. There was a risk. Until the end of 1943 the U.S. would only have equal odds of winning any battle due to the parity of the two navies at this moment in time. This left Japan a window of opportunity.

For Yamamoto a war of attrition was exactly the kind of war he wanted to avoid. Carriers had not shown in the first two carrier battles the sustainability to produce Mahan's concept of a decisive battle. What *Lexington, Yorktown, Akagi, Kaga, Soryu,* and *Hiryu* all confirmed that this type of platform was extremely vulnerable and even one or two hits could destroy them. Yamamoto needed numbers to inflict a decisive battle. So the other weapons at his disposal were submarines or the battle fleet. Did Yamamoto have the vision or imagination to combine the firepower of the various elements that made up the Imperial Navy or would he use airpower alone?

Survivability is also a key element in sustainability. Platforms that can't survive in battle and sustain operations can't establish command of the sea. There are three elements of ship survivability.

(A) Active defense in the form of anti-aircraft guns and in the case of aircraft carriers fighter aircraft. The key to effectiveness was to shoot down an incoming plane before it could launch its weapon. In the two carrier battles both had been ineffective at preventing attacks from hitting the ships.

(B) Passive protection in the form of armor that limits damage if it can't stop it all together. Due to the armament of torpedoes, bombs, and aircraft being carried high in the ship, carriers could not be protected and even a single hit could prove fatal.

(C) Redundancy in the form of damage control and fire-fighting and duplicate machinery. Does the ship have backup systems to keep operational after damage has taken place? Fire and aviation fuel leaks resulted in five carriers destroying themselves after damage all should have survived.

All three elements of survivability must be accounted for to assess ship survivability and carriers were failing all three. Carriers were extremely vulnerable so how could they operate safely? Was there any true way to protect them?

CHAPTER 15: SUBMARINES AT MIDWAY

At 0755, 5 June, the submarine *Nautilus* under the command of Lieutenant Commander William H. Brockman, Jr. was close to the northern edge of her assigned patrol zone when she sighted ship masts. Almost immediately she was sighted by Japanese combat air patrol and attacked with the fighters strafing her deck. She made an emergency dive to a depth of 100 feet. At 08:00, she went to periscope depth and a formation of four enemy ships was sighted: the battleship *Kirishima* the cruiser *Nagara*, and two destroyers. The two destroyers sighted her and attacked. Once again she dove as nine depth charges were dropped over her position. The attack seemed over so she climbed to periscope depth and sighted *Kirishima*. She fired two bow torpedoes but one misfired and the other missed.[249]

At 0830, a destroyer immediately headed for *Nautilus*, which dived to 150 feet (46 m) to wait out the depth charge attack. At 08:46, periscope depth was again ordered. The cruiser and two of the destroyers were now out of range; echo ranging by the third appeared too accurate for comfort. At 09:00, the periscope was raised again and an aircraft carrier was sighted. *Nautilus* changed course to close for an attack. The enemy destroyer followed suit and at 09:18 attacked with six depth charges. By 09:55 echo ranging ceased and *Nautilus* raised her periscope. The carrier, her escorts, and the attacking destroyer had disappeared. Unknown to her skipper at the time, the counterattacking Japanese destroyer *Arashi*, in her rush to rejoin the carrier, was tracked by *Enterprise*'s VB-6, led by Wade McClusky, back to the Japanese task force.[250]

At 1253, a damaged aircraft carrier with two escorts was sighted. The carrier was identified as *Soryu,* but later research suggests it was probably *Kaga*. An hour later, *Nautilus* had moved into attack position. Between 1359 and 1405, after the battle was largely over, *Nautilus* launched four torpedoes at the carrier from less than 3,000 yards. One failed to run, two ran erratically, and the fourth was a dud (a familiar problem for the Mark XIV), impacting amidships and breaking in half. *Nautilus* reported flames appeared along the length of the ship as the first hit, and

---

[249] Lord, Walter, *Incredible Victory*

[250] Ibid.

the skeleton crew which had been aboard began going over the side, with the air flask of the dud torpedo acting as a life preserver for Japanese sailors.[251] The *Nautilus* went to 300 feet as a prolonged depth charge attack commenced.

At 1610, the submarine rose to periscope depth. The carrier, *Kaga* burning along her entire length, had been abandoned. The *Nautilus* resumed her patrol, having expended five torpedoes and survived forty-two depth charges. The faulty torpedoes were a major problem handicapping U.S. submarine operations. This problem would not be rectified until mid-1943. In the first four months of the war 300 torpedoes were fired during 136 attacks on Japanese shipping but only ten Japanese ships had been sunk. There were at least three problems with the Mark 14 submarine launched torpedo. Pre-war the U.S. was in the Great Depression; torpedoes were expensive so during practice they had test warheads that were lighter than the real warheads. Once the heavier explosive warheads were attached the torpedo ran with a head down trim with depth errors between four and eleven feet. It would not be until August 1942 that this problem was fixed by a trim repair kit.

The second problem was a depth sensor. It was designed for a slower running speed and the pressure gradient over the torpedo at high speed gave the sensor the wrong information to set the proper depth. This problem was fixed by placing the sensor in a neutral position.

The magnetic exploder was designed for a northern latitude and did not work well in the warmer waters of the South Pacific. The effects were failure to explode or to explode prematurely. The British and German Navies had already ordered their magnetic exploders disabled. The U.S. would follow but not until June 24, 1943. The conventional contact exploder was again designed for slower speeds. The higher speeds resulted in higher inertial impacts that would cause the crosswise mounted firing pin to miss the exploder cap. This resulted in dud torpedoes. September 1943 the first torpedoes with new contact pistols rectified this problem and finally the U.S. torpedoes became a truly reliable weapon.

I-168 commanded by Tanabe Yahachi had spent June 1-5 looking for American warships to no avail. He had seen anti-aircraft fire from Midway and even attempted a bombardment using his 4" deck gun but search lights illuminated his sub so he dived firing only six rounds. He was attacked by aircraft once and then received orders from Yamamoto to sink a crippled U.S. carrier. He found *Yorktown* at 0530 on June 6th. Over-cautious use of his periscope resulted in getting

---

[251] Ibid.

too close to the carrier so he circled to starboard reaching a distance of 1330 yards and fired four torpedoes and then quickly submerged to 200 feet. One torpedo hit *Hammann* which was alongside *Yorktown* and two more hit *Yorktown*. Within two minutes *Hammann* was clearly sinking so the executive officer Lt. Ralph Elden ordered abandon ship. Captain Buckmaster ordered *Yorktown* abandoned as the carrier settled deeper into the water. At 0501 she sank stern first.

Meanwhile the destroyers *Gwin*, *Hughes*, and *Monaghan* attempted to sink *I-168*. They dropped sixty depth charges and one sprang the hatches to number one torpedo tube. The crew stuffed sacks of rice into the tube to slow the flooding. Her battery room was also damaged which put out the lights. Eventually all went quiet and Yahachi took his damaged sub home using only two engines reaching Sasebo twelve days later.

The sinking of *Yorktown* was significant for future battles. The United States after the battle would only have parity with the Japanese due to their more plentiful smaller carriers. *Junyo*'s sister *Hiyo* would soon join the Japanese fleet and though smaller than *Hiryu* or *Soryu* they were only slightly smaller. *Wasp* would soon be transferred to the Pacific to replace *Yorktown* but the next fleet carrier *Essex* would not join the fleet until 1943. This left *Saratoga, Hornet, Enterprise,* and *Wasp* to hold the line until then.

Many scholars believe this was the decisive battle of the war. It was certainly a decisive U.S. tactical victory but it does not rise to the level of Mahan's "decisive battle." Mahan quotes British Admiral Nelson, one of the greatest admirals of all time.

> ***"What the country needs is the annihilation of the enemy. Only numbers can annihilate. If ten ships out of eleven were taken, I would never call it well enough if we were able to get the eleventh."***[252]

At Midway the U.S. destroyed five ships but ninety-two ships escaped and Japan had plenty of fire-power remaining to contest control of the seas. This would require more battles to be fought and more blood would have to be spilled. Genda's concept that carriers could sweep the seas of enemy ships was also proving to be just as delusional as the German U-boat campaign against a

---

[252] Mahan, Alfred T. *Alfred Thayer Mahan on Naval Warfare* at 80-82.

superpower economy. Such delusions were leading to the direct defeat of the Imperial Japanese Navy. Time was not allied to Japan and every day that passed the United States Navy only grew stronger. If Yamamoto could not bring about Kanji's "quick engagement, quick showdown" then Japan's defeat was inevitable.

CHAPTER 16: GUADALCANAL

July 2, 1942 Letter from King to Nimitz:

> 02 2100 COMINCH to CINCPAC, Info COMSOWESPACFOR, C0NSOPAC. Handle this with utmost secrecy. This is part one of three parts. The United States Chiefs of Staff have agreed upon this joint directive for offensive operations in the Southwest Pacific Area. Leary pass to MacArthur. Quote para 1 objective. Offensive operations will be conducted with the ultimate objective of seizure and occupation of the NEW BRITAIN, NEW IRELAND-NEW GUINEA Area. Para 2. Purpose. To deny the area to Japan. Para 3 Tasks Affirm Task One seizure and occupation of Santa Cruz Islands, TULAGI and adjacent positions. Baker. Task 2 seizure and occupation of the remainder of the Solomon Islands, of LAE, SALAMAUA, and Northeast Coast of NEW GUINEA. Cast. Task 3 seizure and occupation of RABAUL and · adjacent positions in the NEW GUINEA - NEW IRELAND area.[253]

After the victory at Midway King wanted to take advantage of this and go on the offensive. The target islands would be Tulagi and Guadalcanal in the Solomons, which were captured during the Battle of Coral Sea. In addition General Douglas MacArthur's men would take Lae and Salamaua and advance toward Rabaul. The operation would be called Watchtower and it would be the first time American troops captured territory and pushed Japanese expansion back. It would also be the first test to determine if the Japanese could hold their defensive perimeter.

On August 7, 1942 the landings took place with little resistance. The Japanese fled into the jungles as the Marines went ashore. Admiral Richmond Turner was in command of the amphibious landing, Admiral Frank J. Fletcher the covering force TF 61, and Major General Alexander Vandegrift was the Marines. Admiral Robert Ghormley was the overall commander for the South Pacific. In response to the landings the Japanese initially attacked with G3Ms and G4Ms from their main base at Rabaul. Admiral Yamamoto also ordered Vice Admiral Gunichi Mikawa to engage the enemy ships off Lunga Point, Guadalcanal. At his command were the heavy cruisers *Chokai, Aoba, Kako, Kinugasa,* and *Furutaka.* He also had the light cruiser *Yubari* and one destroyer *Yunagi.* The bombers struck first on August 8, 1942. Admiral Fletcher reported to Admiral Ghormley in a memo dated July 8, 1942.

---

[253] Nimitz, Chester. *Chester Nimitz Gray Book*, Vol 1 at 605.

> 08 CTG 61.2 to COMSOPAC, CTF 61. Squadron X-ray attacked 0100 GCT 8th by about 40 type 99 twin-engine torpedo planes and 8 high altitude bombers. JARVIS hit in forward part of ship by torpedo disabled am towing into shallow water. ELLIOTT on fire amidships from bomb hit. Not known yet whether ship can be saved. At least 12 enemy planes shot down probably more by ships and fighters. 5 08 1951 CINCPAC to COMINCH info COMSOPACFOR.[254]

Fletcher had approached his assignment with the perspective once the Marines had been safely put ashore his job was done. This was not consistent with the fundamental principles of sea power. Corbett, for example, emphasized that for an expeditionary operation the role for a Navy does not stop with simply transporting the troops to its objective. It also must establish control of the seas around the objective, support the troops on land with gunfire support, use the transportation highway for logistics and supply and deny the use of this highway to the enemy twenty-four hours a day until the land forces have accomplished their objective.

Unfortunately, protecting the expedition also nails the foot of the task forces to a geographical location.

This allows the enemy to easily find and locate the task force and if carriers are present they must stay within range of the objective. It was the carriers' recently proven vulnerability that led Turner to say that carriers should not be tied to the expedition. The tactics and the objectives are in contradiction: protect the landing force or protect the carriers. At this early stage of the war the U.S. Navy had not established clear doctrine for joint operations.

Only carriers could provide friendly aircraft, the principal offensive tool in use in this period, until the airfield at Lunga Point was repaired and land-based planes could be sent in. It should also be pointed out that the Marines were in support of airpower not the other way around. Their objective was to establish an airstrip and once done defend this airstrip. Had aircraft never been invented this landing on these islands would have never happened.

After the U.S. Navy's greatest success at Midway would come its greatest defeat in the Battle of Savo Island. Mikawa in his flagship *Chokai* led his ships down "the Slot" passage through the Solomons Islands. He arrived in the sound in the very early hours of August 9. His objective was simple; sink as many Allied ships as he could. He was on the offensive. He was hoping to achieve surprise by not

[254] Nimitz, Chester, *Chester Nimitz Gray Book*, Vol 1 at 639.

being detected and morale on his ships was high. He had concentrated all available ships and all ships were taking part so concentration and economy of force were both satisfied. Flexibility will be determined by sustainability. He has no logistical support so he will have to return to Rabaul to replenish fuel and ammunition.

Savo Island was a small unpopulated island that was just west of Lunga Point where the Marines had landed. It formed two straits in which one could enter the sound for a western entrance and a northern entrance. The destroyer *Blue* was guarding the western entrance. As Mikawa closed he slowed his ships down so they would not produce much wake. They sighted *Blue* at 11,000 yards but the destroyer did not react to the Japanese ships, totally unaware that thirty-four 8-inch guns were all pointing directly at her. The dark grey paint of the Japanese ships blended into the black silhouette of Savo Island. At 0123 Mikawa ordered his task group "independent command" allowing each ship's captain to conduct his own attack. At 0131 he gave the order to attack. His force increased speed to twenty-six knots and they then sighted the destroyer *Ralph Talbot* guarding the northern entrance, but she too did not react.[255]

On Mikawa's bridge a third "destroyer" was spotted now, but it was not a destroyer at all, it was the Australian cruiser *Canberra.* This sighting was followed soon after by *Chicago.* At 0138 Mikawa gave the order to open fire and *Chokai* launched four torpedoes at 5,000 yards. One of his pilots from the cruiser float planes, which had taken off earlier in the afternoon to reconnoiter the sound, dropped red flares to illuminate the Allied ships upon seeing the initial salvos and the cruisers turned on their searchlights.[256]

General Quarters was sounded on the Allied ships but it was too late. Two torpedoes hit *Canberra* and one hit *Chicago.* Shells smashed into the ships' superstructure. The *Canberra* fired two torpedoes and a few shells as she started to list to starboard. She was sinking and power went out. *Chicago* with a severed bow attempted to get into the fight but could not find the Japanese ships. As soon as they appeared they had disappeared into the black night. Mikawa now headed north and sighted three U.S. cruisers, *Astoria, Quincy,* and *Vincennes.* The men aboard were asleep and the gunfire to the south had not alerted them to the danger closing in on them. At 0155 Mikawa's ships opened fire again with both guns and torpedoes at 5,500 yards.[257]

---

[255] Dull, Paul S., *The Battle History of the Imperial Japanese Navy* at 187.

[256] Ibid at 187-188.

[257] Ibid.

At 0155 the gunnery officer on *Astoria* sighted an enemy cruiser force bearing about 230 degrees relative. Shortly thereafter the enemy searchlights were turned on. The enemy commenced hitting on the fourth or fifth salvo. By this time the batteries of *Vincennes, Quincy*, and *Astoria* had been trained out and commenced firing. About 0156 the fourth Japanese salvo landed near the bow. One 8" projectile passed through the paint locker and started a small fire. The next Japanese 8-inch salvo hit amidships setting afire the boats on the boat deck and the three planes in the hangar. One 8" projectile set "ready service ammunition" at gun No. 8 on fire and knocked out No. 3 blower serving No. 2 fire room. This fire room was then secured and later abandoned. The sixth 8" salvo hit the face plate and barbette of turret I putting it out of action and killing the personnel within the turret and the barbette. From then until 0200 the enemy was hitting with large and small caliber projectiles with increasing rapidity. At some time during this period an 8" projectile entered No.1 fire room and killed all of the crew in this space.

About 0200 *Astoria* had to turn right to clear *Quincy*'s line of fire. This brought the stern of *Astoria* through the enemy's line of fire resulting in hits on the starboard side from the foremast aft. Soon the port and starboard secondary batteries, except gun No. 1, were completely out of commission due to direct hits and to the fire amidships on the upper deck. From 0200 to 0206 *Astoria* was under an extremely heavy concentration of fire. About 0202 the forward engine room was abandoned because a hit above this space filled the engine room with smoke. This reduced the speed to nine knots. About 0206 director II was hit and put out of action. During this period all fire-main risers forward of frame 103 were ruptured; no water was available for fighting fires.[258]

The enemy's fire gradually diminished from 0206 until 0215 when the enemy ceased firing and retired to the northwest. At 0208 course was changed to the left and the stern was again brought through the enemy's fire. About 0209, No. 4 fire room had to be abandoned due to the intense heat from the fire on the well deck. Two minutes later No. 3 fire room had to be abandoned. About this time *Astoria* had a near collision with the blazing *Quincy* which was on an opposite course. Just as the collision was averted, steering control was lost on the bridge and transferred to aft steering. At 0215, when the enemy had ceased firing, the engine room was abandoned due to intense smoke. This resulted in the loss of all power on the ship. The commanding officer immediately ordered bridge and foretop abandoned

---

[258] U.S.S. *Astoria* Action Report.

as ammunition in the clipping room above the bridge was exploding, endangering surviving personnel. Sometime during the action *Astoria* developed a 2-30 degree port list.[259]

Survivors from the forward part of the ship collected on the forecastle with the commanding officer in charge. Survivors on the stern collected on the fantail with the executive officer in charge. Each party existed without the knowledge of the other as they were separated by the intense fire raging on the main deck and the upper deck amidships. Dense smoke and fires cut off fore and aft passage on the second deck. Bucket brigades were organized by both parties. About 0300, when smoke was reaching down into the lower deck spaces, the small arms magazine and one group of forward 8" magazines were flooded. A short time later the other forward 8" magazine was flooded. The forward 5" magazines were not flooded apparently because the hand operating station on the second platform deck could not be reached and power was not available for operation of the electrical controls on the second deck. About this time the stern group flooded the after 8" magazine. The fire by now had reached the lower 5" and hoists as frequent explosions were heard below decks.[260]

At 0330 a rain squall passed over the ship. This reduced the intensity of the fires, but not sufficiently to permit the bucket brigade to get the fires under control. A little later *Bagley* came alongside the starboard bow and took off all survivors forward. At this time the stern and bow groups realized the existence of each other, and at daylight *Bagley* took off the wounded from the stern group. After the transfer of the wounded, plans were made for salvaging the vessel. The fires had moderated except for a fire in the wardroom country. Both engine rooms and No. 4 fire room were accessible at this time. At 0700 *Hopkins* came alongside and made arrangements for towing. Two attempts were made, the latter successful.[261]

About 0900 *Wilson* came alongside and assisted in the fire-fighting for one hour when both *Hopkins* and *Wilson* were called away. Fire in the wardroom increased in intensity and frequent small explosions were heard below deck. As a result of these explosions the hull must have been ruptured, as a port list gradually developed. This list was 100 degrees by about 1130 when a heavy explosion took place on the port side in way of the forward 5" magazines. The ship listed about 150 degrees to port. *Buchanan* came alongside to help fight the fire but the list had

---

[259] Ibid.

[260] Ibid.

[261] Ibid.

increased to such a point that the shell holes on the second deck, port side, were shipping water. It was obvious that the ship was going to sink. By 1210, as the salvage party abandoned ship, the port waterways of the main deck were awash. *Astoria* capsized to port, settling by the stern and disappeared at 1215.[262]

On board *Quincy* at 0155, as enemy searchlights were trained on *Quincy* from abaft her port beam, the main battery was trained out and commenced firing. About this time the ship received her first hit in the gun mounts on the main deck aft. One or two 9-gun salvos were fired when *Quincy*'s course was changed to the right, bringing her stern through the enemy's fire. While she was in this swing, she was raked fore and aft by large and small caliber hits. The planes in the hangar were set on fire, the bridge hit, the clipping room in the foremast hit, battle II hit, and turret III was hit and jammed in train. Turrets I and II were trained around to starboard and brought to bear upon the enemy.[263]

About 0205, while in the beginning of this turn *Quincy* was "struck" control was lost and the port side was hit by two torpedoes, probably from a submarine,[264] one after steering station: in way of fire rooms III and IV and the other just forward of the blowers either I.C. room about frame 45. About two 6-gun salvos had been fired room the fires amidships to starboard by the forward two turrets when turret II was struck, probably by an 8" A. P. projectile. This projectile entered the gun chamber where exposed projectiles were, detonated and powder was set on fire. The turret was completely gutted and left burning like a torch. At the same time, turret I was put out of action due to a fire in the upper powder room and a hit on the shell deck. Director I was jammed in train as the forestay had carried away due to damage, and caught around the radar antenna. During this period the bridge was hit again killing most of the personnel, including the Commanding Officer. Fragments from the hit also severed steering leads which resulted in the loss of steering control. The ship kept turning in a large circle to the right until power was lost at 0215.[265]

At 0215, when the enemy ceased firing, the ship was out of control, all main and secondary guns out of action, and all fire rooms out of commission. Both engine rooms were intact. The ship was listing rapidly to port, water was coming over the upper deck to port, and fires were blazing intermittently throughout the

---

[262] Ibid.

[263] U.S.S. *Quincy* Action Report.

[264] No Japanese submarines were present and the torpedoes came from Mikawa's cruisers.

[265] Ibid.

whole length of the ship. The surviving personnel realized that it was necessary to abandon ship as quickly as possible. Life rafts and life nets and other floatable objects were thrown overboard, and the senior surviving officers present directed personnel to abandon ship. As nearly as can be determined, this occurred between 0235 and 0240. The ship then capsized to port, the bow went under, the stern raised, and the ship slid from view.[266]

The enemy searchlights were trained on *Vincennes* at 0155 and the main battery was directed to train out and fire. A minute later the first enemy salvo struck, hitting the bridge, the carpenter shop, the hangar, battle II and the antenna trunk. Fires were started in the carpenter shop and the airplanes in the hangar. From this time on the enemy was hitting continuously until he ceased firing at 0215.[267]

Course was changed to the left and speed increased; however, at no time was it greater than 19.5 knots. About a minute later, direct hits were received on sky aft and sky forward, blowing the after director overboard. Attempts to extinguish fires failed as all fire-main risers had been ruptured. Further hits started fires in the movie locker and the cane fender stowage in the after end of the searchlight platform. The fire in the cane fenders was very intense and could not be extinguished. About 0200, attempts were made to evade enemy fire by turning hard right. While in this turn, one torpedo hit (possibly two) was received probably from the submarine which was reported fired on by gun No.1. No. 1 fire room was put out of action at this time. The left side range finder hoods of turrets I and II were struck.[268]

About 0205, when beginning to make a left turn, steering control was lost in the pilot house. Control was shifted to the after steering station. About this time all steam power was lost due to blowers either being destroyed or drawing smoke and flames from the fires amidships into the fire rooms. Diesels were started and they supplied power to turrets I and III. They were still able to fire in local control. Numerous hits during the early part of the action put out most of the guns of the secondary battery.[269]

About 0209 turret II was struck on the face plate by an 8" shell which penetrated without exploding and set exposed powder on fire. Another projectile hit

---

[266] Ibid.

[267] U.S.S. *Vincennes* Action Report.

[268] Ibid.

[269] Ibid.

the barbette of turret number 1 on the starboard side and jammed the turret! At this time all turrets and secondary battery except turret III and gun No.1 were out of action, and all power had been lost.[270]

At this time, while still under heavy fire from the enemy, the ship began to list appreciably to port. The crew was about to abandon ship when all at once the enemy extinguished searchlights and ceased firing. During the next fifteen minutes the list increased rapidly and it appeared that there was no possibility of saving the ship. The Commanding Officer then gave orders to abandon ship. About 0250 *Vincennes* capsized to port and went down by the head in 500 fathoms of water.[271]

Mikawa now headed for home and did not attempt to establish command of the sea. He did not attack the roughly fifty transports carrying the supplies for the Marines which were located just to his east. These ships should have been his strategic target. Given the close-run nature of the land combat that followed on Guadalcanal, interference with the Marines' supplies might have tipped the balance. Mikawa had won a great tactical victory against the U.S. covering force but missed an opportunity to deliver a strategic victory consistent with Corbett's principles. Mikawa was afraid' possible air attacks on his ships by daylight. He had no way of knowing Frank J. Fletcher had retired and there were no aircraft on Guadalcanal at this time. He headed for Kavieng and ran into the U.S. sub *S-44* which promptly sank the cruiser *Kako* with three torpedoes. Yamamoto gave Mikawa official praise but was upset that the opportunity to inflict a strategic blow was once again missed.

Admiral Frank J. Fletcher notified Admiral Robert Ghormley of the attack:

> FLETCHER to COMSOPAC. FLETCHER sending to GHORMLEY Following summary of messages delivered from Turner. Quote at 081645 surface' attack on screen coordinated with use aircraft flares. CHICAGO hit torpedo, CANBEERA on fire. At 2100 GCT. Heavy actions continue to westward. More of our ships in trouble. Submarines in area. At 2152 GCT. QUINCY sunk by torpedoes and gunfire. Air attack enroute. At 2325 GCT. VINCENNES sunk by gunfire and torpedoes. 0245 casualties heavy. At 2358. ASTORIA has fire in wardroom destroyer ordered to pump and ASTORIA to tow through LUNGA channel to ROSES as chance to save her. Movements requires protection which I am unable to provide. Unquote. Direct TURNER to make reports direct to you info to me.[272]

---

[270] Ibid.

[271] Ibid.

[272] Nimitz, Chester, *Chester Nimitz Gray Book*, Vol 1 at 638

Nimitz knew from codebreaking of Japanese ships concentrating at Truk to the northeast of Rabaul. It was clear that a major action was shaping up. On August 12 Nimitz sent Robert Ghormley this message warning him of the Japanese build-up.

> 12 0216 Air Base suggests probability of formation of strong striking force for employment in BISMARCK-SOLOMONS in near future. Preliminary organization seems to be First Air Fleet ·task force: HIEI, KIRISHIMA, SHOKAKU, ZUIKAKU, RYUJO, HOSHO, TONE, CHIKUMA, KUMANO plus another cruiser. 2nd Fleet task force; HARUNA, KONGO, MYOKO, HAGURO, MAYA, TAKAO, 2 DesDivs. Need for logistic arrangement plus necessity assemble destroyer screen from present escort missions indicate movement surface reinforcements will not materialize for seven - ten days. Para. Every means available must be employed to strengthen our position in RINGBOLT CACTUS area prior to arrival above force in area. Cover must be furnished by carrier aircraft as long as necessary and carriers while' within range enemy air bases should be given maximum protection by action of shore-based air against these bases.[273]

Admiral Ernest J King sent Nimitz this message promising reinforcements:

> 12 1750 COMINCH to CINCPAC In view Japanese concentrations that appear to be directed toward RABAUL you should consider advancing 3 to 5 battleships of Task Force 1 to BLEACHER. Desire your comment. Am directing JUNEAU to join SOUTH DAKOTA. SOUTE DAKOTA's ETA _PANAMA _August. 12.[274]

Nimitz's response:

> 12 2337 CINCPAC to COMINCH Utmost Secrecy. Following comments your 112030 and 121750 are based upon present estimate enemy intentions which may be further clarified before our next moves. Enemy strength appears to be destined for NEW BRITAIN - SOLOMON area therefore consider improbable serious attack against MIDWAY and even less against OAHU. A raid in force is of higher probability but opposing it with one carrier task force would be ineffectual and might well result in loss of carrier without compensating damage to enemy. Para. Unable provide logistic support in SoPac area for battleships task force 1 with ships now available and doubt BB usefulness unless we can operate them in close support CACTUS area. Consider we can best oppose enemy that area with shore-based air, carriers and fast forces including new battleships. Therefore while developments next few days may change my opinion I believe that maximum carrier strength will be needed in South and that this can be obtained best by an overlapping relief of Carrier Task Forces on that station. Para. Am bringing Task Force 1 into Pearl Harbor for possible use against landing

[273] Ibid at 646

[274] Ibid at 638

> attack this area. For reasons above I will not send any of the slow battleships south unless so directed by you. Para. For reasons given in my 310215 and because additional planes being dispatched So Pac from HAWAII I again urge the air reinforcements requested in that dispatch.[275]

Both sides were building up their forces and it would result in the third cattier battle of the war This would be the first carrier battle were the United States had a modern battleship participate in *North Carolina.* She would play a significant role in the battle.

[275] Ibid at 639

CHAPTER 17: BATTLE OF THE EASTERN SOLOMONS

The Americans formed three task groups around the carriers *Saratoga, Enterprise*, and the newly arrived *Wasp* to cover the lines of communication between Tulagi, Guadalcanal, Espiritu, Noumea, and Australia. The forth task group formed around *Hornet* would stay at Pearl Harbor to guard the Midway Pearl Harbor line of communication.

The three carrier task forces which participated in the initial Solomons attack operated to the southeastward thereafter. Their mission, briefly, was: (a) to support the Tulagi-Guadalcanal garrisons, (b) to cover the Espiritu Santo-Noumea line of communications, (c) to cover the movement of our aviation ground crews, equipment and supplies into the Solomons, and (d) to destroy enemy forces encountered. The combined strength was approximately three carriers, one fast battleship, five heavy cruisers, one light cruiser and eighteen destroyers.

The fourth and remaining carrier task force, built around *Hornet*, was kept in readiness at Pearl Harbor, and on the 17th, when events indicated that the enemy would commit a large part of his strength in the South Pacific, was dispatched to the scene of impending conflict. However, the *Hornet* group arrived on the 29th, too late to participate in the action under discussion.

About 1910 on the 22d Admiral Fletcher received a dispatch from Ghormley:

> 22 0910 COMSOPAC TO CTF 61 Indications point strongly to enemy attack in force on Cactus area 23-26 August. From available intelligence believe following enemy forces now within radius of about 600 miles from Kavieng. 1 possibly 2 other BB, 10 CA, 5 CL, 10 or 11 Desdiv, 8 or 9 Subdivs including South Pacific. An undetermined number PT and other small craft additional to those previously known Island based and sea planes New Britain and southeast probably increasing steadily over current estimate of 8O fighters and 80 to 100 bombers all types. Land forces include 1 division available Rabaul. 1 from Truk and a force enroute from Davao. Presence of carriers possible but not confirmed. Only evidence sighting you is Cincpac 140159. Realize communications not satisfactory. Making every effort to improve. Important fueling be conducted soonest possible and if practicable one carrier task force at a time retiring for that purpose. Your 211120. This from Com-

> sopac to Comtaskfor 61 info Comtaskfor 62, 63 and Cincpac. Am sending Flatte and Cimarron from Roses daylight tomorrow Sunday accordance by 220911.[276]

Wasp was sent south to top off her fuel which only left the *Saratoga* and the *Enterprise* task groups.

Task Force FOX

Carrier: *Saratoga* (flagship of Admiral Frank J. Fletcher)

27- F4F-4, 33 SBD-3, (30 operational) 13 TBF-1, and one photo recon F4F-7

Heavy cruisers: *Minneapolis, New Orleans*

Destroyers: *Phelps, MacDonough, Dale, Farragut, Worden*

Task Force KING

Carrier: *Enterprise* (flagship of Rear Admiral Thomas Kinkaid) 28 F4F-4 (27 operational) 35 SBD, (33 operational) 16 TBF-1 (14 operational) and one F4F-7

Battleship: *North Carolina*

Heavy cruiser: *Portland*

Light cruiser: *Atlanta*

Destroyers: *Balch, Maury, Benham, Ellet, Grayson, Monssen*

Land-Based Aircraft

Marine Air Group 23 at Guadalcanal, 13 F4F-4, 11 SBD-3

11th Heavy Bombardment Group at Espiritu Santo, 25 B-17, 21 PBY-5A, P-400 (export version of P-39)

Admiral Yamamoto's code name for this operation was KA. He still didn't suspect the JN-25 codes had been broken. For operation KA he had two objectives. The first was to destroy the U.S. Pacific fleet in the area. This would be accomplished by placing Rear Admiral Hiroaki Abe's Vanguard Force ahead of CarDiv1 and Nagumo's carriers. His hope was to have the Vanguard force draw attention away from his carriers. Nagumo had the task of destroying any U.S. carriers. Abe's force would be joined by Kondo's Advance Force, 2nd Fleet and if needed, Yamamoto's Support Force Main Body to destroy whatever remained.

The second objective was to get 1,500 troops to Guadalcanal safely. Mikawa was to use his four cruisers to bombard the airfield during the night of August 24. 8th Fleet, Outer South Seas Force under the command of Rear Admiral Raizo

[276] Ibid at 808

Tanaka would escort the transport fleet to Guadalcanal. To provide additional cover Rear Admiral Chuichi Hara's Mobile Force would be stationed 190 miles northeast of Guadalcanal to provide fighter support.

Admiral Yamamoto and the Combined Fleet were on the strategic offensive choosing the time and place for the operation. He was not using all of his assets. The carrier *Junyo* was available as was the battleship *Mutsu* but these two capital ships would remain in port for operation KA. He was using Abe's force as bait then applying a coordinated effort to combine carrier aircraft and battleships fighting power. Abe's main objective was to divert U.S. carrier strike onto himself and thus shield Nagumo's carriers from attack. Hopefully he could achieve surprise and out-range U.S. carrier strikes. Morale of his men was now apprehensive and cautious. Before the Battle of Midway, victory was assumed; now after such a defeat this level of confidence was shattered.

The operation still called for Corbett's division of forces with the sacrifice of operational flexibility and cooperation. This was hoped to increase security by preventing all the various task groups being discovered. No tankers were part of the operation so the various task groups can only stay at sea for a few days and then they will be forced to return to port. This implies Yamamoto was not establishing sea control but continued to perform strike warfare. Sustainability would generally be limited to air-wing attrition and individual ship survivability. There was a large force of G4Ms and A6Ms that can perform scout, strike, and combat air patrol missions at Rabaul. The operation was scheduled for August 24-25, 1942.

Support Force Main Body, Admiral Yamamoto

Battleship: *Yamato* (F)

Carrier: *Taiyo*

Destroyers: *Akebono, Ushio*

CarDiv1 Vice Admiral Chuichi Nagumo

Carriers: *Shokaku* 27 A6M2 (26 operational) 27 D3A1 18 B5N2 *Zuikaku* 27 A6M2 (25 operational) 27 D3A1 18 B5N2

Destroyers: *Kazagumo, Yugumo, Makigumo, Akigumo, Hatsukaze,* and *Akizuki*

Mobile Force, Rear Admiral Chuichi Hara

Carrier: *Ryujo*, 24 A6M2 (23 operational) 6 B5N2

Cruiser: *Tone*

Destroyers: *Amatsukaze, Tokitsukaze*

Vanguard Force, Rear Admiral Hiroaki Abe

Battleships: *Hiei, Kirishima*

Heavy cruisers: *Kumano, Suzuya, Chikuma*

Light cruiser: *Nagara*

Destroyers: *Nowaki, Maikaze, Tanikaze*

Advance Force, 2nd Fleet Vice Admiral Nobutake Kondo

Heavy cruisers: *Atago, Maya, Takao, Myoko, Haguro*

Light cruiser: *Yura*

Destroyers: *Kuroshio, Oyashio, Hayashio, Minegumo, Natsugumo, Asagumo*

8th Fleet, Outer South Seas Force, Rear Admiral Raizo Tanaka

Light cruiser: *Jintsu*

Destroyers: *Suzukaze, Kawakaze, Umikaze, Kagero, Isokaze, Mutsuki, Yayoi, Uzuki*

Transport Force with 1500 troops

Transports: *Kinryu Maru, Boston Maru, Daifuku Maru*

Patrol Boats: *No.1, No.2, No.34*, and *No.35*

Covering Force: Rear Admiral Gunichi Mikawa

Heavy cruisers: *Chokai, Kinugasa, Aoba, Furutaka*

6th Fleet: Vice Admiral Teruhisa Komatsu At Truk: fourteen submarines

11th Air Fleet at Rabaul: Vice Admiral Nishizo Tsukahara

51 A6Ms, 41 G4Ms, 9 D3As, 2 Irvings, 8 Mavises, and 3 Emilys: 114 total

Standby Force attached to 2nd Fleet, but not at sea.

Carrier: *Junyo*

Battleship: *Mutsu*

Destroyers: *Harusame, Samidare, Murasame*

Nimitz notified King on August 22:[277]

> The consolidation of positions in the TULAGI area continues with Fletcher's striking forces standing by to prevent Jap reinforcements. A comparatively large number of enemy cruisers, destroyers, transports, and freighters have been sighted recently in the RABAUL area. This constitutes a threat to our Marines, but also offers a fine target for

[277] Pearl Harbor is a day behind local time at Guadalcanal so it is August 22 at Pearl Harbor and August 23 at Guadalcanal.

> Fletcher if they ever come within his reach. A force of 1 CL 2 DD and 4 AKs was thought heading toward GUADALCANAL. Attack planes took off, but as the force turned away, no contact was made.[278]

The strike aircraft were from *Saratoga* in the form of thirty-one SBDs and six TBDs and Guadalcanal sent out twenty-three aircraft. Rear Admiral Tanaka knew he had been sighted so he turned his ships to the northeast escaping the strike. *Saratoga*'s planes landed on Guadalcanal planning to return to *Saratoga* the next morning. *Saratoga*'s planes returned to the carrier at 1130 minus two SBDs that had to return to Guadalcanal. Task Force Fox and King pursued a northerly course during the night of the 23rd, the two carrier groups proceeding together tactically but actually separated by about five miles.

At 0800 on the 24th the two carriers were east of Malaita Island. The weather cleared to a marked degree during the early forenoon, making operating and flying conditions excellent. However, the wind was from the southeast. Frequent turns into the wind by *Enterprise* and *Saratoga* to launch or retrieve planes delayed effort to close the enemy to the north.

Enterprise planes again made the dawn search, 20 SBD's taking off at 0630 to cover a sector from 290° to 070° T., to a distance of 200 miles. No contacts were made and all planes returned at 1050. The *Enterprise* had picked up a report from COMAIRSOPAC that one of his planes at 0935 had sighted a Japanese force consisting of one carrier, two heavy cruisers, and one destroyer. This was the Mobile Force in command Hara with the carrier *Ryujo*.

Fletcher was not satisfied with the available information and at 1210 ordered *Enterprise* to conduct another air search and informed Admiral Thomas Kinkaid that the *Saratoga* striking group was being held in readiness pending receipt of more definite word concerning the enemy. *Enterprise* launched a 23-plane search to cover sector 270° to 090° to a distance of 250 miles.

At 1220 *Ryujo* had reached her assigned position and launched six A6Ms and six B5Ns to attack Guadalcanal. Nine more A6Ms were launched at 1248 to attack Guadalcanal in a second strike. At 1440 *Ryujo*, a heavy cruiser, and three destroyers were sighted again but the report did not reach *Enterprise* until 1548. The delay was attributed to the fact that fighter direction was using the same general frequency employed by the scout planes, which could have drowned out the contact reports, and to the existence of local interference which developed when the carrier was operating at high speed.

---

[278] Nimitz, Chester. *Chester Nimitz Gray Book*, Vol. 1 at 832.

At 1500 two large carriers, four heavy cruisers, six light cruisers, and at least eight destroyers were sighted bearing 340° T., distance 198 miles from the American force. This was Nagumo's CarDiv1. *Enterprise* did not receive this report until the scout plane returned to the ship at 1840. On the basis of these contacts, the enemy formation was spread out through an arc 60 to 80 miles wide, centered at about longitude 162° E., steering south.

Fletcher felt he could not wait any longer and decided to attack *Ryujo*. The *Saratoga* attack group, which had been held in readiness pending the outcome of the second *Enterprise* search flight, was launched at 1435. The group originally consisted of thirty SBDs dive bombers and eight TBF torpedo planes. One SBD bomber and 1 TBF torpedo plane were forced back by mechanical difficulties. Fifty-three F4F fighters made up the combat air patrol for the two carrier task groups.

Task Force 61 had been spotted by the *Chikuma*'s float plane and at 1455 Nagumo launched a strike of fifty-four D3As and ten A6Ms. The IJN strike found the USN carriers with all of their F4F-4 fighters present. Seven had been detailed as escorts for a strike just in the process of departing, but all were made available for the CAP. At the time of the second radar sighting, *Saratoga* and *Enterprise* had a combined CAP aloft of forty-two F4Fs plus an additional eleven readied on the two carriers. Four of the aloft CAP were low on fuel and about to land. Eleven had already been sent out along the approximate bearing of the strike with sixteen more following close behind.

The D3As split into two groups, eighteen attacked *Enterprise* and nine attacked *Saratoga*. The dive bombers were at 16,400 feet and the F4Fs struggled to climb to altitude. One F4F shot down one A6M. Four F4Fs came close to intercepting the D3As but the bombers escorts attacked them and shot down one. The A6Ms had split so that three were ahead of the raid in a fighter sweep with the other six in close support of the dive bombers. The D3As attacking *Enterprise* began their dives. Four F4F were in pursuit downing one just as it dropped its bomb and it missed. Three D3As disintegrated by the anti-aircraft fire. Excerpts from *Grayson*'s report:

> The first plane crossed from starboard to port, coming up on Grayson's starboard quarter at an altitude of about 300 feet, strafing as he passed. This fire slashed the canvas top to No.3 gun, and wounded several of the gun crew and adjacent 20-mm. crew. Grayson's after 20-mm. groups trained on the plane and poured in a well-directed, concentrated fire. It was almost impossible to miss. The plane staggered, then crashed close aboard on the port beam.
>
> The next three planes to get clear of Enterprise came along the starboard side of Grayson. The first of these was brought down by the North Carolina, whose volume of fire was so great that the ship ap-

> peared in flames amidships. The second, passing at what appeared to be slow speed, provided a close target for Grayson's 20-mm. battery. This plane was hit repeatedly, and crashed about 100 yards on Grayson's port bow. The third plane, and the last to pass near the Grayson, was fired on only by one 20-mm. gun, for the others in the starboard battery were reloading or firing at distant targets. This plane flew into the terrific low altitude barrage being laid by the North Carolina and Atlanta and was not seen thereafter.[279]

Three of the D3As bombed *North Carolina.* The first planes observed were diving on *Enterprise.* These the battleship engaged with one group of three of her twin 5-inch 38 caliber mounts. Two minutes later she was under dive bombing attack herself. Without shifting her protective barrage from over *Enterprise, North Carolina* opened fire with three other 5-inch mounts on the planes attacking her. Two bombs fell within fifteen yards and the other within about twenty-five yards, knocking gunners down, shaking the ship, and deluging her decks with water, but causing no further damage.[280]

Enterprise sustained three direct hits and several close misses. Near the end of the third minute of the attack a near-hit barely cleared the flight deck on the port quarter, striking the water under the fantail. The resulting explosion under the overhang of the flight deck raised the deck about a foot, bulging the steel plates, and shattering the wooden deck. A gunner in a 20-mm. sponson projecting abaft the fantail was hurled up in the air and fifteen feet across the flight deck, landing in another gun sponson on the port quarter. He was not seriously hurt. A few seconds later, while many gunners were recovering from the shock and deluge of sea water thrown over the stern by this near-hit, a large bomb struck the forward starboard corner of the No. 3 elevator on the flight deck, penetrating to the third deck before detonating. The explosion wrecked compartments for as much as sixteen frames on the second and third decks, bulged and ruptured decks, started numerous fires, cut fragment holes in the side plating, and killed about thirty-five men.[281]

All power failed on the after 5-inch guns as a result of the first bomb hit, and thereafter they had to be trained, elevated, and loaded by hand. This reduced the rate of fire by more than half. Shortly after the first hit a second large bomb struck about 20 feet away, exploding in the No. 3 gun gallery. The blast set off ready powder, put both 5-inch guns out of commission and killed all men at the guns

---

[279] U.S.S. *Grayson*'s Action Report.

[280] Office of Naval Intelligence: *The Battle of Eastern Solomons at* 64-67.

[281] Ibid.

(about 38). The only members of the gun crews who escaped had just left their stations to assist in fighting fires started by the first bomb.[282]

The third hit followed closely upon the other two. This bomb, apparently the flight deck at frame 137 starboard just abaft the island structure. It exploded before completely penetrating the flight deck. Damage, other than the crippling of the No. 2 elevator, was not great.[283] Near-hits which caused appreciable damage exploded under the port fantail, raising the port after corner of the flight deck about a foot, tearing lose all degaussing cables for a length of 30 feet, springing the third and fourth decks, and causing minor deflection of the side plating; (2) near frame 80, port side, resulting in numerous fragment holes above the water line, rupturing gasoline mains, one fire-main riser and one damage-control riser, damaging arresting wires No. 1 and 2 and the first barrier, and resulting subsequently in the grounding out of the starboard steering motor. Fires started by the hits near the No. 3 elevator were stubborn, mainly because of the large quantities of inflammable materials in the aviation issue storeroom and the chief petty officers' quarters, which were affected. *Enterprise* had increased speed to thirty knots, and the battleship, unable to maintain station, gradually dropped astern. At the end of the engagement she was some 4,000 yards from the carrier. Assigning credit to ships for shooting down enemy aircraft proved difficult.[284]

The nine D3As detailed to attack *Saratoga* not only had further to travel, they had to make the journey without fighter escort. They were attacked by a fresh section of three F4Fs well short of their target. When one of the overflown F4F sections got altitude and added four more F4Fs to the fight, the formation leader decided that the better course was to attack *Enterprise*. A further four F4Fs tried to join the fight before the D3As could dive, but four escorting A6Ms arrived in time to disrupt further CAP attacks on the bombers.[285]

During this battle two D3As went down to the F4Fs while three F4Fs were lost to either the A6Ms or AA. All seven of the remaining D3As bombed targets, with three targeting *Enterprise* and another four her escorting battleship. None hit, with one of the D3As attacking the carrier shot down by the CAP after its attack. Now the IJN strikers had to withdraw. Seventeen D3As and eight A6Ms started

---

[282] Ibid.

[283] Ibid.

[284] Ibid.

[285] Heinz, Leonard, *Aircraft Carrier Defense in the Pacific War: The Carrier Battles of 1942* at 66-72.

back to their carriers, but only nine D3As and four A6Ms would return to their carrier decks six D3As and two A6Ms being shot down by the combat air patrol. Two A6Ms ditched and two D3As ditched due to battle damage.[286]

The second IJN wave of twenty-seven D3As failed to find either U.S. task force. Four planes were shot down by U.S. fighters and one damaged that was forced to ditch. This was very fortunate for the United States because *Enterprise* was crippled with her rudders jammed and circling. No Japanese aircraft attacked *Saratoga* so once again having the formations separate but close enough for mutual support paid dividends.[287] The final tally from the first strike was eleven D3As shot down by F4Fs, four A6Ms by F4Fs, five D3As shot down by anti-aircraft fire, two D3As shared between anti-aircraft and the F4Fs that ditched due to damage and two A6Ms shared between anti-aircraft and the F4Fs that ditched due to damage. Four F4Fs were shot down by A6Ms.

This was a far greater performance for anti-aircraft guns than in the two previous carrier battles. The U.S. was learning that it was not the number of ships in the task force that mattered most but the concentration of guns close to the target ship. *North Carolina* with four secondary battery directors could help protect *Enterprise* while she was under attack herself simultaneously. Absent an enemy battleship her primary role was to protect lesser ships so they could fulfill their mission.

Carrier admirals from this battle forward wanted battleship protection.

This had a major impact for future operations. Admiral Fletcher wrote:

> 02 0337 CTF 16 to CINCPAC Info CTF 62, 17, 18, COMSOPAC, COMINCH, CTF1. The present of a fast battleship in task force 16 during past several weeks and particularly during action on 24 August was a distinct asset because of her demonstrated fire power against attacking aircraft and her inherent strength against possible surface contacts. From Comtaskfor 16 action Cincpac. Because of slight deficiency in speed and acceleration and slight inherent slowness in starting a turn the station of the NORTH CAROLINA in cruising disposition and particularly in tight screening disposition during air attacks should be downwind from carrier as was the case on 24 Aug with thoroughly satisfactory results.[288]

---

[286] Ibid.

[287] Ibid.

[288] Nimitz, Chester. *Chester Nimitz Gray Book*, Vol. 2 at 909.

The combat air patrol only prevented four D3As from attacking the ships despite having forty-nine F4Fs in the air. The main problem was altitude and the slow climb speed of the F4Fs. The escort A6Ms also did very well at preventing the F4Fs from intercepting the D3As. *Saratoga*'s main strike effort was directed at the light carrier *Ryujo*, arriving about an hour before the IJN strike on the U.S. carriers. The strike consisted of twenty-nine SBDs in two squadrons and seven torpedo-armed TBFs, cruising with the SBDs at 15,000 feet and the TBFs 3,000 feet below. It attacked about fourteen minutes after sighting *Ryujo* and her small group of escorts. Initially, the strike leader assigned one squadron to attack *Ryujo* and split the second squadron between *Ryujo* and an escorting heavy cruiser *Tone*.[289]

Ryujo had five A6Ms in the air and immediately launched two more raising her combat air patrol to seven fighters. No A6Ms intercepted the SBDs until after they had made their bombing runs. The first squadron attacking *Ryujo* all missed the carrier who was maneuvering to avoid the bombs. The second squadron then aborted its attack on *Tone* and attacked the carrier. Four A6Ms attacked before they could make their bombing runs without any results. The second squadron scored three bomb hits and one damaging near miss.[290]

The TBFs now made their attack runs. Two TBFs were shot down by A6Ms but five others made an anvil attack scoring one torpedo hit. The remaining U.S. aircraft withdrew without further loss and none of the seven A6Ms were downed either. Anti-aircraft guns for the Japanese had totally failed to bring down a single plane. Two scouting SBDs did find the Japanese fleet carriers and attacked *Shokaku* but missed but were able to withdraw safely.[291]

Admiral Robert Ghormley informed both King and Nimitz:

> 25 1326 GHORMLEY/Info: COMINCH, CINCPAC, CTF 61 62 63 17 MacArthur, COMSOPACFOR. Handle as most secret. Operations 25th. Preliminary reports indicate enemy forces yesterday and today consisted at least 4 groups. 1 consisting: 1 BB some cruisers attacked by our carrier air groups some hits. 1 group consisting 2· large CV's, 4 CA's 6 CL's 8 DD's discovered too late for attack. Planes this group believed those which attacked our carriers resulting some damage ENTERPRISE 1 group consisting RYUJO 1 CA 2 DD attacked by our B-17's and SARATOGA air group, set on fire and believed badly dam-

[289] Heinz, Leonard, *Aircraft Carrier Defense in the Pacific War: The Carrier Battles of 1942* at 66-72.

[290] Ibid.

[291] Ibid.

> aged by latter. Group including BB at 1100 L (-11) today appeared to be retiring to northwest at Lat. 04-18 Long 16240. During last night ENTERPRISE and SARATOGA their task forces· retired to southward to fuel WASP ordered to support GUADALCANAL.[292]

Yamamoto withdrew as did the transports carrying the 1,500 men. Operation KA did not achieve any of its objectives and it cost the Japanese another aircraft carrier. Kondo joined with Ade's forces and attempted to engage the U.S. carriers but *Enterprise* was able to get her rudders un-jammed and the Americans withdrew safely. This was a major problem with strike warfare. Long ranges produced a failure in economy of effort. Much of the task force's firepower was wasted and aircraft attrition once again was horrible for the Japanese. Of the attacking D3As 72% did not make it back to their carrier and 60% of the A6Ms did not come back.

What is difficult to explain is that after the strike on the U.S. task force Yamamoto still had forty-one A6Ms, twenty-five dive bombers and thirty-four torpedo bombers that were immediately available. His two fleet carriers had not been damaged. Yet he was fully aware that at least one U.S. carrier had been damaged.[293] Why did he withdraw?

On the American side all but two strike aircraft came back. The Battle of Eastern Solomons was a U.S. tactical victory but in a war of attrition neither side had achieved a major strategic victory. On September 15th *Ryujo* would be avenged when submarine *I*-19 sank *Wasp* with a spread of six torpedoes. Three of the torpedoes struck home, causing heavy damage. With power knocked out due to damage from the torpedo explosions, *Wasp*'s damage-control teams were unable to contain the ensuing fires, she was abandoned and scuttled.[294]

The remaining three torpedoes from the same spread (torpedo salvo), often incorrectly attributed to a second Japanese submarine, hit the U.S. battleship *North Carolina* and the destroyer *O'Brien*, and the latter later sank. Significant damage had been sustained by *North Carolina*, which underwent repairs at Pearl Harbor until November 16, 1942. This single torpedo salvo thus sank an aircraft carrier and a destroyer, and severely damaged a battleship, making it one of the most damaging torpedo salvos in history.[295]

---

[292] Nimitz, Chester, *Chester Nimitz Gray Book*, Vol. 1 at 658.

[293] Dull, Paul S., *The Battle History of the Imperial Japanese Navy* at 206-207.

[294] Frank, Richard B., *Guadalcanal* at 248.

[295] Ibid at 248-249.

The sinking of *Wasp* brought U.S. carrier strength to three fleet carriers: *Enterprise, Hornet* and *Saratoga.* Japan still had greater carrier strength in *Shokaku, Zuikaku, Junyo, Hiyo,* and several smaller carriers as well. The torpedoing of *North Carolina* resulted in her withdrawal. She would be replaced by her sister *Washington* and the new *South Dakota.* Yamamoto had *Yamato, Mutsu, Kongo, Hiei, Kirishima,* and *Haruna* all immediately available yet he only used *Yamato* as a command base and even among the other Japanese ships she was being called "Hotel *Yamato.*"[296]

The failure of operation KA left the reinforcement of ground troops on Guadalcanal unfulfilled. The Japanese began to use fast destroyers that could bring in reinforcements at night and escape the range of SBDs stationed on Guadalcanal before sunrise. These regular reinforcements were nicknamed the "*Tokyo Express*" by the Americans. The airstrip was named after Marine Corps Major Lofton Henderson, commanding officer of VMSB-241 who was killed during the Battle of Midway, and was known as Henderson Field.

Neither side had established command of the ocean surrounding Guadalcanal. The Japanese surrendered command of the seas by day time hours. During the night when aircraft were largely grounded they would bring in troops and supplies. Henderson Field was becoming a serious threat and often referred to as an unsinkable aircraft carrier by the Japanese. With the knowledge of the Japanese using night time hours to bring in their reinforcements and occasionally bombard Henderson Field on October 12, 1942, Ghormley ordered Rear Admiral Norman Scott to establish command of the sea at night and deny its use by the Japanese. This would lead to the second surface battle in Iron Bottom Sound.

---

[296] Stille, Mark, *Yamamoto Isoroku* at 43.

CHAPTER 18: BATTLE OF CAPE ESPERANCE

Scott's task force was Task Force 64 and it was made up of two heavy cruisers, his flagship *San Francisco* and *Salt Lake City*; two light cruisers, *Boise* and *Helena*, and five destroyers, *Farenholt, Buchanan, Laffey, Duncan*, and *McCalla*. Scott's objective was to blockade the western entrance into the sound and deny the seaway to the Japanese. His second objective was to annihilate any Japanese forces that attempt to use the seaway. He had the advantage in the principle of security. He was aware of Goto's forces and Goto was unaware and this also gave Scott the principle of surprise.

At 2228 he lined his ships into a single column and was north-northeast of Cape Esperance and was sailing toward Savo Island. This placed him in an advantageous position for any ships wishing to transit the western strait into Iron Bottom Sound by capping their "T". This traditional perpendicular formation inherently created concentration and economy of force because it put the maneuvering fleet able to train all its guns on the enemy force which could only use its guns located on the bow of their ships. Now all he needed was cooperation between his units.

Mikawa ordered Goto to take three heavy cruisers *Aoba, Furutaka, Kinugasa* plus two destroyers *Hatsuyuki* and *Fubuki* to enter the sound and bombard Henderson Field in preparation for bringing in a large group of transports bring in the 17th Army to retake the airfield.

Goto's primary mission was to bombard Henderson Field but if opposed he must first gain command of the sea to complete this mission. His second objective was to provide cover for the Tokyo Express made up of two seaplane tenders and six destroyers. Goto did not send any destroyers or aircraft to scout the entrances to the sound. He simply made an assumption that he would not be opposed, perhaps because the Americans had not committed surface ships to stopping the Tokyo Express before. For whatever reason, this assumption gave Scott the very important advantage of surprise. Goto's force would need to live up to the principles of flexibility and cooperation to overcome this error in security.

At 2308 *Helena* picked up the Japanese force on her SG radar which was the latest and best aboard the U.S. ships. She did not transmit this data until 2323 to the flagship and Scott. More messages started to come that were more confusing then helpful between 2343 and 2353 when the entire column had to reverse course by way of a 180-degree turn. The destroyer *Duncan* began an attack run leaving the U.S. column assuming everyone knew where the Japanese were. At 234 *Helena* informed that the enemy could be seen at 5,000 yards and no longer waited for the order to open fire. She snapped on her searchlights and fired her fifteen six-inch guns in rapid succession. The rest of the U.S. ships quickly followed suit and opened fire on the still unsuspecting Japanese force.[297]

When *Helena* turned on her search lights and opened fire on *Aoba*, Goto's bridge exploded in hot steel fragments and fire and he was mortally wounded. He saw his "T" was capped and sent out a signal to turn to starboard. The heavy cruiser *Furutaka* was set ablaze, her guns firing as she attempted to reverse course and head northwest. *Aoba* turned to starboard taking most of the punishment but fighting back the best she could.[298]

Kinugasa and *Hatsuyuki* reversed course by making a port turn with *Aoba* shielding them as she went to starboard. This maneuver protected them from taking serious damage. *Fubuki* was illuminated by search lights and all of Task Force 64 opened fire on her. She never had a chance and was sunk within minutes.[299]

Scott had achieved his first objective: as the Japanese attempted to withdraw, he had denied them access to Iron Bottom Sound. Now he formed a line ahead column in pursuit to annihilate the enemy. *Kinugasa* recovered first from the shock of surprise. She opened fire on *Salt Lake City* at 2400 at a distance of 8,000 yards. The American cruiser avoided torpedoes. Then *Kinugasa* opened fire on *Boise* for four minutes. *Boise* was hit on her main belt at frame 90.5 which cut the degaussing cable but no further damage. Hit two struck the captain's cabin at frame 61.5 detonating on impact. It blew a four foot by five foot hole in the bulkhead. Furniture within the cabin was wrecked and fires were started but alert damage control parties put out the flames in twelve minutes. Fragments damaged the gun barrel of 5-inch gun mount No. 3 and three men were injured.[300]

Hit three and four struck the ship simultaneously at frame 58 and passed through the ship without exploding. *Salt Lake City* seeing *Boise* hit tried to place

[297] Dull, Paul S., *The Battle History of the Imperial Japanese Navy* at 215-221.

[298] Ibid.

[299] Ibid.

[300] U.S.S. *Boise* Action Report, Summary of Battle Damage. October 12, 1942.

herself between *Kinugasa* and *Boise*. *Boise* was hit by another four shells. One 8-inch shell hit the faceplate of turret three. Hit five was another eight-inch projectile striking the barbette of turret one breaking up in the process but jamming the turret. Hit 6 struck at frame 31 and was six feet below the waterline. This shell impacted the water first penetrated the side shell and the penetrated another bulkhead before exploding within the upper handling magazine for turret two. There was a huge explosion as her magazines detonated. This hit killed all the men in the forward turrets, handling rooms and magazines. Hit seven struck the ship at frame 17. Some thought that *Boise* had been hit by a torpedo. Compartment A303-L was flooded and the starboard windlass was damaged. The last hit bounced off the side armor of turret two.[301]

Furutaka was hit at 0149 on turret three and at 0151 her number two torpedo mount was destroyed. At 0154 her starboard engine room was destroyed and one minute later her port engine room was hit. By 0205 all her guns were silenced. Dead in the water her captain gave the order to abandon ship at 0220.[302]

Aoba was hit on turret two and three. Turret three exploded. She would take an estimated forty hits but was able to withdraw. *Kinugasa's* only damage was to two motor boats. *Hatsuyuki* received two hits but her damage was minor. The *Duncan* initially opened fire on *Furutaka* and then took on *Hatsuyuki*. In the duel her engine room was destroyed and then slowing down the Japanese destroyer hit her repeatedly. She eventually sank the next day. *Farenholt* was hit by both enemy and friendly fire in the mêlée. Her damage was moderate but she withdrew safely.[303]

Scott by denying the access to Iron Bottom Sound was the victor and in command of the sea. His battle to annihilate the enemy did not go as well.

One light cruiser was severely damaged. One heavy cruiser lightly damaged, one destroyer sunk, and one destroyer suffered moderate damage. In return one Japanese heavy cruiser was sunk, one destroyer sunk, and another heavy cruiser seriously damaged.

---

[301] Ibid.

[302] Dull, Paul S., *The Battle History of the Imperial Japanese Navy* at 215-221.

[303] Ibid.

The Japanese casualties were mainly caused because the element of surprise was with the Americans. The Japanese in return recovered quickly due to pre-war training for night battles. The new Type 91 projectiles produced a magazine hit that almost sank *Boise*. However, other type 91 projectiles simply passed through the ship without exploding and some broke apart upon hitting armor due to their long fuse delay and lack of a true armor-piercing cap to protect the shell's nose.[304]

The Americans hadn't trained as much for night battles in restricted waters before hostilities had begun. Scott didn't place his flag on the ship with the most advanced radar and didn't have a good tactical picture of the battle. Communication between his units was poor. Worse, he left Iron Bottom Sound which allowed the Japanese transports to continue their mission and unload their supplies and troops. This was reminiscent to the Battle of Savo Island in reverse. While victory was achieved tactically the strategic target or the troop transports were untouched.

Yamamoto was not finished with attempting to bombard Henderson Field. He ordered Kurita to take his two battleships into the restricted waters to smash the field and put it out of action. What he had called stupid at Midway was now being carried out in restricted waters that neither navy believed was the proper place for battleships.

Just after midnight on October 14, 1942, Kurita watched from the bridge of the battleship *Kongo* as her main battery of eight 14-inch guns fired into U.S. Marine positions on Guadalcanal. Beside him was Captain Tomiji Koyanagi who would later become his chief of staff. Together they watched *Kongo* fire 430 heavy caliber rounds. Her sister battleship *Haruna* fired approximately 483 rounds, thereby setting ablaze the U.S. fuel depot, destroying aircraft and cratering Henderson Field in the most successful bombardment of the U.S. Marines during the Guadalcanal campaign.

Upon receiving his orders for this mission from Yamamoto, Kurita was initially opposed. The restricted waters around Guadalcanal negated the advantage of his ships' big guns and their ability to outrange an opponent. These waters were the domain of the light cruiser and the destroyer according to Japanese naval doctrines and tactics. Any surface battle within these waters would be relatively short-ranged and nothing more than a brawl.

---

[304] Japanese 8-inch and 6-inch type 91 projectiles could be considered semi-armor piercing shells due to the lack of a true armor piercing cap that would protect the projectiles nose when striking face-hardened armor.

Kurita's ships were not opposed by the Americans and his force gained control of the seas off Lunga Point where they hammered the U.S. positions for two hours. Ninety U.S. aircraft were operational before the bombardment. Afterward only seven dive bombers and thirty-five fighters with virtually no fuel remained. He then followed the orders given beforehand by Yamamoto and he took his ships back north, toward Rabaul returning command of the seas back to the Americans. Ironically, the success of Kurita's bombardment set in motion a U.S. response that changed the outcome of events in the South Pacific.

Vice Admiral William F. Halsey had recovered from a skin rash that had made him unavailable for the Battle of Midway in June 1942. When he was medically cleared for duty he was assigned to command a carrier task force in the South Pacific but his ships were not ready. On October 15, 1942 he took a plane to Noumea, within New Caledonia to familiarize himself with the area. Nimitz sent this message to King on October 16 and received the response that follows.

> 16 9937 CINCPAC to COMINCH for Admiral Ernest J King only. Ultra from Cincpac. Halsey his Chief of Staff and Intelligence Officer will be with Ghormley sixteenth our date. In view Ghormley's 160440 and other indications including some noted during my visit I have under consideration his relief by Halsey at earliest practicable time. Request your comment. If Halsey becomes Comsopac would expect him utilize Ghormley as long as needed.[305]

> 16 0245 COMINCH to CINCPAC for Admiral Chester Nimitz only personal and secret. Most secret. Your 16 9937 approved.[306]

He arrived at Noumea on October 18, but before he could report to Ghormley he was met by a member of Ghormley's staff and handed a sealed envelope. It was a message from Nimitz and it read:

> YOU WILL TAKE COMMAND OF THE SOUTH PACIFIC AREA AND SOUTH PACIFIC FORCES IMMEDIATELY.[307]

When Nimitz learned of Kurita's successful bombardment he concluded that the U.S. Marines on the island were barely holding on and the campaign was in jeopardy of being lost. He believed Ghormley had become dispirited and exhausted and decided to have him relieved by Halsey while he was in route to Noumea. Kurita's and Halsey's destiny would be intertwined from this point forward. Ghormley had serious doubts that the Marines could hold their position and

---

[305] Nimitz, Chester, *Chester Nimitz Gray Book*, Vol 2 at 895.

[306] Ibid.

[307] Frank, Richard B., *Guadalcanal* at 335.

didn't want to risk a repeat of the Bataan death march. Halsey was an aggressive and emotional commander and made it clear he had no intention to withdraw but would attack and establish control of the island. His actions would set up the fourth carrier battle of 1942.

CHAPTER 19: THE BATTLE OF SANTA CRUZ

Yamamoto would send the Combined Fleet South again in late October in another attempt to fight Mahan's decisive battle, using carrier air strength as the primary weapon. He continued with Corbett's method of division.

Selection and Maintenance of the Aim — Yamamoto's objective was to destroy U.S. naval forces in the Guadalcanal area.

Offensive — He was on the strategic offensive choosing the time the operation would take place. The carrier *Hiyo* had engine trouble and was not available for this battle.

Morale — of his officers and men was cautious optimism. Security would mainly fall on Japanese float planes from their surface units and land-based aircraft flying from Rabaul.

Surprise was lost due to the U.S. reading the JN-25 codes.

Economy of effort, flexibility, and *cooperation* were all compromised by the use of division vs. concentration. Yamamoto was planning to concentrate three carriers with *Shokaku, Zuikaku,* and *Zuiho* all operating together. *Junyo* was to act separately to the west of the Advance Force. *Junyo* was a converted passenger ship and she did not have the survivability of a warship, so by division and operating in the rear it was hoped she would not be discovered. Yamamoto made tankers available for refueling but the principal issue that would determine if sustained operations could be continued would be the survivability of his carrier aircraft.

JAPANESE FORCES[308]

Combined Fleet, Admiral Isoroku Yamamoto (at Truk)

Carrier Striking Force, Vice Admiral Chuichi Nagumo

Carriers, *Shokaku* (19 A6M2, 20 D3A1, 24 B5N2, 1 D4Y1) *Zuikaku* (19 A6M2, 23 D3A1, 20 B5N2), *Zuiho* (20 A6M2, 9 B5N2)

Heavy cruiser: *Kumano*

---

[308] Dull, Paul S., *The Battle History of the Imperial Japanese Navy 1941-1945* at 234-235.

Destroyers: *Hatsukaze, Yukikaze, Maikaze, Hamakaze, Amatsukaze, Tokitsukaze, Arashi, Teruzuki*

Advance Force, Vice Admiral Nobutake Kondo

Heavy cruisers: *Atago, Takao, Myoko, Maya*

Light cruiser: *Isuzu*

Destroyers: *Makinami, Kawakaze, Suzukaze, Naganami, Umikaze, Takanami*

Carrier Division 2, Rear Admiral Kakuji Kakuta

Carrier: *Junyo*, 20 A6Ms, 17 D3As, 7 B5Ns

Destroyers: *Kuroshio, Hayashio, Harusame, Murasame, Samidare, Oyashio, Yudachi*

Support Group, Vice Admiral Takeo Kurita

Battleships: *Kongo, Haruna*

Destroyers: *Oyashio, Kagero, Harusame, Murasame, Samidare, Yudachi*

Vanguard Force, Rear Admiral Hiroake Abe

Battleships: *Hiei, Kirishima*

Cruisers: *Tone, Chikuma, Suzuya*

Light cruiser: *Nagara*

Destroyers: *Makigumo, Akigumo, Urakaze, Kazagumo, Fugumo, Tanikaze, Isokaze*

Supply Group

Destroyer: *Nowaki*

Tankers: *Toho Maru, Kyokuto Maru, Kokuyo Maru, Toei Maru*

Outer Seas Force, Vice Admiral Gunichi Mikawa

Assault Unit: *Akatsuki, Ikazuchi, Shiratsuya*

Bombardment Unit, Rear Admiral Tomatsu Takama

Light cruiser: *Yura*

Destroyers: *Akizuki, Harusame, Yudachi, Murasame, Samidare*

Advance Expeditionary Force, Vice Admiral Teruhisa Komatsu

Submarine Force: *I-4, I-5, I-7, I-9, I-15, I-21, I-22, I-24, I-174, I-175, I-176*

October 25 the Main Body Carrier Striking Force was discovered by U.S. search planes so they turned to the north fearing a trap. The Vanguard force continued to the south. From his own reconnaissance Nagumo knew the U.S. task force was East of Rennell Island and north of Ndeni Island in the Santa Cruz group.

At 1800 on October 25 the carrier striking force turned south again but there was much anxiety about the upcoming battle. *Shokaku* and *Zuikaku* had thirty-eight operational A6Ms, 43 operational D3As, and 44 B5Ns ready for operations. In this battle *Zuiho* would provide fighter cover and search capability for *Shokaku* and *Zuikaku* and steam together with them. After several days of bombardments, air strikes from and against Henderson Field, assaults by the Army, the opposing carrier forces squared off to fight on 25-26 October.

The U.S. only had two operational carriers left. *Lexington* was sunk at Coral Sea and *Yorktown* at Midway. *Wasp* had been sunk by a submarine in September and *Saratoga* had been torpedoed and damaged by another submarine in the same month. *Ranger* was considered too small, too slow, and too lightly protected for service in the Pacific. That left only *Hornet* and *Enterprise* on the front lines. *Hornet* was in the area as the Japanese efforts began, while *Enterprise* came out from Pearl Harbor to join her.

Selection and Maintenance of the Aim – The U.S. objective was to inflict serious losses on the Imperial Japanese Navy and stop any replenishment mission to Guadalcanal. Moral after the Japanese bombardment by Kurita's battleships was quite low. Ghormley did not believe the Marines could hold and was relieved by Halsey who sent out a message to Kinkaid "Strike, repeat, strike!"[309] This would be the first test of that message. Security would be provided by the SBD scouting squadrons from his carriers as well as land-based planes from Henderson Field, Espiritu, and New Caledonia.

While surprise might be achieved the Japanese were fully aware that American carriers were in the area because as long as there were troops on Guadalcanal this nailed the American carriers to this geographical area. Economy of effort flexibility and cooperation were advantages for the Americans. *Hornet* and *Enterprise* were divided but they will only be ten miles apart so they could still mutually support each other. The U.S. was far more flexible with Henderson Field in U.S. control. The U.S. forces were on the strategic defensive and sustainability would rest on the attrition rate of the carrier planes, pilots and of the survivability of the ships themselves.

U.S. Forces[310]

Task Force 16, Rear Admiral Thomas C. Kinkaid

---

[309] Franks, Richard B. *Guadalcanal at* 336.

[310] Dull, Paul S., *The Battle History of the Imperial Japanese Navy 1941-1945* at 234-235.

Carrier, *Enterprise* (32 F4F, 23 SBD, 13 TBF)[311]

Battleship: *South Dakota*

Heavy cruisers: *Portland*

Light cruiser: *San Juan*

Destroyers: *Porter, Mahan, Cushing, Preston, Smith, Maury, Conyngham, Shaw*

Task Force 17, Rear Admiral George D. Murray

Carriers *Hornet*, 32 F4Fs, 24 SBDs, 13 TBFs

Heavy cruisers: *Northampton, Pensacola*

Light cruisers: *San Diego, Juneau*

Destroyers: *Morris Anderson, Hughes, Mustin, Russell, Barton*

Land-Based Aircraft Henderson Field: 16 x F4F-4, 20 x SBD-3, 2 x TBF-1, 6 x P-39, and 6 x P-400

Espiritu Santo/Efate: 24 x F4F, 39 x B-17E, 32 x PBY-5A, 5 x OS2U

New Caledonia: 15 x P-38, 46 x P-39, 16 x B26, 13 x Hudson

Kinkaid sailed northwest on October 25. *Enterprise* would handle inner patrols, combat air patrols and scouting while *Hornet* maintains a strike group on ready alert. Initially no contacts were made until 1120 when two battleships, four heavy cruisers, and seven destroyers were sighted by land-based air searches. At 1250 two carriers had been sighted about 360 miles from the American task forces. The battleship force was approximately 60-80 miles south of the carrier group so Kinkaid ordered more search planes to gather more intelligence on the enemy disposition. *Hornet* maintained her strike group.[312]

Enterprise sent out search groups at 1430 and by 1530 sent a strike group to follow up but ordered to return if no Japanese ships were found. The strike was made up of eleven F4Fs, twelve SBDs, and six TBFs. Then word came that the Japanese ships were heading north and would soon be out of range. The strike returned to *Enterprise* but six planes were lost due to low fuel. Five planes had been lost earlier due to routine operations.[313]

---

[311] Lundstrom says that the USN carriers had 74 F4Fs and 72 SBDs available, but only operated the numbers shown during the battle. Lundstrom, *First Team: Guadalcanal*, 348.

[312] Office of Naval Intelligence: *The Battle of Santa Cruz*.

[313] Ibid.

On Guadalcanal the Japanese Army was engaged with the Marines and broke the American line at Lunga Ridge and radioed that they had captured Henderson Field. This spurred the Japanese fleet to head south again.[314] At 0612 October 26, search planes from Espiritu Santo spotted the light carrier *Zuiho*. By 0730 two battleships had been spotted one heavy cruiser, and seven destroyers sighted. *Enterprise* launched sixteen SBDs to scout the contacts each loaded with a 500-lb. bomb and working in pairs. At 0750 Lt Comdr. James R. Lee and Lt. (jg) William E. Johnson, searching reported sighting *Shokaku* and *Zuikaku*. Lieut. Stockton B. Strong and Ens. Charles B. Irvine dive-bombed *Zuiho* with one bomb hit aft which prevented her from recovering aircraft but she could still launch her strike. They escaped five A6Ms that attempted to intercept. Nagumo ordered *Zuiho* to retire after she launched her strike.[315]

The use of SBDs as scouts enabled the U.S. to attack targets of opportunity. The Japanese tended to conduct searches with land-based air or float planes off their surface ships so they could maximize the carrier aircraft for strike missions. The use of SBDs as scouts paid off because one Japanese carrier was put out of the battle at the outset. The U.S. Navy in this battle had a large advantage in the way it managed its security. Ten of the SBDs found the main IJN carrier force or the Advance force. Ensign Howard R. Burnett and Ensign. Kenneth B. Miller, reported and attacked the Japanese cruiser *Tone*. Four of the six that found the carriers were intercepted by fighters, but no SBDs and no A6Ms went down.

Kinkaid ordered an attack group launched to strike *Shokaku* and what was thought to be *Zuikaku*, now steaming about 210 miles to the northwest of Task Force King. The strike was launched at 0830 in three waves. The first consisted of fifteen SBDs escorted by four F4Fs and six TBFs escorted by four F4Fs. The second wave took off at 0910 and consisted of nine SBDs, nine TBFs, with seven F4Fs as escorts. *Enterprise* began launching three SBDs, nine TBFs[316], and eight F4Fs as the third wave. In order to save time and fuel, each of the three waves of planes proceeded toward the target independently.[317]

At 0920 the first *Hornet* wave, which was in the lead, had progressed about sixty miles from the task force. The *Enterprise* aircraft were slightly behind to starboard, with four fighters on either bow about 1,000 feet above. Radar installed in

---

[314] Ibid.

[315] Ibid.

[316] One TBF was unarmed as a command aircraft for the strike.

[317] Office of Naval Intelligence: *The Battle of the Coral Sea*.

Shokaku picked up *Hornet* strike at seventy-eight miles. The Main Carrier Striking Force had twenty A6Ms close to the carriers at two different altitudes, plus three more headed south to protect the Vanguard force of battleships, cruisers and destroyers.

At 1015 *Hornet*'s SBDs reported an enemy task force consisting of two battleships, one heavy cruiser, one light cruiser, and seven destroyers was sighted. This was Abe's Vanguard Force. Three A6Ms over the Vanguard force attacked the SBD escort and the TBF escort in succession. They shot down one F4F from the SBD escort and one from the TBF escort while losing two A6Ms. The surviving F4Fs were separated from the strike aircraft, with two from the SBD escort aborting. The SBDs turned off their base course to avoid the A6Ms, heading for some clouds, but the TBFs continued straight on. The turn by the SBDs took them right to *Shokaku* and *Zuiho. Zuikaku* had separated to launch her contribution to the second Japanese strike was not spotted. The SBDs saw the Japanese carriers about thirty-five minutes after Japanese radar had detected the strike. While the SBDs were now headed toward their prime target, the TBFs did not hear their radio transmissions and never turned to follow them.

Within five minutes of sighting the carriers, the SBDs were under attack from the combat air patrol. A6Ms from *Shokaku*, *Zuikaku*, and *Zuiho* all joined in the attack, The A6Ms killed two SBDs and caused two more to abort. Four more A6Ms would join in during the SBDs withdraw. They lost one A6M to the SBDs' fire, one to a midair structural failure, and one damaged and later ditched. Five of the combat air patrol remained at low level to guard against torpedo planes, while two guarded *Zuikaku.*[318]

Ten out of eleven SBDs bombed *Shokaku*, starting about forty-three minutes after *Shokaku*'s radar had sighted the strike. The SBDs made at least three 1,000-pound bomb hits in the big carrier's hangar and on her AA guns. She was out of the battle with serious fires, but her strike aircraft had already left and her ability to steam was unimpeded. The eleventh SBD bombed a screening destroyer but missed. The SBDs were attacked by more A6Ms as they withdrew, but without losses to either side. Fifteen A6Ms had attacked the SBDs and their F4F escorts downing two SBDs and an F4F, causing another two SBDs and an F4F to abort with damage. Five A6Ms were lost.

---

[318] Heinz, Leonard, *Aircraft Carrier Defense in the Pacific War: The Carrier Battles of 1942* at 72-83.

The six TBFs from the *Hornet* strike searched in vain for the Japanese carriers and finally, running low on fuel, attacked the heavy cruiser *Suzuya* in the Vanguard group at 0931. Only five of the six torpedoes dropped; none hit.[319] The second strike launched from the American carriers came from *Enterprise*. It consisted of eight torpedo-armed TBFs, the air group commanders in an unarmed TBF, three SBDs, and eight escorting F4Fs. The small number of SBDs in the *Enterprise* strike reflected the fact that many had been detailed to conduct the morning search. The strike was at 6,000 feet and slowly climbing when the first Japanese strike spotted it a bit more than sixty miles out from the American carriers. The opportunity proved too much for the Japanese strike escort to resist, and nine A6Ms peeled off the ambush the U.S. strike.[320]

The result was a bloody brawl. Two TBFs and three F4Fs went down, as did four A6Ms. Two more TBFs and an F4F were forced to abort. All of the surviving A6Ms returned to their carriers rather than rejoining their strike, with one severely damaged. In addition to the aircraft downed and aborted, the A6M ambush also caused the escort F4Fs to shed their drop tanks prematurely. The F4F had a significantly shorter combat range than the SBD or the TBF. The fighters relied on auxiliary fuel drop tanks to stay with the strike aircraft. With the escorts' drop tanks gone before the fuel in them had been fully used, the strike leader had to decide whether to press on without the escorts or turn back when the escorts had to. The decision was for the latter, with the result that the strike did not search long or far enough to locate the Japanese carriers.[321]

As with *Hornet*'s torpedo bombers, the *Enterprise* strike attacked the Japanese Vanguard force. The SBDs dive-bombed the heavy cruiser *Tone* resulting in one near miss, while the four TBFs with torpedoes tried for another heavy cruiser, *Suzuya*. One torpedo refused to be dropped, the other three missed. The only combat air patrol opposition was encountered by the SBDs, which were attacked by three A6M without result.[322]

The last U.S. strike of the day flew from *Hornet*. It consisted of nine SBDs, nine bomb-armed TBFs, one unarmed TBF with the air group commander, and seven F4Ds for escort. *Hornet* SBDs selected targets from among the Vanguard

---

[319] Ibid. One torpedo failed to release.

[320] Heinz, Leonard, *Aircraft Carrier Defense in the Pacific War: The Carrier Battles of 1942* at 72-83.

[321] Ibid.

[322] Ibid.

forces. They attacked the heavy cruiser *Tone* without result. The TBFs and their escort continued to search for a while further, but turned back to bomb the same heavy cruiser attacked by the SBDs of the *Enterprise* and next *Hornet* strikes. Nine TBFs executed a glide-bombing attack, dropping thirty-six 500 pound bombs. *Tone*'s detailed action report sights being attacked by fifty-one planes from 0857-1000. The TBFs were intercepted by two A6Ms before attacking, but escorting F4Fs ended the threat by killing one before they could score against the strike planes. The result of the American strike was ten A6Ms shot down, five F4Fs shot down and one forced to abort, with two SBDs shot down and one forced to abort. Two TBFs shot down and two forced to abort.[323]

The Japanese first strike consisted of sixty-four aircraft. Twenty-one A6Ms, twenty-one D3As and twenty-two B5Ns. Two B5Ns were unarmed so that they could scout the U.S. formations and radio back intelligence to Admiral Nagumo. Nine A6Ms separated from the main group to attack the U.S. strike seen heading for the Japanese carriers. This left only four to protect the B5Ns and eight to protect the D3As. The combat air patrol was made up of fifteen F4Fs from *Hornet* and twenty-two F4Fs from *Enterprise* at 10,000 feet. The two American carrier groups were operating ten miles apart with the weather being partly cloudy. Communication failures hampered the U.S. combat air patrol. The strike was first seen on radar at seventy miles but this was not communicated until the strike was thirty-five miles out. The American fighters once again were too low and needed to climb for altitude. The D3As approached at 17,000 feet and the B5Ns were at 14,000 feet and the Japanese A6Ms fighter escort was at 21,000 feet.[324]

Hornet's Fighter Direction Officer all of *Hornet*'s F4F fighters engaged the D3As as they began to descend to 12,000 feet. Twelve of the fifteen actually intercepted and attacked shooting down four D3As, with the loss of one F4F shot down by the D3As. Twenty-one of *Enterprise*'s combat air patrol were able to intercept the B5Ns but only shot down one before they made an attack. They would engage the D3As after they attacked. Both the D3As and B5Ns made a coordinated attack on *Hornet*. The surviving D3As split into three groups and the first group of six planes began their dives. One was shot down by anti-aircraft guns before it released, its bomb and one was shot down by an F4F while it was in its dive prior to releasing its bomb but the last four all made an effective attack hitting *Hornet* four times. One of the first dive bombers scored a hit on the starboard side of the after

[323] Ibid.

[324] Ibid.

end of the flight deck. Then came two near-hits on the starboard side abreast of the bridge. At the same instant two 500-pound bombs landed on the after part of the ship, one penetrating to the fourth deck before exploding, and the other detonating on piercing the flight deck. A third heavy bomb reached the third or fourth deck and exploded near the forward messing compartment, starting fierce fires and killing a number of personnel.[325]

Next a dive bomber with machine guns blazing crashed into the stack, spraying gasoline over the signal bridge, and plunged part way through the flight deck in the neighborhood of the first bomb hit. This suicide plane apparently was armed with one 500-pound and two 100-pound bombs. One 100-pound bomb demolished the signal enclosure, causing many casualties, and partly destroyed the stack. The plane itself, and probably the other 100-pound bomb, exploded on piercing the flight deck, causing a large fire there and in the compartment below. Fortunately the 500-pound bomb proved to be a dud. The fire on and under the flight deck burned for two hours, finally being extinguished by the efforts of a bucket brigade which carried foamite to the scene since all water pressure had been lost at 1015. This dive bombing attack had been delivered from the port quarter. Almost simultaneously a torpedo attack developed from the starboard.[326]

Six bombers of the second group began their dives. None were successful at hitting *Hornet* but one crashed into the ship having been hit by anti-aircraft fire. The third group of five D3As was intercepted by the *Enterprise*'s F4Fs shooting down one D3A before it could release its bomb. The remaining four all dove on *Hornet* but scored no hits and two were shot down by the F4Fs during withdraw.

The B5Ns split into two groups of eleven planes and nine planes to make an anvil attack on *Hornet*. The first group of eleven B5Ns were escorted by four A6Ms. The second group of nine did not have an escort. The A6Ms did their best to protect the bombers shooting down one F4F. Nine of the original eleven B5Ns headed for *Hornet*. Two B5Ns were shot down by anti-aircraft guns before they dropped their torpedoes. Seven B5Ns dropped their torpedoes scoring two hits at 1015. The two hits in the engineering spaces disrupted all power and communications and caused a 10½° list to starboard which slowly improved to 7°-8°. Two more B5Ns fell to anti-aircraft guns as they withdrew.

Two B5Ns attempted an attack on a heavy cruiser with one being shot down by anti-aircraft guns before it dropped its torpedo and the last B5N dropped it

---

[325] Office of Naval Intelligence: *The Battle of Santa Cruz*.

[326] Ibid.

torpedo but it missed and an SBD shot it down as it withdrew. Two minutes later, an unarmed and flaming torpedo plane attempted a suicide dive from dead ahead. It miscalculated its approach and crashed into the port forward gun gallery, exploding just outboard of the No. 1 elevator shaft, the wreckage lodging in the pit.[327]

Of the second group of nine one was lost to a F4F from *Enterprise*, three aborted due to damage, two were downed by anti-aircraft guns and four dropped their torpedoes but all missed. One B5N attempted to crash into the *Hornet* but fell short and into the sea. Eight A6Ms engaged seven F4Fs with two A6Ms and two F4Fs being shot down. One A6M escorting the B5N torpedo planes was shot down either by an F4F or anti-aircraft guns or a combination of the two. A total of thirty-six F4Fs were able to engage Japanese strike aircraft; all fifteen of the *Hornet's* and seventeen of the *Enterprise's* made intercepts. Anti-aircraft fire shot down seven B5Ns, four were lost to F4Fs, and three were damaged and forced to abort. Anti-aircraft fire shot down two D3As and F4F fighters shot down five D3As.[328]

By 1021 *Hornet* was dead in the water, with several large fires burning, a decided list to starboard, many of her personnel killed, many more injured, and power and communications so disrupted that all efforts to reestablish them failed. Unless *Hornet* could get moving again, she would be a sitting duck for the next Japanese strike which appeared fifteen minutes after the last attacks from the first strike. This strike actually came on as two waves, the first of nineteen D3As and five A6Ms and the second of sixteen torpedo-armed B5Ns, one B5N search and contact plane, with four A6Ms as escort. *Enterprise*'s radar picked up the first wave only about forty-five miles from her task force.[329]

The second strike's objective was *Enterprise* not *Hornet.* The dive bomber found *Enterprise* with eight F4Fs at altitude over the carrier and another thirteen low. Altitude issues again plagued the combat air patrol. The D3As were coming it at 17,000 feet, while the high combat air patrol was at 10,000 feet. Four of the F4Fs were dispatched to make a distant intercept but only two managed to engage shooting down one D3A. But most of the combat air patrol was well under the

---

[327] Ibid.

[328] Two B5Ns are shared with F4F fighters.

[329] Heinz, Leonard, *Aircraft Carrier Defense in the Pacific War: The Carrier Battles of 1942* at 72-83.

dive bombers and clawing for altitude when the D3As tipped over, about fifteen minutes after *Enterprise*'s radar first saw them.[330]

What the combat air patrol lacked, the AA fire from *Enterprise* and her screen supplied. The carrier had just been refitted with sixteen 40-mm automatic anti-aircraft guns, and these immediately proved their worth. Anti-aircraft fire downed the first four of the first seven D3As to dive, while none of the seven scored any hits. Three F4Fs that had climbed up from low altitude joined the fray as the D3As continued to dive in, dropping another D3A before it could attack and one more after attacking. Anti-aircraft fire continued to prove its worth, killing another three D3As in their dives. But the D3As also began to score, making two hits and a damaging near miss.[331]

The A6Ms apparently never engaged and the F4Fs did not pursue the departing D3As. The strike left ten of its dive bombers behind: three down to the combat air patrol and seven to the anti-aircraft fire. One of the bomb hits passed through the bow structure of *Enterprise* before exploding, doing little damage. The second hit was potentially much more serious, detonating in the ship's hanger were aircraft were being armed and fueled. While the hit started fires, the hanger crews were able to jettison any aircraft in danger of adding to the flames. In this they were aided by *Enterprise*'s open hanger structure, which permitted the crews to roll aircraft over the edge of the hanger deck and directly into the sea. The hit also had the more lasting effects, jamming the forward elevator in its up position.[332]

Enterprise's radar detected the B5N wave of the second strike about twenty minutes after the last of the D3As had attacked, although it took another five minutes for the radar plot to confirm that the sighting was an incoming strike. The combat air patrol fighters were now running low on both fuel and ammunition. It seems that none of them had landed since the first raid, when all but five had fought. Five had also fought in the second raid, with at least one of those five having fought both raids. As the B5Ns swept in, *Enterprise* had eleven F4Fs climbing over her and another fourteen orbiting close by at low altitude. Weather favored the raid, as it would be attacking through a squall quickly making up to the

---

[330] Ibid.

[331] Ibid.

[332] Ibid.

northwest of the *Enterprise* task force. It formed into two sections of eight B5Ns each before diving through the squall.[333]

Eight of the combat air patrol headed out to try to intercept the raid. Six of fighters (one without ammo) managed to contact one group of eight B5Ns and their A6M escorts, downing one B5N and crippling another before the four escorting A6Ms intervened. The A6Ms and the F4Fs dueled for a time, but neither side scored against the other. The B5Ns pressed on, with the crippled aircraft crashing a screen destroyer, one other B5N killed by *Enterprise* anti-aircraft as it attacked from dead astern, and five B5Ns dropping torpedoes on *Enterprise*'s port quarter. The carrier managed to dodge all of their torpedoes, which had begun dropping less than fifteen minutes after the raid was first seen on radar.[334]

A low F4F and anti-aircraft combined to splash a B5N from the other group of eight B5Ns. Two of the group attacked *South Dakota*, with one of them being downed by anti-aircraft before it could make an effective drop. Five attacked *Enterprise*, with one killed by anti-aircraft after attacking and two more falling to F4Fs while trying to withdraw. None scored any hits on *Enterprise*, although three of their torpedoes dudded against a screening heavy cruiser at the end of their runs.[335]

As with the other raids, the torpedo plane raid resulted in about half the strike planes lost over the U.S. task force. In this case, one B5N crash-dived a destroyer after damage, one was shared by combat air patrol and AA, three went down to CAP, and three to anti-aircraft fire. In addition to the obvious point that combat uses up ammunition, combat flying also consumes fuel at a rapid rate.[336]

The *Junyo* also had a strike. This took the form of seventeen D3As and twelve A6Ms, which appeared on *Enterprise*'s radar about fifteen minutes after the last B5N of the previous strike left the immediate area of her task force. The radar sighting had the strike only twenty miles away, with the first D3As diving in only about six minutes after the radar sighting. Earlier warning would have made little difference, as most of the combat air patrol was now very low on fuel and with little or no ammo.[337]

---

[333] Ibid.

[334] Ibid.

[335] Ibid.

[336] Ibid.

[337] Ibid.

None of the D3As were intercepted before they attacked, but all had to deal with low cloud cover that made target selection difficult and resulted in shallow dives through holes in the overcast. The first eight D3As to attack did manage to find *Enterprise* through a hole in the murk, but none of their bombs struck home. One damaging near miss opened some seams and caused some minor flooding. Anti-aircraft downed three of the D3As in their dives. None of the remaining nine dive bombers targeted *Enterprise*; four dove against *South Dakota* for one hit while five dove against *San Juan* for one hit (which passed right though the ship before exploding under her keel) and one damaging near miss. All nine attacked out of a low overcast that blunted the effectiveness of anti-aircraft fire.[338]

The D3As had a rougher time withdrawing at low level, where they were attacked by both combat air patrol fighters and F4Fs returning from strike escort duties, and seven SBDs and TBFs. Five D3As fell in the withdrawal. While it is hard to apportion credit for these victories, it is likely that most of the dive bombers fell to four returning escort F4Fs, as these aircraft had the most ammo remaining. The escort A6Ms had their own victories at this time, downing one F4F and one TBF. Another F4F was lost to anti-aircraft. Once again the IJN lost about half of its strike aircraft for little gain. Eight of seventeen D3As went down close to the task force; three more would ditched due to damage.[339]

That concluded the strikes against *Enterprise*, as the ship withdrew from the battle area and was not spotted again. More IJN strikes pounded *Hornet* and sealed her fate. Six B5Ns from *Junyo* put another torpedo into her at the cost of two B5Ns down to anti-aircraft. That was followed by a dive bombing attack from two D3As that scored a damaging near miss and resulted in a decision to abandon ship. Six B5Ns from *Zuikaku* followed that up with a level bombing attack from 8,000 feet that results in one hit and a series of misses astern. The final attack by four of *Junyo's* D3As resulted in yet another hit that sparked a large fire. The Americans attempted to scuttle the battered ship, but although five-inch gunfire set her on fire from stem to stern, she refused to sink. The Japanese completed the job the following day, as Japanese forces swept south to exploit their victory.[340]

Looking at the entire series of Japanese strikes, eighteen Japanese aircraft were shot down by the F4Fs, twenty-four aircraft were shot down by antiaircraft fire with three more ditching as they attempted to withdraw. One was shared be-

---

[338] Ibid.

[339] Ibid.

[340] Ibid.

tween anti-aircraft fire and a F4F. This totaled forty-six aircraft out of ninety aircraft that attacked the U.S. ships. However, only one of these aircraft shot down was an A6M the other forty-five came from the sixty-six attack aircraft. Leaving only twenty-one attack aircraft from all four carriers remaining. The attrition of the Japanese attack aircraft was 69% and how many of these that did return but were too badly shot up for further use is unknown. After one strike four Japanese carriers became combat-ineffective as their air wings had been demolished.

The American combat air patrol and fighter direction still assumed torpedo bombers would come in at low altitude and this left their fighters too low to engage the Japanese dive bombers. This handicapped the F4Fs with their slow rate of climb. The great majority of the Japanese bombers were able to make attacks.[341] What the Navy was learning was that it was not the number of ships within a screen that mattered but the concentration of guns close to a target ship that mattered. Battleships with four secondary gun directors could engage four aircraft simultaneously.

The new fast battleships had the most concentrated anti-aircraft gun batteries making them the most efficient aircraft killers.

This continued a trend begun at Eastern Solomons, where battleships and anti-aircraft cruisers were incorporated close enough to the carrier that even 20-mm guns on the screening ships could effectively engage raiders. The performance of *Enterprise* and her screen was a particularly good example of effective maneuver combined with an effective anti-aircraft screen.[342]

---

[341] Ibid.

[342] Ibid.

CHAPTER 20: THE NAVAL BATTLE OF GUADALCANAL

For eleven months the carrier fleets of the United States and Japan had fought each other to a draw. Each side had one operational carrier in *Junyo* for Japan and *Enterprise* for the United States. Four great carrier battles had sunk thirteen naval combatants combined.[343] The purpose behind Mahan's decisive battle was to annihilate the enemy so that the vanquished could no longer contest the seas of the victor and in theory the war would be over and the killing stopped. The stalemate at Guadalcanal had tied the great fleets to the South Pacific. By so doing the U.S. carriers broke one of the principles of sea power by being attached to an invasion, which prevented their ability to roam. In the process the United States lost two more fleet carriers and submarines had crippled a third in the *Saratoga*.

For Yamamoto's conviction that carrier warfare would be more efficient than the battle fleet had been a colossal failure in that it produced a war of attrition and the type of war he most wanted to avoid.

The attrition on air wings had been enormous, making carriers into single strike platforms unable to sustain operations.

Sustainability, the tenth principle in the operational art, was the key to naval power and carriers were too vulnerable. Yet, the question of who would control Guadalcanal remained. Yamamoto would attempt to regain Henderson Field one more time in early November when he attempted to bring in the 38th Division of the Japanese Army. This would result in the Naval Battle of Guadalcanal fought from November 13-15, 1942. The selection and maintenance of the aim remained the same to bring in reinforcement to Guadalcanal and sweep any enemy naval units from the area. Yamamoto and his staff focused on Henderson

---

[343] *Shoho, Lexington, Kikuzuki, Sims, Akagi, Kaga, Hiryu, Soryu, Mikuma, Hammond, Yorktown, Ryujo, Hornet*. Technically *Hammond* and *Yorktown* were sunk by submarine and *Hornet* sunk by surface ships so ten were sunk by airpower, Carrier warfare was inefficient at producing decisive battles of annihilation.

Field as the most important geographical area to secure for victory but this was not the most important geographical area.

The most critical geographical area was Iron Bottom Sound. Whoever controlled the sound could suppress the airfield and reinforce their army ashore while denying access to Guadalcanal to the enemy. The Sound was an extension of territory and whomever seized this territory held the key to final victory of the campaign. Neither side was willing to stay forward deployed so that this geographical position was under control 24 hours a day. This resulted in a war of attrition on land, air, and sea. Both sides were striking at each other but neither side was willing to establish blockade and maintain forward deployment.

Admiral Yamamoto would once again send two battleships with a large screen to bombard Henderson Field. This time it would be Abe's *Hiei* and *Kirishima* with *Kongo* and *Haruna* serving as distant cover with *Junyo*. Yamamoto was still on the offensive choosing November 14-15 to reinforce the Japanese Army using eleven transports of 77,606 tons with supplies for 30,000 men, 31,500 artillery shells, and 7,000 troops. Admiral Raizo Tanaka would command the transport force with eleven destroyers. The first part of the operation would be to bombard Henderson Field on November 13. This force consisted of the battleships *Hiei* and *Kirishima*, Light cruiser *Nagara*, and destroyers *Ikazuchi, Inazuma, Akatsuki, Yudachi, Harasame, Amatsukaze, Teruzuki, Yukikaze, Asagumo, Murasame,* and *Samidare*. A Japanese appreciation prepared in late October observed:

> It must be said that success or failure in recapturing Guadalcanal Island and the vital naval battle related to it, is the fork in the road which leads to victory for them or for us.[344]

Admiral Turner had recently resupplied the Marines but left a significant portion of his screening force behind to confront the Japanese forces under the command of Admiral Callaghan in the heavy cruiser *San Francisco* and Admiral Scott in the light cruiser *Atlanta*. The heavy cruiser *Portland*, light cruisers *Helena, Juneau,* and destroyers *Cushing, Laffey, Sterett, O'Bannon, Aaron Ward, Barton, Monssen,* and *Fletcher* rounded out Task Force 64.

The night of November 12 Abe's force had to endure a tropical storm that made visibility very low as it closed on Savo Island. The storm also broke up his formations. As they began to enter the sound Admiral Hiroake Abe was unsure of where all his ships were and the visibility remained very low. Admiral Callaghan in *San Francisco* made the same error Scott did in the Battle of Cape Esperance by

[344] Franks, Richard B., *Guadalcanal* at 492.

not placing his flag on the ship with the most advanced radar. As messages began to come in they did more to confuse him than help him. The two forces collided and when *Hiei* opened her search lights on the cruiser *Atlanta* the range had been reduced to 4,500 yards. Instantly *Atlanta* opened fire on *Hiei* and in return the battleship fired at *Atlanta* wrecking her forward gun battery. *Laffey* avoided a collision with *Hiei* by only a few feet and then raked her superstructure and bridge only to be torpedoed and raked by *Kirishima* as she passed *Hiei*. Abe was wounded, ordered an immediate withdrawal and cancelled the bombardment mission. *Hiei* was hit on her forward lookout platform, anti-aircraft platform, machine gun platform, radio room, and bridge. Fires were ignited and her pagoda superstructure acted as a huge smoke stack drawing the flames up.

Kirishima passed *San Francisco* on her starboard side smashing her with her main and secondary guns and killing Admiral Callaghan. The light cruiser *Nagara* passed *San Francisco* on her port side firing simultaneously with *Kirishima*. *San Francisco* hit *Atlanta* by accident killing Admiral Scott. *Portland* was struck by a torpedo that jammed her rudders. *Barton* was cut in half by a torpedo and quickly sank. *Juneau* was hit by a torpedo that broke her back but she remained afloat. *Atlanta* absorbed over fifty hits and one torpedo and was dead in the water. *Cushing* was sunk and *Helena* was hit six times by 14" gunfire. *Aaron Ward* was crippled. *Akatsuki* was sunk, *Yudachi* was crippled. *Helena* reported to Halsey:

> November (GCT) HELENA to COMTASKFOR 67. Info COMSOPAC etc. 14 0001 TG 67.4 engaged apparently 2 enemy forces containing BBs and cruisers plus DDs to SE of SAVO about 0124 bearing 312 range 27100. We approached in long column 4 DDs, 1 CLAA, 2 CAs, 1 CL, 1 CLAA, 4 DDs via LENGO CHANNEL on 280 along north coast close in. Changed course to about 310 True then 000 then 315 at 0137, then 270 closing to about 3000 yards of enemy. Enemy force believed coming in to south of SAVO from NW in 2 or 3 groups. Bearing and distance of groups by sail George radar from HELENA: 5 ships 250 True range 4200 course 120 speed 20, 6 ships 315 True range 7000, 4 large ships 290 true range 10000. At 0143 DDs instructed to launch torpedo attack. At 0145 ordered to stand by to fire. At range of about 3000 yards to group on port bow while turning to course 270 commenced firing at 0148. Enemy turned on searchlights and commended firing at short range just prior to our opening fire. 0158 changed course to 000 on signal and speed 28 knots. ATLANTA fell out to left and believed on fire at 0210. SAN FRANCISCO hit heavily especially bridge area and Rear Admiral Callaghan and all staff but one killed. JUNEAU hit by torpedo forward engine room type unknown. PORTLAND believed hit by torpedo and lost steering control prior to 0218. Mêlée resulted in which events uncertain but destroyers both sides very active. Numerous ships afire including one large ship capsized and one large BB or CA stopped and completely enveloped in flames and passed both close aboard. At 0212 attempted to assemble forces remaining. At 0226 gave course 092 True speed 18 Form 18 to ships able

> to comply. At 0240 contacted SAN FRANCISCO on port bow and she formed up. FLETCHER reported in SEALARK CHANNEL. STERRETT and O'BANNON in LENGO CHANNEL. At 0310 reported condition PORTLAND to radio TULAGI and requested tow and air coverage. After transiting SEALARK destroyers formed screen. At daylight picked up JUNEAU in INDISPENSABLE STRAIT near MALAITA Island. Instructed to join up. Took course to southward and speed 10 knots until SAN FRANCISCO made temporary repairs. Transferred medical assistance to SAN FRANCISCO and sent O'BANNON to position to transmit report on force position and intentions. O'BANNON rejoined at 1530. At 0826 course 180 speed 17 knots Zigzag No. 8 all speed JUNEAU could make. At 1101 torpedo fired from about 260 relative running on or near surface passed astern of HELENA and ahead SAN FRANCISCO and hit JUNEAU (then down 4 feet by head) on port side of fantail (location of hit debatable but aft) as she was Zigging 15 deg. to the right. JUNEAU was third ship in formation about 800 yards on quarter of SAN FRANCISCO due to steering difficulty using one screw and as requested by commanding officer. There was a single enormous explosion filling the area with debris and large cloud of yellow black and brown smoke. Debris fell to such an extent and volume. As to cause belief of high level bombing attack. Remaining ships increased to maximum speed and radical course changes.[345]

When *Hiei* attempted to withdraw an 8-inch salvo hit her stern just aft of her steering compartments where during her modernization they added thirty feet to her stern. Water entered the motor room to her rudders which shorted out. Manual steering was immediately applied but communication with the bridge had been cut off so the men did not know what direction the ship should take.[346] The *Hiei*'s crew placed the rudders on the centerline but then flooding of the manual steering compartment made this impossible and the rudders slammed hard to starboard as the crew vacated the rapidly flooding compartment. In addition there was an unexploded shell aft wedged into her hull. *Hiei* circled to starboard only 1000 meters from Savo Island. The *Kirishima* left her sister as ordered and headed north. [347]

The sun rose at 0407 and *Hiei* saw the crippled destroyer *Aaron Ward* at 24,000 meters and opened fire. After four salvos the American destroyer had disappeared. Her captain told the crew the enemy warship had been sunk to raise the crew's morale. At 0505 twenty aircraft attacked and scored two bomb hits and one tor-

---

[345] Nimitz, Chester. *Chester Nimitz Gray Book*, Vol II at 1000. The *Juneau* was hit by torpedoes from submarine I-26 that detonated her magazines. The five Sullivan brothers were on board and none survived.

[346] Kazuyoshi, Miyazaki, *Tragedy at Savo, Hiei* under concentrated fire at 3.

[347] Ibid at 4.

pedo hit. The bombs wrecked her boat deck and the torpedo hit amidships did not cause significant flooding.[348] *Kirishima* was ordered back to help tow *Hiei* and she turned around at 0950. B-17s attacked *Hiei* without result. The third air attack resulted in another torpedo hit that blew part of her bulge up over her gunwale and flooded her forward windlass room. With each air attack she was forced to get underway again and the aft steering compartments would re-flood compromising all efforts to get the rudders unjammed and remove the unexploded projectile. Abe had enough and decided to have *Hiei* scuttled. Her captain refused the order initially but eventually gave the order to abandon ship. The crew vacated the ship in an orderly fashion to waiting destroyers. She was listing ten degrees to starboard. Once the crew was off he ordered a few men to flood the ships shell magazines and leave the ship open. She would eventually founder on her own. At some point before 2300 hours she disappeared.

Mikawa with *Chokai, Maya,* and *Suzuya* bombarded Henderson Field on the night of November 13 unopposed. They fired 1,370 shells at the field but were unable to suppress it completely. *Enterprise* aircraft attacked Tanaka's transports sinking seven of the eleven transports. With four transports continuing south Yamamoto ordered Kondo with *Atago, Takao,* and *Kirishima* to once again bombard Henderson Field. Kondo issued the following battle instructions for Emergency Bombardment Force:

> Tonight we face a high probability to encounter a number of enemy cruisers and destroyers in the vicinity of Savo Island; in that case the bombardment [of the airfield] will be temporarily suspended until the enemy surface force has been destroyed. The primary objective [i.e. the bombardment] will be realized thereafter.[349]

Kondo based on his intelligence reports expected to be confronted with two U.S. heavy cruisers and four destroyers which had been sighted before nightfall. Up until this time the American battleships had always stayed close to the American carriers and there had been no reason to expect anything had changed. Kondo sent Hashimoto on *Sendai* to sweep the northern entrance to the sound and ordered Kimura in *Nagara* ahead to intercept any U.S. forces within the sound. By Japanese doctrine these restricted waters were the domain of the light cruiser and destroyer. He would keep his two heavy cruisers and the battleship *Kirishima* clear of the action while U.S. forces were in the area were swept away by the lighter forces. Hashimoto sighted what he believed as two heavy cruisers and four de-

---

[348] The *Kongo* class amidships and outboard her boilers rooms had five liquid loaded compartments of fuel. If these were ruptured she would not have lost any reserve buoyance.

[349] Goldstein, Donald M. And Dillon, Katheryn V. *Pacific War Papers* at 315.

stroyers and this report confirmed what Kondo had expected. With this false perception he felt reassured the light cruisers and destroyers had enough firepower to deal with such a threat. Initially the two U.S. battleships fired on *Sendai* and she made smoke and evaded the fire. Hashimoto had sent one of his destroyers *Ayanami* on a counter-clockwise course around Savo Island while he conducted a clock-wise course. This resulted in *Ayanami* engaging the lead U.S. destroyers slightly ahead of Admiral Susumu Kimura's light cruiser and destroyers.[350]

Halsey stripped *Enterprise* of her battleship screen and sent Admiral Willis Lee with *Washington* and *South Dakota* and four destroyers to stop Admiral Nobutake Kondo and control Iron Bottom Sound. This was a tactical blockade of Iron Bottom Sound to deny the use of passage to the Japanese. Lee's forces had never trained or worked together prior to this battle. This impacted their compliance with the principle of cooperation.

Lee placed Commander Thomas Fraser in *Walke* in command of the destroyer screen simply due to the fact he was senior to the other destroyer commanders. *Benson* and *Preston* lacked radar and so were placed in the middle with *Gwin* last in line. *Gwin* was designated to fire star shells and illuminate enemy forces. The destroyers were deployed in a simple line ahead formation with each destroyer separated by 500 yards; this allowed the inexperienced commanders to stay grouped together. Lee placed these ships 5,000 yards ahead of his battleships which were separated from each other by another 2,000 yards. This force would steam in a clockwise course first to the west and then north around Savo Island and then down its eastern shore heading south and then back again to the west, thus patrolling both entrances to Iron Bottom Sound.

Lee's role as the officer in tactical command was that of a coordinator at the head of a collection of independent formations.[351] Success would depend on subordinate officer's' understanding of the general plan and their role within this plan, however, they were to use their own initiative to fight toward a successful conclusion. Lee's intelligence reports indicated his force was going to be outnumbered and the battle that took shape was the first battleship vs battleship action of

---

[350] *Sendai* Brief action report JT1 National Archives and Ballard, Robert D. and Rick Archbold. *Lost Ships of Guadalcanal*. Warner/Madison Press Books, 1993.

[351] Commander Task Force SIXTY-FOUR: Report of Night Action, Task Force SIXTY-FOUR—November 14-15, 1942

the war.[352] What Lee experienced this night would shape his decisions in the future course of the war, which lends extra importance to the details of this battle.

Lieutenant Imamura Ichiro noted tension on the bridge of Kondo's flagship *Atago* as battle reports kept coming in. At 0024 *Atago* received a report from Commander Eiji Sakuma of *Ayanami* that she was beginning her attack. Soon after Sakuma's report Kimura on *Nagara* reported one enemy heavy cruiser and three destroyers and that he was attacking and opening fire with his force.[353]

Commander Fraser on *Walke*, still the lead U.S. destroyer, ordered a turn to 270 degrees true and reduced speed from twenty-three knots to seventeen knots to search for the enemy at 0024. This turn to the west was not ordered by Lee nor does it appear that Fraser announced this new heading to any of the other ships behind him.[354] At 0026 Fraser spotted *Ayanami* and ordered *Walke* to open fire. She fired for two minutes at a range of 11,000 yards and Fraser believed his target blew up under heavy concentrated fire. At 0028 he increased *Walke*'s speed to twenty-six knots and shifted to a new target (*Nagara*) bearing one point to starboard, range 7,500, yards and resumed rapid fire. Flames were reported on this target along with heavy black smoke before it disappeared behind the northwest point of Savo Island. At 0031 fire was shifted to port. Commander Fraser had mistaken the U.S. battleships to his rear as enemy warships and opened fire on *Washington*.[355]

At 0032 Commander Fraser observed the destroyer *Preston* astern explode. Japanese gun flashes were coming from starboard and *Walke* was being straddled by enemy gunfire. At 0033 a torpedo smashed into the bow at frame 45 and a salvo of shells hit the radio room, foremast, and in the vicinity of the number three gun. The torpedo explosion blew the forecastle and a section of the superstructure deck completely off as far aft as the bridge. Fire broke out throughout the forward section and the forward 20 mm magazine exploded. The bulkhead of the forward fire room was buckled, as was the main deck amidships. All engines were ordered stop immediately and Fraser gave word to abandon ship, as *Walke* was sinking fast by the head. Only two life rafts were left in condition to be freed. Depth charges

---

[352] *Washington*, Action Report, Night of November 14-15, 1942.

[353] *Atago* DAR No. 8 12 to 14 Nov 1942 (submitted 18 Nov 1942) and From Vanguard Force Flagship *Atago* and the Defense Battles of Guadalcanal Island (*Zenshin-butai Kikan Atago to Ga-tô Kôbôsen*) by Paymaster Lieutenant Imamura Ichirô, pp. 333-349).

[354] *Walke*, Surface Engagement with Japanese Forces, November 15, 1942—report of.

[355] *Walke*, Surface Engagement with Japanese Forces, November 15, 1942—report of.

were checked and reported set on safe. At 0036 the ship disappeared, stern last. The bow detached and remained afloat. At 0037 an unknown number of depth charges exploded killing and seriously injuring many men in the water. Total killed or missing in action six officers and seventy-six enlisted men.[356]

On *Benham* Lt. Commander John Taylor noticed that his ship had worked 300 yards to the right of *Walke*. He ordered a thirty degree turn to port so that his ship did not enter *Walke*'s line of fire. *Benham* opened fire on *Ayanami* using radar ranges and gun flashes as points of aim as the Japanese destroyer passed the U.S. line in the opposite direction. The target's silhouette merged with Savo but was seen burning as the rear destroyers took her under fire. Taylor watched the action behind his ship and saw one of the trailing destroyers hit *Ayanami*. He also noted what he thought was a small cruiser off to port and aft firing at the rear destroyers as well.[357] Then new ships appeared forward and to starboard so *Benham* checked fire and then shifted to these new targets. Black smoke soon appeared and the enemy ships disappeared. Just as his ship reached a position behind *Walke* he realized the lead destroyer had continued to veer to port onto a course of 270 degrees west. Suddenly *Walke* suffered an explosion, lost speed, and began to sink by the bow. Taylor ordered hard port rudder to avoid hitting the lead ship but just as she passed *Walke* at 0034 *Benham* took a torpedo on the starboard side only a few yards from the tip of her bow. The long lance torpedo was probably from one of *Nagara*'s destroyers and blew the bow off as far back to the forward bulkhead of turret one magazine. The ship rose out of the water four feet, heeled to port and then rolled thirty degrees to starboard. Her speed fell from twenty-seven knots to five knots and the shock of the explosion ripped through the ship, breaking her back above the forward boiler room. As *Nagara* and her destroyers passed her by, Lt. Commander Taylor ordered hard starboard rudder and also ordered the port engine room to standard speed which drove the ship into a circle. By the time she completed the circle the battle had passed her so she slowly withdrew to the west and away from the battle. Luckily, none of her crew had been killed and all would survive the battle.[358]

Preston did not have any fire-control radar and her search radar had been turned off before the battle. Commander Stormes kept track of the enemy formations visually. Commander Stormes reported at 0025 that *Walke* opened fire

---

[356] Ibid.

[357] The turn to the west placed the U.S. battleships to port and aft of the lead destroyers. There were no Japanese warships to the port side of the U.S. formation.

[358] *Benham*, Report of Action November 14-15, 1942.

and that by 0027 *Preston* had sighted a ship off the southern tip of Savo Island (this would be *Ayanami*). Commander Stormes gave the order to open fire immediately with all four of *Preston*'s guns bearing on the enemy. Star shells were not used because target was visible due to the moonlight. The range was estimated at 9,000 yards and salvos were spotted to the target. The hitting range was established after a few salvos and fire was very effective. The battery was in automatic control using director fire. The enemy ship moved into the shadow of Savo Island but she could still be distinguished and fire on her continued. Approximately one minute after *Preston* opened fire, the enemy returned fire with her main battery plus what appeared to be 40-mm guns. At 0028-30 this enemy ship caught fire and began to burn fiercely.[359]

Fire was shifted to another ship in the shadow of Savo Island at a range of 8,000 yards (*Nagara*). At 0031 *Preston* was hit on the starboard side by two projectiles, probably 5.5-inch from *Nagara*. One projectile hit between the two fire rooms killing all men in them and covering the amidships area with firebrick and debris. Number two stack fell on the search light knocking it over on the starboard torpedo tube. The other projectile hit the gun shelter just aft of number two gun but did not explode. The projectile killed one man, badly injured another and tore a very large hole in the deck. The projectile cut the power cable for number two gun and jammed it in train.[360]

Commander Stormes believed during this part of the action an enemy heavy cruiser came in on the port side of the column virtually undetected.[361] This "enemy" cruiser opened fire at a very close range. At 0032 a few seconds after *Preston* was hit to starboard she was hit on the port side. As near as can be determined the ship was hit by three projectiles. The whole after part of the ship from the stacks

---

[359] *Preston*, Surface Engagement with Japanese Forces, November 15, 1942—report of.

[360] Ibid.

[361] There were never any Japanese ships to *Preston*'s port side. Henry Stewart of *South Dakota* reported in a post war interview–"At the time of the power outage, Commander Uehlinger [exec of *South Dakota*] and I saw the *Washington* open fire to her starboard, *Preston*, a destroyer was hit and burning, and to us it looked as if the *Washington's* fire had caused the accident. I was told by Commander Uehlinger to forget what we just saw." *Washington*'s deck logs are blacked out at this critical time period. It appeared *Walke* had taken *Washington* under fire at 0031 and Commander Taylor of *Benham* also thought he saw a small cruiser to port aft firing at the rear destroyers. After this point Lee would not let *Washington* open fire unless he was sure the target was an enemy ship. *Preston*'s sudden capsizing to starboard in less than 30 seconds may indicate a torpedo hit from *Ayanami* virtually at the same time that the gunfire hit her. The gunfire alone would not cause the sudden capsizing and the ship sinking so fast at the locations given in her report. Certainly Cmdr. Sakuma believed one of his torpedoes has scored.

aft was a mass of blazing, red-hot wreckage. One projectile hit the engine room exploding after it hit the generators. A second projectile hit between the secondary control section and number three gun. The third projectile hit number four gun. Almost every man aft of the after machine gun nest was killed, including the executive officer. The gunnery officer gave the order for the guns one and two to continue firing if possible but the force of the explosion had jammed them both in train and elevation and they could not fire. The ship immediately listed sharply to starboard and began to settle by the stern. At 0033 Commander Stormes gave the order to abandon ship. In less than thirty seconds *Preston* rolled over on her side and sank by the stern. The bow rose vertically and remained in that position for approximately ten minutes. No records, papers, or accounts were saved.[362]

At 0026 *Gwin* fired two salvos of star shells in compliance with Lee's orders but then Lt. Commander John Fellows ordered gunners to switch to AA common projectiles.[363] As *Ayanami* engaged *Preston, Gwin* at 0031 began a steady fire of four gun salvos. She hit *Ayanami* with at least two salvos and observed that the enemy destroyer which had been firing three turrets was now only firing one.[364] At 0032 *Preston* exploded and *Gwin* received her first hit with a 5-inch round striking the starboard side of the after engine room four feet above the waterline. Superheated steam blew into the 20-mm clipping room and the mount 4 handling room. The lights to mounts 3 and 4 went out but emergency lights came on so that neither guns ability to fire was impaired. The blast in the engine room broke all the sheer pins holding the torpedoes in the forward torpedo mount so that three slipped out and into the sea and the other two came half way out.[365] Lt. Commander Cox, the ship's executive officer, ordered hard right so that she passed *Preston* on her starboard side. As she passed she was rocked by exploding depth charges from the sinking destroyer. She maintained her fire at *Ayanami* and then was hit again near her starboard depth charge rack but the shell failed to explode. At approximately 0036 *Gwin* checked fire as she was no longer able to find a suitable target and could not find *Benham.* At 0045 Lt. Commander Fellows received orders from Lee to withdraw.[366]

---

362 *Preston*, Surface Engagement with Japanese Forces, November 15, 1942—report of.

363 *Gwin*, Report of Night Action 14-15 November, 1942.

364 *Gwin*, Report of Night Action 14-15 November, 1942.

365 *Gwin*, Report of Night Action 14-15 November, 1942.

366 Ibid.

Commander Sakuma, commanding the Japanese destroyer *Ayanami,* began his torpedo run at 0024, taking on the entire U.S. formation alone. *Ayanami* hugged the southern shore of Savo Island in an attempt to keep concealed for as long as possible. Japanese naval doctrine was that destroyers in the advance stage of battle should close to as short a range as possible and destroyers should not open fire with guns until after torpedoes have been launched so that their position was not given away prior to the torpedo attack. If possible, screening units were to be ignored and bypassed unseen so that the main body could be attacked.[367]

Sakuma engaged *Walke* with guns and targeted the middle of the U.S. formation with his torpedoes. At 0030 *Ayanami* launched six Type 90 torpedoes at the third ship in the U.S. formation which Sakuma thought was a heavy cruiser but was actually *Preston.* Soon after launching torpedoes, Sakuma gave the order to re-open fire with his main battery. At about 0031 fire was shifted to the fourth U.S. ship (*Gwin*), scoring hits amidships and aft. Return American gunfire hit *Ayanami* and this toppled her number one stack and silenced main gun mounts number one and three. Fires erupted all over the ship and she then took hits to her steering gear and engine rooms and lost all power. Then at 0032 *Preston* was hit by a torpedo and exploded, and a minute later *Walke* was hit by another torpedo. Sakuma believed that his lone destroyer had sunk one heavy cruiser and one destroyer with torpedoes and set on fire a third destroyer with gunfire. He sent a message to Kondo with his results but the message was not be relayed to Kondo until 0045. *Ayanami* slowly lost speed and came to a stop southeast of Savo Island. The fires on board continued to attract gunfire from *South Dakota.* Admiral Hashimoto on *Sendai* passed *Ayanami* at 0036 and radioed Kondo that she was on fire.[368]

Kimura sighted the U.S. formation at 0030 and radioed Kondo. His light cruiser and four destroyers launched 35-40 torpedoes and then engaged with their main batteries. *Nagara* briefly engaged *Preston,* hitting her amidships just before she exploded. His destroyers fired torpedoes at *Walke* and *Benham.* Both destroyers took torpedo hits and *Nagara* made smoke and checked fire at 0036. Kimura ordered a 180 degree turn to port to maintain contact with the enemy, which was completed at 0040, and to reload torpedo tubes for a possible second attack. At 0038 Hashimoto with *Sendai, Shikinami,* and *Uranami* passed ahead of Kimura in

---

[367] Ballard, Robert D. and Rick Archbold *Lost Ships of Guadalcanal.* Warner/Madison Press Books, 1993.

[368] *Sendai* Brief action report JT1 National Archives and Ballard, Robert D. and Rick Archbold. *Lost Ships of Guadalcanal.* Warner/Madison Press Books, 1993.

Nagara and his destroyer column in their attempt to lead U.S. forces to the Japanese main body and possibly gain position for a torpedo attack.[369]

Lt. Imamura Ichiro on *Atago* noted that the battle began as Susumu Kimura's report was received and distant gun flashes could be observed. Suddenly a bright ball of fire appeared ten kilometers off the port bow. There was a silhouette of a ship engulfed in flames and then the ship broke in two and both sections disappeared (*Preston* or *Walke*). The bridge was quiet and several officers took a deep breath for it was not known if the stricken ship was Japanese or American.[370]

At 0024 Lee and *Washington* observed *Ayanami*'s attack but believed the gunfire was from shore batteries on Savo Island. At 0025 *Washington*'s secondary battery opened fire on these believed to be shore batteries. A fire was started at the right tangent of Savo Island which burned for a long time. The bridge reported a target on the starboard bow (*Ayanami)*. Main battery directors were so blinded by 5-inch fire that they could not find a point of aim. By 0027 *Washington's* radar (CXAM) picked up targets bearing 040 relative 340 degrees true range 9,700 yards (*Negara*'s group). At 0028 *Washington* identified targets bearing 356 degrees true moving around the end of the island. Other contacts followed indicating that there were a number of ships rimming the southern side of the island of Savo estimated to be 6-10 ships. At 0032 she observed a target on starboard beam and then saw one of the lead destroyers being hit (*Preston*). One minute later at 0033 two destroyers were observed being hit with *Walke* burning badly and *Preston* exploding having been possibly hit by a torpedo. Lee obtained reports of men in the water dead ahead; one destroyer was sinking; rafts were ordered to be put over as the ship went by; all enemy fire stopped. Then at 0034 *Washington* checked fire for the secondary battery as a result of mount 3 firing wild. (Training Motor kicked out and the pointers were not matched). It was feared the mount might endanger friendly destroyers. The crew of the battleship felt underwater explosions as of depth charges detonated when the lead destroyers sank. Lee changed speed to twenty-six knots. All secondary targets were lost.[371]

At 0033 *South Dakota* suffered an electrical power failure. All power gyros and all electric fire-control equipment out. Circuit breakers on No 14 switch board

---

[369] Ballard, Robert D. and Rick Archbold. *Lost Ships of Guadalcanal.* Warner/Madison Press Books, 1993.

[370] *Atago* DAR No. 8 12 to 14 Nov 1942 (submitted 18 Nov 1942) and From Vanguard Force Flagship *Atago* and the Defense Battles of Guadalcanal Island (*Zenshin-butai Kikan Atago to Ga-tô Kôbôsen*) by Paymaster Lieutenant Imamura Ichirô, pp. 333-349)

[371] *Washington*, Action Report, Night of November 14-15, 1942.

tripped out. Load shifted to No 3 switchboard. Bus transfer panel for No. 56 and 58 5-inch mounts shifted to alternate source on No. 3 board, causing No. 6 generator to trip out. Feeder circuits also tripped. Regained power in plotting room then lost it again almost immediately. By 0034 *South Dakota* reported two enemy ships rounding Savo Island to the eastward, bearing 345°truereported by radar plot. The enemy was firing on with salvo's falling short few, over many, especially for *Washington*. At 0035 *South Dakota* asked *Washington* if she was okay.

At 0035 *Washington's* SG radar reported four ships bearing 330 degrees true (*Atago, Takao,* and *Kirishima* plus destroyers). Radar plot coached the main gun battery on to one reported to be larger than the others. These targets had been obscured by Savo Island up to this time and main battery started tracking. The *Washington* set course of 282 degrees true. She passed the wreckage of the *Preston* at approximately 0035-0036 staying on *Preston*'s port side. At 0040 *Washington* replied to *South Dakota*, "*She is okay.*"[372]

At 0036 *South Dakota* started to turn to port to clear the damaged destroyers ahead but then turned sharply to starboard breaking formation and steadied on a course of 300 degrees true. At 0038 *South Dakota* passed one of the American destroyers abeam to port (*Preston*). A lull in firing enabled her crew to hear survivors shouting for help. Some men in the water were using flashlights. A small electric fire was reported in compartment C-303 and Repair 4 was sent to investigate the fire, also in mount 58. *South Dakota* changed course again to 285 degrees true. Then at 0040 she resumed main battery firing on targets close to Savo Island.[373]

At 0041 *South Dakota* reported a small fire in C-303L extinguished, the SG radar reported inoperative, and gyros were still out. Capt. Gatch maintained fire on *Ayanami* astern and in the process blew two of her own float planes overboard at 0043. At 0046 *South Dakota*'s SG radar was in commission again and she passed the wreckage of *Walke*. Main battery reported difficulty getting ranges and requested secondary battery directors to track, radars in secondary directors 1 and 4 out, 2 and 3 doubtful. Radar plot reported ships bearing 070 degrees right, range 5,800 yards (*Sendai*). This was one of two previous reports at 7,000 yards, but overlooked on bridge while directing fire control on target bearing 112 degrees (*Ayanami*).[374]

---

[372] Ibid.

[373] The *South Dakota*, Action Report, Night Engagement 14-15 November, 1942, with Japanese naval units, off Savo Island.

[374] Ibid.

Then at 0048 *South Dakota* came under fire for the first time. By 0049 *South Dakota* reported first hits sustained, most likely 1.1" clipping room in foremast structure. Capt. Gatch ordered an increase in speed to twenty-seven knots. Received message from *Washington* asking, "*Are you alright?*" replied "*Everything seems okay.*" By 0050 *South Dakota* reported more hits felt, unable to locate them. Approximately 0052-0054, *South Dakota* veered to the south and then turned back north back onto a course of 292 degrees true. At 0053 *South Dakota* reported three enemy ships coming out of Savo Island, estimated range 11,000 yards (*Atago, Takao*, and *Kirishima*). Gatch radioed "*We are taking hits chiefly in foremast structure*".[375]

Washington noted the enemy ships that main battery was tracking had started a change in course to starboard, reversal completed by 0057 (*Atago, Takao*, and *Kirishima*). At 0058 the moon set and visibility quickly dropped from nine miles down to three. At 0059 Lee's lookouts reported "*Transports off the starboard bow, evidently the ships already being tracked.*"[376]

At 0045 Kondo received *Ayanami*'s report that one cruiser and one destroyer were sunk and another destroyer had been set on fire. Ichiro mentions that there was much elation on the bridge but soon after this they received *Sendai*'s message that *Ayanami* was on fire and the bridge quieted down. Kondo after he received *Ayanami*'s message came to the conclusion that the U.S. surface forces were being crushed. At 2347 Kondo ordered a course change to 280 degrees. While heading west, *Takao*'s lookouts reported one enemy battleship and three destroyers in the south. Kondo ignored *Takao*'s estimate of a battleship and was still convinced that he faced only heavy cruisers. More warnings of U.S. battleships began to arrive. According to *Nagara*'s gunnery officer Lt. Commander Kazutoshi Kuhara, his cruiser had engaged a heavy cruiser, effectively silencing it, however at 0051 Kimura onboard *Nagara* recognized *South Dakota* as a battleship and he also sighted *Washington* and noted her strange foremast, resembling the *North Carolina* class. He radioed Kondo, "*Two enemy battleships off Cape Esperance, heading west along north coast of Guadalcanal!*" At 0051 Nobutake Kondo ordered the Bombardment Force to prepare to reverse course to commence the bombardment.[377]

---

[375] Ibid.

[376] *Washington*, Action Report, Night of November 14-15, 1942.

[377] *Atago* DAR No. 8 12 to 14 Nov 1942 (submitted 18 Nov 1942) and FromVanguard Force Flagship *Atago* and the Defense Battles of Guadalcanal Island (*Zenshin-butai Kikan Atago to Ga-tô Kôbôsen*) by Paymaster Lieutenant Imamura Ichirô, pp. 333-349)

At 0052 *Atago*'s course was 000 degrees. *Atago*'s lookouts sighted an enemy vessel bearing 125 degrees distance 10,000 meters (*South Dakota*). Kondo received word that *Nagara* and *Kirishima* had sighted an enemy ship (*South Dakota*). Then at the same moment *Atago*'s lookouts reported "*Kirishima is firing*" Next they reported, "*Kirishima has scored a hit to enemy bridge with her first salvo!*" Kondo watched and observed *Kirishima*'s first salvo strike the foremast of the enemy ship and the enemy ship's main battery goes silent. By 0053 he issued orders to Hashimoto that he planned to bombard the Marine positions and that he should assist *Ayanami*. Hashimoto turned to the north, forcing Kimura and his destroyers into a 360 degree turn to starboard in order to avoid a collision. Hashimoto released *Uranami* to stand by and assist *Ayanami* and these maneuvers effectively took both Hashimoto and Kimura out of the battle. At 0054 *Atago* settled in on a new heading of 130 degrees true.[378]

At 0051 Lt (jg) Michio Kobayashi on the bridge of *Kirishima* was observing *Takao* when he spotted a stationary ship to port partially camouflaged by Guadalcanal. He immediately identified it as a U.S. battleship and it did not appear that either heavy cruiser had spotted her yet. At 0052 Captain Iwabuchi immediately ordered his ship to engage the enemy battleship to port. Then a message was received from *Atago* at 0053 that she was ready to stand by and shell the airfield.[379]

At 0052 Lt. Commander Tsurukichi Ikeda who was in charge of the ship's secondary battery received permission to open fire. The range was 10,000 meters (11,000 yards) and Ikeda's secondary battery was the first to open fire followed quickly by her main battery. He claimed that two rounds from her first salvo hit the target ship's superstructure. More salvos followed in which he claimed two short straddles and two long straddles but no further hits. At 0054 he was ordered to check fire so that *Kirishima* could make a turn. His secondary battery had already reached their maximum train so his guns could no longer bear on the target anyway. He noted in a post-war interview that six minutes later after he checked fire *Kirishima* came under fire from another U.S. battleship.[380]

Battle damage reports began to flood into Gatch on the bridge of *South Dakota*. At 0055 he received a report that the forward main battery director (Director

---

[378] Ibid.

[379] Kobayashi, Michio. "Senkan 'Kirishima' no Saigo [The Last of Battleship Kirishima]." Saiaku no Senjô Gadarukanaru Senki, 1987, pp 350-361.

[380] Shikikan-tachi no Taiheiyô Sensô [Pacific War as Described by the Senior Officers]. Kôjinsha NF Bunko, 2004.

One) was unable to train forward to 040 degrees, probably due to shell hit. At 0056 another report told him a of shell hit to a 1.1 clipping room with the crew of Quad One killed and fires started in the 1.1" clipping room. Flash proceeding down the ammunition hoist to engineering passageways set two life jackets on fire. Some ammunition went off, and the fire was fought by men present. Shell hit and detonation took out RDF2 loop (Radio Direction Finder number 2). Captain Gatch slowed the ship's speed to twenty-six knots and searches for signs of *Washington*. Secondary battery was still firing on enemy ships. Enemy hits were reported in the vicinity of radar plot. Another shell through the radar plot immediately after this killed Ensign Canfield. A steam line was ruptured just outside of radar plot by 6" inch shell that penetrated into radar plot on starboard side and demolished it. Immediately afterwards another shell hit very near the same place. There was some confusion outside of battle two; three shells just went through that space; some men killed, some wounded, several scalded by steam from steam whistle and siren line. The situation quieted down and word was sent for repair parties to extinguish fires in RDF2, and get first aid for the wounded. Damaged ladders made access difficult and life jackets on deck in battle two were catching fire. The fire in this compartment was quite intense, gutting the entire room. Initially CO_2 was used against the fire with no effect at all. It was not brought under control until 0155.[381]

At 0057 Lt. Ichiro noted that Kondo and his chief of staff, Rear Admiral Kazutaka Shiraishi were standing to his right and Capt. Ijuin was to his left. One of the lookouts on the starboard side reported "*A battleship off starboard.*" Shiraishi inquired if the ship could be *Hiei* for her fate was still not known. Then at 0100 Kondo and Ijuin began giving orders at the same time. Ijuin ordered "*Stand by for a gun and torpedo action to starboard!*" "*Ready to illuminate!*" someone shouted and Captain Ijuin at 0101 ordered "*Commence illumination.*" What Ichiro saw was a battleship that he thought was similar in appearance to *Yamato*. She had a high freeboard and layered bridge and *Atago* identified her as a *North Carolina* class battleship. *Atago* began to turn to port.[382]

At 0102 Lt. Yoshiro Watanabe next ordered to stand by for torpedo action starboard and engage enemy battleship steaming on parallel course. "*No, she is not*

---

[381] *South Dakota*, Action Report, night engagement 14-15 November, 1942, with Japanese naval units, off Savo Island. The shells that ripped through radar plot were from the *Kirishima*'s first salvo.

[382] "From Vanguard Force Flagship *Atago* and the Defense Battles of Guadalcanal Island" (*Zenshin-butai Kikan Atago to Ga-tô Kôbôsen*) by Paymaster Lieutenant Imamura Ichirô, pp. 333-349)

making any headway," he corrected himself. "*Stand by to open fire with guns.*" Watanabe had to make one more correction when he suddenly realized "*No wait the target is closing on the opposite course*!" At 0103 the order to launch torpedoes came and *Atago* launched eight Type 93 torpedoes and opened fire with her main battery. At 0104 Capt. Ijuin ordered "*Cease illumination*!" and she fired her third salvo at *South Dakota* which was now bearing 105 degrees. At 0105 she fired her 4th and 5th salvo with the 127-mm and 25-mm guns joining in and fires were seen on *South Dakota*. By 0106 she fired her 6th and final salvo after which Capt. Ijuin ordered "*Cease fire.*" A lookout shouted "*Torpedo tracks to port bearing 030 degrees*!" Ijuin ordered maximum speed and the torpedoes turned out to be a false alarm.[383]

Ichiro saw the first, second and third torpedoes enter the water followed suddenly by an explosion. He realized that one of the torpedoes had exploded prematurely. In his post-war interviews, Kondo stated that he was stunned at this time by the realization that he was engaged with U.S. battleships. The *Atago*'s lookouts reported," *There is another ship forward of the first, a big battleship!*" They identified the second battleship (incorrectly) as an *Idaho* class and that she was awash up to her main deck and sinking by the bow.[384] Medical Officer Lt (jg) Abe, who was standing on the bridge, heard how one of the lookouts shouted; "*Kirishima is totally obscured by shell splashes!*" When Kondo and the other officers on the bridge turned their binoculars toward the battleship, Lt (jg) Abe saw nine 30-meter high splashes rising around *Kirishima*. During the next few minutes some of the stray shells landed near *Atago* as well. Ijuin observed that *South Dakota*'s main battery remained silent but that her secondary guns continue to fire back fiercely. *Atago* took her first hit, to the starboard soy sauce store which began a fire on her bow. Then she received a second hit on her port side at frame 293. The shell was defeated by the main armor belt but fragments opened small holes in the anti-torpedo bulge. At 0108 Lookouts reported, "*Kirishima is burning and she is gradually lagging behind.*" Kondo observed hits being scored on *South Dakota* by *Kirishima* and *Takao*'s gunfire and viewed her as heavily damaged and sinking. He ordered a turn north in a vain hope that he could disengage *Kirishima* but she could follow. The second battleship became his priority and to keep his force be-

---

[383] Yoshino, Kyûshichi. "Senkan 'Kirishima' no Saigo [The Last of Battleship Kirishima]." Maru Extra Vol. 10, May 1998, at 54-57.

[384] *Washington*'s camouflage was giving her this appearance.

tween the U.S. battleship and Raizo Tanaka's transports. Ijuin ordered, "*Hard to port, stand by for a gun and torpedo action to port!*"[385]

At 0100 when *Atago* turned on her search lights, *Washington*'s main battery opened fire bearing 008 degrees true, range 8,400 yards on target, identified as a battleship. Main battery was on full radar control, however her FC and SG radars could not distinguish shell splashes, which thus had to be observed optically. The *Washington* was able to fire her first two main battery salvos before *Kirishima* was able to return fire, which occurred at approximately 0101 hours). The *Washington*'s secondary battery opened fire on two different targets. Director 1 with mounts 51 and 53 fired upon the main battery target. Twice during the firing these guns were observed hitting the target and starting fires in *Kirishima*'s upper works. Director 3 with mounts 55 and 57 were firing on another ship identified as a probable heavy cruiser (*Atago*) that had her search lights trained upon *South Dakota*. Group 2 fired with a 200-yard rocking ladder. First salvo landed short and was spotted up 400 yards. At about the fourth salvo the enemy searchlights went out, however, the secondary battery continued to fire for about 8-10 more salvos. Director 4 provided star shell illumination with mount 59 for main battery beginning after second salvo for a total of sixty-two star shells being fired. At 0102 *Washington* reported spotting a green light on the port beam (the source of this light is unknown). Director 3 guns continued to fire at the ship that had her search lights on *South Dakota* until the lights went out, then shifted to others in turn until their lights also went out. Fires were started on the ship that *South Dakota* was hitting. At 0102.30 *Washington* reported "*Cease Firing*" given by control on receipt of erroneous report that the target was sunk. At 0103 *Washington* reported that enemy was still firing at her apparently with three turrets and was believed to have fired two salvos in the minute and a half during which fire was ceased. *Washington* ordered *South Dakota* to close *Washington* to hear from CTF 64 (Lee) over TBS. This order was acknowledged by *South Dakota*. At 0104 Lee directed from bridge, "*If you can see anything to shoot at, go ahead.*" Main battery resumed fire. Salvo two after she re-opened fire was reported as a short straddle. More hits were obtained. The Japanese battleship continued to fire with only one turret aft. Lee shouted out a warning to keep good look out for enemy destroyers on both bows.[386]

---

[385] *Atago* DAR No. 8 12 to 14 Nov 1942 (submitted 18 Nov 1942) and From Vanguard Force Flagship *Atago* and the Defense Battles of Guadalcanal Island (*Zenshin-butai Kikan Atago to Ga-tô Kôbôsen*) by Paymaster Lieutenant Imamura Ichirô, at 333-349).

[386] *Washington*, Action Report, Night of November 14-15, 1942.

At 0106 Fire Control reported that the forward group (forward main battery turrets) was getting to its limit of train (148 degrees). At 0107 Cease Firing was issued with the main battery target burning, and heading away. The enemy battleship ceased firing. *Washington* fired an additional thirty-six main battery shells for a total of seventy-five 16-inch armor-piercing shells. Her secondary battery fired a total of 227 5-inch AA common shells during this phase. The main battery continued to track the burning ship for ten minutes. During this time she made a 500 degree turn (one and a half circles). A course of 180 degrees was given to *South Dakota* by Lee over TBS but no receipt was received. At 0114 *Washington* reported from spot one, "*looks like someone opening fire on us on the starboard quarter*", ordered to train main battery turrets to 150 degrees relative.[387]

At 0100 *South Dakota* reported secondary directors 1 and 3 were tracking a target. Director 1 controlling mount fired one spread set of star shells. Two hits felt below decks. Capt. Gatch ordered an increase in speed to twenty-seven knots. By 0102 *South Dakota* reported that she was under searchlight illumination from abaft beam (*Nagara*). Sky control was out, secondary battery director 1 was hit and out of commission. Engines were ordered to full speed. Radio antennae were shot away. At 0104 more hits were felt. Secondary battery was still firing. There was no communication with sky control. A shell hit glancing off mount 55, went through the signal store room, across the superstructure and into the after end of mount 54. The 8" shell did not explode and was, later found on deck and disposed of by throwing overboard.

By 0105 *South Dakota* reported more hits felt, power to sky 1 secured. Calls to *Washington* were useless, as the radio antennae are shot down. At 0107 she reported main battery salvo, no data available, and at 0108 she reported cease firing, no targets, no fire from enemy, *Washington* not in sight, no communication by TBS. At 0110 *South Dakota* reported engagement broken off and she was proceeding at full speed on course 235 degrees true. Ship repair parties and personnel not essential wee at damaged stations fighting fires, caring for wounded and estimating damage. She observed splashes on her wake, 1000 yards astern. No enemy ships were observed firing, so possibly the splashes were from one of those left burning. The bridge received word at 0110 that main battery turret three was having difficulty training due to a 14-inch shell hit by gas seal. At 0115 *South Dakota* reported

---

[387] Ibid.

that she was attempting to raise *Washington* but all efforts were hopeless until her antennae were cleared.[388]

Upon *Atago*'s illumination at 0100 Captain Iwabuchi ordered her to resume fire on *South Dakota.* Lt. Commander Tsurukichi Ikeda was positive that his ship was illuminating the enemy as well. He mistakenly reported later that they were facing a "*North Carolina* class battleship." Ikeda could see his gunfire hitting the enemy ship. Ikeda himself felt only a strange vibration and had no idea that his ship was hit. He soon felt his back getting hot, and realized there must have been a fire in the next compartment.[389]

On *Kirishima*'s bridge Lt. jg. Michio Kobayashi remembered that *Washington*'s first salvo was a straddle that sent up huge columns of water that soaked the bridge and ruined the log he was keeping. After *Kirishima* re-opened fire he thought he saw *Kirishima* hit the foremost main battery turret so that its barrels were canted upwards. Then he received reports that the hemp rope "mantelets" that protected the area around the first funnel and search lights had caught on fire. Captain Iwabuchi immediately ordered the crew to douse the fires and firefighting teams succeeded in cutting the ropes and dumping them overboard in no time. Then Lt. (jg) Michio Kobayashi heard a report through voice pipes about fire in aft secondary battery casemates. The XO, Commander Koro Ono, ordered the aft magazines flooded and soon came a report via voice pipe confirming that this measure had been successfully executed. Lt. (jg) Michio Kobayashi had felt several successive impacts, whether from shells or torpedoes he did not know. They were not that heavy in his opinion and could have been *Kirishima*'s own guns firing.[390]

At 0100 Lt. Commander Kyûshichi Yoshino, *Kirishima*'s flooding control officer, heard Capt. Iwabuchi announce a gun battle to starboard and order speed increased to maximum. Iwabuchi also announced that *Kirishima's* shells were laying well but that the enemy was hitting us as well. At his station below decks Yoshino could feel the ship shudder below his feet after every hit. The roar of the guns was deafening, the temperature within the compartment had reached 45 degrees Celsius (113° F), his throat was parched and he was sweating profusely. After only a few minutes Damage Control Central received the first reports about sev-

---

[388] *South Dakota*, Action Report, night engagement 14-15 November, 1942, with Japanese naval units, off Savo Island.

[389] Shikikan-tachi no Taiheiyô Sensô [Pacific War as Described by the Senior Officers]. Kôjinsha NF Bunko, 2004.

[390] Kobayashi, Michio. "*Senkan 'Kirishima' no Saigo* [The Last of Battleship Kirishima]." Saiaku no Senjô Gadarukanaru Senki, 1987, pp 350-361.

eral fires forward and aft and Yoshino could feel the ship developing a list to starboard. Then the aft engine room reported a steadily increasing flooding to that space. He became concerned how his engine room damage-control party was doing. They had to truly fight for their lives since there was no escape through the watertight closed doors. His heart was pounding and he was having trouble hearing all orders that came in through voice tubes. Then Capt. Iwabuchi ordered: "*Flood No. 1 turret magazines immediately*!" Yoshino could hear from his voice how critical the situation was. He forgot to breathe as he raced to flood the compartment, knowing an explosion could wipe out the entire ship in a second. He was able to flood the compartment in time. Throughout the battle he did his best to stop the starboard and aft lists that *Kirishima* was taking.[391]

Lt. (jg) Michio Kobayashi received new reports of rudder failure through voice pipe. He thought the steering room may have been hit by a torpedo. The *Kirishima* had been steaming at full battle speed and now started to circle. By 0110 *Kirishima*'s battle with U.S. forces was over. Kobayashi received reports that there were fires in both the forward main battery turrets and in the aft secondary battery casemate guns. The XO ordered both forward and aft magazines flooded and a starboard list appeared. Fires were being swept into the machinery compartments, Kobayashi reported a machinery breakdown, and speed was lost until *Kirishima* was dead in the water. *Kirishima* had been hit by many shells and multiple fires had broken out both topsides and below decks. First hits smashed her fore turrets and destroyed the forward wireless station. Next she took several hits aft, so that turrets Nos. 3 and 4 main battery turrets lost their hydraulic power and the hull was holed below the waterline. He estimated that *Kirishima* has been hit by twenty main caliber hits and over 10 secondary hits. He speculated five or six torpedo hits below the waterline.[392]

According to Tsurukichi Ikeda the chief damage control officer Lt. Commander Hayashi told him that *Kirishima* had received fourteen major caliber hits above the waterline and seventeen medium caliber hits as well as six underwater hits all rated as major caliber. According to Tsurukichi Ikeda, *Kirishima* fired sixty-eight Type 3 [incendiary], twenty-two Type 0 [HE], and twenty-seven Type 1

---

[391] Yoshino, Kyûshichi. "*Senkan 'Kirishima' no Saigo* [The Last of Battleship *Kirishima*]." *Maru Extra Vol. 10*, May 1998, pp 54-57.

[392] Kobayashi, Michio. "Senkan 'Kirishima' no Saigo [The Last of Battleship Kirishima]." Saiaku no Senjô Gadarukanaru Senki, 1987, pp 350-361.

[AP] 14-inch shells at the enemy battleship. Lookouts reported ten 14-inch shell hits on *South Dakota*.[393]

According to Kobayashi the XO ordered the port voids flooded to correct the starboard list which was quickly corrected. Then a port list appeared and the XO ordered starboard voids flooded and again the list disappeared for a time. Captain Iwabuchi wanted to beach *Kirishima* using the destroyers or *Nagara*'s help to tow his wounded ship. He would then use her as a floating battery until all shells were expended. All signaling devices had been destroyed so Kobayashi lent his flashlight to signal the destroyers in order to pass heavy wire ropes to them. Two or three of the destroyers closed in and *Kirishima*'s bosun was ordered to pass heavy wire ropes to them. Kobayashi was sent to anchor deck to observe the progress of towing operations. On the way he met the Chief Engineering Officer and his aide both heading for the bridge and panting heavily. The engineering spaces were full of flames and smoke and communication by voice pipes was now impossible. Iwabuchi ordered the machinery spaces evacuated and the crew to report to the upper deck. Both men departed to deliver the message but the message came late with heavy casualties among the engineering crew, most likely due to smoke inhalation. Eventually only the centerline engine room remained operational. By 0149 some of the fires were being brought under control. All attempts to steer with engines failed. Divers were sent into the steering compartment but they were unable to penetrate the watertight scuttles.[394]

The Captain of *Nagara* however refused to tow the crippled battleship. Iwabuchi then sent a corresponding signal to C-in-C, Combined Fleet requesting he order *Nagara* to help tow his ship. The port list re-appeared and the XO ordered additional starboard voids flooded and the list again disappeared for a short time. "Commence counter-flooding port voids," Ono ordered with a surprisingly calm voice. There was no result. Just then the DDs started towing, but *Kirishima* did not move at all. "*Towing is impossible*" one of the DDs reported using a blinker. The list was still worsening. Then the starboard list grew steadily and the XO ordered all port voids flooded but the starboard list only grew so that standing on the bridge became impossible The bridge fell silent as the officers realized their ship was sinking beneath them and that they could not stop it. According to Kobayashi, the XO and Captain Iwabuchi had a hurried conversation in which the

[393] *Shikikan-tachi no Taiheiyô Sensô* [Pacific War as Described by the Senior Officers]. Kôjinsha NF Bunko, 2004.

[394] Kobayashi, Michio. "Senkan 'Kirishima' no Saigo [The Last of Battleship Kirishima]." Saiaku no Senjô Gadarukanaru Senki, 1987, pp 350-361.

XO suggested that it was time to abandon ship. Iwabuchi ordered Kobayashi to use his flashlight to signal the destroyers to come along side and begin to take off the crew. He ordered all sailors to report to the upper deck. This time the orders were sent by runners. The bridge was evacuated soon afterwards. On his descent from the battle bridge, Kobayashi noted many dead on the level below and on the upper deck.[395]

Lt. Commander Tsurukichi Ikeda remained at his station, but then all of a sudden he received the order, given for the whole ships company, to descend to the upper deck. At first everything seemed to be in order, but on the third bridge level Ikeda encountered a scene of total destruction; the ladder was twisted in several places and even the foremast tripod legs had become visible. There were dead bodies everywhere. Once on the deck, he could see that there was an increasing list to starboard and several fires raging below decks Ikeda headed for the stern, but in the amidships area he saw two ten-meter wide holes in the deck right above the secondary guns.[396]

Yoshino received an order to report to the bridge. He squeezed himself out of the narrow hatch and climbed topside. He noted that the superstructure was all shot up and he saw several corpses lying amidst the wreckage. The ship was all blacked out. He later learned that this was intended as a measure to avoid enemy PT boat attacks. In the dark he could see sailors emerging from every passage and manhole. The starboard list continued to grow and Captain Iwabuchi ordered the port engine room flooded. "Led by the skipper we sang 'Kimi ga yo' and gave three banzais. Destroyers came alongside at both sides aft. It was still black and evacuating all wounded took quite some time."[397]

According to Michio Kobayashi, *Asagumo* came alongside the starboard quarter and *Teruzuki* to port. Then XO made a short speech and then ordered the ship to be abandoned. The battle flag was lowered and the crew gave three banzais and began to board the waiting destroyers. The officer who carried the Emperor's portrait boarded *Asagumo* first then followed by the wounded. Most of the men had transferred to the destroyers with about 300 men remaining when *Kirishima*'s starboard list shifted over to port. Michio Kobayashi had barely stepped aboard

---

395 Kobayashi, Michio. "Senkan 'Kirishima' no Saigo [The Last of Battleship Kirishima]" Saiaku no Senjô Gadarukanaru Senki, 1987, pp 350-361.

396 *Shikikan-tachi no Taiheiyô Sensô* [Pacific War as Described by the Senior Officers]. Kôjinsha NF Bunko, 2004.

397 Yoshino, Kyûshichi. "*Senkan 'Kirishima' no Saigo* [The Last of Battleship *Kirishima*]." *Maru Extra Vol. 10*, May 1998, pp 54-57.

Asagumo when the battleship's bow upended sharply. With a lurch and the momentum of her turning over to port increasing, *Teruzuki* had to do an emergency back full to avoid being crushed by the capsizing battleship's superstructure. *Asagumo* cut all lines with the sinking ship and also backed away in time. The last 300 men were thrown into the water including Captain Iwabuchi and XO Ono who were later picked up by the destroyer *Samidare*. *Kirishima* capsized to port and then slipped away by the stern into the depths of Iron Bottom Sound at 0323 of the morning of November 15, 1942. [398]

Lt. Commander Tsurukichi Ikeda along with Lt. Commander Hayashi felt the ship suddenly shift her list from starboard to port and had to jump overboard as the ship began to capsize. They were both rescued by the destroyer *Samidare*. Sixty-one officers and petty officers were rescued in addition to 1,031 sailors. Approximately 209 men were killed in action aboard *Kirishima*.[399]

At 0114 Capt. Ijuin ordered a torpedo salvo of four torpedoes to be launched at the enemy battleship bearing 015 degrees port (*South Dakota*). At the same time a course change to 300 degrees was ordered. By 0117 *Washington* was sighted steaming parallel course on port bearing 090. By 0118 Ijuin ordered the next torpedo salvo to be fired and then by 0120 to stand by to open fire from main battery, distance 13,000 meters. At 0122 *Atago* re-opened fire with her main battery bearing 072 degrees to port, distance 14,000 meters. At 0123 the last torpedo salvo was launched and the enemy battleship was seen to turn to starboard to an opposite course. *Atago* turned to 330 degrees at 0128 and by 0129 *Washington* was bearing port 115 degrees. At 0131 Ijuin ordered to make smoke and *Washington* continued to turn to an opposite course. By 0135 contact was lost and *Atago* withdrew from battle. She had fired 55 Type 91 AP and six Type 0 eight-inch shells, forty nine five-inch type AA common shells, fifteen 25-mm shells and nineteen Type 93 torpedoes. *Takao* had fired 36 Type 91 AP shells and twenty Type 93 torpedoes between 0102 and 0114.[400]

At 0117 *Washington*'s main battery shifted to track new targets bearing 120 degrees relative or 049 degrees true at a range of 13,800 yards. The target tracked

---

[398] Kobayashi, Michio. "Senkan '*Kirishima*' no Saigo [The Last of Battleship Kirishima]." Saiaku no Senjô Gadarukanaru Senki, 1987, pp 350-361.

[399] *Shikikan-tachi no Taiheiyô Sensô* [Pacific War as Described by the Senior Officers]. Kôjinsha NF Bunko, 2004.

[400] The *Atago* DAR No. 8 12 to 14 Nov 1942 (submitted 18 Nov 1942) and From Vanguard Force Flagship *Atago* and the Defense Battles of Guadalcanal Island" (*Zenshinbutai Kikan Atago to Ga-tô Kôbôsen*) by Paymaster Lieutenant Imamura Ichirô, pp. 333-349)

was the leading vessel of a group of five. Its type was unrecognized. The other ships were reported as freighters but they were making 26-29 knots during the 22 minutes they were tracked so they were estimated to be destroyers. *Washington* slowed to eighteen knots. At 0119 lookouts reported firing on the starboard quarter. Lee could not find *South Dakota.* At 0120 *Washington* changed course to 340 degrees true. Fire Control reported at 0121 a good solution on target being tracked bearing 068 degrees relative or 046 degrees true. Other targets were reported at 326 degrees true and also at 147 degrees true, 13,000 yards. At 0123 Sky Control reported flares on starboard quarter. At 0132 the lead ship that the main battery was tracking began to make smoke. At 0133 *Washington* changed course by a starboard turn to 180 degrees true and began her withdrawal from the battle zone. She would dodge some more torpedoes from two of Raizo Tanaka's destroyers but she did not open fire again nor did any Japanese fire strike the ship. The battle was essentially over.[401]

In the aftermath of this fast-paced, confusing, and bloody battle, Lee saw that the lack of training and cohesion between the individual U.S. units had almost lead to disaster. A night action could swiftly turn into chaos and confusion as this battle did. Friendly fire and the shock of running over your own men in the water must have had an impact on Lee. Radar alone had not been enough to maintain control of the formation and *South Dakota* had been blinded by gunfire within minutes.

Kondo had attempted to use lesser ships to secure command of the sea against superior numbers of modern battleships. In fairness he was misinformed of what he was up against believing the two battleships were heavy cruisers and this would lead directly to his defeat. By the time he realized his mistake it was too late and *Washington* was able to wreck *Kirishima* within seven minutes. With the loss of his battleship he did not risk his heavy cruisers and stayed at the extreme edge of visibility. This was Japanese naval doctrine for heavy cruisers while fighting in restricted waterways at night. He did not attempt to gain command of the sea and cancelled his bombardment mission while still having superior numbers.

Kondo had almost annihilated the U.S. force due to his greater numbers. For Lee who was acting alone by the end of the battle it was fortunate that Kondo did not press his advantage. A lone battleship was not an effective battle fleet. Once Lee saw Kondo withdraw, he correctly withdrew himself, having completed his

---

[401] *Washington*, Action Report, Night of November 14-15, 1942.

mission in denying access to Iron Bottom Sound. His ability to sustain operations was hampered due to the loss of an effective screen.

THE BATTLE OF TASSAFARONGA

One last surface battle would take place before 1942 would end. The Battle of Tassafaronga on November 30, 1942 would see eight Japanese destroyers running supplies to Guadalcanal engage a U.S. force of four heavy cruisers, one light cruiser and six destroyers. Firing their long lance torpedoes the Japanese sank the cruiser *Northampton*, and severely damaged *Minneapolis, Pensacola*, and *New Orleans* at the cost of one destroyer *Takanami*. With this battle U.S. heavy cruiser strength was significantly reduced. Five heavy cruisers had been sunk since the beginning of the war and another five had been seriously damaged cutting in half the available strength in heavy cruisers the U.S. battle fleet had available for both the Pacific and the Atlantic. Nimitz's ability to supply adequate screening forces to both carriers and surface combatants was extremely strained. It would not be until February 1943 that the U.S. Navy could undertake serious offensive operations again. Yamamoto did not recognize this opportunity and instead focused on his own losses.

Yamamoto's decision to no longer use elements of the Combined Fleet at the end of December sealed the fate of Guadalcanal. This was the true turning point in the war for it altered Japanese strategic policy. The writ of the Combined Fleet did not extend to fundamental shifts in national strategy and when the Navy informed the Army of its decision it came as an extreme shock. The reversal of strategy corroded the already strained relationship between the Army and the Navy. It had been the Navy which had requested the Army to re-capture Guadalcanal on three occasions. Each attempt ended in failure largely due to the Navy's inability to deliver supplies and control the seas. Yamamoto's will to continue the struggle for this island had been broken.

Yamamoto failed to adopt Corbett's words that for expeditions the key was control of communications and by gaining control we deny their use to the enemy. Freedom of passage however was just the beginning. In areas where resistance was expected or encountered the Army required support and Admiral Yamamoto and his staff never coordinated with the Army except in the transportation of men and supplies. To Yamamoto the re-capture of Guadalcanal was an Army problem once he had transported the troops to the island. The duties of the fleet do not end with the protection of the troops during transit but must continue until they have achieved their objective with direct support in securing all lines of communication and denying those same lines to the enemy. This was the main responsibility of the battle fleet but at Guadalcanal Japan used her battle fleet as a strike weapon instead of devising a plan to blockade the seas around Guadalcanal and Tulagi, securing the seas for themselves, and preventing their use to the Americans. Nimitz would not repeat Yamamoto's mistakes in applying these fundamental principles of naval warfare.

CHAPTER 21: OFFENSIVE IN THE CENTRAL PACIFIC

Yamamoto no longer wished to commit his ships for the defense of the Solomons but decided to transfer his carrier planes to Rabaul and conduct massive air strikes on Guadalcanal, Oto Bay, and Port Moresby beginning on April 7, 1943. They sank one destroyer and four auxiliary ships but the attrition to the Japanese aircraft remained high.

Then on April 11, 1943 the 11th Air Fleet sent a message about the intended visit of Admiral Yamamoto to some of the bases in the northern Solomons to boost morale. The message gave his exact itinerary and since the JN-25 codes had been broken it gave Nimitz the opportunity to strike at Admiral Yamamoto personally. Nimitz assigned Halsey to undertake Operation Vengeance and he in turn gave the assignment to Admiral Marc Mitscher, Commander Air Solomons.

> An attempt will be made to intercept an enemy high commander when he makes a projected visit to the BUIN area the 19th. [402]

On April 18 local or April 17 Hawaii Time the attack was carried out by P-38 long range fighters.

> April 17th. (Oahu date) Com 3rd Fleet 180611 is an operation summary for his area. Major SOPAC task forces continue in port. It seems probable that CINC Combined was shot down in a plane over the BUIN area today by Army P-38s.[403]

Yamamoto was killed sixteen months after the war had begun. He had chosen carrier-based air power as his weapon to deliver the political objective of annihilating the U.S. Pacific Fleet so that his Emperor could negotiate a peace from a position of strength. He had failed. He had effectively fought the United States to a draw in his carrier war. This resulted in a war of attrition with an economic superpower, which was what he wanted to avoid. Now the strategic initiative was with the United States and new Japanese commanders would require a plan on how to stop a U.S. advance.

---

[402] Nimitz, Chester, *Chester Nimitz Gray Book* Vol 3 at 1510.

[403] Ibid at 1511.

Operation Watchtower was finally coming to a close with the Japanese withdrawal from Guadalcanal. To maintain the strategic offensive Nimitz looked at studies to bring about Mahan's decisive battle. In January 1943 a direct thrust at the very heart of Japan's defensive perimeter was considered by taking the Island of Chichi Jima only 528 miles away from Tokyo.

> A plan which makes it possible to destroy the air and sea power of Japan is suitable. We should then first determine whether the taking of CHICHI Jima will place our forces in contact with enemy forces in such ratios that we can destroy them. This plan assumes that CHICHI Jima is so vital to Japan that his entire Navy will be employed to defend or recapture it. There is no way of telling whether or not this assumption is correct.[404]

The plan was similar to Yamamoto's Midway plan in that the attack on the Island was only an excuse to bring about Mahan's "decisive fleet action." It was rejected largely due to the same concerns the Japanese Naval General Staff had expressed about the replenishment and logistical strain if Midway was actually captured. Its lines of communication could easily be cut off and there was no guarantee the Japanese fleet would accept battle. The same applied for Chichi Jima.

By February more realistic American plans of taking the Gilberts while advancing up the Solomons began to take shape. Yet the logistical support was still not in place for the first half of 1943 to truly take the type of offensive Nimitz wanted. He would choose blockade and forward deployment as his weapon of choice.

> Contrary to what most now believe, this new phase in the War in the Pacific was primarily a battleship offensive in sea control.

As Corbett had observed it required a huge logistical train to maintain forward deployment.

> February 17, 1943. SECRET' MEMO FOR 16.
>
> Preliminary study indicates the following: (a) It seems entirely feasible to make a simultaneous thrust up the SOLOMONS and in the GILBERTS. Capture of objectives seems probable. Holding in GILBERTS seems doubtful. (b) Because of preparation time required, May 15, 1943 1s selected as· the target date.[405]

---

[404] Ibid at 1311.

[405] Ibid at 1398.

The initial thoughts on how to break the Japanese defensive perimeter were in the making. General MacArthur would continue his offensive along the spine of New Guinea toward the Philippines. Halsey would drive up the Solomons toward Rabaul. A third road would be opened beginning with the Gilberts and then the Marshall, Caroline, and Mariana Island groups, collectively known as the Mandates. Time was still needed and an organized strategy still needed to be developed but the origins of this strategy were already taking shape as early as February 1943. Nimitz faced multiple obstacles that needed to be addressed in order for the U.S. Navy to realize its true potential and maximize its fighting power.

The Japanese had defeated the United States battle fleet at Java Sea, Savo Island, Tassafaronga, and inflicted heavy losses during the Naval Battle of Guadalcanal. The hastily thrown together U.S. forces lacked cohesion. Friendly fire had cost Scott his life and multiple U.S. ships suffered friendly fire and were sunk. The night battles had quickly degenerated into brawls vs an effective use of combat force needed to conduct a proper fleet engagement. The Navy's tactical doctrine had focused on "major tactics" or those tactics that govern a major fleet action. Opportunities for the employment of "major tactics" were lacking in the two years following Pearl Harbor due to the damage inflicted on the American battleships. The surface battles that did occur in the early stages of the war resulted in the heavy use of light forces and long range carrier duels. These developments revealed tactical flaws in U.S. doctrine.

The Navy had neglected "minor tactics" or those that would govern light forces prior to hostilities and commanders were expected to draw up battle plans and doctrines themselves. For this method to be effective individual units had to train together under the same commander in order to become a cohesive unit. The war showed that the tactical situation may change rapidly and units would need to fight as a cohesive unit without such training. This showed that "minor tactics" could not be left to commanders who were not being given adequate time to prepare prior to battle. Initially commanders attempted to communicate through bulletins or memos but this produced inconsistency or redundancy.

Prior to the war U.S. carriers operated only in pairs and this was the case during 1942. However, the fleet was expanding rapidly and additional carriers were about to enter the fleet. While dispersion of carriers when there were only a few made sense as more entered the fleet it would become impractical and multiple carrier formations and tactics were required. Improved fighter direction, improved radar, and mutual support for the carrier formations would evolve and become the primary choice for offensive operations by the admirals in command of the fleet. Multiple carrier formations could operate independently and strike at targets simultaneously without the need of a willing partner. Strike operations were easier to implement and carry out over maneuvering a fleet into position to conduct a fleet action.

Multiple carrier formations however was not without risk. A single carrier formation could be overwhelmed and defeated in detail. Carriers had shown they were not survivable platforms and needed protection from air, surface, and subsurface threats. This required the battle fleet to protect them and the new fast battleships were ideally suited for such a task. This however ran counter to the concentration of force required by the battleships for a fleet action. Carriers had shown they fought a war of attrition but the battle fleet could deliver a blow so severe it might end the war in one afternoon. Nimitz was faced with a dilemma and an approach and tactical doctrines were desperately needed that could balance the power of the carrier and the battle fleet. In June the Joint Chiefs of Staff asked Nimitz to develop an overall strategy and what would be required for a Central Pacific offensive.

> June 15 2220 COMINCH to CINCPAC. Most secret for Adee only. From Joint Chiefs of Staff to. Chester Nimitz. As explained in War Dept. 4952 of 14 June Joint Chiefs of Staff are now considering the employment of forces to mount operations against the MARSHALLS from PEARL or South Pacific about 15 November. Joint Chiefs of Staff direct you submit an outline plan for the seizure of the MARSHALL ISLANDS to include following and occupation: A - List of forces required for seizure. B - Shipping required. C - Positions to be seized. D - Concept of plan. E - Proposed date for initiation of operations. F - Major favorable and unfavorable factors.[406]

The Joint Chiefs of Staff at the Trident Conference in Washington D.C. had agreed with the British for an invasion of Italy and a cross-channel invasion of Europe in 1944. In return the British accepted the strategic plan for the defeat of Japan. This plan called for the defeat of Japan through blockade and cutting off the oil from the South China Sea, followed by a sustained strategic bombing of Japanese cities, and the invasion of Japan's home Islands. Allied forces were to converge on Hong Kong and the China coast. King said that by accepting this plan the British had tacitly turned over control of the Pacific War to the Americans and Nimitz was free to move troops without advance authority from the Chiefs.[407]

---

[406] Ibid at 1606.

[407] Potter, E.B. *Chester Nimitz* at 240-241.

Operation Granite would be the code name for Nimitz's overall strategy. At its heart were two major objectives. The first was to maintain unremitting pressure against Japan and the second was the complete destruction of the Imperial Japanese Navy at the earliest possible date. In order to achieve blockade the fleet would require to stay forward deployed. This would require a large logistical train. Seizure of the Gilberts, Marshalls, Caroline, and Mariana Island groups would make available approximately twenty airfields, fifteen seaplane bases, eight submarine bases, and ten fleet anchorages. Fleet carriers would no longer be tied to amphibious assaults but be free to maneuver. Escort carriers would provide direct support for the amphibious operations.

With the ability to roam the carriers would push the fast pace and maintain the strategic initiative for the offensive. This was in keeping with Admiral Turner's threat of permanency for future operations, so that an enemy would never feel safe in rear areas and would have to expend resources to defend these rear areas. Nimitz's plan also placed a major fleet action as a strategic objective. The destruction of the Imperial Japanese Navy would allow the United States to implement strategic level blockade on Japan without interference and open the Japanese home islands to invasion. Tetsutaro's 1907 nightmare for the defeat of Japan was about to become reality.

Each operation was well planned in advance so Operation Galvanic for the invasion of the Gilberts, Operations Flintlock and Catchpole for the Marshalls, Operation Hailstone for Truk, Operation Longhop for Manus and Operation Forager for the Marianas were all worked out prior to the beginning of Galvanic. Each operation included tactical plans to bring about a decisive fleet action if the opportunity presented itself. By staying forward deployed and establishing tactical blockades around target islands it was felt this would eventually bring out the Japanese fleet and an opportunity for its destruction would present itself.

The tactical blockades would be established by the old battleships of Task Force 1. They would secure the seas around the target island cutting off all lines of communication and providing direct support for the Marines and Army. They would allow lesser ships to do their job without interference. Present in numbers the only way to break such control would be for the Japanese battle fleet to commit to battle. Failure to break such control would doom the Japanese garrison to defeat. Unable to replenish no matter, how well dug in or how determined they fought, the defending Japanese garrison would eventually exhaust themselves while the U.S., having freedom of the seas, could replenish at will and maintain effective fighting units indefinitely. By seizing the island, land-based air units could maintain the blockade as naval forces advanced to the next target and protect the supply train as American forces moved west. This would cut off the lines of communication with any Japanese held islands to the south of the American advance as it moved west toward China.

The fleet carriers required the fast battleships protection and dispersal to raid and maintain pressure on the rear areas but the battleships required concentration to deliver a blow capable of fighting a battle of annihilation. The demands of such a strategy were contradictory and ships and men would have to train to become a cohesive unit. Nimitz chose three surface officers and one aviator to revise the Pacific Fleet Cruising Instructions. Rear Admiral Robert M. Griffin, Captain E. M. Crouch, Captain Roscoe F. Good, and Captain Apollo Soucek produced Current Tactical Orders and Doctrine, U.S. Pacific Fleet, PAC 10. PAC 10 solved two significant problems. First, as noted, the creation of a single, common doctrine allowed ships to be interchanged between task groups, and this in turn enabled the rapid operational tempo Nimitz desired. Second, shifting the development of small-unit tactical doctrine to the fleet level and out of the hands of individual commanders increased the effectiveness of all units, particularly the fast-moving carrier task forces. Tactical and operational plans for the coming offensive were built on this foundation. This would allow the task forces to change from a carrier-centric fleet to a battleship-centric fleet with few instructions. In addition the plan for the decisive battle called for the use of all weapon platforms available. It was not either aircraft or battleships but a combined effort that would maximize all available firepower.

Unrestricted commerce warfare by submarines would also begin as part of the blockade of Japan. The capture of island bases in the Gilberts and Marshalls would allow subs to stay forward deployed. As the surface fleet moved west these forward bases allowed for longer patrols on station. It also restricted the available sea lanes to the Japanese to transport resources from the South China Sea to Japan. Unlike the German U-boat campaign the U.S. submarine campaign would be supported by a massive surface fleet establishing control of the seas as it moved west. With Japan's economy not of superpower status, its 100% dependence on imported oil, and the long distances and lines of communication within a geography that allowed many choke points, the use of submarines as an agent of blockade was to be highly successful.

Spruance would be in command for Operation Galvanic. The operation called for the capture of Tarawa, Makin, and Abemama Islands which would provide airfields to reconnoiter and attack the Marshalls which would be the next step in the offensive. The Americans expected and were hoping for a major Japanese response to the invasion. Tarawa and Makin were to be captured simultaneously.

Estimates suggested that the Japanese could oppose the attack with ten battleships, seven aircraft carriers, and supporting forces all based at Truk. Spruance in his operational orders said:

> If... a major portion of the Japanese Fleet were to attempt to interfere with GALVANIC, it is obvious that the defeat of the enemy fleet would at once become paramount. Without having inflicted such a defeat on the enemy, we would be unable to proceed with the capture and development of Makin, Tarawa, and Apamama [sic]. The destruction of a considerable portion of Japanese naval strength would... go far toward winning the war.[408]

Spruance would require advance warning if the Japanese fleet decided to interfere. Makin and Tarawa were too far apart for mutual support; Makin was closer to the Marshalls and was considered the more vulnerable. He placed the *Idaho, Mississippi*, and the *New Mexico* in the northern attack group and the six fast battleships which were screening the carriers were in a position to intercept any force coming from the north. Rear Admiral Charles A. Pownall who was in command of the carriers kept his force concentrated so the battleships remained concentrated. While this would provide him with nine battleships his plan was to concentrate the entire fleet with additional ships from the southern attack group providing three more battleships, for a total of twelve; nine heavy cruisers; three light cruisers; and twenty-eight destroyers. These forces would be pulled not only from the carrier groups but also the invasion fleets and absolutely required the common doctrines developed by PAC 10 for they would be formed on the spot. This was very much a battleship offensive that established local control of the seas, denied their use to the enemy, and stayed forward deployed and would continue to the next operation without delay.

In this regard doctrine was totally different from the Guadalcanal. Guadalcanal had resulted in six months of attrition as both sides failed to take command of the sea. Now the Navy would stay with the Marines side by side in support until they had accomplished their mission ashore. This would prevent the enemy from reinforcing their own defenses as they were able to do at Guadalcanal. The defender would be surrounded and cut off and this would be maintained until he surrendered or was destroyed. Instead of months to gain control of the island it would be measured in days or weeks. Only then would the Navy move to the next operation. If the sea lanes were vital enough the only way to stop the advance would

---

[408] Hone, Trent, U.S. Navy Surface Battle Doctrine and Victory in the Pacific, Naval War College Review at 78.

be for the Japanese fleet to come out and fight for control of the seas. When it did Spruance was prepared to concentrate all available firepower and annihilate it.

Had airpower never been invented the offensive would still have looked very similar to the one that was actually carried out.

Admiral Mineichi Koga took command of the Combined Fleet after Yamamoto's death. He received intelligence that the U.S. offensive was about to begin and in September and again in October he advanced his fleet from Truk to Eniwetok to give battle. The offensive did not occur so he returned to Truk. With Halsey's forces pushing up the Solomons toward Bougainville he repeated Yamamoto's April operation by transferring the carrier air wings to Rabaul in late October. The results were the same: high attrition rates left his carriers impotent. Operation Galvanic was set in motion November 20, 1943. The Combined Fleet by squandering its carrier aircraft prematurely became unprepared for a major fleet action and could no longer contest the occupation of the Gilberts by the Americans. The Japanese admirals were still thinking in terms of carrier defense and strike warfare instead of taking and establishing command of the sea.

The biggest lesson in the Gilbert campaign was the need for a prolonged preparation to reduce island defenses before the Marines stormed the beach. Spruance had been concerned that the Japanese fleet would respond quickly so his plan called for the quick seizure of the islands to allow his fleet to concentrate for the expected naval battle. At Tarawa the Japanese defenses inflicted high casualties, much higher than what was expected. For the Marshalls the pre-invasion bombardment would be increased from three hours to three days. It was estimated that half the Japanese defenders on Kwajalein had been killed before the first Marine stepped ashore. It was probably the most successful amphibious operation in the entire war.

Admiral Pownall raided the Marshalls attacking Kwajalein and Wotje to maintain the operational tempo but Rear Admiral Marc A. Mitscher took over command of the fast carriers for Operation Flintlock. The attack into the Marshalls required three attack groups. Two would focus on the twin islands of Roi-Namur the major group of Kwajalein and a third on undefended Majuro Atoll. This would provide anchorages for reserve units and staging areas. Operation Catchpole would assault Eniwetok which would provide a port to stage the attack on Truk. On 29 January 1944, Task Groups 58.2 and 58.3 attacked Kwajalein. By February 3, 1944 TG 58.3 was moved farther west toward Eniwetok and Japan's major base at Truk. Battleship Division 7 with *Iowa* and *New Jersey* was present in

TG 58.3. If a major Japanese response resulted from the Marshall invasions TG 58.3 was to fall back and the remaining six fast battleships were to concentrate. However, Spruance's battle plan called for the total concentration of all fifteen battleships being pulled from the carriers and the invasion fleet into one massive force. However, once again there was no willing partner to engage as the Japanese fleet stayed away.[409]

As early as September Nimitz was planning an attack on Truk or operation Hailstone. Truk had been the central naval base used by the Japanese for the great majority of the war. This was a major attempt to destroy elements of the Combined Fleet. It was similar to the attack on Pearl Harbor or the way Yamamoto should have conducted his Pearl Harbor attack.

> 29 September
> CinCPac-ComSoPac conferences continued during the morning. The main topic of discussion was the employment of Pacific Fleet units in support of both GALVANIC and CARTWHEEL. No decisions were reached. Also under discussion was a major strike on TRUK (PEARL HARBOR in reverse). If we could succeed in sinking a good number of enemy combat units anchored in TRUK, it would solve many of our present difficulties.[410]

There was no amphibious element to Hailstone so the fleet was free to maneuver and focus on the destruction of shipping. On February 17, 1944 the attack began. All the fast battleships were concentrated for the expected fleet encounter but once again Koga had withdrawn his major combatants abandoning the base and leaving forty defenseless transports and oilers remaining within the anchorage. With the harbor entrances at Truk blockaded there was no place to run. The few warships that did attempt were intercepted by Battleship Division 7. The cruiser *Agano* was sunk by a submarine and the light cruiser *Katori*, destroyer *Miakaze*, and a lone minesweeper were all destroyed by Battleship Division 7. One destroyer *Nowaki* did escape the blockade and was the only Japanese ship to survive the battle. Battleship Division 7 due to its high speed was designated to hunt down escaping ships as part of the decisive battle plan. In addition submarines would be placed as advanced scouts and target enemy ships if the opportunity presented itself. This would be their major role in the decisive battle.[411] The unique aspect of

---

[409] Hone, Trent, U.S. Navy Surface Battle Doctrine and Victory in the Pacific, Naval War College Review at 79-80.

[410] Nimitz, Chester, *Chester Nimitz Gray Book*, Vol. 4 at 1665.

[411] Hone, Trent, U.S. Navy Surface Battle Doctrine and Victory in the Pacific, Naval War College Review at 80-81.

the new doctrine was the implementation of combined firepower of all available platforms.

Over the next forty-eight hours the forty transports within the harbor were all sunk. The Japanese fleet trapped within the harbor had been annihilated through the combination of sea control and strike warfare. Nimitz did not allow the Japanese any time to recover and maintained the pressure until the job was finished. It still took over forty-eight hours to sink half the number of ships compared to the ninety-nine targets found at Pearl Harbor on December 7, 1941, even with a carrier force significantly more powerful than Nagumo's six carriers. The major point was that sustained operations were required to destroy large fleets. The strategy was sound in that the enemy fleet was prevented from escaping and there was enough logistical support to sustain operations until the objective was met which was the annihilation of Japanese shipping at Truk. This was the strategy that Yamamoto and the Naval General Staff would have had to adopt to succeed in the Hawaii operation. While Nimitz's plan and force structure certainly had the capability of destroying an enemy fleet the Japanese force structure under the Hawaii operation can be seen as totally inadequate to the task at hand. Once again the principle of sustainability rises as the most important principle in the application of power.

On February 23, 1944 Spruance raided the Marianas by attacking Guam, Saipan, Tinian, and Rota and on March 31 and April 1 attacked Palau and Yap. Koga was killed when his plane crashed during a typhoon between Palau and Davao while overseeing the withdrawal of the Combined Fleet from its Palau headquarters on March 31, 1944. His death was not announced until May 1944 when he was formally replaced by Admiral Soemu Toyoda. With the destruction of Truk the naval base at Rabaul was now cut off and MacArthur turned to the invasion of Hollandia on the northern coast of New Guinea. The Joint Chiefs ordered Nimitz to support this operation code named Desecrate II. Mitscher was in command with Spruance staying behind to plan for the invasion of the Marianas and Operation Forager.[412]

Mitscher's battle plan was to take TG 58.1 and raid the airbases at Wakde, Sawar, and Sarmi. TG 58.2 with Battleship Division 7 would support the landings at Humboldt Bay and TG 58.3 with Lee and the other four fast battleships would support the landings at Tanahmerah Bay. This placed his main surface forces in

---

[412] Hone, Trent, U.S. Navy Surface Battle Doctrine and Victory in the Pacific, Naval War College Review at 81-82.

the center where they could easily concentrate if the Japanese fleet responded. Six battleships, ten heavy cruisers, three light cruisers, and twenty-two destroyers were to concentrate under Lee; a carrier group, TG 58.1, would operate in direct support, under Lee's command. In the event, the Japanese Navy stayed back and watched their defensive perimeter crumble as the Army was being overwhelmed and unsupported.[413]

The application of fundamental principles of sea power—taking command of the sea and cutting off the lines of communication with any defending garrison—was resulting in the disintegration of the Japanese defensive perimeter. Command of the sea was being established by local blockades that prevented passage to the objective twenty-four hours a day. This was Mahan's third principle being applied and the concept that islands can be defended through the use of air power was also proving to be a delusion. Until Japan committed her battle fleet in advance so that it could be in position prior to American land forces reaching their objective, defense against invasion was impossible. Unlike the Japanese carrier-focused approach at Coral Sea and Midway, the Americans were now using their battleships in the strategic offensive, and the only tool capable of stopping it was the Japanese battleships.

---

[413] Ibid at 82.

CHAPTER 22: THE BATTLE OF MARIANAS

Operation Forager called for the capture of Saipan, Guam, and Tinian. June 15 was set for the invasion of Saipan with the dates being flexible for Guam and Tinian. Spruance maintained his doctrine of concentration. He planned to use seven old battleships along with seven fast battleships and form a single battle line if the Japanese fleet responded. Supporting ships would be drawn from both the carrier and invasion task forces. The fast carriers began to suppress the airfields in Saipan, Tinian, Guam, Rota, and Pagan on June 11, 1944. More escort carriers were entering the fleet which meant that they could carry out some of the aviation missions, enabling the fast carriers to maneuver freely. The air attacks were sustained for two days and then TG 58.1 and 58.4 were sent north to attack Chi-chi Jima and Iwo Jima.[414]

On June 12 Admiral Soemu Toyoda issued orders to activate operation A-Go "The Combined Fleet will attack the enemy in the Marianas area and annihilate the invasion force. Activate A-Go Operation for decisive battle."[415] A powerful fleet was assembled under the command of Vice Admiral Jisaburo Ozawa, including nine carriers, five battleships, and eleven heavy cruisers. The plan however was again based on strike warfare and this time the strategy of out-ranging the enemy was to be implemented. A-Go called for the strike to be launched at extreme range and outside the range of American carrier aircraft. The strikes would attack the U.S. fleet, land on Guam, re-arm and re-fuel and make a second attack on the U.S. fleet and return to the carriers. The carriers and three battleships, with Ozawa embarked, left their base at Tawi Tawi in the southern Philippines and sailed through the archipelago, transiting the San Bernardino Strait. A second force, with the large battleships *Yamato* and *Musashi,* came north from Batjan in the Moluccas and rendezvoused with Ozawa in the Philippine Sea. American submarines spotted the Japanese fleets and reported their position to Spruance.[416]

---

[414] Hone, Trent, U.S. Navy Surface Battle Doctrine and Victory in the Pacific, Naval War College Review at 83.

[415] Ibid at 84.

[416] Ibid.

On the night of June 14-15 TG 58.1 and 58.4 were recalled from their attack on Chichi Jima and Iwo Jima. Spruance postponed the invasion of Guam on June 16. The widely separated Japanese groups suggested to Spruance two independent task groups. Spruance conferred with Admiral Turner in command of the invasion force. They elected to reinforce TF 58 with five heavy cruisers, three light cruisers, and twenty-one destroyers detached from the invasion forces. In addition the old battleships, three cruisers, and five destroyers were formed into a blocking force and sent west of Saipan. The old battleships provided close support to the invasion beaches on Saipan and TG 58 maintained mobility to pursue a fleet action. Mitscher recommended the battleships be concentrated into a single task group and Spruance agreed forming TG 58.7 under command of Lee. It contained seven battleships, four heavy cruisers, and thirteen destroyers.[417]

Spruance's battle plan was simple. It called for air strikes on the enemy carriers and then strikes to disable enemy surface units. Task Group 58.7 would annihilate the enemy fleet by fleet action or destroy cripples if the enemy retired. On June 18 TG 58.1 and 58.4 rejoined TF 58 and a new submarine contact suggested that the Japanese force was close enough for a possible night action. Mitscher sent the following message to Lee:

> Do you desire night engagement? It may be we can make air contact late this afternoon and attack tonight. Otherwise we should retire to the eastward for tonight. I am requesting TG 58.1 and TG 58.4 to join today.[418]

Lee replied with the following message;

> Do not repeat not believe we should seek night engagement. Possible advantages of radar more than offset by difficulties of communications and lack of training in fleet tactics at night. Would press pursuit of damaged or fleeing enemy, however, at any time.[419]

In Lee's experience off Guadalcanal, where none of his ships had trained or operated together prior to the battle, the results had included friendly fire incidents, his ship running over his own men in the water, his force becoming separated, and a modern battleship being rendered blind in minutes. From this message one can speculate he was not confident in PAC 10 being able to overcome the lack of training. While Mitscher was attempting to implement Nimitz's strategy for decisive battle Lee hesitated. One of the primary purposes of PAC 10 was

---

[417] Ibid at 85.

[418] Dickson, W. D., *The Battle of the Philippine Sea at* 87.

[419] Ibid.

the realization that adequate training for confused night actions was unrealistic under the demands of war. There was never going to be a perfect opportunity and the sole objective in the decisive battle was to inflict such a huge blow on the enemy that it could end the war. Nimitz wanted to stop the war of attrition. This was the primary reason for placing the destruction of the Imperial Japanese Navy as a strategic objective in Operation Granite.

Soon after Lee responded, Spruance decided against night action. Mitscher recommended detaching TG 58.1 and operate it to the northwest to cut off the Japanese escape route but Spruance favored concentration and when Mitscher recommended close at night to get the battleships into position and attack at dawn, Spruance again declined preferring to stay back. Due to these decisions the strategic offensive was left to the Japanese to initiate the battle. Spruance's decisions led to exactly what Ozawa wanted, the opportunity for the Japanese to strike first while staying out of range of any return attack. Japanese airpower would be put to the test once again to see if it could achieve Mahan's vision of decisive battle on its own.

Vice Admiral Charles A. Lockwood, commander of the Pacific Fleet's submarines, stationed four of his boats in a square surrounding the area in which he believed Ozawa's forces would operate. *Albacore* and *Cavalla* found the Japanese fleet. They transmitted its location frequently and the Japanese were aware they were being shadowed. This was part of the American strategy of using submarines as scouts.

Early on June 18 nine G4M left Yap and found the American CVEs southeast of Saipan. Yap sent eleven A6M and six PTY and Palau sent thirty-eight A6Ms and one D4Y to attack the CVEs. The strike found the fleet oilers and were able to hit the *Saranac*, *Neshanic*, and *Saugatuck*. The latter two ships had to go to Eniwetok for repairs. Rear Admiral Sueo Obayashi of the Third Fleet ordered an attack immediately with sixty-seven aircraft but Ozawa cancelled the attack. Three B6Ns and nineteen A6Ms were already airborne when the strike was cancelled with one A6M lost upon recovery.[420]

> The attack of 18 June was canceled because its execution was impossible without staging through land bases. The decision was made to attack with all forces on the 19th, the day of the decisive battle. An attempt would be made first to annihilate the fleet carrier groups of the enemy as they steamed out from the western side of the Marianas archipelago. For this purpose we planned as follows; we would come up

[420] Ibid at 88-89.

> from the south at the outset of the attack, keeping at a distance of three hundred nautical miles from the advancing enemy carrier groups. We would be 580 nautical miles from the archipelago, so that if the carrier groups materialize we would be able to attack the vicinity of the archipelago the same day. Further, should a night reconnaissance make contact with the enemy mobile force, a search strike would be carried out. In accordance with the above, the van was detached and disposition made for air combat.[421]

Obayashi did not explain his reasoning for launching this attack to Ozawa but it was based on the principle of getting the advantage of the first strike in a carrier duel, which had been one of the keys in the carrier duels of 1942. If it had been carried out, it could certainly have been a surprise attack but this potential opportunity was lost.

> Under these conditions it would be better to be prepared for an attack immediately after discovery of the enemy. And in case there is a risk of our operation being already known on the day of the attack, it is admittedly necessary to launch a night flanking movement on a large scale in order to administer the first blow on the enemy. If the 3rd flying squadron under the circumstance had reported its plan of attack to the flag commander of the fleet, there would not have been any blunder. And in receiving the order of cancelling, if it had any confidence in itself at all, it should have proposed its opinion.[422]

Ozawa wished to advance in parallel to the line of the Marianas, which extended from Guam in a north-northeasterly direction to Rota and Tinian and then Saipan. Ozawa's force was now proceeding SSW (200°) with three ACS trailing astern after recovering aircraft, when Commander Mobile Force received information from Toyoda that the target to the north was false. Based on this new data he issued CMF Dispatch Operation Order No. 19 (DTG 181817) which stated that the enemy west of the Marianas was the target for the next day's attack. At 1900 FMF changed course to 140° and speed to sixteen knots.[423]

At 2020 Ozawa broke radio silence to advise Guam of his movements and intentions for the next day. He felt that the risk of discovery was outweighed by the advantage to be gained by a coordinated effort. U.S. Navy high-frequency direction finding (HF/DF) stations received the transmission and identified its source as "Commander First Mobile Force" estimating the accuracy of the fix as 100 miles. Nimitz passed this valuable information onto Spruance, who received it at 2200. The coordinates were 13° N, 136° E, and were accurate within 40 miles Ozawa's

---

[421] Evans, David, *The Japanese Navy in World War II* at 321.

[422] Dickson, W. D., *The Battle of the Philippine Sea* at 90.

[423] Ibid.

location. Mitscher did not receive the message until 2245. At 2230 a message from Admiral Lockwood to the submarine *Stingray* located at 12° 12' N, 139° E. concerning one of *Stingray*'s earlier messages had been badly garbled and this was then assumed it was being jammed by the Japanese. Spruance and his staff believed she had found the main body of the Japanese fleet and they also believed the message sent out by Ozawa was fake. At 2325 Mitscher, after reviewing the HF/DF intelligence, which indicated that the Japanese were no longer closing and that TF 58's present course and speed would keep the present interval between the fleets, allowing the Japanese to attack outside U.S. strike range, suggested that TF 58 change course to the west at about 0130 to be in position to launch aircraft as soon as possible the next day. He reasoned: [424]

> That the indicated probable course and speed of the enemy fleet, if combined with a reversal of course to the west on our part, would result in our force attaining the ideal striking distance of 200 to 150 miles at 0500.[425]

Mitscher and his staff felt that the old battleships and escort carriers should be able to handle any flanking Japanese groups reasoning:

> Even if the Japanese were successful in sending a portion of their fleet undetected to a position northeast of Ulithi it was believed that this was not a serious consideration so long as the major portion of the Japanese fleet could be engaged to the westward. The United States had a large force of old battleships, escort carriers, cruisers, and destroyers which could successfully engage any portion of the Japanese fleet, other than their new battleships, in a surface action. In an air action the Japanese would have inflicted some casualties, but the number of fighters in the eves would have made this attempt by the Japanese extremely expensive to them. In addition, such a small diversionary force after it once attacked could no longer remain undetected. It could be defeated or beaten off by our forces concentrated primarily for the defence of the amphibious operation, or it would be outflanked by our Fast Carrier Task Force in a sudden reverse to the south if our carrier force was not then engaged with the main Japanese fleet. The worst that could probably happen would have been some losses on our side before the southern diversionary Japanese carrier force could be destroyed. The decision was then reached that even if the Japanese chose to make such a suicidal attempt, our forces could still attack the main Japanese fleet if it approached directly from the west or southwest. It was believed that this decision was in accord with the desires of the Commander in Chief to fight a decisive battle. It appeared that there was nothing the Japanese could do with their fleet to affect seriously the occupation of the Marianas so long as the Fast Carrier Task Forces could engage the major por-

[424] Ibid at 90-91.

[425] Ibid.

tion of the Japanese fleet. There appeared no reason for not steaming directly for the Japanese fleet as long as our Fast Carrier Task Forces were intact. Even the slight possibility of damage to our landing forces could be avoided if the Fast Carrier Task Forces did not go more than 300 miles from the Marianas without some definite indication as to the location of the main Japanese force, for we could attack a diversionary force as easily from a position 300 miles west (downwind) of the Marianas as we could from the near vicinity of Saipan.[426]

At 0038 Spruance advised Mitscher of his decision regarding the proposed course change:

> Change proposed does not appear advisable. Believe indications given by Stingray more accurate than that determined by direction finder. If that is so continuation as at present seems preferable. End run by other carrier groups remains possibility and must not be overlooked.[427]

Mitscher's staff were surprised at Spruance's decision. They had not intercepted the *Stingray* dispatches. In fact, the submarine had had a fire in her superstructure and her radio difficulties had nothing to do with Japanese fleet movements. From battle experienced Spruance was aware that the Japanese used the principle of division with widely separated forces so he did not wish to be drawn out and away from the beachhead. However, one of the major advantages of PAC 10 was to free the fleet carriers from the beachhead and not tie down the carriers. Spruance enumerated his reasons for not going west that night as:

A. The position of the force located by direction-finder bearings was not definite, being within 100 miles.
B. The originator of the enemy radio transmission was not known positively.
C. The size and composition of the enemy force concerned was not known.
D. It was of highest importance that our troops and transport forces on and in the vicinity of Saipan be protected and a circling movement by enemy fast forces be guarded against.
E. There was the possibility that the enemy radio transmission was a deliberate attempt to draw our covering forces from the vicinity of Saipan.
F. The fact that a Stingray transmission at 2346K in the vicinity of latitude 12-20 N, Longitude 139-00 E had been jammed by the enemy indicated that Stingray might have made contact in that vicinity. Stingray's position was 435 miles, 246° from Saipan.

By 0300 the ships of the Japanese First Mobile Force had reached the positions designated to launch their attack. C Force formed a vanguard 100 miles in ad-

[426] Ibid at 91-92.

[427] Ibid at 94.

vance of the main body, which was composed of A Force and B Force. A Force was directly astern of C Force, while B Force was fifteen kilometers north of A Force. The ships of C Force were in three circular formations with a carrier at the center of each formation and the battleships, cruisers and destroyers in a circle around the carriers. That force was formed in a line abreast with ten kilometer intervals between groups at a right angle to the disposition axis. The six carriers of the main body were in two circular formations screened by battleship *Nagato*, cruisers and destroyers.

Imperial Japanese Navy FIRST MOBILE FORCE[428]

A Force

Carriers: *Taiho, Shokaku, Zuikaku* (79 A6M fighters, 77 D4Y and D3A dive bombers, 51 B6N torpedo bombers)

Heavy cruisers: *Myoko, Haguro*

Light cruisers: *Yahagi*

Destroyers: 7

B Force

Carriers: *Junyo, Hiyo, Ryuho* (81 A6M fighters, 36 D4Yand D3A dive bombers, 18 B6N torpedo bombers)

Battleship: *Nagato*

Heavy cruiser: *Mogami*

Destroyers: 8

C Force

Carriers: *Chitose, Chiyoda, Zuiho* (62 A6M fighters, 26 B6N torpedo bombers)

Battleships: *Yamato, Musashi, Kongo, Haruna*

Heavy cruisers: *Tone, Chikuma, Suzuya, Kumano, Atago, Chokai, Maya, Takao*

Light cruiser: *Noshiro*

Destroyers: 8

U.S. Navy TASK FORCE 58

TG 58.1

[428] Ibid at 95.

Carriers: *Hornet, Yorktown Belleau Wood, Bataan* (135 F6F Fighters, 77 SB2C dive bombers, 53 TBF torpedo bombers)

Heavy cruisers: *Boston, Baltimore, Canberra*

Light cruisers: *Oakland*

Destroyers: 14

TG 58.2

Carriers: *Bunker Hill, Wasp, Monterey, Cabot* (124 F6F Fighters, 65 SB2C dive bombers, 53 TBF torpedo bombers)

Light cruisers: *Santa Fe, Mobile, Biloxi, San Juan*

Destroyers: 12

TG 58.3

Carriers: *Enterprise, Lexington, San Jacinto, Princeton* (123 F6F Fighters, 55 SB2C and SBD dive bombers, 49 TBF torpedo bombers)

Heavy cruiser: *Indianapolis*

Light cruiser: *Reno, Montpelier, Cleveland*

Destroyers: 13

TG 58.4

Carriers: *Essex, Langley, Cowpens* (88 F6F Fighters, 36 SB2C dive bombers, 38 TBF torpedo bombers)

Light cruisers: *Vincennes, Houston, Miami, San Diego*

Destroyers: 14

TG 58.7

Battleships: *Iowa, New Jersey, Washington, North Carolina, South Dakota, Indiana, Alabama*

Heavy cruisers: *New Orleans, Wichita, Minneapolis, San Francisco*

Destroyers: 11

On the morning of June 19 Ozawa's search aircraft made contact and the first strike was made up of sixteen A6M fighters, forty-five A6M fighters carrying two 250 lb. bombs, and eight B6N torpedo planes launched at 0807 by Obayashi's three carriers, *Chitose, Chiyoda*, and *Zuiho*. A second strike was launched at 0856 made up of fifty-three D4Y dive bombers, twenty-seven B6N torpedo bombers and forty-eight A6M fighters. *Taiho* launched a D4Y (Judy) equipped with fifteen packages of window radar reflective. This aircraft's mission was to proceed to a point northeast of TF 58 in an attempt to draw off some of the American combat air patrol. Just as this strike had left the U.S. submarine *Albacore* torpedoed the carrier *Taiho* and ruptured her gasoline tanks. In a very similar fate to the *Lexington* at Coral Sea fumes built up from the ruptured tanks and at 1530 a massive explosion took place and she erupted into flames. The fires quickly went out of control and at 1728 she sank with a loss of 1,650 men.[429] In another Japanese mishap the second strike flew over Kurita's Vanguard force which mistook it as enemy aircraft and opened fire. Two Japanese planes were shot down and another eight damaged and forced to abort.[430]

The weather could not have been better for TF 58. The ceiling and visibility was unlimited. Lack of clouds allowed the combat air patrol to see the incoming strikes at unusually long ranges.[431] TG 58.7 picked up the first attack wave at 1004 at 125 miles out. Fifty F6F fighters were vectored to attack the sixty-nine Japanese aircraft. The Japanese formation was stacked with fighters on each flank and high cover above and behind at 20,000 feet. The combat air patrol dove in shooting down 26-29 of the Japanese aircraft and breaking up the formation so that the survivors made uncoordinated attacks on TG 58.7 in small groups. The destroyers *Yarnall* and *Stockham* in the outer screen were attacked and one A6M scored a direct hit on *South Dakota* killing twenty-three men and wounding twenty-three but the ship's combat capability remained unaffected. *Minneapolis* and *Wichita* took a near miss but suffered no damage. Nine to thirteen aircraft were shot down by the battle line. Forty-two Japanese aircraft were lost. Twenty-one A6Ms and six B6Ns returned to their carriers. The Japanese air coordinator, noting the devastating fire of the battle line, advised later raids to take courses to avoid this group. This transmission was intercepted by TF 58 radio intelligence personnel and was assumed to be the reason for the offset approach of raids three and four.[432]

Ozawa launched a third strike at 1000 of fifteen A6M fighters, twenty-five A6M fighter-bombers, and seven B6N torpedo planes. This strike did not find the U.S. carriers but did lose seven of the 15 A6Ms escort to the combat air patrol F6Fs. At 1130 a fourth strike of thirty A6M fighters, nine D4Y dive bombers, twenty-seven D3A dive bombers, six B6N torpedo planes, and ten A6M fighter-bombers took off for the American fleet. This last strike the majority missed the U.S. carriers and jettisoned their bombs and headed for Guam. Twenty A6Ms,

---

[429] Ibid at 110.

[430] Ibid at 108.

[431] Ibid at 105.

[432] Ibid at 116.

twenty-seven D3As, and two B6Ns were intercepted over Guam attempting to land in which thirty were shot down and those that did land were so severely damaged that they could no longer fly the next day. The remainder of the strike did make an attack on *Wasp* and *Bunker Hill* but did no damage. Seventy-three out of eighty-two planes were lost from strike four.

At 1222 *Cavalla* fired six torpedoes at 1,200 yards distance from the carrier *Shokaku* with four striking the ship. The destroyer *Urakaze* immediately attacked the U.S. sub dropping approximately one hundred depth charges in her vicinity but she managed to escape. Sixty-five aircraft went down with *Shokaku* which sank at 1510.[433] Ozawa had sent out 326 aircraft and had lost 288 including the sixty-five lost on *Shokaku* without seriously damaging a single U.S. ship. What became known as the Marianas Turkey Shoot was really a success in radar and fighter direction. Where in 1942 air strikes were intercepted at twenty to thirty miles out these strikes were intercepted at over sixty miles from their targets. With more time the more effective the combat air patrol was. In addition all the task forces while separate were still close enough for mutual support. Flight decks were kept clear so fighters could land and re-arm.

Japanese fighter pilots were far less aggressive than they were in 1942. The bomber formations broke formation rather quickly and this enabled American fighters to isolate individual Japanese planes. This was a reflection of the less experienced Japanese pilots. Their aircraft were still vulnerable and easily set on fire. The American fighters had improved significantly in the F6F over the older F4F. The Japanese strike coordinators instructions were intercepted by the Americans who communicated and vectored American fighters to where the enemy aircraft were being instructed to go. Despite the overwhelming success of the combat air patrol Japanese aircraft were still able to penetrate the air space to make attacks on the ships. The attacks proved to be uncoordinated and unsuccessful partly due to increased anti-aircraft firepower and lower skill of the Japanese pilots. Twenty-seven Japanese aircraft were shot down by ship's anti-aircraft guns.[434]

Ozawa began to withdraw to the northwest. Early morning American searches on June 20 found nothing. An extra mid-day search flown by F6F fighter pilots also came back empty. Finally at 15:12 a garbled message from one of the *Enterprise* search planes indicated a sighting. At 15:40 the sighting was verified, along

---

[433] Ibid at 123.

[434] Reilly John C., *Operational Experience of the Fast Battleships*, Naval Historical Center at 103.

with distance, course and speed. The Japanese fleet was 275 miles out, moving due west at a speed of twenty knots.[435] The Japanese were at the limit of the strike range of Task Force 58, and daylight was slipping away. After the first attack group had launched, a third message arrived, indicating the Japanese fleet were sixty miles farther out than previously indicated.[436] The first launch would be at their limits of fuel, and would have to attempt landing at night. Mitscher canceled the second launch of aircraft, but chose not to recall the first launch. Of the 240 planes that were launched for the strike, 14 aborted for various reasons and returned to their ships; the 226 planes which continued on consisted of 85 F6F Hellcats with drop tanks, 54 TBF Avengers (21 of which were torpedo equipped, the remainder carried four 500-lb. bombs), 51 SB2C Helldivers with drop tanks and 26 SBD Dauntless dive bombers. The Task Force 58 aviators arrived over the Japanese fleet just before sunset.[437]

At 1840 Lt Commander J. D. Blitch, Commander Bomber Squadron 14 from *Wasp,* decided that the U.S. Fleet would have a great advantage in a stern chase if the Japanese train was destroyed, causing them to retire at economical speeds. His air group struck the oilers disabling *Gen yo Maru* and *Seiyo Maru,* both of which were later scuttled, after the Americans retired. Fleet oiler *Hayasui* was hit once and received two near misses suffering slight damage.[438]

When the American attackers arrived, *Zuikaku* was on course 320°, 24 knots, screened by the heavy cruisers *Haguro* and *Myoko,* together with the light cruiser *Yahagi* and seven destroyers. The carrier was in the process of recovering her afternoon search aircraft as the Americans approached. *Zuikaku* apparently had two four-plane divisions of A6Ms as a combat air patrol airborne. *Zuikaku* launched the nine A6Ms remaining aboard as the Americans approached and ten A6M fighters were lost in the battle out of the seventeen total. The individual Japanese formations were well conceived to repel air attack, however their disposition of each task group was not. This comes from the uneven distribution of heavy screen units required by the straight line thrust attack disposition of the previous day. C Force no longer stood between the U.S. Fleet and the main body of A Force and B Force.[439]

---

[435]Taylor Theodore, *The Magnificent Mitscher* at 231.

[436] Ibid at 232.

[437] Ibid at 232.

[438] Dickson, W. D., *The Battle of the Philippine Sea* at 150.

[439] *Zuikaku* Detailed Action report.

TBFs from *Yorktown,* SBDs from *Enterprise,* and TBFs from *San Jacinto* made an attack run on *Zuikaku.* Most of the TBFs were armed with four 500-lb. bombs. Because of this and the fact that TBFs were not stressed for dive bombing they had to use the less accurate glide-bombing technique.[440]

On signal, the Japanese formation opened fire with all of its weapons from the 8-inch guns of the two heavy cruisers to the 25-mm and 13-mm heavy machine guns mounted on all of the ships.

> ***The Japanese employed colored bursting charges to assist director officers and the effect was similar to a fireworks display; red, white, yellow, pink, black, burgundy, lavender bursts together with the incendiaries filled the sky.***

Zuikaku managed to avoid the two torpedoes dropped, but she was hit by 'several' bombs and received five near misses. The hits caused aviation gasoline fires in the hangar deck, which quickly became unmanageable. At first the damage control parties were unable to slow the flames and the order to abandon ship was given but before it was carried out progress was made and the ship was saved.[441]

Admiral Joshima's B Force was about twenty miles southwest of *Zuikaku* on course 300 degrees, speed 24 knots. The flagship *Junyo* was in the center with the battleship *Nagato* on her starboard bow and the heavy cruiser *Mogami* on her port bow, the carrier *Hiyo* was on *Junyo*'s port quarter and the light carrier *Ryuho* on her starboard quarter; all were at 1500 meters while the eight screening destroyers were evenly spaced on a 2000 meter circle. Containing three carriers, this formation naturally drew many attackers. It also had the largest fighter contingent; thirty-eight fighters and fighter-bombers.[442]

Lt Commander Weymouth noted that the *Zuikaku* group was under attack by the *Enterprise* groups and decided to attack B Force. They were met by eight A6Ms which were quickly distracted by the F6F Hellcats as Weymouth pushed on. His group passed north of B Force and then turned to attack the southern carrier, which was *Hiyo,* but it seems that AG 16 concentrated most heavily on *Junyo.* All of the TBFs of the group were armed with four 500-lb. bombs rather than torpedoes. The aircraft reached their push over point at 1904. The pilots estimat-

---

[440] Dickson, W. D., *The Battle of the Philippine Sea* at 151.

[441] Ibid.

[442] *Junyo* Detailed Action Report.

ed that they hit *Junyo* with seven 1000-lb. bombs and nine 500-lb. bombs, and that they hit *Hiyo* at least once. The Japanese records show that *Junyo* received two direct hits near the superstructure and six near misses, making air operations difficult, but her navigational powers were not impaired.[443] There was no indication in Japanese records whether *Hiyo* was hit in this attack. Air Group 16 withdrew through the Japanese disposition and was now attacked by four A6Ms. In the attack the group had lost one F6F, one TBF and one SBD. The survivors joined up at 1918 and set course 100 degrees to return to the ship.[444]

The light carrier *Ryuho* was the object of attention of four TBF Avengers. In their glide bomb attacks the TBFs were taken under heavy fire by the battleship *Nagato*, including her 16-inch guns, but the aircraft managed to drop their weapons, claiming eight 500-lb. bomb hits. The Japanese action report states: slight damage incurred by near misses, but fighting and navigational powers not impaired' in regard to the damage suffered by *Ryuho* during the battle.[445]

The carrier *Hiyo* was not as lucky as her sisters. She had come under dive bombing attack by Air Group 16 as mentioned previously, but her damage, if any, from that attack had been superficial. The next attack was to be fatal. Lt (jg) George Brown, leader of *Belleau Wood*'s torpedo planes (four TBF Avengers with torpedoes), had vowed that he was going to get a hit on a Japanese carrier regardless of the cost. As his formation approached the Japanese fleet he entered a cloud, hoping to emerge close to the Japanese fleet at attack level. In fact, as his group of three TBFs emerged from the cloud at attack altitude they still had 5000 yards to run before they reached their drop position and the Japanese obviously saw the dreaded torpedo planes because they were immediately greeted by intense anti-aircraft fire from the screen of B Force.[446]

Brown picked *Hiyo*. His aircraft was hit and a bad fire started in the crew compartment. Brown climbed to an altitude sufficient for his two air crewmen to bail out, which they promptly did. The other two aircraft were also buffeted and hit by Japanese gunfire as they fanned out to widen the torpedo spread, but Brown's aircraft seemed to take the brunt. The flames went out as he reached his drop point. After he dropped his weapon, he flew the length of the Japanese carrier

---

[443] Ibid.

[444] Dickson, W. D., *The Battle of the Philippine Sea* at 153.

[445] *Ryuho* Detailed Action Report and Dickson, W. D., *The Battle of the Philippine Sea* at 153.

[446] Ibid.

drawing some of the anti-aircraft fire from his wingmen. Lt (jg) B. C. Tate and Lt (jg) W.R. Omark pressed on to their drop points. It seems that at least two of the three torpedoes hit *Hiyo*. When the second torpedo hit *Hiyo,* she went dead in the water and lost all power. The big ship immediately began to list to port and fires spread rapidly from deck to deck. It seemed obvious she would not survive and the orders were passed to abandon ship. A destroyer stood by as the remainder of B Force continued westward. Radioman E. C. Babcock and Gunner G. H. Platz, Brown's crewmen, watched the big carrier go down as they floated nearby. They would be rescued the next day by a float plane from the cruiser *Boston*. The three torpedo planes now headed back for TF 58. Omark was attacked by two D3As and an A6Ms as he left the Japanese formation, but managed to drive them off. Tate's plane ran out of fuel and ditched but he was later rescued. Both pilots saw Brown's heavily damaged aircraft after the battle and reported he appeared to be severely wounded. (He was lost in the return flight.)[447]

Because of the attack disposition of the previous day Ozawa's three smallest carriers were the best protected ships in his force. The three light carriers were in three circular formations spaced ten kilometers apart, approximately ten miles south of B Force. The entire formation was on course 300°, speed 24 knots. From north to south they were formed as follows:

Chitose Unit: *Musashi, Atago, Takao* and three destroyers.

Zuiho Unit: *Yamato, Chikuma, Tone, Kumano, Suzuya* and three destroyers.

Chiyoda Unit: *Kongo, Haruna, Chokai, Maya, Noshiro* and two destroyers.[448]

The entire group had but twenty-two aircraft, of which thirteen were fighters and fighter-bombers. As in the other formations the carriers were at the center of each group, with the battleships and heavy cruisers on a 1500 meters circle and the light cruiser and destroyers at 2000 meters, evenly spaced. As the Americans approached, the carriers were in the process of recovering the sixteen plane raid which had been launched at 1600 against the false contact. Seven of these aircraft were shot down in their landing circle by U.S. aircraft and only two A6M were reported over the entire formation, one of which was shot down by U.S. aircraft. The real defense of this group was its anti-aircraft guns, including the 18-inch

---

[447] Ibid at 153-154.

[448] Ibid at 156-157.

guns of the battleships *Yamato* and *Musashi.* Three U.S. Air Groups picked the light carrier *Chiyoda* to attack.[449]

They hit the carrier with two 500-lb. bombs aft destroying two torpedo planes and damaging one fighter and one torpedo plane. Twenty *Chiyoda* crewmen were killed and thirty wounded. The ship also suffered splinter damage from several near misses. After her fires were put out she recovered her fighting and navigational powers.[450] The attackers also hit *Haruna* on her deck aft and on an aft main battery turret. It was necessary to flood the aft magazines and damage to her shaft brackets restricted her speed to twenty-seven knots. Her fighting power was otherwise unimpaired. The heavy cruiser *Maya* suffered a near miss, which caused a fire on her port torpedo deck, but no serious damage. The only Japanese aircraft carriers which were not attacked were *Zuiho* and *Chitose,* the most heavily defended ships in the Japanese fleet due to their close escort of *Yamato* and *Musashi.*[451]

As the attackers withdrew they were attacked by six or seven A6Ms, which were driven off by two F6F Hellcats from *Bunker Hill,* but not before two SB2C Helldivers were lost. With this strike the battle ended but due to the long range only 115 U.S. aircraft made it back to their carriers. Twenty aircraft were lost over the Japanese fleet and ninety-one ditched into the sea due to lack of fuel or battle damage.[452] The Japanese outranging tactic prevented a second strike by U.S. forces and inflicted high and unnecessary losses on the first U.S. strike. Luckily, for the U.S. many of the pilots were rescued. With the successful withdraw of the Japanese fleet due to the long ranges fought the war of attrition continued. Another battle would still be required.

Nimitz in his June 1944 summary;

> There may be disappointment to some in the fact that in addition to the successful accomplishment of our purpose--the occupation of the Southern Marianas--there was not also a decisive "fleet action," in which we would naturally hope to have been victorious, and to have thereby shortened the war materially. It may be argued that the Japanese never had any intentions of evading task Force 58 with part or all of their forces, and making their major attack against our shipping at Saigon. From this premise it can be proved that our main body of carriers

---

[449] Ibid.

[450] *Chiyoda* Detailed Action Report.

[451] Dickson, W. D., *The Battle of the Philippine Sea* at 156-157.

[452] Y'Blood, William T., *Red Sun Setting: The Battle of the Philippine Sea* (1981).

> and gunnery ships could have pushed to the westward without concern for the expeditionary forces, and that had it done so, a decisive fleet air action could have been fought, the Japanese fleet destroyed, and the end of the war hastened.[453]

After his defeat on June 21 Ozawa was second guessing himself and his tactics. He told his staff that had he been in command of the entire Combined Fleet instead of just the Mobile Force he would have ordered all units to advance on the night of June 19 to engage in a surface battle.[454] It was too late and his carriers headed for Japan while the battleships of the Second Fleet headed for Singapore, dividing the Imperial Japanese Navy due to fuel shortages. The loss of tankers at Truk and in raids on Palau had left the fleet's ability to replenish in extreme shortage. The loss of two more oilers in this battle may have been more costly than losing the carriers. The capability of sustainability was being destroyed for the Japanese Navy and with it the true source of naval power was being eliminated. A force that can't sustain operations has no ability to maintain command of the sea. For the American offensive to be stopped the Japanese Navy would have to seize and maintain control of the seas around an island that required defensive support. Nimitz was implementing this principle which was primarily a battleship offensive but to create conditions for the decisive battle Nimitz needed a willing partner.

This would be the last carrier duel of the war and quite possibly the last in human history. Airpower had sunk one Japanese carrier and two Japanese fleet oil tankers. American submarines did sink two more Japanese carriers and the destruction of Japanese air wings had all but made their carriers strategically impotent. Once again attrition rates on the carrier air wings left the Japanese fleet unable to sustain operations. Japanese admirals continued to approach the war as if battleships were obsolete but carrier warfare was failing them and continued to create the conditions for attrition based warfare that Japan could not win given the vastly different economic power between the United States and Japan. Now all that remained to stop the U.S. advance were the Japanese battleships. Since the Japanese carrier aviation had been squandered their battleships would have to fight without adequate air cover against an enemy with un-matched air power while still being outnumbered in surface combatants. The once sought after 70% ratio the Japanese so desperately believed they needed to achieve victory had fallen to 30% by 1944. The U.S. blockade was moving west and unrestricted submarine warfare with the support of air and surface power was cutting the lines of com-

---

[453] Potter, E.B. *Chester Nimitz* at 303.

[454] Evans, David, *The Japanese Navy in World War II* at 326.

munication between Japan and the South China Sea. The inability of Japanese admirals to come up with a plan to combine the firepower of their carriers and surface ships was leading directly to their defeat. Nimitz had come up with a superior plan that combined the strengths of battleships, carriers, and submarines, but needed his admirals to carry it out, and in this first opportunity they had failed to seize it.

CHAPTER 23: THE BATTLE OF LEYTE GULF

Nimitz now placed Halsey in charge. What had been called Fifth Fleet under Spruance was called Third Fleet under Halsey. He was following Corbett's philosophy that prolonged blockade required two admirals so that one could relieve the other to keep fresh. Halsey's initial operations after taking command of Third Fleet were against the Palau, Mindanao, and Visayas Island groups, and he covered the assaults on Morotai, Palau, and Ulithi islands. The lack of resistance to these operations allowed him to advance the date for KING II—the invasion of Leyte Gulf in the Philippines—to October. Prior to the landings Halsey ordered Mitscher's' fast carriers to suppress the Japanese airfields just as they had during the Saipan landings. The sequence of attacks was as follows: October 10, 1944, airfields located on the island of Okinawa; October 11, Northern Luzon in the Philippines; finally on October 12, Formosa. The result was an air-sea battle that resulted in hundreds of Japanese land-based aircraft being destroyed in both the air and on the ground. Despite Japanese efforts (and claims) the Third Fleet didn't suffer any significant losses and the raids were considered very successful by the American forces.

Admiral Soemu Toyoda developed several SHO (SHO means Victory in Japanese) plans for where the Americans might strike next. SHO 1 was for the defense of the Philippines, SHO 2 in defense of Formosa, SHO 3 in defense of Shikoku, Honshu, and Nanpo Shoto, and SHO 4 for Hokkaido.[455] The primary objective was to position a large surface force capable of attacking and destroying U.S. surface ships and then the landing force. The goal was to strike this enemy fleet within two days of landing while the Japanese aircraft carriers provided air support for the surface combatants. In November, Ozawa's carriers were to have newly trained pilots to replace those lost at the Battle of the Philippine Sea.

For SHO 1 and the defense of the Philippines, the battle would wait for the invasion of the main island of Luzon; the Army was informed that this was when the decisive battle would take place. The first line of defense would be land-based

---

[455] *United States Strategic Bombing Survey (Pacific) The Campaigns of the Pacific War* Naval Analysis Division, 1946, *XII Philippine Campaign* at 280-323.

air forces on the Philippines and Formosa. The Army was to counter-attack MacArthur's forces while the Navy was attacking the American fleet. Toyoda needed reliable intelligence to find the enemy quickly so his forces could mobilize and strike within two days. For this plan to work adherence to two principles, timing and security, was necessary. The plan did follow the principles of objective, offensive, mass, unity of command and simplicity. However, cohesion and logistics were lacking. Many pilots had only had the most basic training; the battle fleet had not had sufficient time to train together, and fuel was almost gone.

Though the Japanese fleet would remain outnumbered in this action and the odds of success would be against Japan, the plan was soundly based on the operational art.

Toyoda knew this was the final fight. He expected the Americans would attack the Philippines in November and keep General Douglas MacArthur's promise to return. Capture of the Philippine islands would cut off the South China Sea and the vital oil and other supplies that were desperately needed in Japan. Toyoda would need every ship and every drop of fuel that could be made available. He moved the Fifth Fleet, based at Ominato, and assigned it to the first Mobile Fleet under Ozawa. The Second Battleship Division consisting of *Yamashiro* and *Fuso* was pulled from training duties in the Inland Sea and sent to join Vice Admiral Takeo Kurita's Second Fleet. Admiral Soemu Toyoda himself moved his headquarters to land so his flagship, the new light cruiser *Oyodo*, could join Ozawa's carrier force. Fuel continued to be the weak point. There wasn't enough in the home islands to supply the entire fleet. Many of the tankers had been sunk so there were no replenishment ships available. This forced Toyoda to split his forces and prevented him from concentrating as he preferred. The carriers stayed home in hopes that new replacement pilots would arrive before the next battle.

The Second Fleet under command of Kurita was sent to Lingga Island where fuel was still available. This was a powerful surface force which would be the center of gravity for the Japanese fleet in the upcoming battle. This was the first time that the majority of Japan's battle line would be aggressively committed to battle. Admiral Toyoda hoped that in November Ozawa's forces could join Kurita's force and concentrate the entire Japanese navy.

In September and early October 1944 the Japanese were planning a major fleet action centered around the battleship. This would be the largest fleet action since the Battle of Jutland in World War I. However, the fast pace of U.S. operations would disrupt everything and catch Japanese forces not yet prepared.

Plans began to change October 9, when Tokyo dispatched a message to Toyoda that they had received diplomatic intelligence that the United States intended to attack Formosa with support from the Chinese 14th and 20th air force. On the same day a plane that had been launched from Kanoya suddenly lost contact halfway between Okinawa and Iwo Jima. October 10, Okinawa was attacked. Toyoda alerted the land-based air forces for SHO 2 and the defense of Formosa. October 11, airfields on northern Luzon were attacked; October 12, Formosa was attacked by over 600 aircraft. October 12, Toyoda activated SHO-2. Land-based aircraft, the first line of defense, attacked the American fleet. With initial reports suggesting success he sent the Third Carrier division's air wings to Formosa to support the attacks. The result was a catastrophe: total of 329 planes destroyed and not a single U.S. carrier was sunk. Toyoda's gamble to send Carrier Division 3's air wing, now mostly destroyed, now made the Japanese Navy unable to provide its own air cover.

Toyoda had to start over and he developed a plan in haste. His original plan that the Navy would commit to battle after the invasion of Luzon was abandoned, Toyoda ordered the fleet to immediately contest the invasion of Leyte. October 18 at 0100, the Second Fleet set sail for Brunei on the west coast of the Island of Borneo. They arrived without incident on October 20, where they were to receive their final orders for the SHO 1 operation. October 20 at 1533, Admiral Toyoda dispatched the following orders to Kurita and the Second Fleet:

> The enemy while employing a part of his strength in the Indian Ocean area to divert us is directing his main force to carry out landings in the Central Philippines. It is the intention of the Combined Fleet to direct all of its power, cooperating with the Army, against the advancing enemy to destroy him. 1-YB (2nd Fleet) will break through to the Tacloban area at dawn on the 25th (X-day) and after first destroying the enemy's surface forces, will cut down his landing forces. Coordinating its actions with those of 1-YB, the Mobile Force will maneuver in the area to the east of Luzon for the purpose of luring the enemy to the north. At the same time utilize any opportunity to attack and destroy him. CinC Southwest Area Fleet will command all of the naval air forces concentrated in the Philippine area, and in coordination with 1-YB break through will carry out destructive attacks against the enemy's carrier and landing forces. At the same time, in cooperation with the Army, counterattacks will be carried out against the enemy's land forces. The main strength of the 6th base Air Force will be deployed as to make possible the carrying out of an all-out attack against the task force on the 24th (Y-Day). For this purpose it will be placed under tactical command of CinC South West Area Fleet. Advance Expeditionary Forces (Submarine) will continue to act in accordance with previous or-

> ders. All other SHO forces will continue with their present assignments unless subsequently specifically ordered otherwise.[456]

Rear Admiral Tomiji Koyanagi remembered the operational orders and how the staff interpreted them,

> Such large scale penetration tactics as confronted us had never been practiced in peacetime. As studies progressed the difficulties of our task became more apparent. But training gave us confidence that we would be able to withstand enemy air attack, and the idea developed that we could put up a good fight. We felt sure that the problem of penetrating the anchorage could be solved. The Combined Fleet policy that our force should destroy enemy transports at anchor, and not engage his carrier task force in decisive battle, was opposed by all of our officers. The U.S. Fleet, built around powerful carrier forces, had won battle after battle ever since attacking the Gilbert Islands. Our one big goal was to strike the U.S. Fleet and destroy it. Takeo Kurita's staff felt that the primary objective of our force should be the annihilation of the enemy carrier force and that the destruction of enemy convoys should be a side issue. Even though all enemy convoys in the theater should be destroyed, if the powerful enemy carrier striking force was left intact, other landings would be attempted, and in the long run our bloodshed would achieve only a delay in the enemy's advance. On the other hand, a severe blow to the enemy carriers would cut off their advance toward Tokyo and might be a turning point in the war. If the Takeo Kurita force was to be expended, it should be for enemy carriers. At least that would be an adornment for the record of our surface fleet, and a source of pride to every man.[457]

To complicate matters more at 1006, the Chief of Staff, Combined Fleet Headquarters advised Kurita by dispatch that:

> The staff of Combined Fleet Headquarters had concluded that it would be preferable to proceed to and break into the enemy anchorage in two groups. One from the north through San Bernardino Strait and the other from the south through Surigao Strait, rather than to approach with a whole force as a unit.[458]

This wasn't an order but a suggestion that Kurita and his staff would need to study. Prior to this message the plan was to keep all seven Japanese battleships together. What would be the advantage of a double penetration of Leyte Gulf over concentration? No answer could be given because his orders didn't specify the

---

[456] Combined Fleet Headquarters Detailed Action Report, October 17 to October 28, 1944.

[457] *The Japanese Navy in WWII, In the words of former Japanese Naval Officers*, Admiral Tomiji Koyanagi, David C Evans, 1969.

[458] Bates, Richard W., *The Battle for Leyte Gulf, October 20th to October 23rd* Strategic and Tactical Analysis, Vol. III, Naval War College, 1957. PP. 160. And First Battleship Division Detailed Action Report, October 17 to October 28, 1944.

route he was to take, the timing or the coordination that would be required if he should separate his forces. There had been no consideration of a double penetration before.

Kurita decided to send the Second Battleship Division, the heavy cruiser Mogami and four destroyers across the Sulu Sea and pass through Surigao Strait. He would take the rest of the Second Fleet, sail past the west side of Palawan, through Mindoro Strait, into the Sibuyan Sea and pass through San Bernardino Strait, then sail south along the Coast of Samar Island toward Leyte Gulf. This formed two separate pincers. The key to success would be that the majority of the American carrier strength had to be diverted north by October 23. This implied Ozawa's force would be discovered by October 22 at the latest. This would allow Nishimura and himself to penetrate the Philippine archipelago during the day on October 24 without interference from American airpower. The two forces would attack in coordination with each other so that the American battleships in support of the invasion would focus on Kurita's larger fleet allowing Nishimura to slip through the back door and attack the transports unopposed.

KING II's tactical plan called for the quick seizure of the Leyte Gulf and Surigao Strait area in order to establish air, naval, and logistics bases to expand operations into the Philippines. On October 17, mine sweepers began clearing away obstacles and underwater demolition teams began to clear the beaches. At 0800, the Sixth Ranger Battalion landed on Suluan Island and by 2000 Dinagat Island. These islands guarded the entrance to Leyte Gulf. On October 18, TG77.4 commenced air operations. By 1045, elements of the Sixth Ranger Infantry landed on Homonhon Island and with all the entrances to the Gulf secured the remainder of the invasion forces arrived that evening. [459]

The invasion force would be commanded by MacArthur and the Seventh Fleet was commanded by Vice Admiral Thomas Kinkaid. Seventh Fleet contained 738 ships. Most of these were amphibious warfare and support ships, not combatants. The landing vessels were divided into two forces: the Northern Attack Force TF 78 under Rear Admiral Daniel Barbey, and the Southern Attack Force TF 79 under Vice Admiral T.S. Wilkinson. TF 77.1 was commanded by Admiral Thomas Kinkaid in his flagship the U.S.S. *Wasatch*.[460]

The Bombardment and Fire Support Groups for Seventh Fleet were a combination of TG 77.2 and TG 77.3. Rear Admiral Jesse B. Jesse B. Oldendorf in his

---

[459] Morison, Samuel Eliot, *Leyte June 1944-January 1945*, University of Illinois Press, 1958.

[460] Vice Admiral Thomas Kinkaid, CTU 77 Action Report, January 31, 1945, RG 38

flagship, the heavy cruiser U.S.S. *Louisville*, was in command. It consisted of six battleships, four heavy cruisers, four light cruisers, and twenty-nine destroyers. Ironically, five of the six battleships he had at his command were present at Pearl Harbor on December 7th. The *West Virginia* and *California* had been sunk at Pearl Harbor and raised from the mud and modernized. *Tennessee* was heavily damaged at Pearl and was also modernized. *Maryland* was slightly damaged and had fought through the Central Pacific offensive with only modest modifications. *Pennsylvania* had been in dry dock at the time of the Pearl Harbor attack and was slightly damaged but did receive new 5-inch twin gun mounts for AA defense. She was the sister to *Arizona*. The *Mississippi* represented the most modernized battleship prior to Pearl Harbor of all the older battleships and was in the Atlantic at the time of the attack. These veterans would now have the opportunity for revenge against the two Japanese battleships determined to break through to Leyte Gulf.[461]

Admiral Thomas Kinkaid's carrier groups were divided into three task units. Rear Admiral Thomas Sprague commanded Task Unit 77.4.1 from the carrier *Sangamon*: this task force included the carriers *Sangamon, Suwannee, Santee, Petrof Bay*, and the destroyers *McCord, Hazelwood, Trathen, Richard S. Bull, Eversole, Richard M. Rowell*, and *Coolbaugh*. Sprague was the senior commander for all three carrier task units.[462]

Rear Admiral Felix B. Stump in *Natoma Bay* commanded Task Unit 77.4.2, which included the carriers *Natoma Bay, Manila Bay, Marcus Island, Savo, Ommaney Bay, Kadashan Bay*, destroyers *Haggard, Hailey, Franks*, and destroyer escorts *Oberrender, Abercrombie, Richard W. Suesens, Walter C. Wann*, and *Le Ray Wilson*.[463]

Sprague in *Fanshaw Bay* commanded TU 77.4.3. This unit consisted of the carriers *Fanshaw Bay, Kalinin Bay, White Plains, St. Lo, Kitkun Bay, Gambier Bay*, destroyers *Hoel, Heermann, Johnston*, and destroyer escorts *Dennis, Samuel B. Roberts, John C. Butler*, and *Raymond*.[464]

Seventh Fleet also had its own supporting submarines in TG 71.1: *Darter, Dace, Angler, Bluegill, Bream, Raton*, and *Guitarro*.[465]

---

[461] Ibid.

[462] Ibid.

[463] Ibid.

[464] Ibid.

[465] Ibid.

A-Day (invasion day) was set for October 20, MacArthur ordered the Sixth Army, commanded by General Walter Krueger with the X Corps and XXIV Corps for a total of 60,500 men and support units, to take Tacloban-Dulag area and seize the airfield and base sites. They were to advance rapidly through Leyte Valley to seize and occupy the Capoocan-Carigara-Barugo area and finally open San Juanico and Panaon Straits. It represented the largest amphibious assault to date by U.S. forces. By 1000, October 20, the 1st Cavalry Division landed at "White Beach" in the vicinity of San Ricardo; the 24th Infantry Division had landed on "Red Beach" in the vicinity of Palo; the 21st Regimental Combat Team (RCT) landed on "Green Beach" near Panaon and the 7th Infantry Division landed near Dulag on the "Blue and Orange" beaches. By late afternoon the beachheads were reported secure, the town of Dulag had been taken and troops were advancing toward Palo and Tacloban. The only Japanese response was an air attack on TG 79.2 and its only success was putting a single aerial torpedo in the light cruiser *Honolulu* at 1615 in the afternoon. On October 20, William Halsey assigned TG 38.1 and 38.4 to support the landings and strike targets on Leyte, Mindanao, and Visayas Island groups. TG 38.2 and 38.3 included all the battleships. They were commanded to search the north for any Japanese fleet coming from the direction of the Japanese home islands and Formosa.[466]

MacArthur planned the KING II operation believing that the Japanese would react quickly and decisively to any Philippine invasion. Therefore, KING II relied upon the quick unloading of supplies once the beachheads were established. From October 20-24, the Northern Attack Force unloaded 114,900 tons of supplies and disembarked 80,900 men. The Southern Attack Force unloaded 85,000 tons of supplies and 51,500 men. What remained of Seventh Fleet's supply ships waiting to unload by the evening of October 24, were thirty-six ships. Three hundred and fourteen ships had already unloaded their supplies and left Leyte Gulf.[467]

Nimitz gave Halsey specific instructions, "In case opportunity for destruction of major portion of enemy fleet offers or can be created, such destruction becomes the primary task!" Nimitz wanted his fleet action and believed Halsey's aggressiveness would provide it, in contrast to the more cautious Spruance. If Third Fleet's attachment to the joint operation was removed, Halsey was free to act the way Mahan would advise, and seek out a decisive battle that would destroy the enemy fleet. However, there was a contradiction because Nimitz also gave Halsey

---

[466] Ibid.

[467] Morison, Samuel Eliot, *Leyte June 1944-January 1945*, University of Illinois Press, 1958.

the assigned task of "Strategic support" of the Leyte Operation. This was to cover and support Southwest Pacific Forces and assist in the seizure and occupation of the Central Philippines.[468]

Halsey's orders to Third Fleet were; "Particular effort will be made to gain a position from which a pre-dawn carrier strike may be launched concurrently with release of fast heavy striking force from a favorable attack position. Development of a favorable tactical situation will be effected by dispatching TF 34 and carrier air groups to attack enemy. The approach will be so conducted as to give TF 34 an opportunity to strike from a favorable position and so coordinate its offensive effort with those of carrier air groups." He wanted the battle line positioned to strike with both surface and air power at the same time. The Japanese fleet would be overwhelmed and a battle of annihilation would result.[469]

Halsey placed his flag on board the battleship *New Jersey*. Third Fleet consisted essentially of Task Force 38 (nominally under the tactical command of Vice Admiral Mitscher) and logistical support units that were divided into five separate task groups.[470]

TG 38.1 was under command of Vice Admiral John S. McCain in the carrier *Wasp* and had three fleet carriers, two light carriers, four heavy cruisers, two anti-aircraft light cruisers, and fourteen destroyers. TG 38.2 was commanded by Rear Admiral Gerald F. Bogan in the carrier *Intrepid* and had one fleet carrier, two light carriers, two battleships, three light cruisers and sixteen destroyers. TG 38.3 was under command of Rear Admiral Frederick C. Sherman in the carrier *Essex* and had two fleet carriers, two light carriers, four battleships, three light cruisers, one anti-aircraft light cruiser and seventeen destroyers. TG 38.4 was commanded by Rear Admiral Ralph E. Davison in the carrier *Franklin* and had two fleet carriers, two light carriers, one heavy cruiser, one light cruiser and eleven destroyers. [471]

TG 30.8 under the command of Captain J. T. Acuff was the logistical support group to Third Fleet. This task group consisted of thirty-three fleet oilers, eleven escort carriers with replacement planes, eighteen destroyers, twenty-six destroyer escorts, ten fleet tugs and thirteen ammunition ships. This task group gave Third Fleet its staying power and ability to maintain control of the seas for months.

---

[468] Vice Admiral William F. Halsey, CTU 38, Action Report, November 13, RG 38.

[469] Ibid.

[470] Ibid.

[471] Ibid.

Without this task group the unremitting pressure and fast pace of the Central Pacific offensive would have been impossible.[472]

No Japanese naval forces immediately appeared; both Halsey and Kinkaid relaxed and started to believe that the Japanese would not resist these landings. On October 22, Halsey detached TG 38.1 and TG 38.4 to head to Ulithi to refuel and rearm. In addition, he dispatched two battleships from TG 38.3 and assigned them to TG 38.4. This left four battleships in the operational area and only TG 38.2 and TG 38.3 to maintain operations. The Army occupied Tacloban and Palo on October 22. So far the landings had been a complete success.[473]

In the evening of October 22, the submarine *Darter* sent a message reporting the sighting of three large unidentified ships at 7°31′ north and 115°22′ east, course 020°speed 21 knots. This was all the information available to the Allied forces on Japanese fleet movements.[474]

Kinkaid received additional sighting reports from his submarines on the morning of October 23. At 0200, *Darter* reported three probable battleships. At 0350, Thomas Kinkaid received another message, "*Darter* at 0300, enemy position 8° 37′ north, 116° 37′ east, course 039°speed 15 knots, at least nine ships with many radar." Then *Darter* reported at 0430, "Two *Aoba* class cruisers 14° 05′ north, 119° 40′ east, course 070°, speed 19 knots." By 0630, *Darter* had attacked and signaled she had sunk one cruiser with at least four hits on another. In addition, at 0700 the submarine *Dace* reported she had made five hits on what she believed to be a *Kongo* class battleship and sank her and that the enemy task group consisted of at least eleven ships.[475]

Kinkaid and Halsey realized that the Japanese were moving major elements of their fleet and that the landings at Leyte would be opposed. Upon receiving these submarine reports, Halsey immediately recalled TG 38.4. TG 38.1 continued to Ulithi to refuel and rearm. Third Fleet would fight the upcoming naval battle with TG 38.2, TG 38.3 and TG 38.4, with TF 34 being pulled from these three formations.[476]

---

[472] Ibid.

[473] Ibid.

[474] Vice Admiral Thomas Kinkaid, CTU 77 Action Report, January 31, 1945, RG 38.

[475] Ibid.

[476] Vice Admiral William F. Halsey, CTU 38, Action Report, November 13, RG 38.

Vice Admiral Takijiro Onishi arrived at the 201st Air Group located at Mabalacat, fifty miles from Manila on October 18 and immediately summoned a conference of the staff officers. The 201st Air Group was commanded by Captain Sakae Yamamoto, currently hospitalized with a broken leg in Manila. The executive officer was Commander Asaichi Tamai, commander of the 201st Air Group. Captain Rikihei Inoguchi was the senior staff officer of the First Air Fleet responsible for the Philippine air defense. [477] Three other men were in attendance: Staff officer Chuichi Yoshioka of the 26th Air Flotilla and two squadron leaders of the 201st Air Group, Lt. Ibusuki and Lt. Yokoyama. Onishi was in the midst of a phone call when the staff entered the room but soon finished his conversation. He addressed the staff:

> The situation is so grave that the fate of the empire depends on the outcome of the SHO operation. Missions have been assigned. A naval force under Takeo Kurita is to penetrate Leyte Gulf and there annihilate enemy surface units. The First Air Fleet has been designated to support that mission by rendering enemy carriers ineffective for at least one week. In my opinion this can be accomplished only by crash-diving on the carrier flight decks with Zero fighters carrying 500-lb. bombs.[478]

The room remained silent as the officers realized what was truly being commanded. Tamai broke the silence when he asked Chuichi Yoshioka of the effectiveness of a plane carrying a 500-lb. bomb crashing into a carrier's flight deck. Yoshioka answered that the odds of gaining a hit would be increased through such tactics and the damage may require several days to repair. Tamai responded that as executive officer he couldn't make such a decision without asking his commanding officer Captain Sakae Yamamoto. Onishi informed Tamai that his conversation on the phone had been with Yamamoto several minutes before the meeting. Yamamoto had instructed him that he should consider Tamai's opinions his own and that he would leave everything up to Tamai.

All eyes turned to Tamai, so he asked permission for a short recess so that he might consult with the squadron. He discussed the request with the squadron pilots Lt. Ibusuki and Lt. Yokoyama who would carry out these new tactics. When the conference resumed, he reported that his force was ready to cooperate and ended with a prayer that these special attacks were left to the group itself. He then requested permission to organize the unit.

---

[477] Captain Rikihei Inoguchi is the brother of Rear Admiral Toshihira Inoguchi who was in command of the battleship *Musashi*.

[478] Evans, David C. (Ed.). *The Japanese Navy in World War II.* Naval Institute Press, 1986; Inoguchi, Rikihei 415 to 439 and Inoguchi, Rikihei, Nakajima Tadashi and Rodger Pineau, *The Divine Wind,* Bantam Books, 1958.

According to Captain Rikihei Inoguchi the admiral's expression was one of sadness but relief. Onishi confided in his senior staff officer:

> Several months ago, when Captain Eiichiro Jyo kept insisting on this kind of attack, I was loath to accept his idea. But when I came to the Philippines and saw the actual state of affairs, it was clear that these tactics would have to be adopted. The situation here evidenced how poorly our strategy had been developed. We have been forced into these extreme measures although they are a complete heterodoxy of all the lessons of strategy and tactics. People do not understand my actions today, and in a hundred years from now people will still misunderstand the course I am forced to follow.[479]

Tamai needed a volunteer to lead the unit and he preferred someone who had graduated from Etajima. This would inspire others if they saw naval academy officers volunteering. He chose Lt. Yukio Seki who was considered to have outstanding character. He summoned the young officer, informed him of the plan and that they wanted him to lead the squadron. Seki leaned forward and rested his head into his hands, with his elbows resting on the table. His head was inclined downward and his eyes were closed. He had just been married in Japan before leaving for the Philippines. There was a long silence and his fists were clenched.

Then he stood up and ran his hands through his hair and spoke in a clear but quiet voice, "Please do appoint me to the post."[480]

After informing the remaining pilots of the plan, twenty-one of the twenty-three pilots volunteered. Tamai decided to call this unit "Shimpu", which is another way of reading the characters for kamikaze. The squadron consisted of twenty-six fighter planes: half were designated kamikaze and the remaining were escorts. These planes and pilots would be split into four units, Shikishima, Yamato, Asahi, and Yamazakura. All but the Yamato unit would be based at Mabalacat. The Yamato unit would be based at Cebu. Seki would command the Shikishima unit.

The pilots fully understood their role was to hit the U.S. carriers and disable as many flight decks as possible before Kurita's fleet came within range. Onishi spoke with Shigeru Fukudome and requested that he organize special attack

---

[479] Ibid.

[480] Ibid.

groups too. Fukudome refused, he feared such tactics would further reduce the morale of his men due to certain death. His remaining air strength would launch conventional attacks during the SHO operation. October 20, Onishi went to the Southwest Area Fleet Headquarters and asked for Kurita's sortie to be delayed until after kamikaze planes had a chance to strike. He arrived two hours too late; the orders to sortie had already been given. The die had been cast and all was in motion now.[481]

Dawn of October 23, and Kurita's flagship, the heavy cruiser *Atago*, was just west of the Palawan Island leading two columns at sixteen knots. In the port column was *Atago* followed by *Takao, Chokai*, and *Nagato*. The starboard column consisted of the *Myoko, Haguro, Maya, Yamato*, and *Musashi*. Both columns were about to zigzag in an attempt to avoid submarines and the port column had just finished a port turn. The morning ASW patrol by the fleet's float planes had not been launched.[482]

At 0533 *Atago* was hit by four torpedoes almost simultaneously. The four hits occurred at frames 30, 125, 180, and 260. Her anchor windlass compartment immediately flooded as well as boiler rooms No. 1, No. 2, and No. 6 with fires spreading to boiler No. 7 and her main gun plotting room. Her No.4 engine room, aft generator room, and the powder and shell magazine for number 4 main gun turret was also flooded. The *Atago* quickly took an 8° starboard list which quickly grew to 23°.[483]

Captain Tsutau Araki immediately ordered engine room No. 3, boiler room No. 7, and all port voids forward flooded in a vain attempt to control her list and bring her back onto an even keel. Her speed was reduced to eight knots. Progressive flooding continued and she lay practically on her side with a 54° list to starboard within ten minutes of being hit. At this point Captain Tsutau Araki ordered abandon ship and signaled the destroyers *Kishinami* and *Asashimo* to come alongside. Kurita and his staff were forced into the water. At 0553, *Atago* rolled over and sank by the bow, taking 350 men and Captain Araki with her. The destroyers managed to save approximately 700 men and rescued Kurita and his staff by 0558.[484]

---

[481] Ibid.

[482] Bates, Richard W., *The Battle for Leyte Gulf, October 20th to October 23rd Strategic and Tactical Analysis,* Vol. III, Naval War College, 1957.

[483] Ibid.

[484] Ibid.

The heavy cruiser *Takao* was just behind *Atago* and at 0534 was hit by two torpedoes. The first hit occurred at frame 180 flooding No. 4, No. 6, and No. 8 boiler rooms. The second torpedo impacted at frame 335, damaging the rudder, both starboard propellers, and her starboard engines. The *Takao* listed at 10° but counter-flooding helped correct the list. Her crew was successful in containing the damage but she was out of the battle. She would get back underway later that evening and return to Brunei, escorted by the destroyers *Asashimo* and *Hiyodori*.[485]

Minutes after *Atago* slipped beneath the surface of the sea, the heavy cruiser *Maya* at 0557 was hit by four torpedoes from *Dace*. *Haguro* had turned hard to starboard in order to avoid two more torpedoes fired at her by *Dace*. *Maya* didn't have a chance. The first torpedo ripped into her hull at frame 25 and flooded her anchor windlass room. The second torpedo hit below turret one at frame 66 and fires began to burn in her powder and shell magazines. The third torpedo slammed into her hull at frame 182 flooding No. 7 boiler room and the fourth torpedo's hit at frame 240 flooded the No. 3 engine room. She immediately rolled over to 30°port list and the fires in her forward magazines exploded at 0605. The destroyer *Akishimo* rescued 769 men but 336 men perished. Most of the survivors from *Maya* were eventually transferred to the battleship *Musashi*.[486]

The Japanese destroyers launched depth charge attacks in a vain attempt to find the American submarines. At 0730, Kurita ordered Matome Ukagi onboard *Yamato* to temporarily take command of the fleet until he could be transferred to *Yamato*. Kurita wanted to be aboard *Yamato* by 1300; however, the Japanese fleet continued to see phantom submarines. Between 1100 and 1430 seven submarine alarms were sounded with both destroyers and aircraft dropping depth charges on the ghosts. It would not be until 1540 that *Kishinami* was brought alongside *Yamato* and Kurita was able to transfer to the battleship. He and his staff would not resume command until 1630. Despite the upheaval, the command and control facilities on *Yamato* were superior to what was on *Atago*, so he and his staff felt that the loss of their original flagship had a negligible effect on their ability to command and control the fleet, although some subsequent commentators have speculated that the experience of having *Atago* sunk out from under him may have adversely affected his frame of mind.

Shortly after midnight on the morning of October 24, Thomas Kinkaid received more reports from his submarines. At 0030, *Guitarro* reported an enemy

---

[485] Ibid.

[486] Ibid.

task force of fifteen to twenty ships including three battleships at position 13° 00′ north, 119°30′ east, course 080°, speed eighteen knots. The next report came from *Angler* at 0340, reporting an enemy task force heading south through Mindoro Strait at twenty knots. He then received the surprising report from *Dace* at 1350 that *Darter* had run aground on Bombay Shoal. *Darter* had to be scuttled and *Dace* took off her crew and fired twenty-one rounds from her deck gun into *Darter* (adding the unusual distinction of an "own goal" sunk submarine to an already lengthy list of kills). The *Dace* then withdrew from the combat zone on her way to Perth, Australia.[487]

On October 24, Halsey distributed his forces to cover all the major passages through the archipelago. TG 38.3 was furthest north near Polillo Island. TG 38.2 was in the center off San Bernardino Strait. TG 38.4 was the most south and east of Samar. TG 38.2 only had two battleships so his battleship strength was widely dispersed. The Japanese ships were spotted early in the morning and clearly Kurita's force was the greater threat. Halsey ordered TG 38.4 to launch an attack on Nishimura's forces to the south but then concentrate toward San Bernardino Strait. He also ordered TG 38.3 to concentrate at San Bernardino Strait and attack Kurita along the way. TG 38.2 would also strike at Kurita. As these carrier attacks were taking place, Halsey issued a preparatory battle order to form TF 34 under the command of Lee at 1512. This message was specific and it would be carried out only when Halsey determined the time was right. Only TG 38.2 and TG 38.4 were close enough to bring their battleships together so TF 34 would consist of four battleships, five cruisers and ten destroyers. Halsey would have to make do with the forces he had available.[488]

At dawn 24 October, sixty miles northeast of the southern end of Samar, *Enterprise* launched sixteen fighters loaded with rockets and twelve dive bombers loaded with two 500-lb SAP bombs each in two search/attack groups in order to search sector 230-250°to a distance of three hundred and twenty-five miles. Lt. Raymond E. Moore led the second group and made contact at 0830 with Nishimura's force. He immediately radioed back that this force consisted of two battleships, one cruiser and four destroyers.[489]

At dawn of October 24, Nishimura turned southeast toward the Mindanao Sea and launched a scout plane to reconnaissance the area around Leyte Gulf. 0700,

---

[487] Vice Admiral Thomas Kinkaid, CTU 77 Action Report, January 31, 1945, RG 38.

[488] Vice Admiral William F. Halsey, CTU 38, Action Report, November 13, RG 38.

[489] Air Group-20, U.S.S. *Enterprise*, Commander Dan F. Smith, RG 38.

the plane reported there were four battleships and two cruisers to the north of the bay. Four destroyers and some torpedo boats near Surigao Strait. There were eighty transports off the landing area. In addition there were twelve carriers and ten destroyers in position forty miles southeast of Leyte. Nishimura transmitted the report to Kurita who received it at 1410 in the afternoon. This report would be the only intelligence that either Nishimura or Kurita would receive about U.S. ships located at Leyte Gulf for the entire battle.[490]

At 0910, Nishimura's force was sighted by approximately twenty carrier aircraft, which made an immediate attack. *Fuso* took one bomb on her stern that destroyed a catapult and two planes. The fire burned for about an hour but no significant damage was done. One bomb hit the forward gun turret of the destroyer *Shigure* killing the crew in the gun house. She managed to control the fires and continued with the rest of the fleet. After this single air attack none followed. His small task force of two battleships, one cruiser and four destroyers continued on course.[491]

At 1015, Kurita received a report that *Yamato*'s radar detected two B-24 aircraft at a distance of 54,800 yards. Ten minutes later a second group of aircraft bearing 70° distance 32,880 yards was detected. Ozawa's carriers had not yet been detected by the Americans and now Halsey's carriers were in position to strike Kurita's battleships as they attempted to penetrate the Philippine archipelago during the day. One of the keys to success for Kurita's plan was already broken. He would have to endure major air strikes without any support.

At 1026 on October 24 the world's largest battleship fired her guns in anger for the very first time. The Battle of the Sibuyan Sea had begun. *Yamato*'s lookouts counted twenty-five aircraft in the raid. *Yamato* was in the center of the formation and most of the attacking planes focused on her sister, *Musashi*. Two attacked *Yamato* and dropped a near-miss bomb that caused no damage. Seventeen minutes later the air attack was over and the U.S. planes withdrew. By 1043, Morishita reduced her speed back to eighteen knots. He received a report at 1046 that she scored a hit on a U.S. aircraft which was seen to fall.

At 1025 Kobe on board *Nagato* had received a report from his lookouts that the U.S. formation was twenty-six SB2C aircraft, twelve F6F aircraft and three SBD aircraft, now bearing 100° starboard, 21,920 yards. *Nagato*'s main gun turrets swung out loaded with Type 3 incendiary rounds. At 1027, he gave the order to

---

[490] USSBS Interrogation No. 390 Commander Shigeru Nishino.

[491] USSBS Interrogation No. 390 Commander Shigeru Nishino.

open fire with her main and secondary battery to starboard. Immediately her guns erupted with flame and smoke and she joined the Battle of Sibuyan Sea.

At 1012, *Kongo*'s lookouts saw an incoming raid bearing 170° to starboard. She attempted to support her flagship when U.S. planes came within range—opening fire with her 5-inch battery from 1015 until 1021. Rear Admiral Kazue Shigenaga on *Haruna* gave permission to open fire at 1026 at nine planes as they passed and fired her main battery for the first time at 1037, but checked fire by 1040.

Eight SB2C dive bombers peeled off from the rest of the formation and singled out *Nagato*. Her gunners put up a hail of anti-aircraft fire as the dive bombers closed within range. 1029, two of the aircraft dropped two near-miss bombs off her starboard bow. As the planes passed, she engaged the aircraft with her port-side AA batteries. Then the battle was over when the U.S. aircraft withdrew by 1040, and Yuji Kobe checked fire. She suffered no damage and passed her first test under fire. By 1048, *Nagato* reduced speed to twenty-two knots to conserve fuel.

After this first attack, Kurita received word that the Fifth Cruiser Division flagship *Myoko* had taken a torpedo hit aft and her speed had fallen to twenty knots. He gave instructions to the cruiser *Haguro* to transfer Vice Admiral Hashimoto to her. *Haguro* would be the new flagship for the Fifth Cruiser Division. When the transfer was completed, he ordered Captain Ishiwara, commander of *Myoko*, to withdraw to Brunei. Ukagi reported the First Battleship Division had received word from Inoguchi that *Musashi* had taken a single torpedo and several near-miss bombs had caused some minor flooding forward. Her main gun range finder was disabled due to shock damage, a matter of concern. She was still capable of full speed. *Nagato* had not been damaged during the raid.

The second raid was spotted at 1125, bearing 120° at a distance of 10,960 yards. This time the lookouts counted thirty-two U.S. aircraft approaching. Morishita, the captain of *Yamato,* issued orders to bring the giant battleship's speed up to her maximum of twenty-seven knots; she aimed her big guns which opened fire at 1146. *Yamato* remained undamaged and wasn't directly attacked during this raid. Another wave of U.S. aircraft attacked at 1115 and three appeared ready to target *Kongo*; her commander Rear Admiral Shigekazu Shimazaki ordered air alerts, but held fire as the planes passed by at 1132.[492] During the second raid at 1125 *Nagato* was completely ignored. Her detailed action report has no record that she opened fire because this raid focused on *Musashi*, which was to the *Naga-*

---

[492] *Kongo* Detailed Action Report. (24 October to 26 October 1944).

to's starboard side. She was not in a good position to assist in *Musashi's* defense, it was likely she would hit *Musashi* with friendly fire.[493]

At 1200, twenty-four aircraft were detected approaching *Yamato*. The pattern was repeated: *Yamato* increased speed, turned in a circular direction to avoid bombs and torpedoes and fired all the guns that she could bear at her attackers.[494] The waves of U.S. planes now seemed to be coming non-stop. A third raid of twenty-eight enemy aircraft was sighted bearing 88° to starboard at 1204, distance 16,440 yards. *Nagato* increased speed to twenty-five knots and opened fire. *Nagato* wasn't attacked during this raid, so she checked fire and reduced speed to eighteen knots by 1219.[495]

Morishita sighted the fourth raid at 1312, bearing 300°. *Yamato* was spared again when the U.S. aircraft focused on other ships. By now, Kurita was frustrated that he had received no word from Ozawa, Combined Fleet Headquarters or the South West Area Fleet Headquarters about their plans to attack U.S. forces. Their attacks were to spare his fleet from U.S. air attacks and they were obviously failing their mission. At 1315, Kurita sent a message to Ozawa and the South West Area Fleet Headquarters: "*We are being subjected to repeat enemy carrier-based air attacks. Advise immediately of contacts and attacks made by you on the enemy.*"[496]

At 1331 twenty-four aircraft attacked *Yamato*. At 1342 one medium-sized bomb hit her at frame 70 on the port beam. The blast blew out the side shell between frames 54–78 creating a hole 46' long x 16' wide between the tween and lower deck just above the waterline. Consequently, twenty heavy-fuel oil tanks were flooded, 710 tons of water flooded void tanks. At 1358, she reduced speed, spotted the next wave of enemy planes and increased her speed to twenty-four knots by 1403.[497]

A formation of approximately twenty-nine U.S. aircraft was seen along the horizon forming for another attack. By 1426 Morishita gave the order to re-open fire. Four minutes later another medium-sized bomb struck the forecastle deck at frame 33. It first made a 1.2' hole, passed through the upper deck to make a 1.5' hole, continued through the tween deck to create a 3' hole and exploded below

---

[493] *Nagato* Detailed Action Report. (24 October to 26 October 1944).

[494] *Yamato* Detailed Action Report. (17 October to 28 October 1944).

[495] *Nagato* Detailed Action Report. (24 October to 26 October 1944).

[496] *Yamato* Detailed Action Report. (17 October to 28 October 1944).

[497] Ibid.

the waterline. The bomb blew two holes in the outer shell: the first was 3' x 6' and the second was 6' x 12' on the port side. An officer's bedroom on the upper deck was moderately damaged, dental operating room on tween deck seriously damaged and the forward windlass room was flooded. Warehouse compartment number seven was flooded and the ship took on 3,000 tons of water. In addition, the hull indicated a variation in heel of 2-3° to port and in trim of 10' down by the bow. Her maximum speed was reduced from twenty-seven to twenty-six knots.[498]

A sixth raid estimated to be eighty-five aircraft attacked before the fifth raid was completed. Morishita maintained *Yamato*'s fire on U.S. aircraft until 1525 when the last U.S. aircraft withdrew. His ship was strafed by fighters but no further bomb or torpedo damage occurred. Morishita received more reports of damage to his ship. Minor damage from fragments was found in the boat garage, Warrant Officer Room frames 19-21 on port side suffered fragment damage. The 7th and 5th AA guns were disabled, there were nine broken communication circuits and the left catapult had an electrical wire broken. Twenty-four aerial wires were down and the port side boat hoist was unusable. Despite this *Yamato's* combat capability was unimpaired. She was capable of twenty-six knots, all of her fire-control instruments and her main and secondary batteries remained intact.[499]

On *Nagato* another air alert was sounded at 1315 and at 1321 more enemy aircraft were detected bearing 255°, distance 38,360 yards. The formation turned 190° by 1326. At 1331 forty enemy aircraft were advancing bearing 5° starboard, distance 10,960 yards. At 1426, four dive bombers attacked and dropped four near miss bombs off her starboard bow. Approximately 700 fragment holes were opened in her hull between frames 24 and 25. These were plugged by the crew over the next forty eight hours. At 1514, twenty-five U.S. aircraft attacked her. Two bombs hit her amidships at 1520 but speed was maintained at twenty-two knots. At 1534, she checked fire and reduced speed to eighteen knots.[500]

The first bomb struck the boat deck just aft of the main pagoda superstructure, penetrated this deck and exploded next to the port side No. 4 casemate gun. Ready ammunition for casemate guns No. 2, No. 4, and No. 6 exploded within the No. 2 crew compartment and disabled all three casemate guns on the forecastle deck. The air intake to No. 1 boiler room was damaged, which forced the No.

---

[498] Ibid.

[499] Ibid.

[500] *Nagato* Detailed Action Report, 24 October to 26 October 1944.

1 boiler room to shut down and reduced her top speed to twenty-two knots. Due to the secondary explosions, fire spread to the deck below, disabling the No. 4 casemate gun on the upper deck level as well. Fragments disabled the starboard side Type 91 director for her starboard 5-inch guns.[501]

The second bomb entered the ship's galley through the sky window, detonated in the rear of the command communications room, killed two officers and twelve men, with six more seriously injured. The machine shop, laundry room and passageway were destroyed. In total three officers and thirty men were killed, another three officers and thirty-three men wounded. During the day's action she claimed to shoot down eight planes and damage six others. Although she had taken two bomb hits, her fighting ability wasn't impaired. She regained use of her No. 1 boiler room later that evening and her top speed returned to twenty-five knots before the Battle of Samar. Kobe reported her damage and results to Ukagi on board *Yamato*. The Battle of Sibuyan Sea had ended for *Nagato*.[502]

At 1520 a group of three planes attacked *Haruna's* starboard bow and three more targeted her port side aft. Shigenaga ordered a hard turn to port at 1521 and then an equally hard turn to starboard. One of the planes on her bow was shot down before it could drop its bomb. The other two dropped near-miss bombs off her port bow. A second plane crashed after it had released its bomb. All three planes that attacked from aft released their bombs, but she turned hard to starboard and her stern swung to port. The three bombs fell into the water on her starboard side. Shigenaga reported two of the planes that attacked from aft also fell shortly after releasing their bombs. By 1539, she reduced her speed to twenty knots and checked fire by 1541. Her hull was damaged by fragments due to the three near-miss bombs.[503]

Over the next five hours 250 American aircraft would attack Kurita's ships in six major waves. A single torpedo would force the heavy cruiser *Myoko* to head back toward Brunei. *Yamato*'s sister *Musashi* absorbed the brunt of these attacks. Rear Admiral Toshihira Inoguchi took command of *Musashi* on August 15, 1944. Known to be one of the best gunnery officers in the Japanese Navy, he fully believed his giant battleship could defend itself against air attack. Like her sister *Yamato* she had been held in reserve for most of the war. This operation represented the first mission which called upon her to take offensive action. At 1000,

---

[501] Ibid.

[502] Ibid.

[503] *Haruna* Detailed Action Report, 24 October to 26 October 1944.

Musashi's search radar detected approximately forty planes bearing 110° at a distance of sixty-three miles. Two B-24 bombers bearing 200° distance thirty-five miles with an attitude of 13,152 feet were identified soon after the first contact was made. At twenty-five miles approximately forty aircraft were reported off the port bow. Air alerts were ordered and the fleet speed was increased to twenty-four knots. 1025, *Musashi* opened fire with her 6.1-inch and 5-inch guns. Her main battery didn't participate in the defense of this wave. *Musashi* claimed seventeen aircraft attacked her and she claimed to shoot down four aircraft, but U.S. records can only confirm the loss of two planes from *Cabot* with a third badly damaged and forced to abort his mission due to heavy flak.[504]

Musashi suffered four near-miss bomb explosions. The first bomb fell off the starboard side at frame 25 and a second bomb detonated off the port bow at frame 20. The near misses caused flooding within her forward peak tanks in the bow. The third near-miss landed off her port side at frame 135 while fourth near miss detonated to starboard at frame 145. A fifth bomb landed directly on the roof of the main gun turret, number one, but was unable to penetrate the heavy armor. It failed to detonate and caused no damage. Then at 1029 a torpedo slammed into her starboard side at frame 130 and flooded her No. 11 and No. 7 boiler rooms. Pumps kept the flooding in No. 11 boiler room under control for the time being but No. 7 boiler room completely flooded. The ship took a 5.5° list to starboard which was quickly reduced to 3° by counter-flooding port void tanks. Her speed and her combat capability were unaffected and she maintained her position within the formation. Two additional torpedoes had been reported to the chief engineer at frames 140 and 150 to starboard but no damage or leakage occurred, so the chief engineer believed the reports of these two hits to be erroneous.[505]

Shock damage from the torpedo disabled the main battery director which ruined Inoguchi's plans to use the main battery for *Musashi*'s AA defense. By 1047, the air alert was over when the remaining U.S. planes disappeared over the horizon. The *Musashi* expended 48 6.1-inch projectiles and 160 5-inch projectiles during this attack. The next wave of U.S. aircraft came between 1136 to1149 bearing 088°, range nine miles. *Musashi* was their main target and sixteen planes made an attack. At 1136, *Musashi* opened fire with her main battery under local control, but a shell in the center gun of turret one exploded and the elevating gear was disabled. *Musashi's* records reported eight SB2C and eight TBF bombers at-

---

[504] *Musashi* Detailed Action Report. 24 October 1944

[505] Ibid.

tacked her. She claimed two dive bombers were shot down and one torpedo plane forced to abort due to damage.[506]

The dive bombers scored two hits. The first struck at frame 15 on the forecastle deck, passed through the ship's head and exited the shell plating above the waterline without exploding. No flooding resulted at this time. The second bomb struck at frame 138 six to eight feet to port from the stack ahead of 5-inch gun No. 4, it penetrated two decks and detonated in crew space No. 10. This cut steam lines to the No. 2 port inboard engine room and it filled with smoke and steam. It had to be abandoned and was never manned again, leaving only three engines operational. The revolutions per minute (RPM) of the other three engines were increased so her overall speed wasn't affected. Four near-miss bombs fell between frames 10 through frame 60 on the starboard side and another near-miss bomb landed close to frame 70 on the port side.[507]

Musashi took her second torpedo at frame 145 just outboard of the port outboard engine room and the port hydraulic machinery room. The hydraulic machinery room eventually flooded but there was only minor leakage into the engine room. After this attack she remained on an even keel since the port torpedo acted as counter-flooding to the 3° starboard list noted earlier. The chief engineer received reports of two additional torpedo hits to port: one at frame 80, another at frame 110. These may have been bombs that were near misses because no inboard flooding occurred, so the chief engineer discounted the report of two additional hits. In this attempt to defend herself *Musashi* had expended nine 18.1-inch Type 3 projectiles, seventeen 6.1-inch projectiles and 117 5-inch projectiles.[508]

At 1217, the next wave of U.S. planes appeared. Four SB2C dive bombers, four TBF torpedo bombers and five F6F fighters attacked *Musashi*. She claimed five U.S. aircraft shot down but this can't be confirmed. Her main battery fired thirteen more rounds in a desperate attempt to down the U.S. aircraft at long range. *Musashi* suffered two near-miss bomb hits on the starboard side at frame 180. Then a torpedo hit on the starboard side at frame 60 in the bow making this her third confirmed torpedo. This torpedo flooded several large storerooms and brought her trim down by the bow by 6.5 feet. She only assumed a minor starboard list from this damage because the hit was so far forward in her narrow bow. Her secondary battery expended forty-three 6.1-inch projectiles and one hundred

---

[506] Ibid.

[507] Ibid.

[508] Ibid.

ninety-four 5-inch projectiles during this raid. After three attacks *Musashi* was still able to maintain speed and remained combat effective.[509]

On board *Musashi* at 1315, an estimated forty aircraft were sighted to starboard bearing 005°, range six miles. Twenty aircraft headed for *Musashi* who claimed to shoot down eight of the attackers. Reports stated that four bombs and four torpedoes scored direct hits. The first bomb impacted at frame 135 starboard and then three bombs struck to port at frames 45, 65, and 70. One torpedo hit at frame 70 to port and another hit at frame 70 to starboard. The effects of these two torpedoes plus the earlier hit at frame 60 in the third attack resulted in the complete flooding of the bow from frame 54 all the way to the armored citadel in front of turret 1. Her bow settled and the forecastle deck was just above the waterline. Due to the heavy bow trim she lost speed and slowed to sixteen knots. A third torpedo hit at frame 130 starboard and immediately flooded the starboard hydraulic pump room. A fourth torpedo was reported at frame 138 starboard, outside the starboard outboard engine room. Now the No. 11 boiler room damaged in the first attack flooded and had to be abandoned. Two other inboard boiler rooms were also no longer operational due to broken steam lines. This left three operational engine rooms and nine operational boiler rooms. Toshihira Inoguchi ordered her speed reduced to twelve knots for safety and more port voids were flooded to remove her list so she returned to an even keel. At this speed she was no longer mission-capable but she was not in danger of sinking.[510]

Halsey gave the Japanese no respite and at 1425 a fifth wave of aircraft attacked. Fortunately for *Musashi* she was ignored during this attack as it focused on *Yamato*. At 1521, a sixth wave attacked and *Musashi* was their main target. At least seventy-five U.S. aircraft attacked the badly damaged battleship that had clearly slowed down. Ten more bombs struck the ship plus ten more torpedoes.[511]

The first bomb hit the heavily armored roof of main gun turret #1 and didn't penetrate the armor. The second bomb hit on the port side of the forecastle deck at frame 62. The third bomb hit at frame 79 on the starboard side and detonated in the ward room. The fourth and fifth bombs hit at frame 115 starboard, detonated on the forecastle deck and caused extensive topside damage. The sixth and seventh bombs detonated at frames 108 and 115 port side and destroyed a nearby radio room. The eighth and ninth bombs struck at frame 120 port and centerline

---

509 Ibid.

510 Ibid.

511 Ibid.

at the 08 level of the pagoda superstructure and wounded Rear Admiral Inoguchi. The tenth bomb hit at frame 127, struck the tower on the 02 level but caused only minor damage.[512]

The first two torpedo hits were reported as duds striking at frame 145 port and no damage was sustained. The third torpedo hit was at frame 75 port, next to turret 1 magazine. The magazines on the lower two levels were flooded. The fourth hit was near frame 125 port and flooded No. 8 boiler room immediately and No. 12 boiler room eventually. The fifth torpedo hit was at frame 145 port and flooded the port outboard engine room. The sixth hit was at frame 105 starboard which flooded the AA magazines immediately forward of the machinery compartments. The chief engineer didn't have details about the last four hits other than location. The final four were located at frames 40, 60, and 165 port with the last torpedo hit at frame 80 to starboard.[513]

Musashi also suffered four near-miss bombs frames 130-140 on the starboard side and two near-miss bombs to frames 135-140 on the port side. The *Musashi* absorbed seventeen torpedoes[514], seventeen bomb hits, and eighteen near-miss bombs and had finally suffered fatal damage. Though she struggled to stay afloat until 1920 when the order was given to abandon ship. Finally, at 1935 she lost her stability and capsized to port. Her bow sank quickly and as her stern rose vertically the men who had somehow clung to her upturned hull were desperate to get off the ship. The men who fell off the stern plummeted hundreds of feet into the water's surface or hit her propellers that rose out of the water. When she plunged water was pulled back into the gaping holes left by the torpedoes and created a whirlpool as she sank from the surface. Finally, she exploded below the surface which killed or severely wounded many men in the water. The destroyer *Hamakaze* and *Kiyoshimo* didn't immediately approach the area due to the heavy thick oil left on the water's surface. They rescued 1,376 men from the original crew of 2,399 and continued rescue operations until 0215 in the morning. Rear Admiral Toshihira Inoguchi wasn't among them—he chose to go down with his ship. *Musashi*'s Executive Officer, Kenkichi Kato, was among the living who recounted *Musashi*'s ordeal after the war.[515]

---

[512] Ibid.

[513] Ibid.

[514] Only fifteen torpedoes detonated.

[515] *Musashi Detailed Action Report.* (24 October 1944): PP 1-27 and Technical Mission to Japan, Index No. S-06-2 Ships and related targets, Loss of the *Musashi.*

The loss of *Musashi* required more aircraft than the planes allocated against the U.S. Navy targets at Pearl Harbor, which makes the idea of "air dominance" a questionable one. It is almost pathetic that it required this much force to sink one individual ship. By absorbing the great majority of the U.S. effort *Musashi* had saved the rest of Kurita's fleet from significant damage. After the sixth attack Kurita decided to turn his force around and headed west to keep his fleet in the more open waters of the Sibuyan Sea. The principal reason Kurita pulled back temporarily was geography. He was approaching San Bernardino Strait which would require him to form his ships into a line ahead formation that would stretch thirteen miles. He needed enough room to maintain a circular formation if air attacks continued instead of lining his ships up like ducks at a shooting gallery. Rather than "retreating under air attack", he was simply opting to avoid giving the enemy a tactical advantage. Had he been in the open sea he would not have withdrawn. At 1600, he radioed Toyoda the following dispatch:

> Originally the main strength of the First Diversion Attack Force had intended to force its way through San Bernardino Strait about one hour after sundown, coordinating its moves with air action. However, the enemy made more than 250 sorties against us between 0830 and 1530 the number of involved and their fierceness mounting with every wave. Our air forces on the other hand were not able to obtain even expected results causing our losses to mount steadily. Under these circumstances it was deemed that were we to force our way through we would merely make ourselves meat for the enemy, with very little chance of success. It was therefore concluded that the best course open to us was temporarily to retire beyond reach of enemy planes and reform our plans. At 1600, we were on course 290° speed eighteen knots.[516]

As the fleet sailed west they passed *Musashi*. This had a demoralizing effect on all who witnessed her plight. Ukagi sent orders to ground her but was at a complete loss to find any words that would help her morale. He grieved for the loss of this ship. He was convinced that his fate was linked to *Yamato*'s. He wrote in his diary,

> I learned that Kurita had appealed to the higher command that it thought it better to advance to the decisive battle scene after attacks of the land base air forces had made some effect. Certainly it seemed that we would expend all our strength before we got there, if and when we were continuously attacked like this. Still we had no choice but to go ahead. This taught us a lesson that it would be best to take up a case which could be the more easily settled when dealt with case by case. That we could do nothing else but go ahead determined to die was

---

[516] Combined Fleet Headquarters Detailed Action Report, October 17 to October 28, 1944.

> what I thought at the time. However, I noticed that it would be more advantageous for tomorrow's fighting if we could deceive the enemy by turning back once before evening.[517]

Kurita's forces turned north at 1630, turned northwest at1648 and sent messages to Ozawa and Shoji Nishimura of his delay. However, by 1714 no more air attacks had materialized and Kurita felt that the U.S. air attacks had ended. He still had not received a reply from Combined Fleet Headquarters and decided to resume the mission. When his staff reminded him that Toyoda had not responded he replied, "*That's alright. Let's go.*"[518] With this his fleet turned east again toward San Bernardino Strait to complete the operation. Upon receiving Kurita's message at Combined Fleet Headquarters, Toyoda focused upon the word "retirement" and his reply at 1815 stated Kurita should, "*Advance counting on Divine Assistance.*" In his post-war interrogation Toyoda explained the meaning of this order as follows:

> The meaning of that order was, while it does not appear in the wording of the orders, that damage couldn't be limited or reduced by turning back, so advance even though the fleet should be completely lost. That was my feeling when sending that order; consequently I am safe in saying that the Second Fleet wasn't restricted in any way as to the damage it might suffer.[519]

With the widely separated forces it was exceedingly difficult if not impossible to maintain a well-orchestrated timetable. Each commander was largely on their own and without full knowledge of the situation that had developed with the other task forces. This is why Mahan preferred concentration over division. Kurita expected but had not received the support from Japanese land-based air neutralizing the American carrier groups. It was also evident that Ozawa had not diverted them north so the original concepts that the SHO 1 plan had assumed for victory were already in disarray.

The Japanese land-based air units struggled to fulfill their assignment in the SHO 1 operation. Fukudome moved his headquarters from Formosa to Manila on October 22. He transferred approximately 450 planes, the remainder of the Second Air Fleet, to the First Air Fleet squadron of 100 planes already stationed in the Philippines. The planes arrived on October 23 and they were to attack the U.S. fleet in route, but no contact was made with the U.S. forces. Most of the Japanese pilots had incomplete training. Many could not fly out of sight of land.

---

[517] *Fading Victory The Diary of Admiral Matome Ugaki*, 1991.

[518] *The End of the Imperial Japanese Navy* by Masanori Ito, 1956.

[519] USSBS Interrogation No. 378, November 13-14, 1945 Admiral Soemu Toyoda.

The weather on October 24 was very bad, with a rain front that stretched from Manila to the north coast of Luzon. In the Central Philippines clear weather prevailed and a scout plane made contact with a carrier task force. Fukudome immediately transmitted the report but the pilot had made an 80° error when he noticed the U.S. forces. Shigeru Fukudome launched a series of attacks with approximately 250 aircraft but most were unable to locate the enemy.

The planes that did attack were successful in damaging the light carrier *Princeton*. While she fought the fires raging onboard, the light cruiser *Birmingham* came alongside to assist her. Then disaster struck when *Princeton* exploded and killed many men on *Birmingham* too. The fires were out of control and *Princeton* eventually sank. *Birmingham* and three destroyers took damage when *Princeton* exploded. Fukudome sent fourteen fighters to cover Kurita's passage through the Sibuyan Sea. American reports state they saw four Japanese fighters and Kurita reported he saw none. Time was running out and the SHO plan was failing.

When Ozawa received Fukudome's report with the location of the enemy, he prepared to launch his strike aircraft. The weather was so poor he instructed his pilots to head for land bases after the attack if a return to the carriers was uncertain. At 1145, the strike was launched and forty fighters, twenty-eight dive bombers, six torpedo planes and two reconnaissance planes flew off. The distance to the U.S. carriers was approximately one hundred and fifty miles. Ozawa transmitted that he had launched his attack to Toyoda but the message was never received due to the bad transmitter on *Zuikaku*.

Ozawa received reports that Kurita was under heavy air attack and had taken significant damage. The decoy effort had not worked. He had expected to be sighted by U.S. submarines on the 23rd, but this had not occurred and his forces remained undetected by the enemy. The only offensive fire power that remained was in the hybrid battleships *Ise* and *Hyuga*. At 1439, Ozawa ordered Rear Admiral Chiaki Mutsuda in command of *Ise* and *Hyuga* to take four destroyers, *Akitsuki*, *Hatsuzuki*, *Wakatsuki*, and *Shimotsuki*, proceed south and attack the U.S. carriers in a night surface action. By 1500 Mutsuda's forces had left Ozawa's carriers.

A single American search plane was spotted high above the fleet at 1635. Ozawa on his flagship *Zuikaku* confirmed that the search plane had transmitted their position and received acknowledgement from its base, overhearing the U.S. pilot's radio reports. Two fighters were launched to intercept but the search plane escaped. Ozawa never received any report about his strike. Only three planes returned to his carriers though thirty landed on land-based airfields. He now had nineteen fighters, five fighter-bombers, four torpedo planes and one dive bomber. Ozawa had finally been discovered but his orders were not to get his force annihilated but to divert the American carriers north. Ozawa however interpreted his orders that his force should be sacrificed in order to complete his mission. Instead of attempting to stay outside of American strike range and get the Americans to chase him he maneuvered his force so it could be attacked. Many scholars have praised Ozawa for diverting Halsey north but his Emperor needed a "fleet in being" at minimum to ever gain the political goal of getting the United States to the negotiation table. Allowing his force to be attacked and destroyed only served the United States strategic objective of annihilating the Imperial Japanese Navy. Despite the operational deficiencies of the Japanese carriers, their survival was critical to maintaining this last strategic playing card.

When night fell on October 24, U.S. air power had failed to control the seas. The destruction of a single Japanese battleship and the withdrawal of one cruiser did not force the Japanese to stop their advance. As night approached the carrier planes could no longer attack and control of the seas shifted back to the surface ships. Mahan's philosophy that a battle fleet was required to destroy an enemy battle fleet still held true.

Similarly, Japan's air forces had failed to destroy or decoy the Third Fleet. The destruction by air power of the carrier *Princeton* was completely insufficient to advance Japanese strategic purposes. The failure to decoy Third Fleet directly led to the loss of *Musashi* and more importantly disrupted the timing of the double penetration between Kurita and Nishimura. With the SHO plan's timing disrupted, disunity of effort between Kurita, Ozawa, Nishimura, and Shima was inevitable.

When Kinkaid received Halsey's preparatory battle order to form TF 34, he didn't notice this was a preparatory order and assumed Halsey had formed TF 34 with the intent to guard San Bernardino Strait. With the northern flank protected, his mind quickly focused on Nishimura's force and he could concentrate all his firepower on this threat as espoused by Mahan. Kinkaid sent out his battle plan at 1443, issued his orders to the Seventh Fleet then informed Halsey, Nimitz and King in Washington D.C. of his decisions. His orders were as follows:

> Prepare for night engagement. Enemy forces estimated two battleships, four heavy cruisers, four light cruisers, ten destroyers reported under attack by our carrier planes in eastern Sulu Sea October 24. Enemy may arrive at Leyte Gulf tonight. Make all preparations for night engagement TG77.3 assigned to CTG 77.2 as reinforcement. Station maximum number of PT boats lower Surigao Strait to remain south of 10° North during darkness.[520]

---

[520] Vice Admiral Thomas Kinkaid, CTU 77 Action Report, January 31, 1945, RG 38.

Jesse B. Oldendorf and his six battleships would guard the center at the top of the Strait. The cruisers would be on both the left and right flanks. This permitted maximum use and effectiveness of firepower from his large caliber rifles. Destroyers and PT boats would then be sent down the strait and situated to conduct torpedo attacks from each side prior to the gun duel. This concentration of forces was consistent with doctrine and the operational principles of war. Kinkaid understood that the Japanese Northern force couldn't break U.S. control of Leyte Gulf. An air strike by such a force might sting his fleet but it could not occupy the Gulf. This made the Japanese carriers irrelevant to Kinkaid's mission, providing close support to the invasion when threatened by an enemy battle fleet.

On board *New Jersey*, Halsey's staff compiled the day's results. Rear Admiral Bogan of TG 38.2 presented the following:

- One *Yamato*-class battleship damaged by three torpedoes hits.
- One *Yamato*-class battleship damaged by one torpedo hit and two bomb hits (possibly same).
- One *Nagato* class battleship damaged by one torpedo and one bomb hit.
- One *Kongo* class battleship damaged by two torpedo hits and six bomb hits.
- One *Mogami* class heavy cruiser damaged and possibly sunk by torpedo.
- One *Nachi* class heavy cruiser damaged by one torpedo hit.
- One Tone class heavy cruiser damaged by one torpedo hit.[521]

Rear Admiral Sherman of TG 38.3 estimated as follows: One battleship badly damaged, two battleships damaged, four heavy cruisers damaged, two light cruisers damaged.

Rear Admiral Davison of TG 38.4 reported:

- One *Yamato*-class battleship damaged by torpedo and down by the bow, probably sunk.
- One *Yamato*-class battleship damaged by one to three torpedoes and two bomb hits.
- One *Kongo* class battleship damaged by one bomb hit.

---

[521] Vice Admiral William F. Halsey, CTU 38, Action Report, November 13, RG 38.

- One heavy cruiser damaged, one light cruiser sunk, one destroyer sunk, one destroyer probably sunk, four destroyers damaged. [522]

Halsey and his staff believed that the Japanese Center Force was rendered combat-ineffective. Halsey had no way of knowing that the majority of the claimed hits were all on the same ship. No one imagined that a single battleship could absorb all the damage that *Musashi* had therefore it was logical to Halsey's staff that both *Yamato*-class battleships had taken serious damage. When the Japanese Center Force turned around and headed west, Halsey believed that this force had indeed suffered heavily. Nevertheless, Halsey received additional reports that this Center Force had turned back east and was informed by later reports that all the navigation lights for San Bernardino Strait had been turned on. Lee suggested that the Center Force would still come through San Bernardino Strait that night and recommended that TF 34 be formed. Halsey needed to decide which Japanese force posed the greater threat to his mission of protecting Seventh Fleet and destruction of which Japanese force constituted Nimitz's other strategic goal expressed in Operation Granite.

When Ozawa's northern force had been detected at 1540, it was reported as three BB, six CA and six DD with a second contact of four CV, three CA and three DD. This report made the northern force appear far more formidable than it was. Halsey's staff came up with three options. The first was to stay and concentrate on the Center Force. Halsey dismissed it because it left the Northern Group free to attack unmolested and forced Halsey to remain stationary. This static posture was contrary to his overall battle plan; he wanted to maneuver his forces at night into a position to allow both his carriers and battleships to attack simultaneously. This would remove any option for the Japanese commanders to accept or decline battle. The Japanese decision to use division over concentration was complicating the U.S. response. Nimitz wanted his admirals to concentrate all available firepower to be able to deliver a blow that would produce a battle of annihilation. Carrier warfare had not shown it was capable of striking such a blow.

The second option proposed to Halsey was to split his forces and attempt to attack both Japanese task forces. Halsey didn't like this plan because their total firepower was diminished and might be insufficient to provide a decisive blow to either Japanese force. Another complication was the wide separation of the four major task groups that made up the Third Fleet at that time.

---

[522] Ibid.

The third proposal was to concentrate all his firepower on the Northern Force (Ozawa's carrier force) and allow the Center Force (Kurita's battleship force) to come through unmolested. A concern was whether the Center Force had enough firepower available to destroy Seventh Fleet. Halsey's staff didn't view the Center Force as a serious threat. They believed there was plenty of time for Seventh Fleet to destroy the Southern Force (Nishimura's battleships were fewer in number) and defend itself from the Center Force in the morning. Seventh Fleet was required to remain stationary because its mission was to protect MacArthur's forces. However, the Japanese carrier group could attack from the north and this group was viewed as the greater threat. Halsey decided to advance at night and attack at dawn with both his carriers and battleships simultaneously. The Northern Force in the open ocean was the only Japanese force that provided him the freedom to maneuver and carry out his battle instructions. After he annihilated this force he could return and mop up what remained of the Center Force.

At 2032, he ordered Mitscher to attack the Northern Force with all of the Third Fleet. He sent a message to Thomas Kinkaid that all three groups of Third Fleet would attack the Northern Force at 2024. He felt this communication was sufficient to let Kinkaid know that Third Fleet was no longer guarding San Bernardino Strait and that Seventh Fleet had to adjust to the new tactical plan.[523]

Kinkaid believed that TF 34 had already been formed and made up a forth group, so when he received Halsey's message that three groups were going north under Halsey's command, he assumed that TF 34 was to remain and guard his northern flank. The disunity of effort was both commanders made assumptions that the other understood his intentions. Halsey believed he had communicated sufficiently that he was taking all of his forces north and leaving San Bernardino Strait open. Kinkaid believed Halsey had now four groups with the formation of TF 34 and assumed Halsey was splitting his forces by taking his carriers north but leaving his battleships to guard San Bernardino Strait.

At 2000, Halsey issued orders to the Third Fleet to rendezvous at 14° 28′ north, 125° 50′ east. TG 38.1 was to refuel from TG 30.8 at 15°00′ north, 130° 00′ east and then rendezvous with the rest of Third Fleet on October 25. On October 24, at 2345, TG 38.2, TG 38.3 and TG 38.4 had joined together. Halsey instructed Mitscher on board *Lexington* to take tactical command and attack and destroy Ozawa's Northern Force. The last report received by *Lexington* with Ozawa's location was at 0235. The pilot reported that Ozawa was approximately

---

[523] Ibid.

one hundred and thirty miles to the northeast of Luzon; this was an error and the distance was approximately two hundred and fifty miles between Third Fleet and Ozawa. The pilot did give their correct course of 150° but it was nine hours after receipt of this report before Mitscher knew exactly where the Northern Force was located. At 0240 on October 25th, TF 34 was formed with six modern U.S. battleships, seven heavy cruisers and seventeen destroyers under the command of Vice Admiral Lee. This task group was placed ten miles ahead of the carrier groups. At 0430, Mitscher ordered the first strikes loaded, prepared to launch at dawn in the event Ozawa maintained his course overnight. It didn't happen. The Japanese had turned to the north instead of continuing south. Mitscher launched search planes at 0540 to determine where the Northern Force had gone. He didn't wait for the Japanese fleet to be found; he launched the first strike by 0600. It would be ready to strike when search planes located the enemy.[524]

Kurita received Toyoda's message to resume the attack at 1915. It was met with anger and disgust on board *Yamato* by his staff. His officers jeered:

> Leave the fighting to us. Not even a God can direct naval battles from shore. Ignorant of enemy attacks they can order anything. It would've been more realistic to say, 'Believing in annihilation, resume the attack!'[525]

This open insubordination of a superior officer showed the level of animosity toward Toyoda and his impersonal command. Soon after he received Toyoda's message, Kurita received a message from Nishimura that stated,

> Our force will storm the center of the eastern shore of Leyte Gulf at 0400 on October 25.[526]

Coordination between Kurita and Nishimura was now impossible. Kurita's staff revised their schedule and dispatched a message to all other forces at 2145. It read:

> Main Force of First Diversion Attack Force plan to pass through San Bernardino Strait at 0100 on October 25, proceed southward down east coast of Samar and arrive at Leyte Gulf at 1100 on October 25. Third Section will break into Leyte Gulf as scheduled and then join forces with Main Force about ten miles northeast of Suluan Island at 0900 on October 25.[527]

---

[524] Vice Admiral William F. Halsey, CTU 38, Action Report, November 13, RG 38.

[525] Ito, Masanori, *The End of the Imperial Japanese Navy,* at 132.

[526] *Yamato* Detailed Action Report, 17 October to 28 October 1944.

[527] Ibid.

Kurita didn't want Nishimura to charge into Surigao Strait. He wanted a feint in order to delay deep penetration until both task forces could coordinate their actions and divide U.S. reaction. It wasn't known if Nishimura ever received this message. However, a coordinated attack by Kurita and Nishimura was imperative to the SHO operation or the double penetration strategy was meaningless.

Then at 2213, he sent an additional message to reassure Combined Fleet Headquarters of his intent,

> We were subjected to repeated enemy carrier-based plane attack all day long on the 24th resulting in considerable damage to us. Powerful enemy task forces to the east and to the north of Legaspi are exceedingly active. Main Force of First Diversion Attack Force, chancing annihilation, is determined to break through to Tacloban anchorage to destroy the enemy. The air force is ordered to carry out full strength attack against task forces.[528]

Kinkaid waited on his flagship for the Japanese Southern Force to commit to battle and attempt to run the gauntlet Oldendorf had prepared. He listened intently as reports came in. At 2310, on October 24, *PT-128* made contact with the enemy's southern group ten miles southeast of Bohol Island. *PT-127* reported two contacts at 0039, ten miles off Camiguin Island bearing 310°. More reports followed from other PT boats that the Japanese Southern Force had reached Taancan Point at 0123. Battle seemed imminent. At 0200, *PT-134* announced an unidentified enemy ship was headed north near the southern tip of Panson Island and *PT-134* had begun its attack. By 0210, *PT-134* reported undetermined results and the Japanese had attempted to drive away the PT boats with gunfire. Surface radar contact was made on Oldendorf's flagship *Louisville* at 0215, bearing 178°, range 53,000 yards, speed of enemy undetermined, course generally north. At 0225, PT boats reported the Japanese had successfully passed the first line of defense. Commander Destroyer Squadron 54 reported it intended to proceed south and make an attack at 0226. By 0235 Jesse B. Oldendorf ordered TG 77.2 to set condition one. [529]

At 0259, DesRon 24 was ordered to attack. It proceeded down the west coast following the other groups then retired to the north behind a smokescreen. At 0301, the destroyers *Remey*, *McGowan*, and *Melvin* launched torpedoes. At 0311, ComDesRon 54 reported two large and one small enemy ships, all headed north in one column. The destroyer *McDermut* and the destroyer *Monssen* launched tor-

---

[528] Ibid.

[529] Vice Admiral Thomas Kinkaid, CTU 77 Action Report, January 31, 1945, RG 38.

pedoes next. At 0317, ComDesRon 54 reported firing completed. Five targets were observed—two may have been hit and slowed. Finally at 0320, ComDesDiv 108 reported a hit and big flare on one ship. The flare was also seen by the crew of *Louisville* and units of the right flank cruisers. At 0327 Section 2 of DesRon 24 launched torpedoes. At 0330, Section 1 of DesRon 24 launched torpedoes. By 0335, DesRon 56 was ordered to launch an attack and the large ship was their primary target. By 0338, surface radar on *Louisville* indicated an enemy group bearing 178°at 28,000 yards. Estimated to be four ships, one medium the remainder small, course 345°, speed 15 knots.[530]

At 0344, *Louisville* reported a large explosion off the starboard beam. The right flank cruisers reported destroyers had hit the enemy with 5-inch guns and one of the enemy ships appeared dead in the water. At 0350 all U.S. ships were ordered to open fire. At 0351 the U.S. cruisers opened fire. By 0353, U.S. battleships opened fire and the enemy appeared to retire at an increased speed. By 0355, Section 2 of DesRon 56 launched torpedoes. Then three minutes later Section 3 of DesRon 56 launched torpedoes. By 0400, the battle line located north of Hibuson Island was headed east and was instructed to reverse course to 270° west. The leading enemy group turned west to retire. At 0402 the U.S. battleships checked fire; they reversed course to 270° west by 0403. At 0405, Section 1 of DesRon 56 attacked. The right flank cruisers reversed course to 270°west. U.S. battleships resumed fire by 0407. By 0410, ComDesRon 56 reported Section 1 had retired in the middle of the channel and had received friendly fire. Oldendorf ordered all fire checked immediately. Kinkaid listened to the battle reports and felt all was well until he realized he had never received confirmation that TF 34 was on guard at San Bernardino Strait. At 0412, Thomas Kinkaid wanted confirmation of TF 34's location and sent dispatch No. 241912 to Halsey, "*Is TF 34 guarding San Bernardino Strait?*"[531]

Oldendorf sent Kinkaid a message at 0420 that suggested he ready air attacks to engage Japanese units headed south and prevent their escape. At 0424, the left flank cruisers were ordered to resume fire. At 0425, Sprague of TU 77.4.1 ordered Stump of TU 77.4.2 to ready search requirements as ordered by Kinkaid. At 0429, Oldendorf received word the destroyer *A.W. Grant* was badly damaged and dead in the water, bearing 171° distance 8,500 yards from *Louisville*. By 0432,

---

[530] Ibid.

[531] Ibid.

lookouts reported all enemy ships either dead in water, on fire or headed south to retire.[532]

All U.S. ships changed course by column movement to 180° south at 0451 and the right flank cruisers proceeded south along the west coast of Surigao Strait. At 0457, DesRon 56 was ordered to form a screen ahead of left flank cruisers. Then at 0520, PT boats reported four large ships headed north up the strait. At 0524, the left flank cruisers were ordered to open fire. *PT-144* reported at 0530 she was sinking and would attempt to beach on southern Leyte Island. At 0539, all U.S. ships checked fire. Enemy units retired to the south. The Battle of Surigao Strait ended with Nishimura's fleet destroyed, only the destroyer *Shigure* survived. Shima's force also quickly retired and what remained headed toward the Sulu Sea. The southern pincer had been stopped; Kinkaid and Oldendorf had accomplished the first stage of Nimitz's battle of annihilation.[533]

On *Zuikaku*, Ozawa received Toyoda's message that all units should advance counting on "*divine assistance*" at 1910. Then at 2000, Ozawa received a message that summarized Kurita's message he sent at 1600. If Kurita had retired it placed Ozawa in a very dangerous position. He was a decoy—if Kurita abandoned his mission then Ozawa's mission as a decoy was irrelevant. As a consequence, Ozawa had sent Mutsuda to engage in a night battle that was suicidal if Kurita had turned around. So he recalled Mutsuda with an order to turn back north and rejoin his force by 0600. By 2110 Ozawa had received Kurita's additional messages further explaining his actions. Ozawa now understood that Kurita was continuing with his mission but the delay in receiving these messages had resulted in considerable confusion. He decided not to change Matsuda's orders to re-join his force after he received this new information.[534]

At 1920, Matsuda stood on the bridge of his flagship *Hyuga*, and saw flashes of light on the horizon. His staff thought it may be gunfire but Matsuda remained skeptical and thought lightning was more likely. Nevertheless, he traveled forty minutes toward where the flash had been seen. At 2010, he received the message from Ozawa to rejoin his force to the north. He continued south, forty minutes later he turned southeast, still in search of U.S. forces. By 2241, with no contact made, he turned north to rejoin the Main Force by 0600.[535]

---

532 Ibid.

533 Vice Admiral Thomas Kinkaid, CTU 77 Action Report, January 31, 1945, RG 38.

534 *Zuikaku* Detailed Action Report, October 21 to October 25, 1944.

535 *Hyuga* Detailed Action Report, October 20 to October 29, 1944.

Yamato sailed through San Bernardino Strait; the time had come to find out if Ozawa had successfully lured the U.S. armada north. Kurita's staff and crew were not optimistic and they fully expected to have to fight their way out. Some felt the greatest threat would come from submarines, while others anticipated a surface battle. The night was clear and Kurita could determine the fleet's position visually while it traversed the narrow passage. Part of the crew rested while other crew members manned battle stations in multiple shifts and heavy fatigue affected every man. Lookouts scanned the horizon while her search radar continued to seek out targets but no contacts were ever made. At 0037, October 25 *Yamato* sailed past the southern tip of Luzon into the Philippine Sea and not a single American ship in sight. Did Ozawa succeed or were the Americans waiting for daylight? Kurita directed his fleet to the east until 0300 and then turned southeast toward Leyte Gulf. He deployed his forces in a night search formation that covered a thirteen mile front of six columns. He was blind with no usable information on the location or size of the American navy's disposition. He spread out and hoped he could make contact, but found nothing in the area. [536]

Kurita's staff waited for word from Nishimura reporting any success of the southern pincer. He had received a message at 0230 that Nishimura was entering the Strait and at 0335 he had sighted three enemy ships. Nothing had been heard for two hours. On *Yamato*'s bridge his staff remained hopeful that good news would arrive soon. Then at 0532 a message from Shima notified them that both *Fuso* and *Yamashiro* had been destroyed, *Mogami* was afire and that he was retiring. Penetration into Leyte Gulf had to be accomplished by the Center Force alone. The failure to coordinate meant that both Japanese surface groups could be defeated in detail. His gamble to achieve a double penetration into Leyte Gulf had failed. Kurita had not heard from Ozawa and he didn't believe Third Fleet had been lured away. Instead, he suspected that Third Fleet had pulled back to entrap his fleet.[537]

At 0645 October 25, *Yamato*'s lookouts spotted ship masts on the horizon. Kurita had run into Sprague's TG 77.3 or Taffy 3 of six escort carriers, three destroyers, and four destroyer escorts. The weather was poor and Sprague quickly seized this advantage and headed east into a rain squall while his carriers began to launch aircraft. At 0659 *Yamato* opened fire and the Battle off Samar had begun. *Yamato* and *Nagato* opened fire on *White Plains* at 34,000 yards and on *Yamato*'s third salvo

---

[536] *Yamato* Detailed Action Report, 17 October to 28 October 1944.

[537] Ibid.

one of her Type 1 AP projectiles designed to dive exploded under the keel of *White Plains*. It shook the carrier violently and she lost steering and circled throwing up a huge black cloud of smoke that made it appear she had been hit severely. She was able to regain her steering and continue with the rest of the American task group.[538]

Kurita had ordered a general attack when he first sighted the Americans but then held his destroyers back to conserve their fuel. His cruisers and battleships formed a very loose battle line and followed the American ships to the east and into the rain squall. *Johnston* and *Hoel* made a counter-attack at 0720 and *Johnston* fired ten torpedoes with one hitting *Kumano* blowing off her bow and knocking her out of the battle. *Yamato* hit *Johnston* with three main battery projectiles and three secondary projectiles that took out half of her machinery and reduced her speed to seventeen knots at 0727. She disappeared into the rain squall giving Kurita the impression she had been sunk. *Hoel* fired five torpedoes but all missed and was heavily damaged by *Haguro* at about the same time. The Japanese fleet was now under constant air attack from the carrier planes and the cruiser *Suzuya* was knocked out of the fight by bomb damage.[539]

Sprague turned his ships to the southwest around 0730 and then ordered a counter-attack by his screening destroyers while still in the rain squall. Smoke screens and the poor weather made visibility poor. Seven torpedo attacks were all made within seven minutes of each other by five ships beginning with *Hoel*'s second attack at 0753. This forced *Yamato* and *Nagato* north and away from the battle for ten minutes. *Hoel*'s torpedoes missed but *Yamato*'s and *Nagato*'s guns did not. The U.S. destroyer was raked and then as the Japanese battleships passed her again they fired into her at point blank range sinking her at 0840.[540]

None of the torpedoes fired by the American destroyer escorts scored a hit but the counter-attack did allow the six carriers to open the range. The weather began to clear and around 0810 a second carrier group was sighted to the southeast. This was Admiral Felix B. Stump's TG 77.2 or Taffy 2. At 0820 *Yamato* scored a hit on *Gambier Bay* which crippled the carrier and she was later sunk but *Yamato* with the rest of the battleships drifted in the direction of Taffy 2 while Sprague turned his ships to the west opening the range even further. This gave Kurita the perception he was engaged with faster fleet carriers and that they were escaping. The level of

---

[538] *Yamato* Detailed Action Report and U.S.S. *White Plains* action report.

[539] *Yamato* Detailed Action Report, 17 October to 28 October 1944.

[540] *Fanshaw Bay* and *Hoel* Action Reports.

U.S. air attacks and their coordination was increasing so at 0911 thinking the enemy had escaped he called off the attack so his forces could re-group. In the two and a half hour battle he had sunk one carrier *Gambier Bay*, two destroyers *Johnston* and *Hoel*, and one destroyer escort *Samuel B Roberts*. He damaged three carriers, *Fanshaw Bay*, *Kalinin Bay* and *White Plains*, one destroyer, *Herrmann*, and one destroyer escort, *Dennis*. Taffy 3 was operationally wrecked and had to withdraw immediately. Later after the surface battle land-based air strikes using kamikaze tactics for the first time sank *St. Lo* and damaged two other carriers in Sprague's TG 77.1 or Taffy 1.[541] The battle had cost Kurita the heavy cruisers *Chokai, Chikuma,* and *Suzuya,* and *Kumano* had been crippled and forced to withdraw on her own.

At 1000, Kurita sent a report to Combined Fleet Headquarters,

> SMS251000, 1YB action spot report No. 1 October 25, known results obtained to present; definitely sunk two aircraft carriers of which one was regular large type carrier, two heavy cruisers and some destroyers. Definitely hit, one or two carriers. Enemy carrier-based aircraft continue to attack us. The remaining enemy including six or seven carriers was making use of squalls and smoke screens to make good its retirement to the southeast. Friendly units heavily damaged; Chokai, Chikuma, Kumano. Other's being checked. We are at present proceeding northward.[542]

Kurita sent out orders at 1014 to the rest of the fleet,

> All squadrons under the command of 1YB are ordered to assume #30 alert dispositions, course 0°, and speed 22 knot.[543]

At 1018, Kurita instructed the destroyer *Fujinami* to assist *Chokai* and if she was unmaneuverable to take off her crew and sink her with torpedoes. This was what eventually happened and *Fujinami* then attempted to withdraw alone through San Bernardino Strait. Kurita instructed the destroyer *Nowaki* to aid *Chikuma*. Eventually she too took the crew of *Chikuma* and sank the crippled ship with torpedoes. By the time this was completed she was far behind the rest of the Japanese fleet but she made her way toward San Bernardino Strait alone.

At 1040, Kurita was handed a message sent by *Yahagi* which had been sent at 1030. It read:

---

[541] For minute by minute account of the Naval Battle off Samar see *The World Wonder'd, What Really Happened off Samar* by Robert Lundgren. Nimble Books, 2014.

[542] Combined Fleet Headquarters Detailed Action Report, October 17 to October 28, 1944.

[543] Ibid

> SMS 251030, from Flag 10 Division to the Yamato results obtained by us; one carrier of the Enterprise class sunk and one seriously damaged (its sinking was almost certain) three destroyers. Damage sustained the Yahagi hit but battle cruising not hindered.[544]

Kurita's staff took this as an addition to what *Yamato* and the heavy cruisers had accomplished and didn't factor that the Tenth Division had witnessed the same ships after digesting the news from *Yahagi.* At 1100 Kurita sent a new message to Combined Fleet Headquarters correcting his original report. It read,

> SMS 251100, correct 1-YB's action spot report No. 1 as follows: "Three or four carriers including one of the Enterprise class, have been sunk."[545]

The fleet was ordered to set course of 270° at 1055 and at 1100 the course was set to 255° heading back to Leyte Gulf. At 1115, Kurita and his staff received a message informing them that enemy carrier-based aircraft were using the airfield at Tacloban base, including those from the damaged enemy carriers. This information was based on enemy voice transmissions. At 1118, three enemy planes were sighted bearing 130° and the fleet was turned to a new course of 180° at 1119. At 1120, a new enemy intercept was received:

> Being attacked by an enemy force consisting of four battleships, eight cruisers, and other units. Vice Admiral Willis Lee? Will proceed to and from? Leyte area. Request that high speed carriers go to the attack immediately 0727.[546]

This message was sent by Owada Comm. Unit and based on this intercept it was a combination of several U.S. messages that had been sent in the clear. Kurita was well aware that Vice Admiral Willis Lee commanded the U.S. battleships and from this broken intercept it gave the perception that Lee was being sent to Leyte Gulf to come to the rescue. Kurita did not know exactly where TF 34 was but he did know the Americans knew exactly where he was. With these broken intercepts he determined the Americans must be coming to him.

At 1120, Kurita sent a message to Combined Fleet Headquarters, "Our position Ya Hi Ma 37, course southwest, proceeding to Leyte anchorage. Enemy task force was in position thirty miles to northeast and another large force sixty miles to southeast." At 1123, the fleet came to a new course of 225° . At 1144, another enemy intercept sent from Takao Comm Unit was received and it read:

---

544 Ibid.

545 Ibid.

546 Ibid

> Our force was being attacked by a force composed of four battleships, eight cruisers and others. Proceed to Leyte at top speed.[547]

Kurita ordered *Yamato* to launch *Nagato*'s #1 scout plane, which she had taken aboard before the battle, at 1145 in hopes that he could gain some kind of intelligence on the enemy disposition. This was his last plane available for search operations. The transfer of thirty-six aircraft to shore and the loss of several aircraft when *Musashi* was sunk meant that *Yamato* was the only ship with aircraft remaining on board by October 25. At 1148, the fleet was ordered to a new course of 270° west. Then a message from Combined Fleet Headquarters which had been sent to First Air Fleet and Southwest Area Fleet to attack the enemy task force reported at 0945 "in position, Ya Ki 1 Ka." This placed a U.S. carrier striking task force in a position bearing 5° distance 130 miles from Suluan light. This position placed this task force to his north and again confirmed in his mind he was surrounded.[548]

At 1206, Kurita requested information from Combined Fleet Headquarters as to the targets of the aircraft and the results obtained. At 1230, he received another message sent from Owada Comm Unit which read,

> Kinkaid cancels present orders and ordered addressee to proceed to point 300? Miles southwest of Leyte Gulf in a plain text message.[549]

Kurita had to make the biggest decision of his life. From the enemy intercepts he concluded that the American fleet was concentrating to block any attempt to penetrate the Gulf. In addition carrier-based aircraft were also concentrating at Tacloban airfield. It had been five days since the beginning of the invasion. How many transports were left and how much material had already been landed? It was obvious to him that the Americans had sufficient power to destroy Nishimura's forces as well as Shima's. There were no friendly units to the south to support or offer aid. However, all these details couldn't answer the burning question in his mind? What was the strategic gain for Japan? He could fight the battle for the sake of fighting a battle but what would the nation of Japan gain for the sacrifice? Surprise was lost. The enemy was fully aware of every move he made and now had time to recover.

Kurita estimated the situation:

---

[547] Ibid.

[548] Ibid.

[549] Ibid.

> The wiser course was deemed to be to cross the enemy's anticipation by striking at his task force which had been reported in position bearing 5°, distance one hundred and thirty miles from Suluan Light at 0945.We believed that turnabout, proceed northward in search of this element would prove to be to our advantage in subsequent operations.[550]

Rear Admiral Tomiji Koyanagi in his own words on the turn to the north:

> The enemy situation was confused, Intercepted fragments of plain text radio messages indicate that a hastily constructed air strip on Leyte was ready to launch planes in an attack on us, that Kinkaid was requesting the early dispatch of a powerful striking unit, and that the U.S. Seventh Fleet was operating nearby. At the same time we heard from Southwest Area Fleet Headquarters that a U.S. carrier striking task force was located in a position bearing 5° distance one hundred and thirty miles from Suluan light at 0945.
>
> Under these circumstances, it was presumed that if our force did succeed in entering Leyte Gulf, we would find that the transports had already withdrawn under escort of the Seventh Fleet. Even if they remained, they would've completed unloading in the five days since making port and any success we might achieve would be very minor at best. On the other hand, if we proceeded into the narrow gulf, we would be the target of attacks by the enemy's carrier and Leyte based planes. We were prepared to fight to the last man, but we wanted to die gloriously.
>
> We were convinced that several enemy carrier groups were disposed nearby and that we were surrounded. Our shore-based air force had been rather inactive, but now the two air fleets would surely fight all-out in coordination with the First Striking Force. If they could only strike a successful blow, we might still achieve a decisive fleet engagement, and even if we were destroyed in such a battle, death would be glorious.[551]

Kurita made his decision at 1236 and sent the following message to Combined Fleet Headquarters:

> First Diversion Attack Force abandoning plan to break through to Leyte Gulf. Turning about and will proceed northward along the east coast of Samar in search of an enemy task force. After decisively engaging same, plan to go through San Bernardino Strait.[552]

Believing he was surrounded and TF 34 was to his north and closing in on him, he would turn north to engage this force in the open sea. He believed Lee with TF 34 was two hours away and had no idea the distance would not allow an interception until thirteen hours had elapsed. Had he known this information his

---

[550] Ibid.

[551] Evans, David, *The Japanese Navy in World War II*, pp 355-384.

[552] *Yamato* Detailed Action Report, 17 October to 28 October 1944.

decision to turn north may have been different but his decision was sound. At the time he made the decision TF 34 was indeed heading south. Kurita had correctly determined the situation with only one missing key fact and this was the distance between the two forces. By sending his float planes to land bases, he had violated the sea power principle of security, removing his ability to ascertain the direction and numbers of the enemy. Kurita was operating blind.

Nimitz received Kinkaid's report that his forces had won a great victory at Surigao Strait, but he was concerned that no reports had come from Lee engaging the Japanese Center Force. Like Kinkaid, he too had made the assumption that TF 34 had been formed and was guarding San Bernardino Strait. Lee should have engaged the Japanese shortly after midnight, but no word had been received from him. He called his assistant, Chief of Staff Captain Bernard Austin, and asked him if there were any dispatches from TG 38 that he had missed. Captain Austin replied, "*Will you tell me in particular what you are looking for?*" Nimitz answered, "*I am very concerned, because nothing I have seen indicates that Halsey has left San Bernardino guarded against Japanese units coming through there and getting our ships off Leyte.*"[553] Austin replied that some others had the same concern. Nimitz asked if anything came in to let him know immediately.

The next signal came from Kinkaid in plain language, the message that Halsey received at 0922. Immediately thereafter, Nimitz was handed Kinkaid's previous request that "*Lee proceed top speed cover Leyte.*" Austin could tell Nimitz was deeply troubled as he paced the floor to his office. Nimitz still wanted to know where TF 34 was. At 0944, Austin suggested, "*Admiral, couldn't you just ask Halsey the simple question; 'Where is TF 34?'*" Nimitz thought about it and then replied, "*Go out and write it up. That's a good idea.*" [554]

At 1000, Halsey received a message from Nimitz who had been monitoring the radio transmissions from Pearl Harbor. Alarmed at the calls for help coming from Kinkaid and Sprague his message from Pearl Harbor read; "*Turkey Trots to Water GG Where is Repeat Where is Task Force Thirty-Four RR, The World Wonders.*" The first and last phrase of the message, "*Turkey Trots to Water*" and "*The World Wonders,*" were padding that were supposed to be removed after decoding. This padding was added to confuse Japanese attempts at decoding the message. The problem lay in the last phrase, "*The World Wonders,*" which was interpreted

[553] Potter, E. B., *Chester Nimitz* at 336-339.

[554] Ibid at 336-339.

by the staff on board the *New Jersey* as part of the message; so Halsey received, "*Where is Repeat, Where is Task Force Thirty-Four RR, The World Wonders.*"

Nimitz's orders to Halsey for the KING II operation had specific instructions, "*Destroy enemy naval and air forces in or threatening the Philippine area. Protect air and sea communications along the Central Pacific axis.*" In addition, a late entry which was unnumbered and unlettered read, "*In case opportunity for destruction of major portion of the enemy fleet offer or can be created, such destruction becomes the primary task.*" Even more than this, though, Nimitz instructed Halsey, "*Forces of the Pacific Ocean areas will cover and support forces of the Southwest Pacific in order to assist in the seizure and occupation of objectives in the Central Philippines.*"[555]

Halsey wrote Nimitz on his thoughts and how he interpreted his orders prior to the battle:

> I intend, if possible, to deny the enemy a chance to out-range me in an air duel and also to deny him an opportunity to employ an air shuttle (carrier-to-target-to-land) against me. If I am to prevent his gaining that advantage, I must have early information and I must move smartly. Insomuch as the destruction of the enemy fleet is the principle task, every weapon must be brought into play and the general coordination of these weapons should be in the hands of the tactical commander responsible for the outcome of the battle. My goal is the same as yours– to completely annihilate the Jap fleet if the opportunity offers. [556]

Halsey in his own words of what he felt upon reading the "World Wonders" message:

> I was stunned as if I had been struck in the face. The paper rattled in my hands. I snatched off my cap, threw it on the deck, and shouted something that I am ashamed to remember. Mick Carney [his chief of staff] rushed over and grabbed my arm; "Stop it! What the hell's the matter with you? Pull yourself together!"[557]

An enraged Halsey walked off the bridge with his chief of staff and retired to the admiral's quarters on the 01 level. It was of course the last three words of the message that Halsey perceived his superior officer was mocking him, humiliating him in front of his entire command, having no faith in his command ability, not coming to the aid of a fellow officer, and placing doubt in his own decision-making, just as he was about to carry out Nimitz's strategic vision outlined in Operation Granite.

---

[555] Commander in Chief, U.S. Pacific Fleet, Action Report. October 1944.

[556] Potter, E. B., *Bull Halsey*. Naval Institute Press, 1985 at 279.

[557] Ibid at 303.

At 1055, Halsey returned to the bridge and ordered Task Force 34 to turn around and head south, destroying his entire plan of fighting a battle of annihilation. He ordered TG 38.2 to also turn south and support Task Force 34. Mitscher would take TG 38.3 and TG 38.4 and pursue the Japanese Northern Force. At 1115, the orders were carried out. Task Force 34 had reached a position only forty-two miles from being able to engage the Japanese carrier force, or approximately within two hours. His forces were so far north he couldn't arrive to block San Bernardino Strait until 0100, approximately fourteen hours later. Due to the time delay in which messages were sent, received, decoded, and then given to the respective commanders, he was completely unaware that the Battle off Samar was already over and the threat to Leyte Gulf had ended. Halsey later wrote, "*I turned my back on an opportunity I had dreamed about since my first days as a cadet.*"[558] The only response his mind could offer was to obey what he perceived as a direct order from his commanding officer, to turn back south, and go to the aid of Seventh Fleet.

Task Force 34 made its way south at twenty knots but, unprepared for a high-speed run over the distance required, slowed to twelve knots at 1345 to refuel the destroyers. The battleships *Iowa* and the *New Jersey* were the fastest battleships at his command, so when refueling was completed at 1622, he divided his forces again creating TG 34.5 under the command of Rear Admiral Badger in the *Iowa* along with three light cruisers and eight destroyers. They left Lee and the remainder of TF 34 behind, traveling at twenty-eight knots. TG 34.5 would arrive too late to prevent Kurita from withdrawing through San Bernardino Strait but did intercept the lone destroyer *Nowaki,* sinking her in the early morning hours of October 26.

On board *Lexington*, as the first wave of U.S. aircraft attacked Ozawa's forces, Mitscher prepared a second strike. At 0835, sixteen torpedo bombers, six dive bombers and fourteen fighters took off and would arrive over the Japanese fleet at approximately 1000. Commander David McCampbell from the *Essex* was able to stay over the Japanese fleet and act as a target coordinator and keep Mitscher informed. As strike two arrived over the Japanese fleet, Lt. C. O. Roberts took over as strike coordinator and Commander McCampbell was relieved.[559]

---

[558] Ibid. at 304.

[559] *Lexington,* Action Report, November 22, 1944, RG 38 and Rear Admiral Frederick C. Sherman, CTU 38.3, Action Report, November 15, 1944, RG 38.

Upon conclusion of strike two Lt. Roberts reported that as many as fourteen Japanese ships were still afloat. *Lexington* was approximately one hundred and two miles south of the Japanese fleet. Mitscher launched a third strike beginning at 1145. This strike consisted of approximately 200 aircraft many which had participated in strike one. Commander T. Hugh Winters from *Lexington* relieved Lt. Roberts upon arrival at 1310 as target coordinator.[560]

Strike four took off at 1315 and consisted of approximately thirty-six planes. Mitscher dispatched DuBose forward at 1415 when the distance between the U.S. and Japanese forces were approximately sixty miles. The fourth strike arrived approximately at 1445 and Commander R. L. Kibble took over as target coordinator. At 1610, Mitscher launched a fifth strike with Commander M.T. Wordell in command. A sixth strike was launched at 1710. By the end of the day his carrier aircraft had sunk three Japanese carriers and a destroyer using 527 planes. It would now be up to DuBose to continue to destroy the northern force at night but without TF 34 the Japanese had two battleships that out gunned anything DuBose had available. [561]

Ozawa's main body and Matsuda's task force re-joined at 0701 and formed into two separate groups. The lead group was under command of Ozawa with the carrier *Zuikaku, Zuiho*, battleship *Ise*, cruiser *Oyodo*, and destroyers *Akitsuki, Hatsuzuki, Wakatsuki*, and *Kuwa*. The second group under command of Chiaki Matsuda consisted of the battleship *Hyuga*, light carriers *Chitose, Chiyoda*, light cruiser *Isuzu, Tama* and destroyers *Shimotsuki* and *Maki*. Ozawa had sent out three search planes at dawn but had not heard from them since.[562]

Rear Admiral Takeo Kaizuka was in command of the carrier *Zuikaku* when at 0807 her lookouts reported sighting nine Grumman aircraft and then at 0808 a large formation was detected bearing 160° to port, altitude angle of 5°at a distance of 6,576 yards. At 0815, Ozawa attempted to send a message to Kurita that his force was coming under attack by a large U.S. air raid but unaware that *Zuikaku* had a bad radio transmitter the message was never received. At 0817, the large formation was splitting into two separate groups of aircraft and at 0821 *Zuikaku* opened fire with her AA guns. Her speed was twenty-four knots when at 0829 forty dive bombers and ten fighters attacked. Lookouts reported, "*Torpedo on the starboard beam.*" and *Zuikaku* would heel over to one side as she turned hard to

---

[560] *Lexington,* Action Report, November 22, 1944, RG 38.

[561] Ibid.

[562] *Zuikaku* Detailed Action Report, October 21 to October 25, 1944.

avoid the torpedo. At 0835, another torpedo track crossed her stern and then the ship was shaken by a 500-lb. bomb hit on the port side amidships.[563]

This was quickly followed by a more violent shock at 0837 as a torpedo hit outboard of the number 4 generator room which flooded immediately. *Zuikaku* immediately listed to port 29.5° Her secondary switch board panel, port switch room, No. 8 and No. 10 power conduit lines were flooded and this cut power to her helm. The rudder lost electrical power and direct manual steering needed to be applied. Her port after engine room filled with smoke and progressively flooded and was abandoned. By 0840, her two starboard shafts remained in operation but both port shafts were disabled. Counter-flooding starboard tanks corrected the list to 6° by 0845 and emergency power was restored to aft steering. [564]

Ozawa soon received word that *Chitose* was on fire at 0845. At 0848, Ozawa became aware that her communication equipment was out. Reports of fire on both the upper and lower hanger decks were received at 0850. Eight U.S. aircraft passed her bearing 020° and by 0854 Kaizuka received good news that the fires on the hanger decks were extinguished. Suddenly, the destroyer *Akitsuki* exploded at 0856 which then sank immediately. At 0859, her AA guns were ordered to stand by as the first U.S. attack wave retired.[565]

Ozawa slowly received word as to the damage suffered from the first attack. *Zuiho* had taken a single bomb hit but was still capable of twenty knots. The light cruiser *Tama* had taken a torpedo hit in her number two boiler room and fallen out of formation. The carrier *Chiyoda* had also been hit by a single bomb but the damage was minor. The carrier *Chitose* was listing heavily to port and burning. At 0923, the cruiser *Oyoda* flashed a signal asking "*Notify condition of your communication equipment?*" At 0927, the AA alert was ordered to stand down. At 0950, Kaizuka ordered the ammunition from the aft magazines to be moved to the starboard side of the ship.[566]

Then at 0953, approximately thirty aircraft bearing 160° to port were detected. AA alerts were sounded and the ship was ordered to her maximum speed. At 0958, approximately ten bombers and six to eight fighters attacked and her AA guns opened fire. Two torpedo tracks were observed to pass her starboard stern

---

563 Ibid.

564 Ibid.

565 Ibid.

566 Ibid.

and these planes retired by 1008 and she checked fire. In this attack she had avoided further damage.[567]

Zuikaku was only capable of eighteen knots after her torpedo hit and attempts to steer her manually were proving difficult. It was now clear that her communication equipment was out and Ozawa was having a very difficult time commanding his fleet. He had decided to share the fate of his flagship and had to be persuaded by his staff that now wasn't the time for such decisions. Eventually he gave in to his staff at 1032. Kaizuka ordered *Zuikaku* to come to a stop and by 1051 Ozawa was transferred by boat to the cruiser *Oyoda* who raised the admiral's flag at 1100. With Ozawa back in command of the fleet Takeo Kaizuka could now attend to saving *Zuikaku*.[568]

At 1102, none of the three surviving carriers were in condition to land aircraft and the nine remaining Zeros providing CAP over the fleet had run out of fuel. The planes each made a water landing. Four U.S. bombers were sighted bearing 070° to starboard at 1104. Takeo Kaizuka ordered his AA crews to stand by at 1120 and the ship maintained a speed of eighteen knots. At 1150, another large U.S. formation was detected bearing 240° and AA alerts were sounded. Kaizuka ordered more speed and she increased her speed to twenty knots by 1209.[569]

Ozawa received a message from Kurita that 1YB had sunk one carrier and one cruiser and was in battle with at least four more carriers at 1246. U.S. aircraft were forming for another attack. Kaizuka's gun crews opened fire on a single U.S. plane at 1250 to 1255 without result. A large formation of U.S. aircraft had been detected sixty miles away bearing 240° at the same time. By 1305 the formation was 43,840 yards and closing. By 1306, the lookouts sighted seventy bombers escorted by eight to eleven fighters approaching. Kaizuka knew his ship will be the main target and ordered flank speed. Using all available power the wounded carrier reached a speed of twenty-four knots at 1309 and her AA guns opened fire. [570]

At 1321, *Zuikaku* was hit by two torpedoes on the port side and one direct bomb hit. She also suffered many near miss bombs during the attack. Her list immediately grew to 14° and then climbed to 22°. Kaizuka ordered all starboard tanks flooded but the list was only reduced to 21° by 1327. Her AA guns contin-

---

[567] Ibid.

[568] Ibid.

[569] Ibid.

[570] Ibid.

ued to fire between 1328 to 1337 and 1338 to 1342. Takeo Kaizuka knows his ship was sinking so at 1358 he ordered the crew to the flight deck to prepare to abandon ship. Assembled, they give their final salute to the portrait of the Emperor and then leave their ship. *Zuikaku* sank at 1414. The destroyers *Hatsuzuki, Wakatsuki,* and *Kuwa* were ordered to pick up survivors. Rear Admiral Takeo Kaizuka forty eight officers and seven hundred and ninety-four men perish with the ship. The destroyers *Wakatsuki* and *Kuwa* rescued forty seven officers and eight hundred and fifteen men.[571]

Captain Kuro Sigiura was in command of the carrier *Zuiho.* At 0740, he received word that a large group of enemy aircraft had been detected bearing 230° at a distance of one hundred and ten miles. By 0822, her lookouts sighted approximately 100 U.S. aircraft approaching. Sigiura gave permission to open fire with her AA guns at 0825.5. Six SB2C dive bombers attacked and at 0835 *Zuiho* was hit on the aft section of her flight deck which penetrated the flight deck and detonated in the lower hanger bay. The explosion bulged up the flight deck and lifted the rear elevator. At 0836, a near miss bomb detonated off her stern and then at 0838 she suffered near miss bombs off both the port and starboard bow. By 0845.5, Sigiura received reports that the lower hanger deck was on fire and the ship had assumed a list of 3° to port. By 0855, the U.S. aircraft were retiring and gunfire was checked. Good news was reported at 0856 when the fires on the lower hanger deck were extinguished.[572]

At 0955, another large U.S. formation of aircraft was detected with approximately twenty aircraft. By 0957, *Zuiho* used her 5-inch guns and rocket batteries to engage the aircraft. No damage was suffered during this attack and by 1010 the U.S. aircraft retired. Sigiura noted at 1030, *Zuikaku* was lowering Ozawa's flag and that the admiral was transferring to the cruiser *Oyoda.*[573]

At 1240, he received a signal from *Oyoda* that she has detected another large enemy formation of aircraft approaching. By 1310, lookouts counted at least forty dive bombers and twenty-seven torpedo bombers approaching. At 1317, *Zuiho* took her first torpedo hit on the starboard bow under the forward compass bridge. A small bomb estimated at 100 lb. hit the aft elevator. At 1330, six planes attack which resulted in another torpedo hit on the starboard aft section of the ship, another estimated 100-lb. bomb hitting at frame 170, which exploded in the medi-

---

[571] Ibid.

[572] *Zuiho* Detailed Action Report, October 21 to October 25, 1944.

[573] Ibid.

cal X-ray room, and seven near miss bombs detonated along her hull. The rudders lost hydraulic power and manual steering was then placed into effect at 1034. *Zuiho*'s speed fell to twelve knots due to high pressure pipes to the starboard engine room that were cut. Near miss bombs opened her hull allowing water to enter her number two boiler room and the port side engine room. By 1410, the U.S. aircraft retired.[574]

By 1416, Sigiura and his crew attempted to control the list through counterflooding and seal off the damaged bulkheads to control the progressive flooding. The water continued to advance so he ordered every available man to man the pumps in an all-out effort to save his ship. Then at 1432, twenty more U.S. aircraft attacked which resulted in at least ten more near miss bombs detonating close to her hull. Slowly her port list continued to grow so that by 1437 the list had grown to 13°. By 1445, the list was 16°. He ordered that the Emperor's portrait be taken down at 1449. By 1450, he received word that the port engine room has completely flooded and *Zuiho* slowed to a stop. Orders were given for all secret documents to be destroyed at 1456 and by 1459 the Emperor's portrait had left the ship.[575]

By 1500, the list was 23°. Finally by 1510, Sigiura ordered the flag to be lowered and the crew to abandon ship. There wasn't much time remaining for at 1526, *Zuiho*'s stern slipped beneath the surface of the sea, and then the ship capsized to starboard. She then plunged by the stern at 1526. Sigiura didn't go down with his ship and was rescued by the destroyer *Kuwa* along with fifty-eight officers and 701 men. Six officers including her executive officer, Commander Hozumi Eguchi, and 208 men perished with the ship. [576]

Nakase was in command of the battleship *Ise*. During her conversion to a carrier-battleship hybrid she received many new anti-aircraft guns, mainly 25 mm machine guns. At close range she could put up a tremendous amount of flak. At 0739, her radar picked up a large formation of aircraft bearing 230° at a distance of one hundred and ten miles. Nakase immediately notified the other ships in the formation. By 0817, the aircraft were within 21,920 yards and his lookouts sighted the aircraft as they split into two separate groups. At 0820, Nakase sounded AA alerts to his ship and the battle was joined.[577]

---

[574] Ibid.

[575] Ibid.

[576] Ibid.

[577] *Ise* Detailed Action Report, October 24 to October 25, 1944.

Initially the U.S. aircraft focused on *Zuikaku* and *Zuiho* but by 0840 six bombers and five fighters attacked *Ise*. At 0840, she avoided a torpedo that came toward her port bow and one near miss bomb on her starboard side amidships. At 0858, she took another near miss bomb off her starboard bow and three fighters strafed her stern. At 1000, *Nakase* was informed that another wave of U.S. aircraft has been detected bearing 150°. Again, AA alerts were sounded and his lookouts reported at least fifty aircraft approaching. At 1005, ten U.S. dive bombers attacked *Ise*. A single near miss bomb fell to port but seven near miss bombs, some as close as 33 yards detonated on her starboard side and one direct hit on the roof of turret two at 1008. The direct hit destroyed the 25-mm AA guns on the roof of the turret but didn't damage the turret itself protected by heavy armor. [578]

The next wave of U.S. aircraft approached at approximately 1250, bearing 150° and was detected at eighty-two miles. By 1308, 50 aircraft became visible on the horizon but it wouldn't be until 1430 that *Ise* was targeted again. Two torpedoes approached off the port bow and were avoided by turning hard to port, and then at 1435 two torpedoes approached from the starboard bow and were avoided by a hard turn to starboard. At 1505, one near-miss bomb fell to starboard and three to port. Noboru Nakase reported at least twenty U.S. aircraft attacked *Ise* at this time.[579] By 1700, the Japanese carriers had been sunk and *Ise* now represented the main target for the US aircraft to attack. Noboru Nakase looked astern at 1705 to see an estimated 85 U.S. aircraft approach. From 1707 to 1730 *Ise* was their principle target. A total of eleven torpedoes and thirty-four near miss bombs detonated around her hull but she wasn't directly hit.[580] Rear Admiral Noboru Nakase had somehow maneuvered his ship safely throughout this barrage. At 1820, *Hyuga* and *Shimotsuki* joined up with *Ise* and *Oyoda*. Noboru Nakase fell in behind his division flagship *Hyuga* and would follow the orders and movements during the night.[581]

Captain Yoshiyuki Kishi was in command of the light carrier *Chitose*. At 0810 a large formation of U.S. aircraft was detected bearing 200° at a distance of 76,720 yards. By 0815, the aircraft were bearing 120° to port with an altitude angle of 10° at 43,840 yards the lookouts saw this formation separate into two groups of at

---

[578] Ibid.

[579] Ibid.

[580] Ibid.

[581] Ibid.

least fifty aircraft each.[582] As Captain Yoshiyuki Kishi looked aft over his ships stern, 50 enemy aircraft approached his ship just slightly to starboard at 0823. At 0824, he gave the order to open fire with his AA guns. The range was 16,440 yards. At 0827, ten U.S. dive bombers rolled over into an attack dive and at 0828. He then ordered a 30° turn of the rudder. Two bombs hit the AA guns located on the port side abreast the forward elevator and cutting the port side communication cables. Near miss bombs bracketed the hull.[583]

At 0830, ten more dive bombers descend on her from 110° starboard. A direct hit was scored on the port side aft of the number two elevator, penetrated the flight deck and detonated in compartment number seventeen. Crew compartments thirteen and sixteen were ripped open and on fire. Near miss bombs detonated close aboard. Her outer hull aft on the port side was ruptured and the hydraulic pressure lines to her rudders were severed. Crew compartment seventeen flooded immediately with crew compartment fourteen and sixteen progressively flooding. Four major power lines were also cut so that operation of the rudders became impossible.[584]

At 0834, ten more aircraft dive on the carrier bearing 120° starboard. These bombs produced more near misses that shake the small carrier. At 0835, another wave of ten dive bombers attacked from port bearing 60°. Two direct hits on the side of the ship detonated flooding number two and number four boiler rooms. *Chitose* immediately took a 27° list to port. Captain Yoshiyuki Kishi then received word that the number two communications room was full of CO_2 so he ordered the crew to move to the number one communications room and abandon that space. He also ordered starboard void fuel tanks to be flooded to help correct the list. He then received word that the number three boiler room was on fire so he gave permission to the crew to abandon this space.[585]

By 0836, steam pressure began to drop and the forward port engine began to slow and the number two generator quit. Emergency auxiliary systems immediately took over. Smoke and CO_2 were filling the port side passageways. At 0840, another near miss bomb detonated forward flooding the number 6 crew space. At 0841, the number three boiler room began to progressively flood. Kishi ordered

---

[582] *Chitose* Detailed Action Report, October 25, 1944.

[583] Ibid.

[584] Ibid.

[585] Ibid.

the aft engine rooms to maximum power. By 0845, four more U.S. aircraft attacked bearing 080° to starboard. Those AA guns still in operation opened fire.[586]

The number one boiler room couldn't produce enough steam for the surviving machinery plant. The forward starboard engine slowed and the number one generator steam pressure read zero. The main power circuit was still on. *Chitose* listed to port at 20° but could still make fourteen knots. By 0852, the U.S. aircraft were retiring and all AA guns checked fire. Water had entered the number one boiler room so that the base of the boiler was submerged by 0855. Kishi ordered the crew to abandon the space and lock down the watertight doors after the crew was safely out.[587]

By 0900, *Shimotsuki* was closing to render assistance. Orders were given to the crew to prepare *Chitose* for possible towing. Kishi then received word that the forward engine rooms were beginning to flood. By 0905, flooding entered the starboard aft engine room and the crew abandoned this space. All her boiler rooms, both forward engine rooms, and the starboard aft engine room, were now out of commission. By 0910, the port aft engine slowed and all power was lost by 0915. At this point Kishi ordered all secret documents destroyed and for all surviving crew members to assemble on the starboard side of the ship.[588]

By 0920, the list to port had grown to 28°. The Emperor's portrait was taken down at 0925 and orders were given to prepare to abandon ship. Then at 0930, the list had grown to 30°; Kishi could wait no longer and gave the order to abandon *Chitose*. Only seven minutes later at 0937, *Chitose* disappeared into the depths taking 903 men with her including Kishi. The light cruiser *Isuzu* rescued thirty-five officers and 445 men and the destroyer *Shimotsuki* rescued 121 men.[589]

Rear Admiral Tomekichi Nomura was in command of Rear Admiral Chiaki Matsuda's flagship. At 0810, *Hyuga*'s radar picked up a large formation bearing 210° at 98,640 yards. Nomura increased speed to twenty-four knots at 0813 and by 0816 AA alerts were sounded. At 0817, her 5-inch high angle guns opened fire on a group of planes coming in bearing 30° to starboard. At 0821 approximately

---

[586] Ibid.

[587] Ibid.

[588] Ibid.

[589] Ibid.

thirty aircraft attacked from port which she engaged with her AA guns. As quickly as the attack came it was over and the U.S. aircraft retired.[590]

Matsuda quickly learned that *Chitose* had been hit and was on fire. The light cruiser *Tama* had taken a torpedo hit in her number two boiler room and fallen out of formation. The carrier *Chiyoda* had also been hit by a single bomb but the damage was minor. He ordered the light cruiser *Isuzu* to stand by and assist *Tama*. The destroyer *Shimotsuki* was assigned to assist *Chitose* and *Hyuga* and the destroyer *Maki* to defend the *Chiyoda*. At 0937, *Chitose* sank and *Shimotsuki* stood by to rescue her crew. [591]

Nomura was notified that at 0942 another large formation had been detected bearing 200° at a distance of 71,240 yards. AA alerts were sounded at 0945 and his lookouts reported sighting the enemy at a distance of 42,744 yards. His lookouts counted approximately forty-five aircraft now bearing 170° to starboard by 0950. At 0953, *Hyuga*'s 5-inch guns opened fire and this was followed by her main battery at 0955. The carrier *Chiyoda* became the main target of approximately thirty aircraft and she suffered a direct hit on the port side aft which began a raging fire. She comes to a stop as her crew fought the fires aft and Mutsuda had *Hyuga* and *Maki* circle the wounded carrier in an attempt to drive off her attackers. The U.S. aircraft retired by 1010.[592]

At 1033, more U.S. aircraft were detected at a distance of 27,400 yards and AA alerts were sounded at 1049. At 1055, an estimated 100 aircraft were seen splitting up into five different groups. Without any protective air cover the U.S. aircraft were free to maneuver into focused and coordinated attack groups on the individual Japanese ships. As the U.S. aircraft formed for the next attack *Tama* reported she was capable of thirteen knots by 1150 and Mutsuda ordered her to proceed to Okinawa alone and had *Isuzu* re-join *Hyuga*. By 1155, the fires on board *Chiyoda* seemed to be under control and he ordered *Hyuga* to prepare to take the carrier under tow. The U.S. aircraft now attacked his group and *Hyuga*'s guns opened fire at 1237. The attack focused on *Chiyoda* again and by 1320, Mutsuda ordered *Isuzu* and *Maki* to take off her crew and sink her. *Shimotsuki* had picked up the survivors from *Chitose* and re-joined *Hyuga* and these two ships headed north to join Ozawa leaving *Chiyoda*, *Isuzu*, and *Maki* behind. *Isuzu* and *Maki* were not able to take off the crew of *Chiyoda* due to the fires being too intense.

---

[590] *Hyuga* Detailed Action Report, October 20 to October 29, 1944.

[591] Ibid.

[592] Ibid.

Amazingly, they left the ship. U.S. surface forces found her at 1625 and sank her in thirty minutes. She wasn't able to get out a distress signal, so neither Ozawa nor Mutsuda were aware of her plight.[593]

As *Hyuga* headed north to rejoin Ozawa, Nomura engaged several small groups of U.S. aircraft as they come within range of his guns at 1327, 1350, 1416, 1430, and 1520. None of these aircraft attacked *Hyuga* herself and were likely retiring from attacks made on other Japanese ships. At 1625, another wave of U.S. aircraft was detected at a distance of seventy-one miles. By 1715, the distance had closed to 25,208 yards and AA alerts were sounded. By 1722, both her main battery and secondary battery guns all opened fire. Seven near miss bombs bracketed her hull but there were no direct hits. By 1745, all U.S. aircraft retired and this was the last U.S. air attack of the day on *Hyuga.* At 1820, *Hyuga* and *Shimotsuki* joined *Ise* and *Oyoda* for this was what remained of Ozawa's carrier force. *Hatsuzuki, Wakatsuki,* and *Kuwa* were rescuing the survivors of *Zuikaku* and *Zuiho.*[594]

At 1915, Ozawa received a message from *Hatsuzuki* that she was under attack from U.S. surface forces estimated to be two battleships, two cruisers, and a destroyer squadron. Ozawa immediately sent out a message requesting her position which had not been relayed. There was no reply. Ozawa ordered *Ise, Hyuga, Oyoda,* and *Shimotsuki* south to give battle at 2130. By 2330, *Wakatsuki* and *Kuwa* joined his force and reported that *Hatsuzuki* had quickly laid down a smoke screen allowing *Wakatsuki,* and *Kuwa* to withdraw but nothing had been heard from her since. Ozawa continued south in a vain search but found nothing. Just before midnight he turned back north. The Battle of Cape Engano was over. Now he headed back for home and safety for there was nothing else he could do.[595]

DuBose on his flagship the cruiser *Santa Fe* listened to reports of the carrier air strikes taking place. At 0825 the enemy's position was bearing 115° at a distance of one hundred and fifteen miles. *Santa Fe* was part of Cruiser Division 13. The other cruisers in the division were *Mobile, Wichita,* and *New Orleans.* DuBose received orders to increase speed to twenty-five knots at 0835 to chase the enemy and set course to 010° true. At 0850 CTF 38 gave a preliminary report of the first strike. Two CV hit badly, one CV hit, one CVL untouched. One heavy ship

---

[593] Ibid.

[594] Ibid.

[595] Ibid.

sunk after tremendous explosion on fantail. By 0919, CTF ordered a course change to 000° north.[596]

At 0930, DuBose received a radio signal from the strike planes that the enemy force consisted of four CV, two BB, three or four cruisers, and seven destroyers. One CV had exploded. By 0938 CTF 38 radioed enemy course 330° speed twenty knots. Then Halsey ordered a change in speed to twenty knots at 1012 which didn't make much sense since this speed wouldn't close on the enemy. DuBose had to wait 46 minutes to find out what was happening. Then at 1058, he received word that Commander Third Fleet ordered TF 34 and CTG 38.2 to reverse course and proceed south. He also ordered CTU 38.3 and CTU 38.4 to continue air strikes on the enemy force to the north. At 1114, course was changed to 090° and by 1117 course was set at 180° south. No sooner had this been accomplished when CTG 34 ordered Cruiser Division 13, *Wichita* and *New Orleans* and ten destroyers to re-join TG 38.3 and TG 38.4.[597]

Santa Fe was put about again at 1120 heading back north and sighted TG 38.3 bearing 095° at a distance of eighteen miles at 1246. At 1250 CTF 38 sent information concerning the enemy northern force. Enemy formation was split into two groups. Group one consisted of two CV flanked by three destroyers and followed by a battleship. Group two consisted of one CA speed ten knots, followed by one CV which was dead in the water screened by two damaged cruisers and one battleship which may not be damaged. The enemy was on course 340° at a speed of twenty-two knots. At this point CTF 38 ordered DuBose to take Cruiser Division 13 ahead of TG 38.3 and to keep *Wichita* and *New Orleans* and form a strike group.[598]

At 1300 DuBose had taken station ahead of TG 38.3. The cruisers were in column led by *Santa Fe, Mobile, Wichita*, and *New Orleans*, with a distance between vessels of 1,000 yards. His screening destroyers were *Bagley, Knapp, Caperton, Cogswell, Ingersoll, Dortch, Healy, C. K. Bronson, Cotton*, and *Patterson*. Pilots from *Langley* reported that the enemy was bearing 030° distance eighty-six miles from our strike group at 1330. The *Lexington* pilots reported at 1332 that one CV was on fire with occasional explosions and she was being circled by a CL, one BB,

---

[596] *Santa Fe*, Action Report, November 15, 1944, RG 38.

[597] Ibid.

[598] Ibid.

and two DD. Main target area one CVE sinking by stern and listing to port. Another CVL was on fire but underway.[599]

At 1350 CTG 38 suggested Cruiser Division 13 be sent in after dark to destroy crippled enemy ships. DuBose concurred and replied accordingly. At 1356, CTG 38 warned that the cruisers were now approaching the location of the morning battle and that they should be on the lookout for downed aviators. CTG 38 sent word to CTG 38.3.3 and CTG 38.3.4 to be prepared to make night torpedo attack on any worthwhile target. DuBose was concerned about the two Japanese battleships. As he reviewed the reports from the aircraft it was clear that the four Japanese carriers had been severely damaged, crippled and in sinking condition but the two battleships seemed to remain unscathed. At 1402, Laurance DuBose radioed CTG 38 and said,[600]

> Am of the opinion that if we should be able to get those two battleships together it is going to be tough on the cruisers. However, if you think so we will do it.[601]

Mitscher understood that without the support of TF 34's battleships the Japanese now outgunned him. As dusk fell he would need to be careful not to close the range too close and his cruiser force was no match in a gunnery duel. He kept the light cruiser *Reno* and four destroyers with the carriers and ordered the destroyers *Callaghan* and *Porterfield* to join DuBose. All he could do was to add two destroyers, when he needed to add at least two battleships. By 1410, pilots from *Lexington* reported enemy fleet was now seventy miles ahead, course 030° at a speed of fifteen knots. They were leaving one crippled carrier behind. Laurance DuBose ordered his strike group onto a course of 000° and to increased speed to twenty-five knots at 1429. At 1431, Mitscher stopped his advance with the carriers so they would stay clear of the enemy. He reported that TG 38.3 would remain at latitude 19° 60′, longitude 126° 40′ and operate here. He then ordered DuBose to launch all available float planes to search for downed aviators.[602]

DuBose ordered all cruisers to launch float planes immediately. They were to work in pairs and do rescue work only and be back on board one half hour before sunset. At 1510, *Cotton* rescued a downed pilot. At 1517 *Santa Fe* launched her float plane and it teamed up with the float plane from *Mobile*. At 1519, *Cotton* res-

---

[599] Ibid.

[600] Ibid.

[601] Ibid.

[602] The *Lexington,* Action Report, November 22, 1944, RG 38.

cued another U.S. pilot. DuBose noted at this time his ships were passing through debris and oil slicks from the morning battle. He still had some doubt as to the exact location of the enemy and *Callaghan* and *Porterfield* were well behind his formation. Then at 1605, his Radar III picked up a surface target bearing 029° at a distance of 32,900 yards.[603]

DuBose ordered general quarters at 1610 and told his destroyers to form in the rear of the cruisers. At 1617, he gave permission for the cruisers to open fire when ready. At 1618 he visually spotted an enemy carrier bearing 041° distance 23,300 yards. At 1622, he set course to 020° and at 1624, *New Orleans* was the first cruiser to open fire. By 1628, the course was adjusted to 010°. Then at 1630, pilots from *Langley* reported one battleship and one light cruiser heading north at forty five miles and show no sign they were returning.[604]

At 1631, *Santa Fe*'s main battery opened fire at the carrier bearing 068° with a range of 14,460 yards. By 1635, hits were recorded by *Santa Fe*'s gunners. At 1636 her secondary battery opened fire. At 1637, the wounded carrier returned fire with several shells landing short. DuBose observed the Japanese carrier getting hit frequently and began to burn. She began to list to port and when first approached she was down by the bow but this had changed and she was now sinking by the stern. He saw crew men running along her flight deck and he identified the ship as a *Chitose* class carrier. By 1639, he ordered all cruisers with the exception of *Wichita* to check fire. The *Santa Fe* had expended two hundred and eighty-one 6-inch AP rounds and thirty-one 5-inch rounds.[605]

At 1641, he ordered the destroyers to close and finish her with torpedoes but at 1646 the carrier capsized to port. His destroyer commander replied that the target was going down and she wasn't worth a fish and that he was rejoining the Main Force. At 1655, *Chiyoda* sank with all hands. By 1700, DuBose ordered his force north in search of more targets. Pilots from *Langley* informed him that the next targets were bearing 330° at a distance of twenty-five miles at 1705. Another report of a CA bearing 325° at a distance of thirty-five miles was reported at 1716. At 1720, *Mobile* sighted heavy AA gun fire ahead. DuBose however had to begin picking up his float planes as dusk was almost upon them. At 1724, he began to maneuver to pick up his float planes which, was completed by 1753. Now that this had been accomplished he ordered his destroyers to form three attack groups

---

[603] *Santa Fe*, Action Report, November 15, 1944, RG 38.

[604] Ibid.

[605] Ibid.

behind the cruiser column, increased speed to twenty knots and set a course heading north.[606]

At 1804, the sun set and then at 1810 the flash of AA fire was seen directly ahead. DuBose ordered an increase in speed to twenty-five knots at 1813. At this time two planes from *Essex* reported they were on station and reporting for duty. DuBose sent them ahead ten to fifteen miles and look for enemy ships. Then at 1821, a SB2C bomber made a water landing and *C.K. Bronson* broke formation to rescue the pilots. The planes he sent forward reported back at 1823 they had sighted a contact bearing 340° at a distance of twenty-four miles. By 1825 they reported back one CL and two DD bearing 335° at a distance of twenty-two miles. Radar contact on *Santa Fe* was established at 1835 at a distance of seventeen miles. *Wichita* reported she had made radar contact and DuBose set a course of 030°. By 1841, air forward reported sighting a ship's mast on the horizon and by 1843 radar had established contact on all three enemy ships and that the main battery director was locked onto the closest target. Director 61 reported targets at 28,000 yards with the largest target now pulling away at 1843. At 1851, Laurance DuBose sent out the order:[607]

> As soon as within range and with good setup commence firing, CL's on near targets and CA's on far targets, course change to 050°.[608]

New Orleans didn't take long for at 1852 she was the first again to open fire on the farthest target available. Combat Information Center (CIC) on board *Santa Fe* reported closest target now bearing 330° distance nine miles. At 1859, the target was returning fire. At 1900, Laurance DuBose changed heading to 010° and then received a report from his aircraft above of another contact bearing 005° distance fifty-five miles. CIC reported three contacts bearing 335° distance 19,800 yards, bearing 328° distance 21,800 yards, and bearing 331° distance 27,900 yards. With this information DuBose ordered a new course heading to 330°. At 1905, *Santa Fe* main battery opened fire on the closest target bearing 348° at a distance of 16,950 yards. The targets course was 110° at a speed of thirty knots. The two other targets were heading north. Course heading was changed to 060° at 1906 and then the target made a short turn toward *Santa Fe* and then turned away. *Wichita* radioed that her target was out of range and asked permission to engage closest target which DuBose immediately answered affirmative. At 1907, *Santa Fe* sec-

---

[606] Ibid.

[607] Ibid.

[608] Ibid.

ondary battery opened fire and the range had been reduced to 14,000 yards. Shell splashes were reported falling close and it appeared that the target was taking *Santa Fe* has her target. Course was changed to 080° at 1911 and at this time two direct hits were observed. The return fire was inaccurate with some short rounds and many overs but no straddles. She was seen to turn away on fire and by 1913 the secondary battery checked fire having expended three hundred and ninety-four 5-inch rounds. The main battery continued to fire.[609]

DuBose ordered Destroyer Division 100 to close target and finish her off at 1914. The target was still unidentified and was making stack smoke. She then turned toward the U.S. ships at a speed of twenty knots and the fires seen earlier were now out. Fearing a possible torpedo attack Laurance DuBose ordered a course change to 120° at 1916 and then to 140° at 1918 observed a hit on the enemy warship. At 1919, the main battery checked fire having expended four hundred and ninety-eight 6-inch rounds. By 1920 Laurance DuBose ordered the chase to resume and changed course back to the north with a setting of 030°. The *Santa Fe*'s secondary battery resumed fire at this time with the target bearing 340° at a range of 14,000 yards. A new fire was seen on the target and then an explosion was observed but the targets speed remained twenty knots. The new fire was put out almost immediately and then the target changed course back to a southwesterly course toward the U.S. fleet.[610]

At 1926, *Santa Fe*'s main battery resumed fire with the target now bearing 338° and the range had opened to 15,590 yards. Another hit was observed at this time. The target course was now 168° and she had an estimated speed of eighteen knots. At 1927 DuBose changed course to 060° and the target changed course to 152°, bearing 331°, and had increased speed back up to twenty knots. At 1930, as range opened up *Santa Fe* checked fire with both her main battery and secondary battery to conserve ammunition. She had expended another three hundred and seven 6-inch rounds and three hundred and thirteen 5-inch rounds. At this time his planes reported four or five large targets sixty miles to the north and still heading north at a speed of twenty knots. These must be the Japanese battleships and they didn't appear to be coming back south. At 1933, DuBose set a course of 030° and target swung to the left. Destroyer Division 100 which had given up the

---

[609] Ibid.

[610] Ibid.

chase resumed the chase at this time. By 1942, Laurance DuBose ordered an increase in speed to twenty-eight knots.[611]

At 1945, the target was on a course of 000° at seventeen knots which was the slowest speed yet observed. Planes reported at 1947 the larger ships to the north the distance was now fifty miles. At 1949 DuBose changed course to 060° but a minute later at 1950 changed course again to 340° with his ships in column formation. Then at 1958, the target slowed down to a stop but as she came to a stop she suddenly picked up speed again. Laurance DuBose changed course to 310°. Laurance DuBose ordered his planes to search for the other two original contacts when this group was first sighted at 2005. Destroyer Division 100 closed at 2009 and fired half salvo of torpedoes from astern and then opened fire. The target was observed to return fire on the destroyers. At 2012, *Santa Fe* re-opened fire with both her main and secondary batteries with the target bearing 290° at a distance of 13,370 yards. Target course was now 321° at a speed of twenty knots. The target swung to the west and by 2018 *Santa Fe* checked fire, however DuBose ordered *Mobile* to resume fire. *Santa Fe* had expended another ninety-nine rounds of 6-inch and two hundred and thirty-four 5-inch rounds. By 2019, Target had increased speed to twenty-one knots now bearing 271° on a course of 257°. At 2027, cruisers reformed into column on *Santa Fe*. Then at 2028, the target suffered a large explosion and was covered with smoke at the approximate time the torpedoes should have arrived which had been fired by the destroyers at 2009. At 2033, DuBose ordered *Wichita* to open fire once range had decreased to 10,000 yards. At 2036, his destroyers reported target was a cruiser and *Wichita* opened fire at 2036. Target was observed to be on fire. At 2042, more shell hits were observed and target stubbornly returned fire again. His destroyers then fired star shells to illuminate target at 2043. [612]

The target was now bearing 228° and range had dropped to 6,850 yards and she was slowing down. At 2047, *Santa Fe* re-opened with both main battery and secondary battery at a range of 4,830 yards. The target speed was now zero. Hits now occurred with every salvo and target began to settle by the bow. DuBose ordered the destroyers to close and finish her off and *Porterfield* began her approach. At 2048, Laurance DuBose slowed to twenty-five knots and checked fire with the main battery expending another forty eight 6-inch rounds and the 5-inch expending one hundred and four rounds of star shells and thirty-one rounds of

[611] Ibid.

[612] Ibid.

common shells. At 2056, the target sank before *Porterfield* could close. Six underwater explosions were noted as she sank. DuBose believed the target was an *Oyoda* or an *Agano* class cruiser. Other observers reported the target as a *Terutsuki* class destroyer. The ship they had attacked was the brave destroyer *Hatsuzuki* that had been in the process of rescuing the survivors of *Zuikaku* and *Zuiho.*[613]

The range had decreased to forty-two miles from the Japanese battleships and DuBose didn't wish to tangle with these ships. At 2107, his fleet commenced forming column formation and he set a course south to rejoin TG 38.3. By 2230, he released his aircraft and allowed them to return to *Essex*. At 2330, he reported to Mitscher the following report:[614]

> First contact on CVL which was sunk. Next three contacts about forty five miles north. Two headed north at twenty knots after being fired upon and couldn't be located later by snooper. One evidently with steering trouble but speed of twenty-six knots sank after about an hour's run around and great many direct hits. Believe enemy ship was an Agano type cruiser. Snooper had final contact fifty miles north of us on a course north speed twenty knots, fuel in destroyers precluded thirty knot stern chase. I am returning.[615]

Kurita received a message at 1710 from the South West Area Force reporting that, with exception of one regular carrier being damaged, results obtained were undetermined. At 1744, a group of Japanese bombers arrived over the fleet. Two Japanese dive bombers made an attack on *Yamato* before the aircrews properly identified the fleet below as friendly. Luckily for *Yamato*, no damage was sustained. The air crews asked for directions to the enemy, and *Yamato*'s staff gave them their best estimate to the north. These aircraft returned thirty minutes later reporting they couldn't find the enemy.[616]

By 1830, Kurita had found nothing and decided to end the operation and return to Brunei. He had expected to find the enemy within two hours of turning north, but after six hours, nothing had appeared. Where was TF 34? Effectively blind with no way to ascertain where the enemy was, Kurita shifted his main concern to fuel. Did he have enough to return home?

Exhaustion was also having an impact. Kurita had not slept since leaving Brunei on 22 October. By 1917, Kurita issued orders to all damaged units to make

---

[613] *Hyuga* Detailed Action Report, October 20 to October 29, 1944.

[614] *Santa Fe*, Action Report, November 15, 1944, RG 38.

[615] Ibid.

[616] *Yamato* Detailed Action Report, 17 October to 28 October 1944.

every possible effort to proceed alone but, where this was impossible, to dispose of any damaged warships and transfer the crew to its screening vessel and proceed to Coron. At 1925, Kurita and his staff were handed a message from Combined Fleet Headquarters in response to Kurita's message that they had abandoned the penetration into Leyte Gulf. It read,

> Combined Fleet DesOpOrd No. 374: If there is an opportunity to do so, the First Diversion Attack Force will contact and destroy what is left of the enemy tonight. The other forces will coordinate their action with the above. If there is no chance of engaging the enemy in a night engagement tonight, the Main Body of the Mobile Force and First Diversion Attack Force will proceed to their refueling points as ordered by their respective commanders.[617]

With its focus on attack, the SHO 1 operation suffered for its flaws in reconnaissance and communication. Kurita, unable to conduct his own searches, depended on reports from either the First or Second Air Fleet, and these failed him as it became clear that the report of a U.S. task force to his north had been false. When he might have gainfully conducted a night battle, he had to count on the enemy's conveniently coming to engage him. He had the option of resuming his mission to enter Leyte Gulf, but nothing had changed concerning the strategic significance of such a battle, a battle fought solely for its own sake. To fight a major engagement without a strategic objective was a concept without precedent in sound naval doctrine. Kurita admitted postwar that he never considered a return to Leyte Gulf.[618]

At 2130, his fleet passed through San Bernardino Strait. At this time he sent a message to First and Second Air Fleets,

> In view of the one-sidedness of the decisive action carried out today, the 25th, there is much likelihood of the enemy's attempting to carry out revenge attacks against us with the entire strength of the remainder of his task force. It is probable that such contact would be made in an area in the vicinity to the east or north of Legaspi on the 26th. We are of the opinion that the situation may offer an excellent opportunity for the shore-based air force units to strike the first blow against the enemy and gain control of the air.[619]

---

617 Combined Fleet Headquarters Detailed Action Report, October 17 to October 28, 1944.

618 Robertson, Operational Analysis for the Battle of Leyte Gulf.

619 Combined Fleet Headquarters Detailed Action Report, October 17 to October 28, 1944.

The hoped-for Japanese land-based attacks could not save Japan. Onishi in command of the First Air Fleet met with Fukudome in command of the Second Air Fleet for a third time late in the evening of 25 October. Reports for the past two days showed that thirteen aircraft using the kamikaze tactics had sunk two carriers and a cruiser and heavily damaged at least four other carriers,[620] compared to the 250 aircraft using conventional attacks that had sunk only the light carrier *Princeton*. Onishi argued that the evidence was quite conclusive, and that special attacks were their only hope. Fukudome conceded the effectiveness of these tactics but was still reluctant to adopt them. The meeting went through the night, and at 0200 on 26 October Fukudome finally agreed to adopt kamikaze attacks for the Second Air Fleet. The adoption of these tactics shifted Japan's dwindling fuel reserves away from the fleet, so the Battle of Leyte Gulf would be the last time that the Imperial Japanese Navy would sortie in strength and the last time it had military significance on a strategic level.

After the battle, Halsey sent message 251317 to Nimitz concerning his action's and decisions. He said:

> That there be no misunderstanding concerning recent operations of the Third Fleet, I inform you as follows: To obtain information of Jap plans and movements became vital on 23 October so three carrier groups were moved into the Philippine coast off Polillo, San Bernardino and Surigao to search as far west as possible. On 24 October the Third Fleet searches revealed Jap forces moving east through the Sibuyan and Sulu Seas and both of those forces were brought under attack by Third Fleet air strikes. The existence of a Jap plan for coordinated attack was apparent but the objective was not sure and the expected carrier force was missing from the picture. Third Fleet carrier searches revealed the presence of the enemy carrier force on the afternoon of 24 October, completing the picture.
>
> To statically guard San Bernardino Strait until enemy surface and carrier air attacks could be coordinated would have been childish, so three carrier groups were concentrated during the night and started north for a surprise dawn attack on the enemy carrier fleet. I considered that the enemy forces in Sibuyan Sea had been so badly damaged that they constituted no serious threat to Thomas Kinkaid and that estimate has been borne out by the events of the 25th off Surigao. The enemy carrier force was caught off guard, there being no air opposition over the target and no air attack against our force. Their air groups were apparently shore-based and arrived too late to land on their carriers or get into flight.

---

620 The inaccurate number of U.S. ships sunk or damaged came from the Japanese reports given to Vice Admiral Takijiro Onishi, and this represented his perception at the time he made his argument for Vice Admiral Fukudome to adopt kamikaze tactics.

> I had projected surface striking units ahead of our carriers in order to coordinate surface and air attacks against the enemy. Commander Seventh Fleet's urgent appeals for help came at a time when the enemy force was heavily damaged and my overwhelming surface striking force was within forty-five miles of the enemy cripples. I had no alternative but to break off my golden opportunity and head south to support Thomas Kinkaid although I was convinced that his force was adequate to deal with the enemy force that was badly weakened by our attacks of the twenty-fourth—a conviction justified by later events off Leyte.[621]

Kinkaid's interpretation of the orders from Nimitz for KING II differed dramatically from Halsey's. In 1960 in an oral interview Thomas Kinkaid said,

> As Commander of the Seventh Fleet, I was to transport the landing forces to Leyte Gulf beaches, establish them ashore, and see that they were covered and stayed ashore. The Third Fleet under Halsey was to give us protection during the landing and during whatever actions might take place afterwards. His was a strategic cover; mine was a direct cover and the protection of the landing forces. It's a very important point that I have brought out frequently, because I had a mission and Admiral Halsey had a mission. In spite of the fact that we did not have a common superior, I have frequently said that if both Halsey and I had carried out our respective missions correctly there would have been no confusion.... It has always been my opinion...that one commander would not have been better than two where each of us had a mission...very clearly stated."[622]

In a top-secret message to King dated 28 October 1944, Nimitz expressed two regrets. The first dealt with the loss of the light carrier *Princeton* on 24 October. Concerning the Battle off Samar, Nimitz said,

> My second exception and regret is that the fast battleships were not left in the vicinity of Samar when Task Force 38 started after the striking force reported to be in the north end of the Philippine Sea, and composed of carriers, two battleships, cruisers and destroyers in support. It never occurred to me that Halsey, knowing the composition of the ships in the Sibuyan Sea, would leave San Bernardino Strait unguarded, even though the Jap detachment in the Sibuyan Sea had been reported seriously damaged. That Halsey feels that he is in a defensive position is indicated in his top-secret dispatch 251317.
>
> That the San Bernardino detachment of the Japanese Fleet, which included the Yamato and the Musashi, did not completely destroy all of the escort carriers and their accompanying screen is nothing short of special dispensation from the Lord Almighty; although it can be accepted that the damage the Japs had received the day before in the Sibuyan

---

[621] Vice Admiral William F. Halsey, CTU 38, Action Report, November 13, RG 38.

[622] Wheeler, Gerald E. *Kinkaid of the Seventh Fleet.* Naval Institute Press, 1995, p 406.

Sea undoubtedly affected their ability to steam and shoot when they attacked Sprague's escort carriers.[623]

The Battle of Surigao Strait was a demonstration of the power of command of the sea. Seventh Fleet's battleships were fulfilling their primary mission in securing Leyte Gulf and preventing passage to the Gulf from the Japanese. This allowed the transports to do their job without interference. Only the Japanese battleships possessed the power to break that control. Japanese airpower was incapable of breaking that control and throwing back an Allied invasion. No U.S. amphibious assault was ever stopped even after Japanese conventional air attacks were turned into human guided missiles. Faced with Japanese battleships, Kinkaid called for U.S. battleships to ensure that control of the sea would be maintain.

To affect events ashore command of the sea had to be exercised twenty-four hours a day for weeks or months if needed to be effective which was why the principle of sustainability was the true measure of naval power during WWII.

With it ships could influence events ashore and this enforced the political will of one country over another. This was why battleships remained the final arbiter of sea power through the end of World War II.

Kurita's Center Force came under the most intense aerial attack by any Japanese fleet during the entire war. For three days the U.S. launched hundreds of aircraft in over 18 separate waves without a single Japanese plane in defense. After three days his force had suffered attrition due to these air attacks but remained combat effective throughout. Kurita was forced to withdraw not due to damage received but due to the inability to sustain operations due to lack of fuel. Even if he had pushed on and won in Tsushima-like fashion and gained command of the Gulf he would have be forced to abandon it as his fuel and ammunition reserves would have been exhausted and the Japanese navy no longer had the capability to replenish itself at sea under near continuous air attack. Center Force did not have true power to affect events ashore due to its inability to sustain operations. The window of opportunity where the Japanese battle fleet could have been victorious over the U.S. fleet had already passed by. By focusing on strike warfare in 1942

---

[623] Potter, E. B., *Chester Nimitz* at 344.

and not on command of the sea with the support of strike warfare, Japan's admirals ensured their own defeat.

The U.S. Pacific Fleet carriers and the airpower they brought to naval warfare were the engine that enabled Nimitz's first strategic goal of relentless pressure on the Japanese and maintaining the strategic offensive. This air power prepared the battlefield but another power was still required to actually push back the Japanese defensive perimeter. The ability to control passage and maintain control of the sea was the decisive factor that enabled every amphibious assault to be successful. This required battleships.

Nimitz's second major strategic goal, destroying the Japanese fleet, required a battle, and confirmed Corbett's view that decisive battles would be rare because they needed a willing partner. This applied to both sides. The tactical nature of the fast tempo provided by the carriers diminished the opportunities of the battleships to train and prepare for a decisive fleet action. This led to Lee's decision to decline a night battle on June 18, 1944.

The emphasis on the carrier provided the perception that battleships played only a secondary role in operational planning. This is a myth. Through the Gilberts to Leyte Gulf it was the concentration of the battleships that was foremost in the commanding admiral's battle plans and how to focus this weapon should the Japanese come out to fight. It was only after Leyte when the Japanese fleet was largely immobilized that the fast battleships were evenly distributed among the carriers.

Halsey, Spruance, and Mitscher all focused on the concentration of battleships but never adapted to Japanese use of division; this would have forced American forces to separate. The PAC 10 doctrine provided the United States with a tool that allowed task groups to transform and remain combat-effective yet the admirals did not fully seize this advantage when the opportunities presented themselves. Some observers recognized this. Vice Admiral George D. Murray, commander Air Force Pacific Fleet wrote:

> Concentration though usually sound, may sometimes be pursued too far, with diminished returns. The ability to divide forces cleverly, as developed by the enemy and to un-concentrate quickly may often be an advantage.[624]

---

[624] Hone, Trent, U.S. Navy Surface Battle Doctrine and Victory in the Pacific, Naval War College Review at 94-95.

The failure to recognize and adapt to Japanese asymmetries of the use of division prevented Halsey and Spruance from annihilating the Japanese fleet in a single blow. The great fleet battle never occurred.

Nevertheless, because of the Japanese strategic failure to seek command of the sea via combined carrier and battleship warfare, the Americans were able to create nearly a complete blockade of Japan. In 1944 the U.S. armed forces would sink 4,115,100 tons of Japanese merchant shipping and Japan could only offset this with 1,735,100 tons of new shipping with a net loss of 2,380,000 tons. At the beginning of hostilities Japan's Merchant Marine was just over six million tons of shipping and the leadership believed three million tons was the absolute minimum to maintain industrial and civilian requirements. Unlike the United States or Great Britain the industrial capacity of Japanese industry was proportional to imported materials to maintain the war effort.[625] By the end of 1944 Japan had been reduced to 2,564,000 tons and, even more importantly, with the capture of the Philippines, the sea lanes to the South China Sea had been cut off, making the remaining shipping resources almost useless.

Bauxite imports fell 88% by 1944. Pig iron imports fell 89%, pulp 90%, raw cotton and wool 91%, fats and oils 92%, iron ore 95%, soda and cement 96%, lumber 98%, and rubber and sugar 100%[626] The average caloric intake for Japanese citizens fell 12% below the minimum daily requirements during the course of the war.[627] For the key import of oil the Japanese Navy required 1.6 million barrels a month just to operate. In August 1943 Japan imported successfully 1.75 million barrels but by July of 1944 only 360,000 barrels of oil were reaching Japan. After October 1944 imports fell 91% as the South China Sea was cut off. [628] American submarines sank 1,113 merchant ships for 4,779,902 tons and in addition sank 201 combatants of the Imperial Japanese Navy of 540,192 tons. [629]

---

[625] Poirier Michel Thomas Commander, U.S.N., *Results of the American Pacific Submarine Campaign of World War II* 30 Dec 1999. Strategic Bombing Survey, *Japanese Transportation*, pp. 60, 108-109. This study indicates there was a number of factors that were important, but that in most industries, industrial output was directly linked to imports of primary materials.

[626]Ibid. at 207.

[627] Ibid at 218.

[628] Ibid at 215.

[629] Japanese Naval and Merchant Shipping Losses During World War II by All Causes Prepared by The Joint Army-Navy Assessment Committee NAVEXOS P 468, February 1947 at 4-5.

In addition to the direct loss of merchant hulls already described, the Japanese suffered an important indirect effect of submarine warfare caused by the loss of efficiency due to convoying. This loss of efficiency meant that it took a ship to get from point A to point B. The entire merchant marine (including that shipping throughout the empire that was not convoyed) had a loss of "carrying efficiency" of 8% between January 1942 and January 1944 with a further reduction of 21% by 1945.[630] Moreover, on the critical line between Singapore and Japan, efficiency declined by 45% between May 1943 and May 1944, with further substantial declines later.[631] Not only did Japan have too few ships, but their ships took longer and longer throughout the war to carry badly needed cargoes the same distances.[632]

The American submarine campaign was successful because it was being supported by the forward deployment of a huge surface fleet with tremendous reach due to the air power it possessed. It was a combined effort that used control of the sea to maintain a logistical train allowing both surface and submarines to maintain forward deployment. As the fleet advanced this further restricted available sea lanes and concentrated merchant shipping through various choke points due to the geography of the South China Sea. U.S. carrier-based aircraft sank 359 merchant ships for 1,390,241 tons and destroyed 161 combatants of the Imperial Japanese Navy of 711,236 tons.[633] U.S. Navy and Marine aircraft based on land sank eighty-eight merchant ships for 218,718 tons and eleven combatants for 13,402 tons.[634]

The charts below show the major Japanese combatants sunk per year through 1944. After 1944 the blockade had eliminated the ability of the Imperial Japanese Navy to operate and it lost all strategic value. While the Japanese Navy held a strategic value from 1941 to 1944 the U.S. surface fleet inflicted greater losses on the enemy than did carrier aircraft. In addition the U.S. surface fleet steadily attrit-

---

[630] The Japanese calculated merchant marine efficiency by a factor called *Kakoritsu*. *Kakoritsu* is computed by dividing actual cargo carried (in metric) tons in a given time period by the cargo carrying capacity of ship's in use during that period in that particular service.

[631] Strategic Bombing Survey, *Japanese Transportation*, p. 51.

[632] The delays were caused by the need to await sufficient merchants and escorts to form convoys and by the Japanese tactic of running some convoys near the coast- which lengthened the distances that needed to be traveled.

[633] Japanese Naval and Merchant Shipping Losses During World War II by All Causes Prepared by The Joint Army-Navy Assessment Committee NAVEXOS P 468, February 1947 at 4-5.

[634] Ibid.

ed the Japanese submarines and reduced their opportunities to engage the U.S. battle fleet.

Table 7. Japanese major combatants sunk December 7, 1941 to December 31, 1942.[635]

Surface ships	Carrier air power	Land air Power	Submarine	Shore battery	Mine
I-124	*Kikuzuki*	*Kisaragi*	*Sagiri*	*Hayate*	*Shinonome*
I-23	*Shoho*	*Mutsuki*	*I-173*		
RO-32	*Akagi*	*Asagiri*	*Natsushio*		
I-123	*Kaga*	*RO-61*	*RO-30*		
Furutaka	*Soryu*	*Yayoi*	*I-168*		
Fubuki	*Hiryu*	*Murakumo*	*I-28*		
Akatsuki	*Mikuma*	*Oboro*	*Yamakaze*		
Yudachi	*Ryujo*	*Yura*	*Arare*		
Hiei[636]	*Kinugasa*	*Natsugumo*	*Nenohi*		
Kirishima		*Hayashio*	*Kako*		
Ayanami		*I-15*	*Tenryu*		
Takanami			*I-4*		
I-3					
Teruzuki					
I-22					

[635] Japanese Naval and Merchant Shipping Losses During World War II by All Causes Prepared by The Joint Army-Navy Assessment Committee NAVEXOS P 468, February 1947.

[636] *Hiei* was sunk by combination surface, land based air, and carrier air power. The surface battle crippled her steering which was the primary reason the Japanese gave up on her.

Table 8. Japanese major combatants sunk in 1943[637]

Surface ships	Carrier air power	Land air power	Submarine	Shore battery	Mine
I-1	*RO-102*	*Arashio*	*I-18*		*Makigumo*
Minegumo	*Suzunami*	*Asashio*	*Okikaze*		
Murasame		*Tokitsukaze*	*Oshio*		
I-9		*Shirayuki*	*Isonami*		
RO-107		*Oyashio*	*I-24*		
I-31		*Kagero*	*I-182*		
I-7		*Hatsuyuki*	*Choyo*		
RO-101		*Kiyonami*	*Fuyo*		
Nagatsuki		*Yugure*	*Sunae*		
Niizuki		*Ariake*	*Hakaze*		
I-25		*Mikazuki*	*Numakaze*		
Jintsu		*I-17*			
Arashi		*RO-103*			
Hagikaze		*Mochitsuki*			
Kawakaze		*Tokitsukaze*			
I-178		*Shirayuki*			
I-168					
Yugumo					
Hatsukaze					
Sendai					
Yugiri					
Onami					
Makinami					

[637] Japanese Naval and Merchant Shipping Losses During World War II by All Causes Prepared by The Joint Army-Navy Assessment Committee NAVEXOS P 468, February 1947.

Table 9. Japanese major combatants sunk in 1944.[638]

Surface ships	Carrier Air power	Land air power	Submarine	Shore battery	Mine
I-48	*Naka*	*Harusame*	*Kuma*		
RO-37	*Fumitsuki*	*Yuzuki*	*Sazanami*		
I-171	*Tachikaze*	*Kiyoshimo*	*Umikaze*		
RO-39	*Oite*	*Ume*	*Minekaze*		
I-21	*I-174*		*I-43*		
RO-40	*RO-117*		*Agano*		
I-11	*I-184*		*Tatsuta*		
Maikaze	*Hiyo*		*Shirakumo*		
Katori	*Samidare*		*I-42*		
I-32	*Satsuki*		*Akigumo*		
I-2	*Musashi*		*Ikazuchi*		
I-180	*Wakaba*		*RO-45*		
I-176	*Zuikaku*		*Yubari*		
I-16	*Suzuya*		*I-183*		
RO-106	*Chiyoda*		*Inazuma*		
RO-104	*Zuiho*		*Asanagi*		
RO-116	*Chikuma*		*Minatsuki*		
RO-108	*Chokai*		*Hayanami*		
I-5	*Mogami*[639]		*Kazegumo*		
RO-111	*Akitsuki*		*Matsukaze*		
RO-36	*Kinu*		*Tanikaze*		
RO-44	*Noshiro*		*Shokaku*		
RO-114	*Hayashimo*		*Taiho*		
I-185	*Uranami*		*Hokaze*		
I-6	*Abukuma*		*Usugumo*		
RO-48	*Fujinami*		*Tamanami*		
I-55	*Shiranuhi*		*Oi*		
I-364	*Nachi*		*I-29*		

---

[638] Japanese Naval and Merchant Shipping Losses During World War II by All Causes Prepared by The Joint Army-Navy Assessment Committee NAVEXOS P 468, February 1947.

[639] *Mogami* was heavily damaged in surface battle prior to being sunk by carrier based aircraft.

I-362	*Naganami*	*Kusakaki*
Fuso	*Hamanami*	*Nagara*
Yamashiro	*Shimakaze*	*Otaka*
Asagumo	*Wakatsuki*	*Natori*
Yamagumo	*Kiso*	*Asakaze*
Michishio	*Akebono*	*Yunagi*
Hatsutsuki	*Akishimo*	*Shikinami*
Chitose[640]	*Hatsuharu*	*Unyo*
Nowaki	*Okinami*	*Maya*
I-45	*Kumano*	*Atago*
I-54		*Tama*
I-37		*Akikaze*
I-38		*Jinyo*
I-177		*Kongo*
I-46		*Urakaze*
Kuwa		*Shimotsuki*
Uzuki		*Shinano*
I-370		*Kishinami*
I-371		*Iwanami*
		Shigure
		I-41
		RO-112
		RO -113
		RO-49

The Army, Navy, and Marine aircraft combined for twenty-three merchant ships for 114,306 tons and nine combatants for 48,750 tons. Army and Navy carrier-based aircraft combined for one merchant ship of 6,143 tons and one combatant of 5,700 tons. Army and Navy-Marine aircraft land-based sank fourteen merchant ships for 49,978 tons and six combatants for 21,250 tons. Navy carrier-based and Navy-Marine land-based aircraft sank two combatants for 21,800 tons. Army,

[640] *Chitose* was crippled by carrier based air power and then sunk by surface ships.

Navy carrier-based, and Marine land-based combined to sink eight merchant ships for 58,185 tons.[641]

The battle fleet sank 112 combatants of the Imperial Japanese Navy for 277,817 tons but only eleven merchant ships for 43,349 tons. The battle fleet did combine with airpower for the sinking of four more merchant ships of 29,179 tons and twenty more combatants for 102,303 tons.[642] These figures show that the United States used its submarines and airpower as the primary agents of commerce warfare and the battle fleet to secure the seas and allow the lesser ships to do their job. The U.S. fast battleships and cruisers were not used for commerce warfare like the Germans had attempted in the Atlantic. They were used to secure command of the sea and protect the vulnerable carriers. Aircraft and the submarine assumed the role of Corbett's cruisers in exercising command of the sea and in strategic level blockade and commerce warfare. The battle fleet set the line of scrimmage allowing the carriers and submarines to do their job with minimal interference.

After December 7, 1941 Japanese air power sank zero U.S. battleships, one heavy cruiser, zero light cruisers and twenty-five destroyers. Although the burden of ship defense against enemy air attacks fell largely upon carrier and land-based aircraft. Approximately 7,600-7,800 enemy planes came within shipboard anti-aircraft gun range during the 45 months of the war. Of these, an estimated 2,773, or 36 percent, were shot down by naval and merchant ships. The ten fast battleships which protected the carriers were officially given credit for shooting down 198 Japanese aircraft. The *North Carolina* shot down 24, *Washington* 12, *South Dakota* 64, *Indiana* 18, *Massachusetts* 18, *Alabama* 22, *Iowa* 6, *New Jersey* 20, *Missouri* 11, and *Wisconsin* 3. In addition *Texas* shot down 1, *Nevada* 5, *Tennessee* 16, *Colorado* 11, *West Virginia* 8, *Maryland* 7, *New Mexico* 21, *Idaho* 5, *Arkansas*?, *New York* 1, *Pennsylvania* 10, *California* 3, and *Mississippi*?[643] The "kills" listed occurred within sight of the ships being attacked. An estimated 565 Japanese aircraft fell while returning to their bases and could not be assigned to a particular ship. Of the 2,773 aircraft shot down by the U.S. Navy and Merchant Marine 1,179 were shot down by the Navy and 151 shot down by merchant ships. Kamikaze aircraft accounted for 878 aircraft being shot down before striking a ship. The entire U.S. battle line shot down 286 aircraft with two battleship's total figures being unde-

---

[641] Ibid.

[642] Ibid.

[643] Aircraft shot down taken from individual ship histories.

termined.[644] Considering the battleships represented 0.4% and the smallest number of main combatants within the U.S. Navy their contribution to air defense in shooting down slightly over 10% of all Japanese planes shot down by the entire U.S. Navy was a significant accomplishment.[645] The American admirals used their battleships to secure the seas and this in turn allowed lesser ships such as carriers, cruisers, and destroyers to exercise control of the sea with minimal interference. This was the proper use and implementation of this tool in naval warfare based on Mahan's and Corbett's philosophy. This increased the fighting power of a battle fleet as an overall weapon system when viewed as a whole instead of by its individual parts.

The submarine campaign was successful because it was being supported by the forward deployment of a huge surface fleet. It was a combined effort that used control of the sea to maintain a logistical train allowing both surface and submarines to maintain forward deployment as it moved west. The Japanese Imperial Navy literally was immobilized due to a lack of fuel. It would never again sail in force and had lost its strategic importance by the fall of 1944. This had a major impact on the dysfunctional relationship between the Japanese Army and Navy. After Leyte the Army was forced to fight alone resulted in the Navy losing all political power and quickly became irrelevant from a political standpoint. The loss of face and the diminished political power would result in admirals making the decision of sending the *Yamato* on a suicide mission on April 7, 1945 to defend Okinawa. Attacked by over 300 U.S. aircraft her end largely repeated her sister *Musashi*'s experience on October 24, 1944.

A single battleship was more a national symbol than a military force and when *Yamato* capsized and exploded it resulted in a huge mushroom cloud so large that it could be seen from Japan. An ominous warning of what was to come. Ironically, American airpower could only claim one battleship *Musashi* during the time span where the Japanese fleet held strategic significance. *Kongo* was the only battleship sunk by a submarine in the Pacific. The American battle fleet sank *Kirishima, Fuso*, and *Yamashiro. Hiei* was sunk by a combined effort of surface ships and air power but it was the damage from her surface battle that resulted in her inability to maneuver. This then led to the Japanese giving up on her and allowing her to founder. *Mutsu* was destroyed by an unexplained magazine explosion in 1943.

---

[644] Author unable to locate *Arkansas* and *Mississippi*'s official aircraft kill numbers as reported by the U.S. Navy for WW II.

[645] Antiaircraft Action Summary World War II October 1945, Headquarters of the Commander in Chief United States Fleet.

The Japanese battle line had not been completely defeated at sea but *Hyuga*, *Ise*, and *Haruna* were all destroyed by airpower at Kure on July 24 and 28, 1945. However, they had already been immobilized by lack of fuel and no longer held any strategic value for Japan. Carriers, cruisers, destroyers were also destroyed in these raids which demonstrated that the blockade had rendered the Japanese Navy as nothing more than a group of target ships. Only *Nagato* survived the war and surrendered in Tokyo Bay September 2, 1945 with the prize crew coming from *Iowa*.

The use of kamikaze tactics in the last year of the war gave the Japanese military a false hope that with this tactic they could increase the attrition rate on American ships to inflict Mahan's decisive battle. The tactic did increase the hit rate from 3% using conventional tactics to 6% using kamikaze tactics but even this was not nearly enough. And, by definition, the use of suicide tactics used up the very resources needed to maintain resistance and sustainability. Air power no matter what form it took could not establish control of the seas over a properly defended battle fleet or break either a tactical or strategic blockade on its own. Without the mutual support and combined strength of air power and a battle fleet Japan could not hope to accomplish their strategic objective of decisive battle.

Mahan had demonstrated that any island without the protection of a navy can't be defended. The tactical blockades established through forward deployment destroyed the Japanese defensive perimeter which was based on the island being capable of defending itself through air power. The strategic key was denying the use of the ocean and cutting the lines of communication which isolated the defending garrison. This was how naval power affected events ashore. It is on land that people live and to exert power you must alter the balance of power on land. By preventing the replenishment of the defending garrison while maintaining this ability for yourself through the use of the ocean, the defending garrison is doomed to defeat. This had far greater strategic consequences than simply striking at individual enemy units. Instead of causing attrition, which took effect only slowly, entire bases could be cut off all at once and their combat capability neutralized such as Rabaul or Truk and a strategic level blockade could be implemented against an entire country.

Air power and the submarine came to dominate the post-war. Since the great majority of the ships sunk were sunk by these two technologies it is easy to understand the perception they were dominant in World War II. They certainly were the dominant choice on how to conduct offensive operations during the war by the admirals making the decisions but they were not efficient and resulted in a slow war of attrition. The United States could afford this type of war because it had the stronger economy. Reverse this single variable and give Japan the larger economy and the U.S. victories of 1942 become staggering defeats. Fighting to a draw with an economic superpower would be equal to defeat in a war of attrition.

With no great fleet battle in the historical record, and the success of air power and the submarine, the postwar perspective was that battleships were obsolete. Battleships processed a subtle power that could influence military operational plans by their sheer presence. All lesser ships benefitted and their success could be directly tied to how well the battleships influenced events. They complicated an attacker's position and when present in numbers and with the proper supporting infrastructure of a battle fleet no other weapon could effectively counter their power. Had the admirals successfully carried out Nimitz's objective and battleships achieved a decisive battle in an afternoon, perceptions may have been different!

Post-war there was no new construction of battleships or even heavy and light cruisers. The *Iowa* class served on and off again for the past seventy years becoming four of the most decorated U.S. warships in United States naval history. They represent the last of their kind. What are called cruisers today have no design relationship with their World War Two counterparts. The armored warship disappeared. The United States has not been required to fight for command of the sea since the end of World War Two and it may never have to again.

Corbett wrote command of the sea can be maintained without battleships if there are no enemy battleships to interfere with cruisers or the lesser ships. If no one builds battleships then there is no need for battleships. This is the principal reason they have disappeared. The emphasis on strike warfare over command of the sea and blockade has dominated global naval planning post-war, so no new construction has ever been allocated. Contrary to conventional wisdom, which places the decisive battle of the war at Midway or perhaps Leyte Gulf, the war's outcome was decided at Guadalcanal when *Washington* and *South Dakota* blockaded Iron Bottom Sound preventing its use to the Japanese and sinking *Kirishima.* This broke Yamamoto's will to continue to fight for Guadalcanal, with the profound strategic result that abandoned his resolve to win the war quickly before U.S. industrial strength could take effect. Yamamoto then assumed the strategic defensive which allowed the United States to complete its military buildup. This meant that Japan was now pursuing a political strategy which it knew, before the war, could not be achieved. This is why the Naval Battle of Guadalcanal can be considered the true turning point in the war, and it was decided by battleships.

Japan's abandonment of her battle fleet for the use of air power as the primary tool for offensive operations led directly to her defeat. Sustainability and the ability to deny the use of the seas while maintaining freedom of passage trumped strike warfare each and every time. This was the true measure of naval power and the battleship throughout the war remained the final arbiter of sea power. Its role in implementing this power was largely misunderstood. Blockade ended the Japanese Imperial Navy's ability to operate and opened Japan to potential invasion. Tetsutaro and Saneyuki's theory of how the United States would defeat Japan had come true just as they had predicted in 1907, but an unforeseen technological innovation removed the necessity for a bloody invasion.

Two atomic bombs were dropped on the city of Hiroshima on August 6 and on Nagasaki on August 9, 1945 destroying both cities and killing 129,000 thousand people. On August 9, 1945 in a meeting in an underground bunker below the Imperial Palace Toyoda still argued that Japan must not be occupied and that disarmament and war criminals should be left in Japanese hands. Others argued that the time had come when there was no more room for negotiations. The preservation of "*kokutai*" was considered essential. There was no honor in extinction. The two million Japanese citizens along with the tens of millions of citizens from other countries lost in the war did not justify a single man remaining in political power. However, if *kokutai* was destroyed Hirohito said, "*If this comes to pass, we will be unable to pass on our progeny the country called Japan that we received from our imperial ancestors.*" It was for this fundamental reason he accepted unconditional surrender. [646]

With the atomic bomb, aircraft could inflict Mahan's battle of annihilation against any fleet or even any nation. However, it has also made unlimited war between nuclear powers obsolete. With this tool politics through the use of force can only result in mutual destruction. There have been no total wars or decisive fleet battles since World War II.

---

[646] Drea, Edward J., *In the Service of the Emperor* at 211.

BIBLIOGRAPHY

PRIMARY DOCUMENTS

Bureau of Aeronautics, Navy Department, Airplane Characteristics & Performance: Model F4F-4 (July 1, 1943).

Joint Army–Navy Assessment Committee, Japanese Naval and Merchant Shipping Losses during World War II by All Causes. (1947)

Chester Nimitz Chester, *Chester Nimitz Gray Book* Vol. 1 thru Vol. 8. 1941-1945.

USN Overseas *Aircraft Loss List* June 1942.

Japanese Detailed Action Reports:

Combined Fleet Headquarters Detailed Action Report, October 17 to October 28, 1944.

First Air Fleet's Detailed Battle Report #6. (Midway)

First Battleship Division Detailed Action Report, October 17 to October 28, 1944.

Mobile Force's Detailed Battle Report #6. (Midway)

Atago DAR No. 8 12 to 14 Nov 1942 (submitted 18 Nov 1942)

Ise Detailed Action Report, October 24 to October 25, 1944.

Yamato Detailed Action Report. (17 October to 28 October 1944).

Sendai Brief action report JT1 National Archives

Zuikaku Detailed Action report, June 1944

Junyo Detailed Action Report.

Chiyoda Detailed Action Report

Kongo Detailed Action Report. (24 October to 26 October 1944).

Nagato Detailed Action Report. (24 October to 26 October 1944).

Yamato Detailed Action Report. (17 October to 28 October 1944).

Haruna Detailed Action Report, 24 October to 26 October 1944.

Musashi Detailed Action Report. _ (24 October 1944): PP 1-27.

Zuikaku Detailed Action Report, October 21 to October 25, 1944.

Hyuga Detailed Action Report, October 20 to October 29, 1944.

Ise Detailed Action Report, October 24 to October 25, 1944.

Zuiho Detailed Action Report, October 21 to October 25, 1944.

Chitose Detailed Action Report, October 25, 1944.

U.S. Action Reports

Commander Task Force SIXTY-FOUR: Report of Night Action, Task Force SIXTY-FOUR—November 14-15, 1942

Vice Admiral Thomas Kinkaid, CTU 77 Action Report, January 31, 1945, RG 38

Vice Admiral William F. William Halsey, CTU 38, Action Report, November 13, RG 38.

Commander in Chief, U.S. Pacific Fleet, Action Report.

Air Group-20, U.S.S. *Enterprise*, Commander Dan F. Smith, RG 38.

Lexington, Action Report, November 22, 1944, RG 38

Rear Admiral Frederick C. Sherman, CTU 38.3, Action Report, November 15, 1944, RG 38.

Astoria Action Report August 9, 1942

Enterprise Action Report February 1, 1942.

Vincennes Action Report. August 9, 1942

Quincy Action Report. August 9 1942.

Grayson's Action Report. August 23, 1942

Boise Action Report, Summary of Battle Damage October 12, 1942

Washington, Action Report, Night of November 14-15, 1942.

Walke, Surface Engagement with Japanese Forces, November 15, 1942

Benham, Report of Action November 14-15, 1942.

Gwin, Report of Night Action 14-15 November, 1942.

Preston, Surface Engagement with Japanese Forces, November 15, 1942—report of.

South Dakota, Action Report, night engagement 14-15 November, 1942

Fanshaw Bay Action Report October 25, 1944

Hoel Action Report October 25, 1944.

White Plains Action Report October 25, 1944.

Santa Fe, Action Report, November 15, 1944, RG 38.

Office of Naval Intelligence

The Office of Naval Intelligence. *The Battle of the Coral Sea*

The Office of Naval Intelligence: *The Battle of the Midway*

The Office of Naval Intelligence: *The Battle of the Midway Japanese Account.*

The Office of Naval Intelligence, *the Battle of Java Sea February.*

The Office of Naval Intelligence: *The Battle of Eastern Solomons*

The Office of Naval Intelligence: *The Battle of Santa Cruz*

United States Strategic Bombing Survey (Pacific) The Campaigns of the Pacific War Naval Analysis Division, 1946, XII Philippine Campaign,

USSBS Interrogation No. 390 Commander Shigeru Nishino.

Technical Mission to Japan, Index No. S-06-2 Ships and related targets, Loss of the *Musashi.*

USSBS Interrogation No. 378, November 13-14, 1945 Admiral Soemu Toyoda.

Antiaircraft Action Summary · World War II October 1945, Headquarters of the Commander in Chief UNITED STATES FLEET.

Bates, Richard W., *The Battle for Leyte Gulf, and October 20th to October 23rd* Strategic and Tactical Analysis, Vol. III, Naval War College, 1957.

U.S. Army Field Manual FM 3–0.

SECONDARY SOURCES

Alden, John D. *The American Steel Navy* Naval Institute Press 1972.

Asada, Sadao. *From Alfred Thayer Mahan to Pearl Harbor* Naval Institute Press 2006.

Ballard, Robert D. and Rick Archbold. *Lost Ships of Guadalcanal.* Warner/Madison Press Books 1993.

Clay Blair, Jr. *Silent Victory* Philadelphia: J.B. Lippincott Company 1975.

Clausewitz, Carl Von. *On War,* Everyman's Library 1993.

Julian Corbett, Julian S. *Principles of Maritime Strategy*, London 1911.

Julian Corbett, Julian S. *Maritime Operations in the Russo-Japanese War 1904-5* Naval Institute Press 1994.

Dickson, W. D. *The Battle of the Philippine Sea* London 1975.

Drea, Edward J. *In the Service of the Emperor* University of Nebraska Press 1998.

Dulin, Robert O. Garzke, William H. *Battleships United States Battleships in World War II* Naval Institute Press 1976.

Dull, Paul S. *The Battle History of the Imperial Japanese Navy 1941-1945* Naval Institute Press 1978.

Evans, David C. Peattie, Mark R. *Kaigun Strategy, Tactics, and Technology in the Imperial Japanese Navy 1887-1941.* Naval Institute Press 1997.

Evans David C. *The Japanese Navy in WWII, in the words of former Japanese Naval Officers,* Naval Institute Press 1969.

Franks, Richard B. *Guadalcanal.* Random House 1990.

Friedman, Norman, *U.S. Battleships,* United States Naval Institute 1985.

Friedman, Norman, *Battleships, Design and Development 1905-1945* Mayflower Books 1978.

Goldstein, Donald M., Dillon, Katheryn V. *The Way it Was, Pearl Harbor* Brassey's 1991.

Goldstein, Donald M., Dillon, Katheryn V. *The Pearl Harbor Papers* Brassey's 1993

Goldstein, Donald M, Dillon, Katheryn V. *The Pacific War Papers Japanese Documents of World War II* Potomac Books Inc. 2004.

Inoguchi, Rikihei, Nakajima Tadashi and Rodger Pineau *the Divine Wind,* Bantam Books, 1958.

Ishibashi, Takao. *Nippon Teikoku Kaigun Zen-kansen 1868-1945: Senkan, Jun'yô-senkan [Illustrated Ships Data on Vessels of the Imperial Japanese Navy 1868-1945: Battleships, Battlecruisers]* Vol. 1. Namiki Shobo, 2007.

Ito, Masanori. *The End of the Imperial Japanese Navy,* W.W. Norton & Company 1956.

Kenneth J. Hagan. *This People's Navy: The Making of American Sea Power* N.Y. Free Press 1991.

Lord, Walter. *Incredible Victory* Harper & Row 1967.

Lundgren, Robert. *The World Wonder'd, What Really Happened off Samar* Nimble Books 2014.

Lundstrom, *First Team: Guadalcanal Campaign,* Naval Institute Press 2005.

Alfred Thayer Mahan, Alfred Thayer, *The Influence of Sea Power upon History,* 1660-1783, published by Little, Brown & Co in 1890.

Alfred Thayer Mahan, Alfred T. *Alfred Thayer Mahan on Naval Warfare* Dover Publication Inc. 1999.

Marder, Arthur J. *Old Friends New Enemies* Oxford University Press 1981.

Miller, Edward S. *War Plan Orange: The U. S. Strategy to Defeat Japan, 1897-1945* U. S. Naval Institute Press, 1991.

Ministry of Defense. *War with Japan,* London 1995.

Morison, Samuel Eliot. *Leyte June 1944-January 1945*, University of Illinois Press, 1958.

Poirier, Michel T. Commander, USN, *Results of the American Pacific Submarine Campaign of World War II,* December 30, 1999.

Potter, E. B. *Bull William Halsey* Naval Institute Press, 1985.

Potter, E.B. *Chester Nimitz* Naval Institute Press, 1976.

Shikikan-tachi no Taiheiyô Sensô [Pacific War as Described by the Senior Officers]. Kôjinsha NF Bunko, 2004.

Stille, Mark, *Yamamoto Isoroku* Osprey 2012.

Taylor Theodore. *The Magnificent Mitscher*, Naval Institute Press 2006.

Ulysses S. Grant. *Personal Memoirs of U. S. Grant, Vol. 1,* N. Y., the Century Co., 1917.

Ugaki, Matome. *Fading Victory* University of Pittsburgh Press, 1991

Wheeler, Gerald E. *Kinkaid of the Seventh Fleet.* Naval Institute Press, 1995

Whitley, M.J., *Battleships of World War II an International Encyclopedia* Naval Institute Press 1998.

Y'Blood, William T. (1981). *Red Sun Setting: The Battle of the Philippine Sea* Naval Institute Press 2003.

Articles

Benere, Daniel, E. *A CRITICAL EXAMINATION OF THE U.S. NAVY'S USE OF UNRESTRICTED SUBMARINE WARFARE IN THE PACIFIC THEATER DURING WWII*, NAVAL WAR COLLEGE

Lengerer, Hans, *Contributions to the History of Imperial Japanese Warships*

Heinz, Leonard, *Aircraft Carrier Defense in the Pacific War: The Carrier Battles of 1942.*

Hone, Thomas C., *REPLACING BATTLESHIPS WITH AIRCRAFT CARRIERS IN THE PACIFIC IN WORLD WAR II,* Naval War College Review, winter 2013.

Hone, Trent, *U.S. Navy Surface Battle Doctrine and Victory in the Pacific,* Naval War College Review

Kazuyoshi, Miyazaki, *Tragedy at Savo, The Hiei under concentrated fire.*

Michio Kobayashi, Michio. "*Senkan 'Kirishima' no Saigo* [*The Last of Battleship Kirishima*]." *Saiaku no Senjô Gadarukanaru Senki*, 1987,

Reilly John C. *Operational Experience of the Fast Battleships*, Naval Historical Center.

The 2011 edition of *British Defence Doctrine* (BDD) Joint Doctrine Publication 0-01 (JDP 0-01) (4th Edition) dated November 2011.

Takahashi Fumio. *The First War Plan Orange and the First Imperial Japanese Defense Policy: An Interpretation from the Geopolitical Strategic Perspective*, NIDS Security Reports, and No.5 (March 2004).

Tully, Tony, *Why Japan lost the War*

Weir, Erin M.K., *German Submarine Blockade, Overseas Imports, and British Military Production in World War II,*

Yoshino, Kyûshichi. "*Senkan 'Kirishim'' no Saigo* [The Last of Battleship *Kirishima*]." *Maru Extra Vol. 10,* May 1998,

Robertson, Operational Analysis for the Battle of Leyte Gulf.

Ichiro, Imamura Lieutenant, Paymaster, *Vanguard Force Flagship Atago and the Defense Battles of Guadalcanal Island* (*Zenshin-butai Kikan* Atago *to Ga-tô Kôbôsen*)

Web Sites

UBOAT.Net
Kaigin.com

Index